222, 111, 444, 333, 555, 11:11, 444, 888

Dedication

This book is dedicated to TMH. Regardless of what name you use, we all ultimately praise the same, singular higher power.

My deepest gratitude goes to my grandparents and other departed loved ones. Without their guidance, life would have been a mystery, and success would have been elusive. Their words were my strength, and even when I felt alone, they never left my side. While others ran and ridiculed me, they remained steadfast before and after death.

I also extend my thanks to my angels, ancestors, and spirit guides. We all have them, but belief is key. If you're aware, you understand; if not, I hope my book can shed some light. I didn't grasp it initially, but now I see clearly.

HE IS REAL, AMEN!

I0166570

Introduction

I've debated whether to write again and how to summarize my story without omitting key details. I've written three books, all stolen, lost, or misplaced. I started writing after a 2005 accident to recover memories, believing it would help me remember like assembling a puzzle.

I'm a 47-year-old woman who has felt trapped for over half her life. I've always stayed positive and let others control my life. I couldn't risk wronging anyone because I lacked family or friends. My only constant support was TMH. I learned life's lessons through experience, not guidance. TMH was always there to catch me when I fell and reassure me.

I've endured many trials, and it's my purpose to share my experiences and how TMH saved me. I'm grateful to TMH; without him, I wouldn't have survived. I was never taught about life, and people assumed I'd figure things out on my own because I was "too smart." I thank them now for teaching me resilience, street smarts, and book smarts. I was never sheltered and always struggled.

My life lacked access to mentors or preparation. Every achievement and obstacle came with risks and consequences. I faced tragic events, but I was never truly alone because TMH was always there. When my family and friends didn't care, my true father stepped in. I'm strong enough to endure any obstacle. By sharing my story, I finally have a chance to speak without judgment or interruption.

Please be patient as you read my story. It's written based on my memories, and my memory isn't perfect. If I seem repetitive, it's because I'm expanding on each memory as I go. I hope you enjoy it, and thank you for reading.

They wanted me to believe that I was born in January 1978 and raised in the Anacostia neighborhood of Southeast Washington, DC. My early education began at Our Lady of Perpetual Help, but due to my parents' separation, I transferred to Spingarn Senior High School, where I graduated from the STAY Program. Thai is the life I was trained to remember a story well put together .I later received an Associate's degree in Accounting and Business Management from the University of the District of Columbia.

My family was always a bit unusual, but I didn't realize how much until my parents separated. Before that, life was good. I stayed with Mom, my sister with Dad. We had fun times skating and biking together. I only recently discovered my father was actually my stepfather, and my mother had an affair. This explained why we moved to Durham, NC after the separation. My mother never broke free from the lies and secrets, which ultimately led to her demise.

The urce of my mother's "diseases" was my stepfather and stepmother. The men in her life after my stepfather were paid to participate in sexual rituals and spread diseases, starting with my mother. The hate was real, with a continued grudge after he infected her and decided to steal an inheritance left for me by my grandfather. My aunts and uncles felt I had no right to the inheritance because I wasn't "true blood," which they found out through my sister. Everyone was aware that I was the only one in the dark about this.

My mother, like me, was gifted, but under MK Ultra, and never broke free from their control. For years I wondered why she did anything they asked of her. This explained why no one ever protected or cared for me; the assaults didn't matter, as they were always orchestrated. Sadly, my mother and I revealed our truths to the wrong people - my sister and her own sibling and mother used this to continue using her for her energy and to keep her in bondage.

They tried to break my spirit, but they were unsuccessful. First, they came for me, then they came for my children. My sister, aunt, and cousins conspired against me after my grandmother's passing. They believed I didn't deserve anything, including my inheritance. My sister and my children, whose fathers had been killed and who had been infected with diseases meant for me, worked together to turn my children against me. They hoped I would return to my exes. Thankfully, I was redirected. This was all done to steal my inheritances, including a life insurance policy and funeral that had been fraudulently paid for and enacted. They didn't expect me to survive, as the truth would have been revealed. They all worked together to kill me, but their plots failed. TMH and my ancestors blocked every attempt and warned me of their deception and plans. At first, I couldn't believe it, but as I paid closer attention, the details made sense. They were protecting me and revealing the truth about the poisoning, abuse, and killings I had endured. The corruption extended beyond my family to the government, who had been involved for years.

As I matured, my childhood perception of my stepfather as a flawless and tireless provider shifted. I came to understand that everyone, including my parents, has limitations, and they eventually reached theirs. Although unconventional to some, my parents' comfort with nudity at home was normal to me, but I never grew comfortable with it. The incest and pedophilia within my family have persisted for years. Just as I was auctioned off my entire life, so was my mother. When they had no further use for her, they discarded her. My stepfather and stepmother orchestrated auctions, meetings, and hired hitmen behind the scenes to conceal the diseases and uphold lives they never deserved. My stepmother, sister, and aunts formed a coven, siphoning my energy for years through my partners. After I leave them or they leave me, they connect and absorb my energy to live out the life path meant for me. In return, they paid my exes, among many others—co-workers and F.A.N.S.—to join them in performing rituals to maintain the facade.

Seeing my mother's deep sadness and confusion after separating from my stepdad was devastating. Angry and heartbroken, my mom confronted my stepdad with evidence of his infidelity - herpes. A physical fight followed, leaving my mom bedridden for days with a bruised ankle. We stayed with my grandmother for a while. I've recently realized that both my parents had flaws and neither was honest, which led to disaster and destroyed lives. Everything was a show - the yearly new cars were all part of the payment, and then they kicked her out, boarding up a house which, I would discover, was in my or my mother's name. My sister would later say it was in my grandmother's name. I saw it all, and if that were the case, why were we living in and out of cars and moving to North Carolina? They are all liars, and I'm sick of the lies. I've decided to tell the world in the hopes that it will reach others. Through TMH, all things are possible.

The instability and abuse I experienced in my childhood taught me to react quickly to difficult situations. While other children played, I took solace in writing, as my childhood was filled with insults, beatings, and isolation. After my father gave my mother herpes through infidelity, my parents separated. We briefly lived with my grandmother, where I was exposed to disturbing experiences that continue to haunt me.Despite my academic success and award at Petworth Elementary, my mother, following my grandmother's advice, decided to move us again. We left my grandmother's full house for my cousin's home in Durham, NC. The constant upheaval and abuse I endured made adapting to change easy; it was the only constant in my life. I realized my life would be an adventure. My mom needed me; it was clear her family only used her. They encouraged her to divorce, then abandoned her long before the discovery of HIV. In Durham, NC, my mom enrolled in school and met a man who was kind, loving, caring, and eccentric - an angel in disguise, in my opinion. He even co-signed my mom's first apartment lease in Raleigh, NC. I never understood him; he never lived with us but simply wanted to help my mom. He either wanted to be homeless or maybe that was a pretense.

At the time, my mom was still married but separated. This is why my father cared so much; he and my stepfather were aware of each other. My stepfather believed

I was dead, but despite the lie, he still assisted my mom and would have continued if she had not returned to D.C. as my stepfather and her so-called father had requested. They conspired to keep her bound to them; if she had stayed, she would have broken free and found herself, and they would have lost control.I wonder how he's doing today. I checked online, and it says he passed away in 2022, although my angels are saying he is still living. I'm not sure. I hope he is alive and that he finds me. I thought about calling the number online, but I don't want to cause trouble, and I don't want to alert my family any more than I already have. I've been made aware that the authorities are fully aware of the situation. The question is what they will do and when; this has gone on for decades, and many have been killed to cover this story up and to continue receiving payments and perpetuate lies.

I have many unanswered questions about my past, but I've learned to be patient and trust that the truth will eventually come to light. My recent hospitalization served as a stark reminder of my mortality and reinforced the importance of patience and faith. Despite facing a deliberate attempt on my life, my health and faith were restored by TMH, who reminded me that He always hears my prayers, especially when I am most vulnerable. During a hospital stay for dangerously high blood pressure and an impending risk of stroke, I was visited by my deceased grandparents. My grandmother, appearing as a nurse, comforted me with a touch that reminded me of my mother's soothing presence when I was in ICU at Providence Hospital in 2016. At just fourteen, I was delivering my first son and coded on the table due to a torn artery, a complication not uncommon for someone my age. The physical trauma was compounded by the emotional torment I endured throughout my pregnancy, a result of being sexually assaulted at thirteen. I was judged and ridiculed by those who thought I would never succeed, which mirrored the abuse I endured at home. Boys made unwanted advances toward me, and girls isolated me at school. Followed by years of suicide attempts always coding and awaking TMH never gave up on me and never allowed me to do so either.

Yet, I never forgot my grandmother's words: "People will talk forever; it is what you believe that makes you." She taught me that my actions mattered more than their words. My accomplishments were the best response to those who doubted me. During these times of isolation and feeling unheard, TMH revealed Himself to me. Although it took me years to fully understand her wisdom, I suddenly remembered her teachings in that moment. They became my guiding light, helping me to overcome life's obstacles. I found comfort in my faith when I was abandoned by those who should have protected me. I always turned to TMH when I felt alone and unheard. He was my unwavering support in the midst of turmoil.

Growing up as the youngest in a family of large women, I was always given hand-me-downs that were too big. To make them fit, I had to alter them myself, teaching me to be resourceful with what I had. This taught me to 'make do', but may have led others to perceive me as 'fast'. I would roll my pants at the waist or tie up my shirts - it was simply necessary, not something I thought much of as a child. However, growing up in a household full of negativity, these actions were often misinterpreted and disregarded, leaving me without validation. My mother, influenced by my grandmother and her siblings, prioritized her lifestyle over my well-being, forcing me to keep my son. It was clear that my well-being was not important to them.

Unlike other family members, I rarely received any of the child support benefits they received. The funds were used for everything but me. The exception was when I lived with my aunt in Riverdale, MD. Though she was kind, my time there ended abruptly due to a misunderstanding—or was it? Did she send me to PIW because of what I'd said about my other uncle? It's clear that many uncles and their associates had the opportunity to violate me and control my life for their benefit. I've discovered that I spoke many truths without even knowing it, as they erased my memory and were triggered when I spoke of them. Life has a funny way of repeating unresolved issues until they're corrected. They falsely assumed I was talking about my aunt's husband when I wasn't and misinterpreted my trauma as lies and troublemaking.

People often formed opinions based on my initial words and then clung to that narrative, as it suited their purposes. They never gave me a chance to fully explain myself. It was easier to dismiss anything that didn't fit their preconceived notions. My entire life has been shaped by the mistakes of others, not my own. To believe otherwise would mean that my life was a lie, constructed for the benefit of those who expected me to fail. Despite their expectations, I have overcome every obstacle placed before me.

I became a mother at fourteen. I had already been taking care of my siblings and going to school; now I had another responsibility. Despite the stress of a colicky baby and the hateful names I endured at school for nine months ("slut," "fake-ass virgin," and worse), I was determined to be the best mother I could. My grandmother blamed my experiences on the way I dressed, which made me wonder if it was okay for people to treat me that way because of my clothes. After one of my many suicide attempts, my stepdad told me to let things work themselves out and not to stress because it would kill me. I realize now that what he really meant was that I should move on and stop making a fuss. Many times, he hoped I'd give up, but I never did. I was determined to tell my story without judgment or interruption.

I was homeless and barely surviving, which led to stays in psychiatric wards and hospitals due to depression. I later discovered that these feelings of suicide and poverty were not my own, but were projected onto me in hopes of driving me insane. My sister was sent to check if these methods were working; those around me were never family, but handlers whose job was to keep me down. They are still trying to this day, obsessed with winning by any means necessary for their selfish reasons.

When I reflect on my life, I see myself carrying extra weight while pushing forward. No matter how hard it was, I always took one more step forward, knowing I'll find the strength to carry the rest of the burden. In a moment of despair, I attempted suicide. The doctor warned that if I didn't manage stress and anxieties over things beyond my control, I would worsen, as all my health issues - diabetes, high blood pressure, and other projected illnesses - were not meant for me. They were able to maintain these issues by keeping me in a low vibration until I remembered my self-worth. My son reached out to my stepdad, who visited and echoed the doctor's words. After over 25 years of trauma and a complete lack of paternal love and affection - he was merely a financial provider - I interpreted his words as a strange expression of love. Physical affection wasn't shown in my stepdad's family; after finding out the truth, I realized why his emotional distance seemed normal, but wasn't the same with my siblings. It's funny how most of my achievements were to show my stepfather that I was worthy and could do it on my own, that his efforts while I was younger were not wasted. I had to realize it never mattered, and what was important was that I did it for myself; I shortly learned this after receiving no acknowledgment or sincere love.

My stepfather excelled at understanding and finding solutions, regardless of the situation. He was also skilled at conveying his point, even if it took hours and became heated. However, this was merely one of the many illusions in my life. As a child, I was innocent and joyful, always maintaining a unique perspective. Family outings and dinners were frequent occurrences, something I now treasure as rare. My stepfather, once the love of my life, always made me feel safe and secure, but only to keep me close and maintain appearances for all those they'd told lies to, past and present.

Weekends were filled with adventures like skating on Frederick Douglas Hill and biking from Anacostia to my grandparents' house on 14th Street NW. My grandparents' home was always a haven of warmth, laughter, and delicious food. Their love was genuine and remains so to this day, providing me with unwavering guidance and support. The aroma of Grand Stepdad's fresh-baked rolls and the gentle breezes that accompanied Grandma and me during our porch-side Scrabble and solitaire games are cherished memories, representing moments of relaxation, learning, and joy. As the youngest on my stepdad's side for many years, their home was the epicenter of family gatherings, conversations, and playful activities.

Before my cousin came along, I was the baby of the family. We always found ways to entertain ourselves with games like Atari, table tennis, freeze tag, red light green light, hopscotch, and skating. My cousins often played basketball, and we all enjoyed pitty pat on the front lawn with family and friends. We were never allowed to leave the front yard alone; an older person always had to accompany us.With around thirteen children in the family, excluding my aunts and uncles, we rarely needed to find other friends to play with. My grandparents didn't believe in wasting time on television, so we spent our time with books, board games, and family gatherings. I miss those times, especially the holidays, reunions, and back-to-school trips. I miss many things about my childhood in the 80s, like cassette tapes and quality time with my family, especially my grandmother. We were very close and spent a lot of time playing Scrabble, doing crossword puzzles, and crocheting (which I never really learned).

I wasn't a girly girl; I took shop instead of Home Economics in high school. I struggled to relate to the women on my mom's side of the family; they were always caught up in drama and chaos. My mother was different from my father's side of the family, and I struggled to adjust. I admired the women on my paternal side, particularly my aunts who always dressed elegantly. Sadly, they never liked me and only wanted to steal my light. They said we didn't share the same blood, but family is so much more than that. Family is love, patience, and who you can always go to when things get rough. This was never the case for me; they thrived on my downfalls.

They made sure I would tear myself down with addictions and sex, knowing that if I surrounded myself with these things, I could never uncover my gifts. They were successful in this when I was young and naive, learning many things the hard way without any guidance. Thankfully, God watched over me and never allowed me to fall too far astray. When I did, he would correct me and take it away, as I too had to endure lessons without being aware of my gifts. He was careful not to let any of it destroy me, but for the lesson to be learned so that I would eventually turn them into blessings, just as it was written.

In life, all things are foreseen, and we have different paths based on choices; that is where free will comes into play. Destiny can never really be destroyed; you just have to choose the correct path and unlock the truth and the blessings behind it all. If you choose incorrectly, it will cause delays, but what is destined is destined; only you can change your path in life. In retrospect, I realize that my father's actions, while seemingly right, were not. I am uncovering uncomfortable truths about my family and my past, including secrets and disturbing behaviors that were considered normal at the time, such as family members sleeping with each other.Despite the many trials I have endured in my life, I have been sustained by TMH's love, grace, and mercy. That is why I am writing this book - to express my gratitude to TMH for saving me from myself and loving me unconditionally.The atmosphere at my maternal grandmother's house differed greatly from my own home. My mother was a dedicated homemaker; my grandmother, however, took in patients from St. Elizabeth's Hospital as a source of income. The environment in my grandmother's household was chaotic and unstructured. Patients were exploited and treated as servants, despite their mental health issues. Drinking, fighting, incest, greed, laziness, and drug abuse were all common occurrences.

An elderly woman, who was sweet and often talked to herself, lived within the house and diligently cleaned it every day. She eventually passed away there. The household consisted of two men with contrasting personalities; one was a chain-smoker who constantly ran errands, while the other was quiet and introverted. Despite their differences, they were all united by their shared humanity and capacity for love. My mother's family was notorious for their schemes to get rich quickly. My aunts and grandmother were always filling my mother's head with unrealistic plans, and it seemed like they had a strong influence over her. They were envious of my mother and me because my father always provided for us, buying my mother cars and sending us to Catholic school. They never showed any concern for my well-being. On the other hand, my father, grandfather, and his siblings were always loyal and put their families first.

Life has taught me that things aren't always as they appear. I had to learn about love and life through experience, rather than instruction. Perhaps people assumed I was intelligent enough to figure it out, or maybe they were simply too preoccupied with themselves. Regardless, I had to navigate it on my own. Every success and failure was a learning opportunity, and I realized that I could handle those who intended to harm me, even when they caught me off guard. I've always known I had support, even when I lacked clear direction. We must be courageous and confront our problems directly. Our words carry weight and can significantly impact others' lives. Through dishonesty, exaggeration, or justification, we can inadvertently obstruct someone's path. It's important to find those who will love and cherish us for our true selves, not for our possessions or looks.

I long to be loved for who I truly am. For years, I accepted what I was taught without question, but now I struggle with how to present myself and my beliefs. This has been a difficult time because I value truth. Lies grow and become accepted as truth, which can lead to disaster. Truth is simple and doesn't need to be overthought. As children, we learn everything from others. Instead of looking within ourselves, we rely on external sources for knowledge. This was true for me as well. I was taught the importance of self-belief, understanding consequences, and the inevitability of secrets being revealed. I tend to be introverted by nature. Recounting my life story has been a challenge. It's been shaped by the experiences and assumptions of others, rather than my own truth-seeking. I've only ever heard one side of the story and accepted it as fact. Only after my life had been dictated by the guilt and pain that others shared with me — while they reveled in the laughter and celebration of my rushed decisions and forced failures — did I start searching for the other side. The events of my life unfolded as they did because I had to learn everything through firsthand experience. Growing up, I never questioned our family's actions; I assumed they were normal because my cousins and sister participated without hesitation. My older sister was often the catalyst for these situations. Had we been truthful with ourselves during visits to our grandmother or aunt's house, we would have recognized that my sister instigated the chaos. However, due to embarrassment or fear, no one was willing to acknowledge their involvement.

I am no longer afraid to speak the truth, which is why I am the outlier in the family. They are angry that I didn't wait to speak out after realizing that this "BOO BOO" was wrong. I found that out after being molested and sexually assaulted by family incest and strangers. Family does not sleep with family by marriage or not it is NASTY and WRONG. The lack of consequences for the sexual abuse I suffered throughout my life - starting with my sister, then my uncle, and later my boyfriend, who got me pregnant - normalized these experiences for me. The abduction only reinforced this distorted worldview, where I came to believe that this was simply the way life was. So, my uncle started out tickling and wrestling something he had always done growing up, but he began touching places that made me feel uncomfortable and I would speak of it they were just too wasted to hear or care. I can still hear my mom say, "You know how he plays when he's been drinking", he would always catch me while everyone would be sleeping, and I would be woken by the hot smell of E&J . Always took a deep breath as his hand rubbed on me the same as my sister used to do at first. I would lay still and hope he would go away. Then he would later begin to get on top of me until he would relieve himself on my stomach and get a rag. I would wipe it off and he would say it is OK, go to sleep, and kiss me. To avoid seeing him, I started sleeping on my stomach. But I could still smell the liquor on him, no matter which way he approached me. I kept my eyes closed, terrified and unsure who to confide in.

I thought I found a new friend - a guy across the way. He was much older than me (nineteen to my thirteen), but he assumed I was fifteen. Like my sister, I was trying to be fast and fit in, always talking to someone. I did not know what came with that however because there was never anyone around to ask or inquire, I knew I could not ask my sister because she was pretty but had a hell of a reputation. I thought to myself, but I would later discover there was a reason for this. One night it finally happened my mom aunts and grandparents left to go out of town for my great-grandfather's birthday party and I was left to babysit as usual this night I fell asleep in my clothes still remembering my outfit red tube top, blue jean mini skirt, and when I fell asleep no one was home except me and my baby cousins and I had put them to bed already. I was sleeping and I was on my back and I smelled E&J I took a deep breath in hopes he would just go away or be over in a hurry, but I didn't know anything could go inside of their remember I only knew about rubbing and kissing from my sister and cousins, and him touching me too make spit come out his pecker was my thought process never knew entry was there but whoa would I find I have never felt so much pain in my entire life and as I tried to scream he put his has over my mouth and whispered it okay relax as tears ran down my face terrified and then he was done he told me to go clean myself up because my mom and my aunt should be back soon and I did when my mom arrived. He acted as if nothing ever happened I was so disturbed my mom kept asking me what was wrong with my clothes because my skirt was still sideways I just said I wanted to go home, and when got the car I told my mom I didn't want to go back over there anymore I don't like how he touches me not even realizing that my innocence was gone and would never be replaced. My mom did not listen to me because she was set on the fact that she had to work, and my aunt was the only one able to watch me.

Shortly after a few weeks passed I told my friend what had happened so we began to date more and touching started and one day while in his room we making out but that was all we ever did because I used to tell him I didn't like how it feels because it hurt when my uncle did it, and he was aware because it was the reason I would come over to get away from my uncle. He promised me that it would not hurt because he could show me a better way and I trusted him until he tried to enter me I had a flash of my uncle's face and remembered the pain I felt an instant fear come over me and quickly change my mind he continued while saying you already started now, oh come on you, not even a virgin no more and the more he pushed the more I pushed it hurt badly again and I scratched his face and back up while trying to get him off of me and afterward he told me to get dressed he had to go pick up his little sister instead rode around on his bike showing off his scratches telling everybody he hit. We would break up after that and he would begin to date the neighbor downstairs from my aunt. I kept it hidden as well just assuming this must be the way people showed each other love and it continued for months until he had to move away I would later discover that I was pregnant and was in the process of telling my story to my sister only did not get a chance to tell the entire story the only portion that was quickly outed by sister was the first part of my uncle making me appear as my uncle never touched me assuming that my boyfriend was my son's father and I never said my uncle was my son's father I just said I was molested and sexual assaulted and no one asked by who or let me finish. It did not matter it was just another way to make me out to be something I was not, but it was a way of letting my uncle out of a sexual assault he did now they both were made to look good while they slandered me as the wild, young Jazabel without even hearing the full story. They ventured off and just never said or did anything about allowing my uncle to continue his life as normal, still attending gatherings "Not cool at all" I left and said forget everybody.I had my first son at the age of fourteen years old from molestation and sexual assault be it uncle or boyfriend both were wrong. I was told I was grown enough to lay there and knew what I was doing prancing around with cheerleader outfits, tube tops, half shirts with your fast ass are what was said to me you going to have him and take care of him, but the moment he was born he was no longer mines and I was no longer grown or his mother. I became a kid again and they took my son for a little added funding I remember me trying to leave with my son I walked from East-West Highway in Hyattsville, MD to Benning Rd, NE with him strapped to the front of me covered with my coat and blankets after being pushed away after my mother's and boyfriend house at the time because he decided to go in my room and wear my starter coat (Raiders). My mom surprised me with a special Christmas gift that year. I wasn't allowed to wear it to school, though; my mom was old-fashioned and worried it might get stolen. I could only wear it when I was with her.

My mom's boyfriend was wearing my missing Christmas gift. When my mom got home, she demanded I apologize to him. I refused, and she kicked me out because I had a baby. I later learned he and my aunt were involved in my mother's death. This cycle was a constant in my life and held me back. Although my aunt was money-hungry and living with my uncle was difficult, I always had a place to stay as long as I had a dollar. Eventually, I had to break free and began house hopping, staying on and off with my mom until my aunt would put us out with fake eviction notices. I finally realized that I had to create a more stable and independent life for myself and my son. My grandmother's teachings instilled in me the importance of proving people wrong, no matter what. This has been my driving force, pushing me to rise above challenges and defy expectations. I acknowledge my mistakes and learn from them, refusing to blame others or make excuses. While guilt and heartbreak may linger, I strive to move forward without holding onto grudges.

After my parents' divorce, my mom started dating a deacon who worked at the same school as my stepmom and aunt. He also worked part-time at Pizza Hut, which was fun initially because I loved pizza. We attended Greater Light Missionary Baptist Church almost daily, where I was an usher. However, things took a turn for the worse. I was often left unattended and expected to care for younger family members, despite being a child myself. This was because my older sister was involved in drugs and prostitution, leaving me as the next oldest. The adults would drink and fight, and my concerns about my uncle's behavior were ignored. I felt trapped and unheard, and the constant conflict created a hostile environment.

After my parents' second divorce, which resulted from my stepdad's infidelity, we left Anacostia. The separation was a tumultuous experience, filled with anger and betrayal. My parents' actions—changing locks, boarding up windows, selling sentimental items, breaking into houses, and stalking—made it feel like a war zone.Witnessing this chaos firsthand was formative; it showed me the destructive potential of relationships and the importance of choosing a partner wisely. The reason for their second separation mirrored the first: cheating. Upon our return to DC, I discovered evidence of his affair, which fueled my mom's rage. As a child, I didn't fully grasp her anger. Now, as an adult, I understand her frustration and the difficult choices she faced. Returning to DC and my stepfather meant giving up new opportunities and a fresh start.

My mom had free will and could choose her own path, but the plan was always to trap and ruin her. She probably missed my stepdad, family, and their lifestyle, but it all went wrong. You can't have everything in a relationship; there must be compromise. Their emotions were volatile, quickly swinging from love to hate.They separated, and my mom started working at Sharp Health Elementary, DC with my aunt as a teacher's assistant. It was there she met a deacon who worked there during the day and at Pizza Hut at night on weekends. He was a demon disguised as a deacon. I was used to my parents' hate, but my stepdad never stopped taking care of us and working hard, even with no help.

Unbeknownst to my mom, my stepdad's mistress was also working there with my aunt and her friend, my stepmother. My parents were only separated, not divorced.To escape my grandmother's house, we would often go to Pizza Hut. Eventually, my mom started leaving me at my grandmother's more frequently after she got a part-time job at Kmart. My grandmother resented this; she always viewed me as troublesome, even though I was quiet and kept to myself. I think she feared that as I grew older, I would reveal secrets from her past, present, and future. I spent a lot of time alone writing and wishing I could go home. My sister was no longer around, and my aunts were preoccupied with their own chaotic lives, cheating on their husbands with cousins and maintenance men. No one seemed to have the resources or ability to help. There was always some drama unfolding, and I was caught in the middle of it. For example, one of my aunts had an affair with her first cousin, who tragically shot himself after she refused to leave her husband. In another incident, my mom was accidentally stabbed. I never believed it was an accident. I think she wanted to do that for a while . So much chaos all the time remembering how after the separation they tried to jump my stepdad much more . The closest was when we went to pick my sister up from my father and stepmother's house in Takoma Park, MD because they did the same thing as she was trying to do to me. My stepmother owned two properties side by side before they moved to Bethesda, MD and before that, my sister was staying with my stepdad only would always call my mom to pick her up and complain about my stepdad until finally one day my sister decided to fight my stepmother so the story was told only to once again to keep her trapped and remaining and mom quickly picked her up so she could quickly run away later that evening as usual to prostitute and be a Jezebel with her friends always selling her body for alcohol, drugs, and money living from house to house with different men all the time mom would always pick her up from anywhere no matter what time or place. She consistently showed disrespect, even going so far as to have my mother pick her up just to be rude. My mother, raised in an abusive and addictive family with old-fashioned values, didn't tolerate disrespect. Corporal punishment was the norm during her upbringing, where the saying "Spare the rod, spoil the child" was taken literally.

These same methods were used on me and my children, ultimately leading to their removal. This was all part of a larger plan to control me, orchestrated by those who projected their own issues onto me. I was unaware of this manipulation until I achieved sobriety, isolated myself, and broke free from their grasp. I have spent most of my life in survival mode due to abuse from those paid to harm me. The struggles have always been real, and TMH continues to reveal the truth about my siblings and family. They were all spoiled and never understood survival, only stealing, cheating, and manipulating. They never worked on themselves and were only interested in stealing what others worked for.

My grandmother, my mother's mom, was known for collecting social security, life insurance, and welfare payments. I didn't believe it until they tried to lie on my mother's paperwork and forge her signature on a "do not resuscitate" order against her wishes. My arguments went unheard because I was the youngest, even though I was the only one who truly loved my mom. I now understand the truth: my mom's HIV diagnosis led to her being ostracized and defamed. People were unwilling to care for her, causing her to feel devalued, and ultimately leading to her untimely death. They are now attempting to do the same to me. However, I believe that what they intend as lessons will ultimately become blessings. I will share my mother's story and seek justice for the wrongs done to her. TMH works in mysterious ways to ensure the truth is revealed. They unalived her with a disease to cover up and greed their bad doings and bad health to obtain wealth. Remember those insurance policies I was talking about, yes, whenever they want something new, or things do not go the way they want then they do dark magic to make others sick, unalive, and collect from other deaths. This is what they have been doing for decades. They paid for all that was rumored and profited off others by any means. My parents separated my aunt became my babysitter only not really because she was too busy cheating with the maintenance man who worked the property and half the time my mom was not working she was just enjoying her freedom and on her mission to get back years lost while being married after my stepdad had cheated on her twice that I knew about is why they separated from her side with my step dad it was other things. My stepdad always enjoyed the finer things in life, just like his parents. He married my mom young, and she felt she had to live a more luxurious lifestyle to keep up. My mom's family believed in scams, schemes, and government assistance, while my stepdad's family had a military background. They were structured, hardworking, and valued family.

Amidst this turmoil, I was tasked with caring for my younger relatives, including my youngest aunt's children. Her negligence was apparent as she prioritized her needs and those of her partners, often leaving her children with inadequate meals. Her husband's rapist, a family of notorious con artists, exploited every available opportunity for financial gain, including government assistance and child support.. My sister chose to live with my step dad when my parents separated, but she didn't stay with him. She became known for promiscuous behavior around the Pinnacles and later moved to Trinidad stepdad with a drug dealer who exploited her. My father was unable to prevent my sister from engaging in a risky lifestyle, despite his efforts which is more than what he has ever done for me as he did not view me as his knowing the secret of my biological father. She lived next door to my father and stepmother, but lacked appropriate supervision. As a result, she engaged in drug use, drinking, and prostitution.My uncle was unable to assault my sister, so he assaulted me instead. Or perhaps he didn't need to , as my sister may have offered it to him willingly.

My sister would often visit to see her friends and earn money. She would drop by sporadically, and while there, she would usually meet with friends in the building hallway. One day, one of her friends brought one of his friends and they began talking. My aunt was too exhausted to know her husband was missing from the room through the night for her daily events with her maintenance person lover . She never came to my rescue or caught him. As a child, I slept on the living room floor. My mother had four children and an antique couch that was off-limits. I was considered an outcast for speaking about forbidden topics, and I was always wrong. Even now, the smell of alcohol during sex triggers nausea and transports me back to that time. This unresolved trauma prevents me from forming close relationships. At thirteen, I was terrified and alone, with no one listening or acknowledging my fears. As I matured, I befriended an older boy, hoping he could help me, but I was wrong again. No one was going to save me. Even without any prior discussion about menstruation, when I believed I had started my period, I decided to run away. My mom, not my stepdad, reported me as a fugitive. I was trying to graduate high school on the run during my senior year at Cardozo High School. While I was a fugitive, I continued to go to school on a half-day schedule until I could no longer. I had to get away from my family to improve my life, so I went to someone who would do anything for money. She was solely focused on money, not her children or family. This might have been because she was aware of her husband's actions. I returned to her home due to the lack of consequences for my uncle's actions. He would offer apologies in his own way whenever possible. One day, he said, "I didn't know it would affect you like that." I contemplated revenge, but instead, I ended up in jail due to my aunt's false accusations about me and her boyfriend. I believe she knew about her husband's actions, and they all covered it up. In revenge constantly punishing me throughout life for speaking on it.

Consequently, I left my family after meeting my first genuine boyfriend at the mall. I confided in him about my experiences, and he made me feel loved and cherished. He pampered me with a new hairstyle and wardrobe before our first date. His mother allowed me to stay with them as long as I remained in school. However, when I expressed a desire to leave, he became possessive and abusive, leading to our separation as I believed we outgrew each other. I moved back into my aunt's house, where new problems arose. I stayed with my aunt again after my mom and I agreed that she would give my aunt part of my child support. I re-enrolled in Cardozo HS, which was generally okay. I made a few acquaintances around the way: one who went to school with me, one who I clicked with because we were both pregnant around the same time, and three others. One of the three was considered the "hottest of the hot" until she wasn't anymore, and another was a tomboy who could fight but only because of self-esteem issues. I never considered anyone a friend. People were always judging me based on my appearance and how I cared for myself. They only saw what was going on outside, not what was truly going on behind closed doors. As kids, we are often told "what goes on in this house stays in this house."Despite encouragement to "let go and let TMH" and hide our pain, we often forget the importance of speaking up. Things were going well for me; I had ended a relationship with my high school sweetheart and begun dating my second son's father, who I will always consider my first. We spent a lot of time together, often at his house or on the block late at night, but he always encouraged me to stay in school.

When he was arrested during my pregnancy, I took on full responsibility, managing his affairs and preparing for our son alone while working at Boston Market. I had gotten that job after assaulting my aunt and being arrested for it; she had slapped me after assuming I'd slept with her boyfriend, and I think I tried to kill her. I was tired and my mom was looking for a place to stay she knew my aunt boyfriend father rented rooms out so I was asked to give him her number and ask his dad to give her a call and that turned into me going in the house that evening after my mom dropped me off as I was sitting and waiting on my food to warm since I only had an hour before all the knobs would be removed off the sink and stove and that left me about forty- five minutes before the water would be shut off the knobs removed from tub yes these were my living conditions at the age of sixteen and paying rent that came from my child support and a percentage of my paycheck, as I sat at the table to eat my steak and potatoes from Murray's my aunt entered the room to say so you think you slick round here trying to have sex with people so what did you give him was her question. I did not respond just continued to eat as she approached " I know you hear me talking to you and as I raised from the seat to walk away she slapped my first thought was to stab her instead I slapped her back not knowing my strength she fell and I snapped and began kicking her repeatedly with my cowboy boots until my uncle and cousins grabbed me and restrained me realizing I was still holding the knife when the police arrived. They all came to me and I was not scared. I quickly grabbed my coat and went to my friend's house. When my friend met me outside, I handed them my coat with the knife hidden in the sleeve. Just then, the police got out of their cars, and my cousins and uncle pointed me out to them. I was arrested that night and taken to the youth division in Northeast DC, where they held me until morning. Then, I was transferred to CCB downtown, where a lawyer met with me. My mom had already visited me the night before and told me her boyfriend didn't want me to come back. She said she was tired of me getting into fights, even though this fight was over something she had asked me to do. I was left feeling abandoned.

The lawyer asked if I had any close relatives, and I explained that I didn't. My mom had told me my stepdad had moved on and didn't want anything to do with me. I believed her because I hadn't seen him since the previous Christmas when my stepmother sent us presents. I later realized those gifts were actually from my stepdad's mistress, and a huge fight broke out. I had no way to contact my stepdad, and the only place I felt I could call home was my grandparents' house, which I was about to discover was no longer an option after they passed away. The attorney reached out to my stepdad and to my surprise I released to him and when he came to pick me up I was taken to my aunt's house my grandparents old house where I spent the night and then I would later that evening be moved to my other aunts house in Riverdale, Md where I would continue to go to High Point HS and later be transferred to Bladensburg HS which is would I would find out the guy I met at the mall went to Northwestern and played in the band and my best friend was dating his friend and we would later run back into one another and reconnect briefly but did not work out because we outgrew one another apparently, nevertheless after getting ready to graduate I started going through changes I was having dreams about pass trauma and didn't know exactly how to address it since no one on my stepdad's side new what had happened to me meant having a whole baby and it was never mentioned which was crazy how does your thirteen year old daughter get assaulted three times, by three different people, have a baby, get arrested, and kicked out and there are no questions so I tried to kill myself I took a lot of pills and cut my wrist my aunt found me and I was removed and sent to PIW (Psychiatric Institution of Washington) after a misunderstanding where my therapist misinterpreted my flashback about my uncle's abuse. I successfully completed a program there and was allowed to return home. Things were going well until I started spending time with my ex from the mall and began to feel unloved by my family. The more I expressed my hurt, the more I was labeled as attention-seeking, when all I wanted was love and support.

After being released and grounding myself again, my step dad picked me up. But this time, instead of placing me with my family, he helped me get my own efficient apartment. At sixteen, I was working as a waitress and dishwasher at night while attending school during the day, until my circumstances changed once again due to the lack of adult supervision. My senior year, I found myself in trouble after a fight at school. My tokens had been stolen, and I'd gotten into a fight over it. Despite the trouble, I returned to school the next morning. The guidance counselor spoke up for me, and I received after-school detention; my tokens were also returned. The counselor acknowledged that I was a good student and generally stayed out of trouble. I explained that I worked hard after school to pay for my tokens, and the situation was resolved.

My troubles continued when my sister got into trouble once again. The last time I saw her was around 640 uptown, building 529, where her drug-addicted boyfriend bought drugs from my drug dealer boyfriend and his devil-worshipping brother. I recently discovered I was an offering for a sacrifice to make up for her karma as well as to join a cult or coven. It is truly sad how many people have tried offering me up for gifts I wasn't aware of until recently. They set out to harm me while I was saving them, opening so many doors, offering help, feeding, and caring for children even after my family was destroyed. This has continued from 1999 to the present. Mind you, these are all people she has been with, not me, as I was never given an option to be a teenager and my days consisted of maintaining and providing for myself only. I did not choose to sleep with anyone to obtain any of what I had then or currently. Every day has been a struggle since I could remember. Even now, I am struggling to get what was rightfully mine, as if it was never meant for me or I'm stealing what is mine. I just try to keep my head up and faith high as I pray this will all end someday soon.

She left after the feds raided their apartment and discovered she was pregnant. I remember awaking to go to school only to be told to get back in the house after a night of chaos. My uncle had cornered me in the basement trying to get at me again. My sister had come over just in time. Finally, I thought, someone else to witness it. You see, I was there alone and he was coming on to me. She came in and caught him, only he didn't care because he was drunk, so he locked us in the house. She called her boyfriend at the time, and he came in and threatened my uncle. The next morning S.W.A.T was outside, helicopters and all. Turns out her boyfriend's brother had been holding his girlfriend hostage and she jumped from the window in the middle of the night and exposed him for guns, drugs, and sex trafficking. She was arrested and released.

Against my advice, she moved to Red Springs, NC. Before this, my mother had gone down there because he had stolen from the police chief's mother's house and pawned some items, resulting in her arrest. My mom went to get her and the kids. She then moved to Nova Ave, Capital Heights, MD, with my mom. We were both staying with my mom at the time. My mother put both of us out on a cold night with her kids - this was common in my family, and I often was punished for things my sister did. We walked a long time that night. I was okay, but worried about her kids. We knocked on doors, and after nearly freezing to death, a family arrived home. Hoping they would have consideration for her babies, we asked if they could call the shelter hotline because it was too cold for the babies to be outside. I was determined not to return to jail or foster care, so when the van arrived, I ran away. After some time, I returned to my aunt's house to regroup. It was during this stay that a fight occurred, and I was forced to find a way to pay my bills. I was told that if I didn't work, I wouldn't have money for food or shelter.

Approximately a year after living independently and preparing for graduation, I was abruptly awakened in the middle of the night and instructed to take in my sister, as she had nowhere else to go. Although I was a minor, I had been self-sufficient and managing my own household for over a year. Despite this, I was suddenly burdened with the responsibility of caring for another adult and two children in my small efficiency apartment, which was in my stepfather's name. Being a minor, I felt powerless and had no say in the matter.

While juggling work and school, I discovered that my sister, Jezebel, was using my home as a drug outlet. My checks were stolen and the money was spent on diapers, milk, and other items that were not my responsibility, leaving me unable to pay rent. Jezebel was out prostituting while I was left to care for her hungry and dirty children with soaked diapers. I had no children of my own; my mother had my son. Yet, due to my stepfather's actions, I found myself back in the situation I had worked so hard to escape.

The FBI showed up at my stepfather's house because of my involvement in the Fort DuPont rapist case. I was still living with my mom after being abducted from West Virginia Ave NE and assaulted twice on Rosh Hashanah Day. At first, no one believed me, and I was punished for allegedly making up the story. This is devastating to realize that everything that happened in my life was orchestrated to create trauma and keep me in a low vibration, with the goal of turning me into a drug-addicted crack whore like many in my family. I was gone, but I saw life a little differently. Yes, I drank and even smoked marijuana, but my mindset was always to get away from here. Their mindset was to keep me here so they could continue to harvest my energy and receive funds that were never intended for them.

Eventually, I became a key witness in the trial, and my stepfather simply brought the FBI to our house and left. The trial was successful, and the rapist was sentenced—or was he? I would later discover that he, too, was part of the plot and was paid off. Perhaps it was justice for speaking up and fighting for it. When I returned home, I found that I had been evicted and my belongings were outside. The rent had fallen behind because I was caring for my mom and her children, and my stepfather meant what he said: no work, no food or shelter. Of course, that was only for me. The USAA account rightfully belonged to me, but I was only allowed to use what I deposited through work. I was never made aware that the funds in the account belonged to me, and everyone but me benefited from it. I calmly collected my things, took my tips, and moved into the Walter Reed Hotel on Georgia Ave. NW, WDC.

My sister and her kids came to stay with me, even though she continued to be ungrateful. I was pregnant again, still in school, and working to support myself and my son, as his father wasn't contributing. My sister became involved with a pimp across the hall from my room. One night, I returned to find her and another woman engaging in sexual acts in my room while the children slept. Furious, I demanded she leave. After changing rooms, I continued my life while she remained at the hotel, working for the pimp. We saw each other occasionally and later reconnected when my mother fell ill. I struggled to balance work, school, my child, and my mother's care. Eventually, we moved in with my aunt, but were illegally evicted and ended up in a rat- and roach-infested efficiency apartment where you could actually here the rodents moving in the walls through the night.Thankfully, my mom would take us to my grandmother's to escape the situation during the day and at night i would stay up all night until it was time to leave in the morning . The ceiling eventually collapsed, and we moved again.

During this period, I worked at Coral Hill Seafood in Capital Heights, MD, and Popeye's in District Heights, MD. I also supplemented my income by doing hair on the side. Unfortunately, my apartment flooded due to hazardous waste, which made my son sick. Thankfully, my rent was covered for a year, and we were relocated to a new apartment. My sister secured a place on Nova Ave first, and shortly after, my mom was discharged from the hospital with a severe open wound on her buttocks due to bedsores from neglect. My grandmother took her to my sister's house, where I visited every day after work for about a week to change her bandages. Afterward, she would return to my grandmother's house, and I'd go there after work, relying solely on bus and foot for transportation Sadly, my mom's condition deteriorated; she felt unloved and ashamed, and was giving up. My ability to help was limited because I was a minor and had no say. All I could do was try to keep her alive and myself afloat. I couldn't fail my kids, especially my son, who my mom could no longer care for. He was rebellious at school because he was used to my mom, and living with me was different. I wasn't ready to take on the responsibility, and it was hard for me to even look at him without remembering what happened. After my mom passed, my aunt suggested he stay with my cousin in Lacrosse, VA, and we arranged for him to move in with my cousin. They never truly cared; after all, they were the reason for poisoning my mother, as they knew she was our protector, and without her, we would have no one.

Their goal was and always has been to corrupt my son for their own desires. It was never a fight, to be honest. Many may say I took the easy way out, but only I knew what my heart could stand. I tried correcting it in 1997-2000 when I reopened my door to him after he was brainwashed and sent to bring me down. Before that, they recruited my ex-husband—the devil. They were all part of the same cult/coven unbeknownst to me. I have always been a loner, so I was blinded to the evil things in life. As I said, a lot was hidden, and a lot was stolen.

This plot was well put together. Everyone I have been in contact with since the age of eighteen has been paid to take me down or monitor me to some degree, whether it be employers, exes, children, or many others. There were many up to recently, and it continues. They do this by depriving me of things I have worked hard to obtain and maintain, to keep me in an ongoing cycle of returning to work, exes, and much more. I opted out, and yet I still find myself entrapped, but I know this too will soon be over with. My benefits are often denied or redirected. My life is a mix made in hell, awaiting for TMH to come in and change it all.

The worst moment of my life was losing the only person I knew who truly cared about me. She never explicitly said it, but I knew she believed me. She let them control the narrative until her death, but now, having experienced similar events, I see things differently. They wanted to shame her, but they sent him to her because, like me, she was searching for love in the wrong places. I've started to wonder if they were covering up similar events my mom mentioned – like the time she almost got hit by a car after running out of my uncle's house because he tried to touch her. She never shared details, but I've heard many unfinished stories throughout my life that would lead to the conclusion of the story they couldn't wait for her to tell.

The day she died, no one seemed to care. They raided her belongings, even her jewelry, before she was even cold. She may not have had much, but it was hers, and they probably couldn't tell you where any of it is today. The disrespect was profound, even extending to her boyfriend at the time. Karma caught up with him years later when my cousin died after sleeping with my mom's last partner. Everyone tried to shame my mom because she passed from AIDS, but that didn't stop them from trying to pick up where she left off – mentally, physically, and sexually. All she ever did was love, and in her final days, all she felt was unloved.

After the funeral, everyone went back to my grandmother's house for the re-pass. They were going through her things, but I didn't stay. I was so upset that I called my son's father's godmother and asked if I could go with her down to Lorton, VA. She was one of the drivers who would take people down there from Metro Center. I was still a minor and I went to the one person I thought loved me. He comforted me during the visit, and after that, my journey would begin. My son's father was going to be released from prison soon, and he wanted me to move back uptown. Even though my rent was already paid for the year because my son had gotten sick from raw sewage that flooded my apartment, I contacted his mother and got the information to apply for a property on GA and Decatur St NW, WDC. I was approved and moved in a few weeks before he came home.

Unfortunately, after his return, we had a falling out because he wouldn't spend time with me or watch his son while I worked. This was especially difficult because I had just moved and started a new job. I had the option of asking my aunt to watch my son, but she wanted to be paid upfront. I didn't have the money because my partner had just returned home, and I had already missed work. Missing work resulted in me losing my job, leaving me without income and needing to find a babysitter while also ensuring the rent was paid. I had mistakenly assumed we would function as a family unit, and I would receive the same support I had given when he needed it. Instead, I discovered that his entire family struggled with addiction. I didn't judge them because my own family had similar issues. A person's outward appearance doesn't always reflect their inner character. True beauty comes from within. Energy is transferable, so it's essential to be mindful of who you associate with, especially in intimate relationships. Over time, hidden truths about my partner and his family were revealed.

Time passed, and I received an eviction notice. I still hadn't gotten any help. One day, while I was visiting his mom's house (she lived downstairs in the same building), she showed me a picture of my son's father with a new girlfriend. She assumed he had already told me, but I had no idea. I saw him later that evening and asked him about it. He didn't deny it, and we broke up. Now, I was alone and had lost both places to live. My things were put out, and he had no problem collecting any of my furniture that he thought was valuable enough to keep. His son and I, however, were simply out.I am grateful to God for his mysterious ways! The police officer who worked across from my apartment building used to flirt with me, but I never paid him any attention because he was a police officer from the fourth district. When he saw me struggling with my son's belongings, he asked me what happened and if I had somewhere to go. I thought to myself, "Here we go again, back to my aunt's house."

He found me a room at the Days Inn for a few days and then moved me to 16th Street NE, where my life changed dramatically - or should I say until I almost died, and God stepped in. Unbeknownst to me, my sister had been reaching out to those involved in my life. This was all orchestrated before my eighteenth birthday when I was supposed to receive whatever inheritance remained They all lived off of it while I struggled. They felt I needed to suffer for the decisions my mother made by having an affair and having me. The problem with that is I never asked to be created or born, and it's quite selfish of them, as family ties are deeper than just blood. They all knew each other prior to the eviction or my move from MD to DC. However, they could not control me as I had secured all that was built and then lost it all when I chose what I thought was love; it was only a disaster waiting to happen.

My family's abandonment and poor treatment of me were exploited by both my son's father and my stepdad to establish control over me. They were aware of my vulnerability and isolation. My son's father moved me into an apartment under his name, and in exchange, I was only responsible for paying the rent. Although our interactions were sporadic, he would become controlling and possessive if I didn't answer my phone, often accusing me of infidelity. Despite the power imbalance in our relationship, we rarely had sex. I later discovered that his constant busyness, which I initially attributed to his job as a police officer, was actually due to his involvement in a prostitution ring where he robbed clients. This explained why he didn't hesitate to give me money or pay for my move. Between 1996 and 1998, when I was 18 years old, I was in a relationship with a man who was around 27 years old. I have always tended to attract older men. One day, while I was on the bus and had no reception, this man held a gun to my head. When I got off the bus, my phone had died, so I couldn't call for help.

He held the gun to my head, but I looked him straight in the eyes and said, "Before you shoot, please take my son across the hall so he doesn't have to witness this." He called me "a crazy bitch" and left. TMH was right there, and I hurried to get my son. The following morning, I planned to ask about transferring my lease and apartment because of the upcoming tax season. Later that month, I returned home to discover the babysitter had been evicted. My first ex-husband was there; he'd been trying to reach me about helping to find my son. I had ignored him due to his dangerous lifestyle and followed the advice of my second son's father: never depend on anyone to treat you as well as you treat them, and never put all your eggs in one basket. He had the opportunity to make a move, and he did this all a part of another illusion. We spent an interesting evening talking on my back steps while waiting for her to drop off my son. As he had her phone number, he stayed after she left, and we talked. After my son fell asleep, we walked to the recreation center to smoke, and then he walked me home. He asked to see me again, and I agreed. I should have rejected him from the beginning, remember he comes in many forms. The things we least expect and yet love are used to delay and destroy.

He knew I was unaware of his ongoing relationship with his child's mother. Despite this, he deliberately drove down their street, which I was unfamiliar with. She followed us until he lost her, and we ended up at a playground. We talked and got to know each other on a different level, which led to kissing and eventually going back to my house to make love.The lovemaking was incredible, the best I had ever experienced. It was different from the passion I felt with my son's father. There was chemistry and intense passion, but the touch, kiss, and thrust were unique. We continued to meet up occasionally, and it became more frequent. I eventually moved across the hall, and he disappeared for a while. When he reappeared, he was upset because his child's mother had tried to kill him by ramming her car into his while he held their son. He came to my house, and after I put the babies to sleep, we discussed him keeping his son. I immediately told him I wouldn't be involved and advised him to return his son to his mother, as I wouldn't want anyone to do that to me. He called her, they met, and disappeared for hours. When he returned, we argued about the duration of his absence, but he ended up living with me for a while.

My eldest son, who barely knew me, decided he was tired of living in Virginia and called to move in with me. Despite my confusion, I agreed and made the necessary adjustments to accommodate him. I had just been approved for a new credit card with a $2,000 limit, which I used entirely for moving expenses, furniture, rent, and necessities for my children. Life was good for a short time until I received a life-changing call at work. I was young and foolish to let him back into my life, especially after I realized he was selling drugs. However, during the 1990s, at the age of eighteen, I had a good job that paid at least $50,000 annually, allowing me to support myself and maintain my housing. I gave him money for rent, which he spent on drugs instead.

I have never been on government assistance until it was forced upon me with the lies and destruction—in fact, they wish for everyone to believe I made it off the government when in fact it is the opposite. They brought me down to control my money as well as the narrative. Truth be told, I did get on housing assistance until 2016 after my kids were damn near grown, and before that, I paid regular market rent with no assistance and I maintained very well. They would always do something to destroy all I built, and I would always have to restart. I realize now this was done as a way to destroy my credit and have me in a position with no options. I have paid off debts that have been accumulated for years as I did not want to go through the back and forth until recently I felt as though if I continue to pay I will never get ahead, so I fell back and decided to start reporting all things, although this has not changed my credit report or my circumstances. They just incorporate more people in more places, and in return, I gain more haters and enemies who become obsessed with destroying me as they feel I am way too privileged.

My ex-husband called one day while I was at work to tell me U.S. Marshals were at the house to evict us because drugs had been found. He also failed to mention that he hadn't paid my rent. He got a U-Haul truck, put us up in a hotel room, and was subsequently arrested a few days after. I found another address in Trinidad and held onto it until I could relocate. He was released from jail six months later. We reconnected and resumed our relationship after his release in 2000. My love for him was so strong that I walked from Trinidad to the D.C. Jail the night he was released and waited for him. We walked home together and spent the entire night making love. We were deeply in love, but it was an illusion - a plot for my destruction orchestrated by my family. Unbeknownst to me, he was just one of many handlers.

I was convinced that this was my happily ever after. We were incredibly passionate, making love multiple times throughout the day and night. He awakened a wild side of me that I never knew existed. My life was being redirected towards disaster, and they expected me to stay, but I ran as far away as I could. I always wondered how he kept track of me, but now I realize he was sleeping with over half of my family and casting spells on them. He was hoping to do the same to me and would do anything to maintain control over me. But my love for my children and myself was far greater. We went clubbing, attended gatherings, and were spontaneously sexual anytime, anyplace. I knew he wasn't perfect; he was involved in court cases for assault involving family. This mirrored my own family experiences. There's always been some comparison in every relationship, which allowed me to relate on some level. My family exploited that for their own pleasure. It was all a setup, appearing to be real-life experiences, but it was all staged.

Our relationship lasted for two years, and despite a few minor issues that I ignored, everything seemed to be going well. It's common to overlook warning signs; they may not seem relevant at the time, or they may simply appear insignificant. I never questioned why; I simply trusted, and the pattern would repeat - plans canceled without consideration, feelings disregarded.

Then, an incident occurred where he displayed possessiveness, jealousy, and abusive behavior. We would argue over trivial matters. Why didn't you answer your phone? What took you so long to get here? I felt trapped and suffocated. I would get slapped for rolling my sweatpants and exposing my belly, showing too much, looking at someone for too long, or talking with someone without introducing him. It was irrational, reminiscent of movies like "Enough," "A Diary of a Mad Black Woman," and "What's Love Got to Do with It." I was completely isolated, and being young, I mistakenly believed this was love - but it was a catastrophe. He showered me with endless gifts, but the cost was exorbitant. I would later discover that he was stealing and robbing, endangering my entire family.

The movie "A Fall from Grace" closely mirrors my situation; these individuals watched these movies and then used me to enact them in real life. However, I didn't snap; I became cautious and distanced myself. If I had stayed, with all the disrespect and abuse, who wouldn't have contemplated drastic measures? In my case, TMH had a much safer plan that would alter the entire narrative - one in which I am alive and able to share my story, rather than having it shared by someone who may not have genuinely cared.

Life took a sudden turn from non-stop partying to an endless series of unfortunate events. Things changed after his return. While I had resumed my studies to become a Medical, Coding, and Billing Specialist, he started working at a job I had secured for him through my company. Unfortunately, I later discovered he had quit, which resulted in me losing my job as well. It seemed like he found ways to get me fired from every job I got. He would threaten my co-workers, call me incessantly, or I'd have to conceal bruises and scars. There was always something. Determined to improve my prospects, I decided to go back to school to expand my knowledge in accounting and medicine. My initial goal was to find a stable job for the foreseeable future. However, this goal quickly shifted as we fell into a pattern of excessive partying fueled by e-pills, weed, and alcohol. These substances, which seemed harmless initially, gradually developed into destructive habits that diverted my focus and attention.

Despite a lifetime surrounded by dysfunction, I didn't recognize my own abnormal actions. My children were often left in the care of my husband's cousin or a friend. While facing jail time for a crime I didn't commit and under close police surveillance due to a conspiracy against me, he proposed one evening while we watched television, and I accepted. We planned a simple ceremony with a justice of the peace and a reception at the Skyline rooftop in Virginia. My father and his wife generously used Rewards points to gift us a stay at the Marriott and a crystal ashtray. It was a unique wedding, complete with my aunt bringing Popeyes and a Go-Go music entrance – the world's best orchestrated ghetto fabulous wedding. I should have known then that no real father would have allowed it to happen. This too, like my last one, was a planned wedding.

When I was younger, I didn't know my rights and lacked common sense. If I had known then what I know now, I could have called the police to have the car towed or retrieved my keys from the hotel office since the car was in my name. However, I was upset and fixated on the fact that I only had one car key. He returned home with the car, meant to be my wedding gift, a few days before his court date. I went to court with him, and although he didn't resign that day, he had two weeks until his sentencing. By then, we were married, and despite his suggestion of a divorce,

I refused. I believed in staying married and didn't want to repeat my parents' mistakes. I thought we could resolve our issues.

Weeks later, he turned himself in, and I was alone again. His cousins were supposed to help but never did, leaving me uncomfortable and unsupported. Before he left, he went on a robbery spree, leaving me with all the drugs and money. He told me his cousins would help me get rid of it, but just in case, he showed me how to prepare the drugs for sale. That's when I learned the importance of presentation and illusion. Initially, when my husband was incarcerated, I had access to all his money and drugs. People I knew would inquire if I could supply them, and I'd sell only to those familiar to me. Recognizing the potential for quick and substantial profit, I abandoned school and embraced drug dealing. I had witnessed my second son's father engage in similar activities but remained oblivious to the repercussions and the extensive network it involved. I was deeply committed to my husband and determined to support him until his release, with aspirations of leaving the neighborhood behind.

However, reality proved harsh. Following my new connection's arrest, I spent countless hours traveling to Baltimore. Although he had left me with valuable contacts, they frequently attempted to exploit my situation due to my gender and access to a significant network. Consequently, I needed to establish my own connections. My husband's cousin, residing in Baltimore, understood my predicament and connected me with a reliable individual who became my primary supplier. He always treated me respectfully. Despite a brief romantic encounter, I remained focused on my marriage. Even though my husband had been unfaithful, two wrongs don't make a right. I communicated my desire to maintain a professional relationship with my supplier, and he agreed.

My car's bumper was damaged before my first husband's incarceration. It eventually fell off at a gas station on Brentwood Rd, NE WDC. I put it in my trunk and went to a gas station with an auto shop, where I met my last son's father. He offered to help, and we exchanged phone numbers. The next week, we went to the junkyard for a bumper. He also changed my oil and brakes, and we smoked marijuana. We became friends due to our shared interests; we both smoked, and he helped me sell my product. However, this friendship led to complications. One night, while intoxicated, we had sex. This continued for a period, but I eventually told him it needed to stop because I was married. He knew about my marriage, abuse, and infidelity from the beginning. He'd seen my scars and heard my stories, often questioning why I stayed. My reasons were my vows and loyalty. I never lied to him, and when my first husband was nearing his release, I told him I'd only contact him to reconcile if I needed repairs to my car. He agreed.

He was released from jail after eighteen months, and I moved nearby to Queen Street. Unfortunately, he followed me there, and life took a familiar, unpleasant turn. He continued the pattern of abuse, justifying his actions by claiming I was unfaithful while he was incarcerated.Despite the pain and my guilt over the situation, I forgave him repeatedly, caught between what I had been taught and what I knew was right. During his time in and out of jail, I didn't expect our relationship to last with so much abuse. However, he surprised me, and we were initially happy, enjoying each other's company and spending time together. For the first time, I felt loved and understood.I should have trusted my instincts and not given him another chance. I had forgiven the beatings, the infidelity, the displacement from my home, and even my own arrest because of him. I urge you, please remember, if a man abuses you once, he will likely repeat the pattern/ He will only finish what he did not before, especially if you forgive him.

He reappeared after a few days and asked me to go to court with him so I could get the car, which was in my name. I had only learned to drive two days before he left, so I didn't argue and just went with him. When we arrived, he suggested we get a divorce, and I agreed. We didn't anticipate the obstacle that was about to hit us; he didn't get locked up. However, we both soon realized the price tag for me would be my kids, freedom, and stability. He didn't lose anything because everything was in my name.I had a doctor's appointment near Hechinger Mall and discovered I was pregnant and went grocery shopping.. When I got home, I realized I'd forgotten the ricotta cheese for the lasagna I planned to make for dinner that night. I was shocked to find money, drugs, and guns when I opened the door. He quickly told me not to worry, he had gone on a move, and he was going to have it moved before they arrived home.He asked to come with me to Safeway because he needed baggies. I asked him to put everything away before he left, just in case the kids came home early. I had also noticed a van parked across from my house that I had never seen before. He was cocky, giving the van the finger and saying "F them." He told me he would be back in time, as the kids would go to the rec center after school, and then we would be back.The police were everywhere— front door, street, and alleys. My first thought was to find my boys. The recreation center wasn't closed yet, and it wasn't time for them to be home. But when I got there, the director was closing up, saying he sent the kids home because the air conditioning wasn't working.

I was stuck. I had no one, and the director knew it. I was determined to find my kids before turning myself in. I called my second son's father, but he cursed me out and said, "Hell no." My sister also refused to help. After spending the night in a hotel using the money left behind by the police after a raid, He called his brother to discuss the situation. We agreed that since he had prior convictions and I only had juvenile charges, I would take the fall to protect my children. The same day the feds raided my home, I discovered I was pregnant with my third son and had just lost two children at once. His mother and brother agreed to help, so I turned myself in and was arrested. I was comfortable with this decision because my children were safe. While in jail awaiting bail for child neglect, possession with intent to distribute cocaine, crack cocaine, heroin, and possession of firearms, I accepted a plea deal that would automatically dismiss his case. However, this plea meant I was now facing thirty years in prison.

My life changed drastically due to my jealous sister and greedy husband. Everyone I thought I could trust was involved in a plot against me. I should have paid closer attention when my sister jokingly said she was jealous—she meant every word. It took me 45 years to realize who had been pretending to care and help me all along. My sister envied my life and even used my experiences with domestic violence (including a torn ACL from an altercation on my birthday) to her advantage.. The police raid on my Queen Street house left me with nothing. I had to return to try and salvage what I could. The raid took everything, including food and my children's drinks, that I had just purchased. I had spent $389 on groceries the night before the raid. The police report would later state that my children were found dirty and hungry, even though I had just gone grocery shopping. When I returned to my apartment after the raid, I found Capri-Sun containers and snack wrappers everywhere. The only thing left in the refrigerator was an old meal. They had emptied the freezer and the refrigerator and my clothes purchased for my children were all gone. Afterward, they would spend the next seven and a half years slandering my name and character. During that time, I was trying to stay afloat amidst the constant beating and cheating. While pregnant, we moved to his mother's house, where his sons were staying at The Wingate's on MLK AVE, SE, in Washington DC. The drama continued there, and despite my high-risk pregnancy, I was constantly told that the baby wasn't his. He used this as an excuse to beat and cheat on me

My former partner's mother helped him find a night job, which allowed us to get an apartment in her building. Initially, things were fine. However, he soon took a part-time maintenance job, giving him and his cousins access to other apartments for illicit activities like smoking and prostitution. His family – his mother, cousins, and childhood friends – lived in other units. This quickly became problematic as he repeated his past behaviors from the "Trinistepdad" situation and began selling drugs from our apartment. Recognizing this as a dangerous situation about to escalate, and fearing legal repercussions if caught again, I knew I had to leave.

I went to my aunt's house, my usual refuge offering shelter with minimal cost. While there, my son's father called to see him, and I agreed to a visit. Since I was in the neighborhood, I decided to see a childhood friend. Having recently escaped a dangerous, abusive, and unstable relationship, I felt I deserved some enjoyment. I went out with another childhood friend, someone who had always been protective and respectful. However, I later discovered his true intentions: he had aligned himself with my family, my ex-partners, hired individuals to harm me, and conspired with a former high school acquaintance, now a PG County police officer living nearby, to orchestrate my downfall and seize what was rightfully mine, orchestrated by my sister. At the time, I was still married, and this individual was also married and a friend of my son's father.

When the weekend was over, I went to pick up my son. I had a feeling that something wasn't right. As I was gathering his things, the police suddenly showed up and started banging on the door. We had to go to court the next morning. After he took responsibility, I was released. Despite our reconciliation and eventual move to The Kennebec in Oxon Hill, Maryland, I realized that not all relationships work. It's crucial to maintain civility for the sake of the children, especially when co-parenting. Their plan was different; it involved getting me pregnant, using my children to receive financial aid for their existing relationships, and maintaining a facade of independence while in a relationship.

They targeted me to steal my identity and my children's identities for government assistance and tax fraud to support their habits and family. They kept me stressed and at a distance, hoping my children would be returned to them. He frequently took my car without asking, leaving me and our son alone for hours while he engaged in infidelity and theft. The situation deteriorated further when he and his cousin, despite their lack of knowledge, attempted to fix my car's oil pan. Growing tired of waiting for help that never came, I decided to take matters into my own hands. I had always been independent and resourceful, learning to handle DIY projects and repairs on my own. My faith rested solely in TMH.

I reached out to a friend uptown who had always been supportive, and he provided me with enough money to fix my brakes. Determined to be independent, I contacted the father of my youngest son, a mechanic, who agreed to help despite the strained relationship caused by my ex-husband's return. He repaired my car, allowing me to return home. Later that evening, my ex-husband found the mechanic's number in my phone and questioned me about it, leading to a heated argument. A few nights later, as I lay in bed, I contemplated how I could leave my ex-husband and take my son with me without him knowing. I knew it would be difficult, but he had left me no other choice. Two nights prior, we had a serious argument because I encouraged him to find legitimate work instead of resorting to robbery and theft. I suggested that he could utilize my hairdressing skills to earn money. I went uptown and styled two people's hair, earning $175. With that money, I bought Pampers, milk, cereal, a bottle, and some tree. As a result of my actions, he beat me, leaving a third-degree burn on my left eye and a scar that remains to this day. He also rubbed my face in the carpet, causing severe bruising and burning. Despite the violence, we made up, as we had agreed at the beginning of our marriage to never go to bed angry with each other. In his mind, sex was enough to reconcile. I wanted to escape the situation and get away from him. I took my son to my aunt's house, where she took pictures of my injured face. I then dropped my son off at my sister's house and went to the emergency room at Washington Hospital Center, where they also took photos. I reported the incident to the police but chose not to press charges.

I left the hospital angry and went to my sister's house, but she ultimately told me I couldn't stay because she was taking in another family and didn't have space for me. I spent the night driving around with my son until I fell asleep at the wheel and crashed into a couple's truck in the Third Street Tunnel. Fortunately, they were understanding and their truck was fine, though my car was damaged. When I returned to Kennebec to park my car, he saw me and insisted we talk. I was exhausted and had nowhere else to go, so I reluctantly agreed. Things were calm for a few days until he found the photos my aunt took of my injuries, and the fighting started again. I knew then the relationship was over.

That night, I resolved to leave with my son and whatever belongings I could manage. I put on my pajamas, placed my shoes by the door, and waited for both him and my son to fall asleep, careful to avoid any sudden movements that might attract his attention. He was always suspicious; even a brief absence would prompt him to check on me, and any movement resulted in a tighter grip and questions about where I was going.I knew I had approximately five minutes to disappear completely. Despite the fact that he had torn my ACL in the past, I relied on my high school track experience and sprinted away. However, halfway to Southern Ave SE, WDC, coming off Kennebec, Oxon Hill, MD, my ACL gave out.

Undaunted, I pressed forward. My abuser materialized, attempting to coerce my return upon realizing my escape. Though he had stolen everything, including my children's essential papers, I remained resolute. My son was still in the house, but I would not re-enter without police protection, knowing that doing so could cost either of our lives. In retrospect, I should have followed my first instinct: wake him, take my son, and leave. My children were my only concern as I continued towards Southern Ave, SE, focused on our safety and escape. I decided to walk to the gas station at the top of Southern Ave, SE, WDC, to call my mechanic friend— the only person I knew nearby who owned a car. He arrived promptly. While I waited, my ex-husband and his mistress drove by, taunting me. Unbeknownst to me, they were all conspiring together, leading me to believe I was safe. I would later regret this misjudgment after discovering their plan to impregnate me and repeat the cycle of abuse I had just fled.

After a difficult night where my friend offered support, the following morning I attempted to obtain a restraining order and regain custody of my son at the courthouse, but was unsuccessful as his father had already moved. Earlier, while at a gas station, I was confronted by my partner and his mistress, who I later learned lived in our building. Fortunately, my youngest son's father arrived, and I was able to leave with him. I discovered that my partner's infidelity involved a former high school girlfriend who was also closely connected to my aunt, sister, and a deceptive friend. This deception had been orchestrated before I turned eighteen, and I was completely unaware.

I discovered that my aunt collaborated with my husband's mistress and my sister to ruin my marriage. My husband was frequently outside so he could cheat on me with his mistress, who was my aunt's friend and co-worker. The replacement for me in accounting for the job was lost upon my move back to D.C from Nova Ave, Capital Heights in which another friend would later move there one of which was the guy from the mall. My ex-husband's mistress was also friends with a man he later robbed, and they all worked together in the detailing department.This pattern of betrayal has been a constant theme in my life. They would lie and sabotage any external communication to isolate me and prevent me from receiving help or love. This was only the beginning of their schemes against me because I refused to conform to their expectations. They made me defensive and angry, which resulted in frequent jail time and illness from stress and worry. I know other mothers and single stepdads can relate; our children are precious, and as parents, we are obligated to protect them at all costs. My initial plan was disrupted when I discovered they were manipulating my life and causing my depression. By preventing me from having a family and then taking away the ones I created, they left me feeling empty. They assumed I needed my children to survive not because of taxes or lack of government assistance, but I have always worked. Even without the resources they obtained illegally, I managed to stay afloat. Life was never easy; despite appearing privileged, I never was. I built everything from scratch, only to be subjected to ridicule and mistreatment. This negativity led me to stop caring. As I focused on living for my children, communication decreased, and they began using my kids against me. Although I managed to escape, I was unsuccessful in getting my son back. He consistently used my pending neglect and drug case against me. A plea I had taken to keep our family together was the one that would keep the distance intact, but their plan was already in motion. His paid role was to get me pregnant and destroy my life, leaving me empty and in despair. Initially, it was easy to manipulate me with dark magic and deceit. I never suspected any betrayal and believed they had no connection with my family. The truth was that this was all part of a larger plan.

After my sister complained about my stay, the Victims Advocate Program moved me to a hotel on New York Ave, NE WDC. My sister was in a residential program with my children. A court order restricted my visits to twice weekly for two hours at her home. Soon after a court appearance, he started following me. One day, I went to her door and found him and his cousin attempting to force their way in. I later learned my sister had revealed my location to him. Together, we were able to fend them off, and they left. We decided against calling the police, as my sister reportedly wanted to avoid attention.

For two years, legal proceedings stalled without a hearing, and my case docket vanished. Despite my court-appointed attorney's investigation, I was unable to disprove the false accusations against me. This deadlock persisted for an additional three to six months, resulting in the loss of everything. My ex-husband relentlessly pursued a guilty verdict for neglect and aimed to prove me an unfit mother to gain custody of our son for financial benefit. He intended to leverage the discovery of the jacket against me. My attempts to attend classes and complete tests were futile, as evidence continued to be stolen and destroyed. My sister actively prolonged these hardships to sustain her own lifestyle, exploiting me and my children without considering the damage inflicted. Weeks went by without contact with my children. My eventual court appearance was prompted by my ex-husband's insistence. I had previously avoided visits to shield my children from the injuries he had caused. In court, I falsely claimed a car accident as the cause of my injuries, a statement contradicted by his partner, my own sister.

A court-appointed psychologist deemed me unfit to parent due to alleged mental disabilities, a determination compounded by my sister's exploitation of my injured ACL. The Social Security Administration's rejection of this report was baffling and unfair, exposing a system seemingly driven by influence rather than merit. Suddenly, everything I had built was stripped away and given to an undeserving individual. Their aim was to discredit me, and taking my children, particularly placing my second son in foster care, was their most devastating tactic. My greatest fear materialized. Consequently, my second son, now incarcerated in a maximum-security facility for car theft, became defensive. They had shifted their focus to my children. The only child they couldn't manipulate was the one left alone, yet he was institutionalized. Eventually, he succumbed, becoming defiant and seeking attention and survival through misbehavior. Ultimately, I had to relinquish my children because everything I held dear had been compromised.

Benefiting from her children and their godparents' political connections, she quickly obtained a housing voucher and foster care license because she had my children, which sped up her housing. Although unseen by me then, a betrayal occurred while I was focused on reuniting with my kids and not paying attention. To deal with the pain of losing them, I turned to alcohol and marijuana, which damaged my life and created distance between us, especially impacting my second son. He was much like me, outspoken and resilient. My oldest son's upbringing was different, raised first by my mother and then my cousin, causing him to align with them and resent me after my mother's death. Despite my family's negative portrayal of me, my mother always ensured he knew I was his mother. Later, my sister secured a fully furnished three-bedroom house with a basement and porches using an emergency voucher. Despite the circumstances potentially being at our expense, I never resented her success, as my priority was always the well-being of my children.

Moving to Ashton Heights in Suitland, MD, my immediate concerns were securing employment and regaining custody of my children. My felony conviction created considerable challenges. The ongoing stress from my ex-husband taught me to be cautious in my interactions. Despite past attempts to foster positive relationships with former partners, my focus now centered on progressing for the sake of my children. Co-parenting became essential, despite consistent conflict and his attempts to control the situation. To enable some level of communication, we decided to meet at the recreation center near Trinidad, with his cousin present, as much of his family, who were aware of the plans to ruin my life, lived there. This arrangement, intended to support co-parenting, unfortunately evolved into another source of distress, enabling my ex-husband to continue his emotional abuse and manipulate our son.

After disclosing my new address, my ex-partner began visiting, and our relationship resumed. However, I soon discovered he was still involved with his mistress. He would even use her car to pick me up, claiming it was his. I believed him until I found her lip gloss and other personal belongings inside. When I confronted him, he dismissed it, saying she'd do anything for him. This was the final straw, and I ended the relationship, recognizing his manipulative behavior. I shifted my focus back to preparing to file for divorce. The process in Maryland, where we were married, differed from Washington, DC. My son's father and I had been spending time together and developing feelings for each other. He loved me, but I was preoccupied with my divorce, court cases, and rebuilding my life, and I didn't reciprocate his feelings. Despite my anger, he was there for me every step of the way.

My criminal record, stemming from pending drug and neglect felony cases, prevented me from passing the required background checks for accounting jobs. Consequently, I lost my job and was evicted from my apartment in Ashton Heights, Maryland. Being jobless and separated from my children made me ineligible for government assistance and tax filing. Unbeknownst to me, this was orchestrated by my ex-husband. He appeared at my eviction and suggested I move into a low-income housing program in Atlantic Gardens on 4th Street SE, near his mother. He presented this as an easy transition, but I later understood his true motive: to monitor and control me from afar while he continued his relationship with his mistress in our former building. He would bring my son for visits, but only when he was also in Trinidad. These constant, unwelcome intrusions became suffocating. He acted as though our legal marriage and his custody of our son gave him free rein, even after my son stopped calling me "mom" and used my name instead. When I tried to discuss this, he would cut off contact if I didn't comply. He even attempted to have me killed by orchestrating a robbery of my friend. Sharing my story is essential, and by the end, the reasons will be clear.

While dealing with numerous personal challenges, I routinely visited my other two children in another part of town, often bringing food. Despite my own family's needs, I found myself providing for my daughter, her husband, and their children. They were content simply being together and with my children. It felt as though I was financially responsible for her entire household while she received government assistance like housing, TANF, and child support, including additional funds for my youngest son due to his behavioral issues and anxiety, which led to medication. These funds appeared to be used for their leisure and to impress others.

During a vulnerable moment after consuming alcohol with my youngest son's father, I made a grave error. Instead of seeking strength from my faith, I sought revenge against my former husband and his partner. Weeks later, I awoke in the hospital, paralyzed and without sensation on the left side of my face. My son's father and his mother were present, praying. Upon regaining consciousness, he announced my awakening and kissed my forehead, urging me to remain still while he fetched the doctor. The doctor informed me that I had been in a serious accident, resulting in significant head trauma and facial nerve damage. My memory was gone, and I didn't even recognize my son's father. I never asked about other visitors, as I had always felt alone. I was eventually discharged with lasting facial nerve damage and extensive bruising. Despite undergoing plastic surgery, I remained disoriented for weeks following the accident.

After retaliating by damaging his truck due to his attempt on my life and theft from a friend, I returned to my son's father's home. I had been living there since leaving my ex-husband and family, finding more acceptance from his family than my own.

However, this changed after my accident. His behavior shifted, and he began treating me poorly, similar to others, revealing a preoccupation with money. Surprisingly, a close and previously loyal friend also turned against me for reasons unknown. I later understood this to be part of a scheme to force me back under my family's control. Despite their hurtful actions, I consistently returned to my family, believing that our blood relation equated to love.

I miraculously survived a severe car accident shortly after arriving at my son's father's home in Clinton, MD. The impact caused extensive damage to my car, from the front bumper to the middle of the driver's side, necessitating the use of the jaws of life to remove the roof and extract me. My son's father admitted he believed I had died due to the significant blood loss. Although I have no memory of the event, I am grateful to have escaped with only minor injuries. During my recovery, I was prescribed strong pain medication, including Morphine and Percocet. Unbeknownst to me at the time, while I was heavily medicated to keep me subdued, he was abusing my prescriptions along with his daily cocaine habit. I was only aware of his marijuana and alcohol use then, but the truth would later be revealed.

Our arguments flared up again with my sister when I started seeing my children regularly. Whenever she was mad at me or I didn't agree with her, she'd threaten to interfere with my visits. It wasn't enough that she had already separated us; my oldest lived with her, and a social worker brought my youngest to me for only two hours, twice a week. Even this limited time together became inconsistent because of our constant conflict. She misused money meant for my children's needs, like taxes, spending it on parties, possessions, and her substance abuse. She wasn't even caring for her own two children, whose godparents were always the ones looking after them. Consequently, my children's belongings that I purchased were often used by her sons, which I didn't mind since they were all cousins and boys. This is why I never wanted my children to be around my family, much less live with them. I felt trapped in a terrible situation, one I desperately didn't want my children to go through, as I had experienced it myself, both as a child and an adult. Despite being at a disadvantage, I worked hard with my earnings. I was able to maintain my job, buy a car with cash, and provide a home for us, holding onto the hope that things would eventually get better.

Despite hoping for respite after four years, my sister's relationships with my social worker, therapist, and others involved in my case deepened. Obtaining a foster care license, she portrayed herself as the ideal older sister and aunt. However, her true motive was to dismantle my family to gain attention and usurp the life I had created. Her two prior theft charges were overlooked. She also left Red Springs, NC, after my nephew's father attempted to pawn items stolen from the police chief's mother. Her history included embezzling from multiple companies and a lifelong involvement in prostitution, beginning as far back as my memory serves. She was the one who introduced me to marijuana. Our childhood was spent in a home plagued by addiction, incest, alcoholism, and indolent thieves who consistently sought shortcuts and avoided honest work.

The system, along with family, jealous individuals, and even supporters, neglected to intervene before harm occurred. I was a victim of deception and manipulation, and their scheme succeeded. Driven by financial gain and the theft of a life, they maintained control over one person while destroying the other. My case was intentionally prolonged with fabricated excuses simply to secure payments for an undeserved lifestyle. Despite numerous attempts to provide evidence and lodge complaints, my concerns and my son's objections were consistently dismissed. My eldest son's distress manifested in declining academic performance. This was particularly perplexing given my history of always being involved to resolve or discipline my children's issues. Consequently, my son acted out frequently, seeking negative attention merely to see me. They continued to place him in institutions and respite care, ultimately leading to his molestation in foster care. This sequence of events concluded my neglect case. Shortly thereafter, she reasserted herself into my life by pursuing child support from my oldest son's father, even after his early graduation and departure for college in Delaware. They conducted an entire court case in my absence, a direct consequence of rendering me homeless to create the illusion of my being unreachable. They falsely informed the court of my death from a drug overdose and that his father had died by suicide shortly after. This was done to obtain retroactive child support and an inheritance intended for my son or me; the specifics remain unclear due to my absence and lack of awareness regarding their communications and his death, which a childhood friend later informed me of in 2014, without further details.

Facing sentencing in my criminal case, I initially chose to plead guilty. However, after reviewing all police reports and hospital records, I reversed my decision and informed the judge. My ex-husband, who had started a new life with someone from Kennebec, held me responsible for the consequences of the raid. He accused me of selling drugs to an informant while he was incarcerated. Later, I learned that while I was away in Baltimore, my supposed best friend allowed her daughter's father to sell drugs to my clients from my home, using my identity and without my knowledge. He moved on with my son and his mistress, leaving me to handle the aftermath. My focus shifted to parenting classes, anger management, and therapy for my children and myself. Amidst this, I was enduring physical and mental abuse while struggling to maintain work, housing, and provide for my children. I was a constant presence in their lives. Why, then, did they choose to completely remove them, knowing they were my source of strength? My aspiration was always to build my own family and move beyond my past. I simply desire happiness and peace.

Despite ongoing prayers and hard work, my longing to see my son, taken by my ex-husband, persisted after moving in with my youngest son's father, even though we loved each other. A planned meeting in Trinidad highlighted how my children were often used against me. My children meant everything to me, a stark contrast to many in my family who lacked knowledge of their children's fathers. While they made judgmental comments, I valued that my children's fathers were known and involved, some even living with them—a rarity due to others prioritizing welfare over their children's well-being. I never sought child support, wanting the fathers to remain present in their children's lives without fear of repercussions. Instead of asking for help, I always worked diligently to ensure my children's happiness. I was willing to pay child support if it meant my children were well, regardless of the personal cost, but selling my body for money, like some family members who became pregnant for that reason, was never an option. I never considered assistance and was often denied anyway due to earning too much. The system questioned my choice not to seek child support and seemed to resent my independence. I consciously chose a different path, determined to overcome the negativity from my community, family, and F.A.N.S. While they accepted their circumstances, I believed we were meant to exceed the accomplishments of past generations. The struggles of our elders were intended to pave the way for a better life, not confine us to limited possibilities.

Motivated by my grandmother's encouragement, I resolved to challenge assumptions and prove my detractors wrong. Despite being betrayed and efforts to silence me, I chose to speak out against their deceit. What began as an attempt to assist a family unexpectedly turned into a catastrophe, leaving me bewildered. The police were not involved because my sister moved in with me. This followed her starting a relationship with my aunt's former boyfriend and my uncle's former best friend, with whom she also became intimate. This man, a military veteran who had served with my uncle, was verbally and potentially physically abusive. After my marriage, my sister contacted me, needing shelter because her boyfriend was evicting her and her children. He had discovered her attempt to surprise him with a threesome, which angered him. She explained it as mere experimentation. As I've said, I am not judgmental; everyone has their own approach to life. Consequently, I readily welcomed her into our home. During her initial week in our two-bedroom apartment, our household comprised my two children, her two children, herself, my husband, and me. We adapted by converting our enclosed back porch into a bedroom, giving our bedroom to the children, and my husband and I slept on the sofa bed in the living room. We managed.

One night at Anacostia Park, while our children slept, my husband, his friend, my sister, and I were drinking and smoking. My sister and my husband's friend then decided to engage in sexual activity, which my husband watched. I became enraged and wanted to leave, but he tried to persuade me to join them. A fight ensued between my sister, my husband, and me, during which I injured my hand and sought medical attention the following morning before kicking my sister out. Her flirtatious behavior with my husband, which he encouraged, was unacceptable, especially in front of his friend and my sister. We had all been drinking, and her behavior continued on the drive home. This was the second time I had physically confronted someone over inappropriate involvement with my partners. Lessons learned. Subsequently, my home was raided, significantly disrupting my life. Despite facing increasing hardship, I persevered, maintained my faith, prayed, and trusted that ultimate justice was not mine to enact. Although immediate consequences might not occur, I remained certain that eventually, truth and life would reveal and punish all the wrongdoing. The trauma of losing my home was quickly followed by the devastating loss of my children, which made life feel meaningless for a long time. With the minimal possessions we had left, we gathered $294 in change from water jugs left by the police after they had taken everything, including my children and our food. We used this money for a hotel room. That night, we planned how to get my children back. After exhausting all other contacts, my husband reached out to his mother, who agreed to care for them. We visited them daily. We also discussed the plea deal. Given his prior convictions, he faced a substantial prison sentence if found guilty. I proposed taking the plea for the drug charges, believing that as a first-time offender, I would likely receive probation. He agreed, seeing it as the best course of action.

Planning to surrender to the fifth district police station the next morning, the intention was for him to be released and subsequently arrange for our children to be placed in his mother's care. Finding someone to look after my kids was never an issue, as payment was always involved – substantial amounts, starting at least at $2,000 for both, potentially more or less. It seemed everyone profited from our distress. They consistently found reasons to delay things after their needs were met, often making last-minute changes that caused further setbacks.

Following my release, my ex-husband immediately resumed selling drugs on Queen Street. His intention was to fund our relocation from my former apartment to The Wingates. He concealed the drugs in the apartment above our previous one in Trinistepdad and conducted transactions in the back. I recognized the inherent danger in this decision. Three days later, a police raid occurred, leading to the confiscation of the drugs. Although we were not there, this event further delayed our move and intensified our already difficult circumstances. Consequently, we were compelled to sell my car to my neighbor's girlfriend. Our intention was to use the funds to buy another vehicle and rent a room in Virginia. Unfortunately, the car was later destroyed due to my ex-husband's continued involvement in robberies. After he robbed someone nearby, I was waiting for him on Queen Street, five months pregnant, when I saw a man run towards my car with a cinder block. He smashed it through the front windshield; thankfully, I was in the passenger seat. My ex-husband pursued the man and then came back to check on me. Although I was physically unharmed, I insisted that we had to leave the area, cautioning him that his actions would ultimately lead to our deaths. His history of robbery and theft had created a multitude of enemies. I needed to separate myself from him and his reputation. The horrific robbery on Chesapeake St., SE, in the 1990s, where a young man was killed, heightened my fears, especially after my ex-husband admitted his involvement and I personally witnessed his violent tendencies, which convinced me of his capacity for extreme actions.

Life with my ex-husband became increasingly difficult, marked by traumatic experiences, especially during my pregnancy. We were living with his mother at The Wingate's in Southeast D.C., where my children were already staying in her small apartment on bunk beds provided by CFSA. Pregnant at the time, I slept on the living room floor. His mother, a Wingate's native and well-regarded community member, worked at the front desk. He also worked there, initially during the day in maintenance, which gave him access to vacant units, and later at night at the front desk. This access led to the discovery of his infidelity with female tenants. After my plea bargain, I could no longer tolerate the disrespect. Even during my pregnancy, his behavior caused significant distress. In one instance, at seven months pregnant, I found him flirting at the pool. The ensuing argument led to my collapse in the parking lot. Another traumatic event occurred in the same month when I confronted him about his infidelity. He denied he was the father and, during our argument at his mother's house where we were living, he ordered me inside. When I refused, he physically dragged me by my hair down the hallway until his mother intervened, preventing him from going to his mistress who lived downstairs.

Ending the relationship became necessary due to ongoing abuse, disrespect, and infidelity. I had previously communicated my inability to continue under such circumstances. The discovery of another woman's underwear in our bed linens was the definitive end. Seeking safety and support, I returned to my aunt's home on Lamont St, NW WDC—the same aunt who supported me during my relationship with the Pentacles. She again became a vital source of strength, aiding my recovery. During this period, I also re-established connections with childhood friends. Despite the complexities arising from his friendship with my second son's father and my pending sentencing, he was insistent on providing assistance. However, given my fear of imprisonment and losing contact with my children, especially considering his unsettling activities like selling the apartment he obtained for us after starting his new job, I couldn't take that risk.

Around the time my son was a few months old, I reconnected with my ex-husband to try and co-parent. However, about nine months later, he took our son from me. I was homeless then and still dealing with court cases related to neglect and criminal charges. My aunt offered me a place to stay, but I regretted it because of my uncle. I had intense hatred for him due to the abuse I suffered between the ages of nine and thirteen and wanted revenge since he never faced any consequences for his actions. He disgusted me, and I felt protective of my little cousin, wanting to shield her from what I had experienced. I immediately took her under my wing; she was like a little sister, and her brothers were like my own. I tried to care for all my younger cousins as much as I could. My little cousin lived with her grandmother until she was older, and I often wondered if my aunt shared my fears. I made sure my little cousin was safe, often being the one looking after her. I tried to be away from my aunt's house as much as possible. My friend knew how uncomfortable I was there and frequently invited me to his place downtown near the parks where he worked, which was a welcome escape. When I wasn't there, I was up late at night trying to make money and avoid the police, hustling in my car until the police arrived and cleared everyone out.

Despite my child's father's notoriety within the local drug scene, my good rapport with dealers stemmed from my own independence and willingness to work, not from his reputation. They respected me because I wasn't prostituting myself. This led to a mutual protectiveness. Although I could generally handle my own affairs, I always had other ways to earn a living, such as hairdressing, cooking, or renting property. I believed in resourcefulness and the importance of trying. Sex work was never an option. I remained self-assured and persistent. Taking that initial step forward, with faith, allows for guidance along the journey. Looking back, I realize that others, whom I called the "F.A.N.S.," admired my ambition and wanted to be like me. It's interesting to consider the difference between acting out of necessity and having one's needs already met. My approach was distinctive, and their attempts to imitate me appeared to be a way to improve their own standing without grasping my core motivations. As someone who truly started with nothing, I wasn't insulted by their imitation; I saw it as a form of flattery.

My friend, who worked with my aunt and my ex-husband's mistress (both secretly supporting me), became a pawn in what I believe was a deliberate setup orchestrated by my tracking ex-husband to harm me. He arranged for my friend's car to be stolen and then returned, parked in my spot, in an obvious attempt to frame me. They were all working together, concealing their involvement in these elaborate and malicious plots designed to ruin me.My ex-husband's mother, living across the street, could monitor everyone visiting my house. My friend and I would meet, sometimes at my place. Despite my ex-husband's ongoing affair and refusal to finalize our divorce (a situation that persisted even while I fought in court for my children and to recover from being in survival mode), I believed we had both moved on. However, one evening, as I was starting to rebuild my life, he saw my friend and me being intimate.Later that night, I was at home drinking Seagram's Gin and Juice, expecting my friend after his call saying he was coming over. I fell asleep waiting. Hours later, a phone call woke me. "You set me up," my friend accused, explaining that he had been robbed, and everything, including his car, was gone.

Leaving my residence, I was confronted by my ex-husband, who blocked my return inside. His anger was evident, and he physically attacked me. This assault was triggered by his incorrect belief that our divorce stemmed from my infidelity. The reality was that his violent behavior, including an attempted murder, and his actions of stealing my friend's vehicle and drugs and then staging it at my property, led to our separation. Subsequently, he reached out through my youngest son's father, asking for my contact information and receiving assurance that contacting him was acceptable if I felt ready. I agreed to communicate, secure in my innocence. During a meeting at Hope Village, he confessed to having me followed and hiring someone to kill me based on his mistaken suspicion that I was involved in a robbery. Although we initially considered reconciliation, I ended the relationship after his admission, particularly as he had learned of my innocence.

Amidst a baseless legal battle and the struggle to regain custody of my children, further betrayals led to an overwhelming situation. I decided to leave street life for stability and a fresh start, recognizing the fleeting nature of those connections. My ability to navigate both street and conventional worlds, once a survival mechanism, was no longer beneficial. Returning to my pre-marriage life seemed impossible at that time.I failed to mention that the stolen phone charger belonged to one of my son's fathers, a detail that quickly caused significant issues. Several days later, my hidden rent money, known to only one person, was stolen after a forced entry. Only the savings I had diligently collected were taken. Though consumed by anger and the desire for revenge, I had to remain restrained due to ongoing legal proceedings and the urgent need to regain custody of my children.I later discovered that the same individual was responsible for their removal. He justified his actions by claiming a lack of resources and wanting to provide for his mistress, my son, and her daughter before his anticipated return to prison. Stealing from me and orchestrating my eviction was his chosen method. He had even made arrangements for me at Ashton Heights following my eviction.

Prioritizing inner peace over material possessions, including sentimental items, I've embraced the fleeting nature of life and change, leading to a sense of detachment and an inability to plan for the future due to constant transitions. Despite a restraining order obtained after an assault, its protection was negated by his subsequent, unexplained rearrest. My attempt to retrieve my son with the PG police in Oxon Hill, MD, failed due to a system error. Even with the restraining order and his later incarceration, intervention was denied because his non-maternal companion cited my pending court cases. Referral to DC authorities offered no help due to jurisdictional limits; the DC restraining order was merely one aspect of his broader actions.

Numerous reports filed with the FTC, IRS, and UI yielded no action due to a lack of concrete evidence to initiate an investigation. Although I knew the perpetrator, past experiences led to my claims being dismissed as hearsay, leaving me feeling powerless and unheard in my pursuit of justice. I share this account hoping for guidance or assistance in taking appropriate action.Driven by a desire to retaliate after being displaced, I later discovered his mother and mistress had manipulated him into granting his mother custody, despite him not living with her and her suffering from knee rheumatoid arthritis. Even incarcerated, he maintained control through his mother and mistress, who played a maternal role in my son's life. This arrangement sustained their income while he was jailed and allowed her to fraudulently claim tax benefits—a deliberately executed scheme.

Driven by a desire to recover what I had lost, my actions inadvertently worsened my circumstances. I partnered with someone equally intent on revenge: my son's father, whose judgment was clouded by alcohol and who sought retribution. I formulated a plan targeting his mistress, whom I blamed for taking my son and orchestrating my eviction and the theft of my rent money. My twin shared this desire for revenge and intensified the situation by introducing paint remover. Meanwhile, I drove to Ashton Heights—a location from which I had been previously evicted and where he had quickly moved them after stealing from my friend and me. Prior to this, he had left his car at my home, anticipating harm to me from my friend. My ex-husband had also made attempts on my life. It is important to note that I was not involved in the initial idea; he conceived the plan while intoxicated. I remained in the car while he vandalized their vehicle with paint remover, which led to my arrest, although the charges were later dropped.

Years later, I was arrested again for speeding in my new car while taking my son to his stepfather's house for a regular weekend visit. I was traveling at high speed and was arrested. My son's father was contacted to pick up my son and my car, as I was charged with malicious vandalism. I spent the night in jail, and he later posted my bail. Subsequently, I lost my car after repaying the bond, which had already been refunded after my court appearance. However, he and his mother insisted on repayment, forcing me to sell my car and leaving me without transportation once more. Feeling defeated after losing my career, children, and home, I believed these individuals were destroying my life with the aid of the judicial system. Although I was initially consumed by vengeance, my youngest son's father helped me recognize that there was more to life.

I went through a time of being overwhelmed with generosity – kindness, gifts, cars, trips, and affection were lavished upon me. Yet, the profound pain I harbored kept me from truly accepting these gestures. My thoughts were consumed by the past, which I felt had stolen a piece of me. I was convinced that those who professed their love for me actually intended to harm me financially and through my children. It seemed my family, ex-partners, and acquaintances were taking advantage of my suffering, my efforts, and my setbacks. They weaponized my weaknesses against me, even involving my children, the very beings I carried and birthed. The love I once knew was perverted and turned into a tool against me, leaving me devastated and disoriented. Despite this inner chaos, I remained outwardly calm and resisted isolation. My son's father advised me to move on, but I couldn't; my only concern was the well-being and security of my children. Their actions were based on a false premise that I depended on my children for financial support, which has never been the case, as I have always been employed and supported my family.

At twenty-four weeks into a pregnancy with my youngest son's father, I experienced the stillbirth of a baby boy. He was delivered and pronounced dead. I received a birth certificate with his footprints and his blanket, treasured items that were sadly lost after a painful separation when my belongings were discarded. Before this additional heartbreak, my youngest son's father was manipulated by his friends for about six to seven and a half years while living at his mother's. Eventually, he also turned against me. Even after my legal separation from my husband, the destructive pattern from our relationship continued. My ex-husband would contact me, re-enter my life, and request to meet. Hoping to see my son, I always agreed. However, he would appear without our son and expect sexual intimacy. When I refused, I resumed my relationship with my last son's father, who later learned of my interactions with my ex-husband. I denied these interactions, despite his prior knowledge that I was still married when our relationship began. My ex-husband finally signed the divorce papers after being shot and nearly killed.

A disagreement regarding my communication with a former partner preceded another pregnancy. This pregnancy ended in a distressing abortion at nearly four months, requiring a trip to Florida. Before this, we endured the loss of a stillborn child followed by a miscarriage, both profoundly heartbreaking experiences. The father of my youngest son suspected the most recent pregnancy, along with the prior three, were deliberate manipulations. Instead of providing comfort during this period of sorrow, he resorted to alcohol and recreational activities, showing a lack of empathy and understanding that grief is experienced uniquely. Our situation worsened upon our return to Clinton, MD. Following the death of a close family member and subsequent renewed contact with cousins, he became a frequent user of hard drugs. This triggered painful memories of my first husband's addiction and his attempts to involve me in drug use. The movie "Sparkle," depicting a gifted woman's ruin due to drugs, deeply affected me, as did my own negative encounters with E-pills during my first marriage. I was determined to avoid repeating those past errors.

I made the decision to forgo any future abortions and focus on resolving our relationship issues. I became pregnant again, and despite it being a high-risk pregnancy, there were no other medical complications. During this time, my partner started spending time at his stepfather's house with my son's godfather, who lived nearby. I later found out he was using drugs and being unfaithful. Unbeknownst to me then, he was living a double life. Initially, I felt our relationship was improving, especially after my decision to continue the pregnancy and take responsibility. However, around six months into the pregnancy, I found condoms in his pocket and subsequently learned he had given me chlamydia. This led to a significant argument, and I left, walking from Clinton, MD, to his father's residence in Temple Hills, MD, where I stayed for several weeks before we eventually reconciled after he came to see me.

Seeking to build a family back in Clinton, MD, irreconcilable differences with my partner became apparent through constant arguments. Despite my growing desire for independence and to leave, my partner couldn't grasp this need, given my lack of financial obligations. The situation deteriorated after our son's arrival. I subsequently moved in with my sister, which began a repetitive and emotionally draining pattern of conflict and temporary reconciliation. I would stay to assist her until she no longer needed help, at which point I would be asked to leave. This cycle persisted for several years, hindering my efforts to achieve independence. Although initially offering comfort, my family would manipulate my partners, leading to my isolation.

By the year's end, I finally used my tax refund to purchase a much-needed new car. This became essential after my previous car, left with my son's father, was vandalized and then towed due to complete engine failure while I was pregnant and asleep. This negligent act, depriving me of transportation during a crucial time, was another instance of his jealousy manifesting as a withdrawal of support for both me and our child. However, I had already developed a plan for permanent separation. I had gradually recognized the manipulative patterns within my family and identified the key individuals responsible. The main challenge was breaking free from this cycle and establishing a lasting solution. Even as the manipulation continued, I began to emotionally detach. I would temporarily return to my aunt's or sister's, but my aunt's living situation had changed after her son's death—a loss I view as a tragic consequence of our family environment, as my cousin was simply struggling to survive and improve his life. My family, as always, displayed greed and a lack of empathy. My maternal grandmother allowed drug dealers to operate from her home, inevitably leading to their struggles, a pattern repeated by her children for years. My aunt and sister also neglected their children. My own upbringing in my grandmothers' homes was marked by scarcity and restriction. My aunt would lock the refrigerator and remove appliance parts after 6 pm, creating a restrictive atmosphere that became my normal. My primary motivation was to escape this environment and ensure my own children would never endure such treatment. However, my family seemed determined to keep me isolated and despairing, fostering the belief that escape was impossible. While I may have temporarily succumbed to this hopelessness, I ultimately rejected this imposed reality and embraced my own understanding. To achieve this freedom, I had to confront the truth and let go of the illusions I had been holding onto. I had been consistently deceived, my judgment clouded by a desire for love, and I had given endlessly without receiving anything in return.

Federal agents raided my aunt's home due to illegal activities. She claimed she was unaware of any release from jail and that she and my uncle were out that night. At my aunt's house, individuals approached my cousin, a persistent and clever person always looking for opportunities. He was a constant go-getter, doing everything from sweeping hair to taking out trash, and his family sacrificed him for a new home in Fort Washington, MD. Despite being on the verge of a new job and impending fatherhood, his life tragically ended due to an unloaded gun he unknowingly had. This situation emphasized the significance of living a righteous life for enduring success, as wrongdoings will eventually have repercussions, embodying the idea of "live by the sword, die by the sword." I realized that staying stagnant requires a change in path; repeating the same actions will not lead to different results. Recognizing the worsening circumstances, I decided to change my life.

After relocating to Fort Washington, MD, I managed to create a home for my son and me, and my second son started visiting. While things were getting better, they weren't as stable as I had hoped. It was another challenging period involving rent, childcare, and finding housing, all without any support from my son's father. Strangely, I was even paying him $200 weekly, in addition to my aunt's contribution, even though he was unemployed and refused to care for our son. My work hours and lack of transportation made it impossible to pick up my child from daycare before closing. My aunt offered to watch him until I finished work, despite the daycare being nearby, but expected me to arrange his transportation to her house.

At the age of 29, I was utterly drained by constant disrespect and a self-serving cycle that only benefited others. I was paying rent for a place where I was denied a key, subjected to a curfew, prohibited from having visitors, and repeatedly experienced break-ins, the theft of my possessions, and violations of my privacy.

In addition to this rent, my aunt demanded $175 weekly. It felt as though everyone was profiting from my labor except me. I recently discovered that they were all conspiring to control and manipulate me. My ex-husband and his mistress feigned animosity towards each other in my presence while secretly working together to ruin my life and take it over.

Financially ruined by my ex-husband, his lover, and their relatives, my destroyed credit forced me to pay cash for a Rent-a-Wreck car, significantly limiting my enjoyment of life. One night, driving home from my son's father's, I lost control on a curve and totaled the vehicle. The airbag deployment caused temporary blindness. Thankfully, my father, who was on a call with me, heard the crash and helped me move the car to my aunt's house.

Despite this setback, I saved enough to move out and buy a car. Although I was employed and paying rent, living with my aunt and her rules and curfew felt restrictive. However, my focus was on creating a stable home for my children, so I endured it until I could move. My son and I moved to Courts of Camp Spring in Suitland, MD. Soon after, I received a child support court notice from my ex-husband. Shockingly, my own family betrayed me. My cousin told me my aunt had given my address to my ex after seeing him and my son at the grocery store. This betrayal was deeply painful, considering the trauma and abuse he inflicted, which they witnessed. Ironically, my aunt had even photographed the last incident.

My second son's foster mother, a PG County police officer, called to inform me he was caught having sex with another foster child. Despite it violating my court order, my children always come first, so I picked him up. He was removed from the home and it was later discovered he had been molested by another foster child at a prior placement. This child, with a history of abuse, should not have been around other children. TMH has not disclosed all the details, so the full truth remains unknown to me. My son was released to my care, and I was unaware of the future consequences. Having endured significant hardship, my children were always my priority. He eventually confided in one of his new foster parents, another PG County officer, with whom we had excellent communication. After being unjustly labeled an unfit mother for seven and a half years, he was returned to me without any support. My son asked me not to reveal what happened. Wanting to sue the courts, I contacted several attorneys, but none were willing to challenge the legal system.

The system's blatant unfairness was evident: after deeming me an unfit parent, they easily returned my son—emotionally damaged and resentful from the very environment they claimed I couldn't provide. His subsequent defiance, including skipping school and smoking at my house with friends while I was working, jeopardized my housing situation. Having endured my own violations, I understood his pain. Yet, I was once again left to rebuild my life without court or family support, and those who offered help often had ulterior motives. The cycle of hardship worsened when my car was repossessed, and I lost my job due to his persistent issues. It became clear these repeated problems weren't coincidental; some force was manipulating him, mirroring my own sense of being controlled.

Initially, I attributed these thoughts to trauma, prioritizing helping him. However, allowing visits with his father only made things worse. No matter his misbehavior, I was always blamed and expected to resolve it. I even discovered his father was knowingly allowing him to be truant and spend time at his place. The situation escalated when his father caught him stealing. This validated my earlier suspicions, which arose when I saw my son giving my sister money and buying her groceries. When I confronted his father, his claim that he was the one giving my son the money felt dishonest, leading me to suspect he was teaching him to deceive people instead of preventing him from stealing.

I received a disturbing call from my son, who claimed his father was trying to kill him. Although hesitant, I felt I had to intervene and called the police for a wellness check. By the time they arrived, my son had left, but I eventually found him at his usual spot on Morton St, NW. He seemed lost, searching for himself, and was defiant and uncontrollable. The situation escalated when he stole a car and a gun from his father, leading to further police involvement. He was arrested for his rebellious actions and desire for revenge. During the arrest, he revealed confidential information and even confessed to knowing how to manufacture drugs. My sister, with whom I was still in contact, relayed this shocking news to me. He received a five-year federal prison sentence, marking the beginning of his difficult journey and a continuing one for me. Despite wanting to distance myself, my love for my children kept me involved. I contacted my sister, offering to pay for accommodation. She agreed, and we moved in with her on Tewkesbury Place NW, WDC, after I dropped off some belongings at her shed. However, our stay was short-lived; after about a week, my son's behavior resulted in another eviction. I continued working, and he attended school, but his constant trouble always affected me. One morning, MPD officers came to my house to inform me that my son was under investigation. A young boy had been found dead in an alley, slumped over his bike. My son and a friend had been at the Takoma Park recreation center when the boy's bike was stolen. They were accused of the theft, questioned by the police, who said they would follow up. When I questioned my son, he insisted he was only helping his friend and hadn't hurt anyone.

My sister kicked us out after that incident, which infuriated me. I had already paid for the move and given her money, and now I was suddenly homeless. I was also angry with my son for causing the eviction and for hitting me. Having my belongings stolen was a constant worry growing up, even with everything locked up, so I've always hated thieves. We weren't even supposed to be at my sister's; her voucher put her at risk. When I lost my temper, she intervened, and he ran out yelling for help, claiming I was trying to kill him. He was always seeking his father's attention, which is why he went back to Morton Street uptown, the one place I had warned him to avoid. It frustrated me that he idolized his father, but I never interfered in their relationship, assuming his father would keep him out of trouble. I was wrong. I thought he'd eventually realize his father didn't care, a lesson he had to learn on his own. I found him later, but he ran off again. Amidst all this, he ended up on Lamont St., where I unexpectedly ran into an old best friend. I was happy then, but I would later regret reconnecting. I became homeless, and my son essentially led me into a trap. With nowhere else to go, I had to leave my youngest with his aunt, thinking it was the best option. I assumed she would simply call his father, her brother, but things didn't go as planned. Not all adults are responsible; some just look for someone to blame. I eventually found my second son's father, who suggested I stay with my so-called best friend, unaware he was also sleeping with her. I knew about one of my other friends but didn't realize they were all involved sexually and conducting rituals against me – another setup in the making. It would start well enough, with her dropping me off and keeping my car while I was out of the way working. That was fine until I discovered unpaid tickets and that she wasn't putting gas in the car after I used it. Things had to change. I never intended to stay there long; my goal was to save money and move on.

After discovering she had gotten a ticket without telling me, I stopped letting her drive my car and paying for her gas about two weeks later. One night, I went to her place after work, but she wasn't there. She called and told me she was at a Days Inn in Laurel or Largo, Maryland, asking me to get the key and come there. When I arrived, she suggested we smoke and have a drink before I left. For a moment, it seemed like she was interested in sleeping together, but I declined because her friend knew my son's father. I decided to stay for a smoke and a drink, and I became extremely drunk. I don't remember much, only waking up naked in a Jacuzzi after being punched in the face. I later learned they had put PCP in the weed, which I had never used before. I felt unsteady, and then he accused me of stealing his water bottle, which I knew nothing about. He started hitting me and even tried to drown me in the Jacuzzi while she just stood there screaming. I fought back, grabbing the phone and hitting him to get him off me. As always, TMH intervened when the hotel attendant came upstairs due to noise complaints as she was leaving to meet her daughter's father outside, whom she had called or planned to meet. I also left, but he had my keys and bag, and I needed to get to safety. It's messed up that she didn't help me and was going to leave me there; I wouldn't have been in that situation if it weren't for her. It felt like a setup, but I didn't understand why, as I hadn't done anything to her. However, it started to make sense when I realized she was sleeping with my son's father and wanted me to look bad, or maybe he paid her back for the wellness check I had done on him. I'm not sure, but it was clearly a plan to harm or even kill me. Only TMH stepped in to save me again.

The drive home was silent. After arriving, her daughter's father told me to leave once I explained what happened. She was clearly trying to make it seem like her being there was only because of me. I used the money to pay my storage and gave her some. She asked for fifty dollars and groceries, which I agreed to since I had food stamps. Moving forward, I would pay her $125 each week to stay at her place. While trying to stop my car from being towed, I let her use it. Looking back at how this all got twisted, the same night my son's father gave me money and I saw her, she suggested we go to a bar. We had a good time, but we saw some people my son's father knew, which later made it look like I was flirting with him. I wasn't flirting; I was just having fun and making normal conversation. People often misunderstand harmless interactions. The whole thing was a setup. She was involved with an uptown killer and often made me wait outside. Because of this, I was attacked and got bruises, a head injury, a loose tooth, and my car keys and money were stolen. When her daughter's father asked about what happened on the way back to her apartment, I told him everything. He was angry about her cheating and pretending to be there for me. To make things worse, I had to call my second son's father to get my car back. He was furious, questioning why I was there and about the other man's false accusation that I stole his PCP. Her friend, who smelled like urine and alcohol, came back to my car and later apologized, finding his bottle in her coat. He then offered to buy me alcohol as an apology. I was enraged and couldn't work because of the pain, so I spent two days recovering. When I went to my youngest son's father's house in Clinton, MD, he didn't care, refusing to let me inside and saying I could only sleep in my car in the yard until I found somewhere else. Eventually, I went back to my supposed best friend's house to get my things, but she deliberately avoided me for days. I waited outside with my friend for her to come home before going back to my sister's house.

Living precariously from one paycheck to the next, I depended on a friend for sporadic temporary housing, always ensuring my job-related needs were met. Despite the instability, I coped. Eventually, my hairdresser, who knew my youngest son's father's family, assisted me in finding a place to live. I rented the basement of her brother's home in Capitol Heights. Although the mold and lack of temperature regulation were difficult, it was better than sleeping in my car. My primary goal was to bring my youngest son, who had been living with his father since my homelessness began, back to me. By the end of the year, I arranged to rent his father's house for $1600 per month. The first month went smoothly, but the subsequent month, he started removing his belongings and frequently entered the property, disregarding my requests for necessary repairs. The leaking bedroom ceiling, damaged by a roof issue, was never fixed, and he avoided my calls. The house was in disrepair, lacking heat, with a mildewed basement, and broken locks on both back entrances. Despite these problems, I never complained. I was grateful to have a home and, as I had done previously, I adapted to the situation, repairing what I could and accepting what was beyond my ability to fix.

Despite financial constraints, I enrolled in Everest University's Medical Coding & Billing program. Fortunately, grants, including a $2,000 monthly stipend, provided the financial stability needed to reunite with my youngest son. After three semesters, my second son received early release from his five-year prison sentence and came under my supervision. Recalling my own experience with parental rejection, I agreed, hoping to offer him a better future despite our history of difficulties living together. Their safety remained my paramount concern, influencing my expectations even when they were not in my care. I dedicated as much time as possible to them, hoping they felt my ongoing support despite my limitations. My oldest son, though seemingly sad, displayed resilience and communicated only with me, refusing to speak with social workers. I made sure his needs were met by providing metro passes, shoes, clothes, and a small weekly allowance for times I couldn't be there. Their well-being took precedence over material possessions. Throughout these challenges, I remained resolute, constantly hoping for an end to our hardships, unaware of the personal impact this was having on me. Maintaining focus is crucial; clarity will eventually emerge. I have always trusted my intuition; a feeling of unease often signals a valid issue. My life has been marked by numerous obstacles. People have frequently conspired against me, attempting to erode my self-assurance. While their actions caused me profound pain, I consistently recovered stronger. This resilience appeared to intensify their animosity. Notwithstanding these trials, my prayers were answered with my son's release from prison, just as I had believed. However, my life subsequently took a negative turn. My son contacted my sister, with whom I had been estranged for five years, to arrange a meeting with my nephews. Subsequently, she called me, and we re-established communication. She even visited me at my home in Capitol Heights, Maryland. She appeared to be thriving, now driving her own car.

My son's brief reintegration was disrupted by his return to old habits and acquaintances. While I allowed visitors, renting rooms for income created difficulties. These tenants damaged my property (broken pictures, appliances) and dangerously misused the stove for heat, despite being instructed to use space heaters, ultimately disabling it. They also deleted important files from my computer, including schoolwork and my unpublished book.Growing increasingly frustrated, particularly after a mail-related incident that threatened eviction, I issued a 30-day notice to vacate. My initial plan was to help a homeless woman and her co-worker while also addressing my financial situation. However, the woman repeatedly violated the no-guest rule, left without paying rent, and stole items, making the arrangement impossible. Even with my son back home, the disruptive atmosphere was detrimental. The breaking point occurred when I found my son and his friends with two girls in the basement during a snowstorm, under the influence and engaged in sexual activity. After contacting the girls' parents and having the boys shovel snow for money to buy the girls food, they eventually left. Unfortunately, these events signaled the start of further troubles.
My son's new friendships coincided with his use of Triple C and K2, which led to him acting irresponsibly. During this period, I also lost my car. While I could manage without a car by walking or using the readily available bus service due to the close proximity of everything, it presented challenges for my son, who was used to me driving him and his siblings everywhere. Despite this, I always found ways to transport them, even if it meant paying for it, such as when I picked him up after his release. A friend offered rides for a small fee, but these were only for essential travel, not for recreation. Soon after the incident with the girl, the police contacted me at home. They informed me that my son and a friend had been arrested for stealing steaks and Triple C from the local Shoppers. I later discovered that Triple C was a cough medicine teenagers used to get high. I questioned my son about the theft, as we had food at home, even if he didn't particularly like it. The police brought both boys to my house and released them into my care. Because my son was a minor, but his friend was not, I had to sign a release form for his friend to ensure he would appear in court. A few days later, his friend came to my door to tell me that my son had been arrested again, this time for car theft in our neighborhood. My son had seen someone leave their keys in their car and decided

to steal it because he didn't want to walk or take the bus due to the cold. He was apprehended and returned to jail. After serving five years in federal prison, he would now be incarcerated in PG County. Although Maryland would not file charges, DC would take over the case due to his probation there, and he would have to complete his sentence.

My life took another chaotic turn after my son's arrest. His friend then broke into my home, stealing his shoes and clothes, forcing me to move yet again after reinforcing my doors. It became clear that my son's choices continued to disrupt my life. Despite my attempts to stay hidden, my son compromised my location, resulting in his return to incarceration and further instability for me.Adding to these troubles, I received a foreclosure notice. I discovered the property had existing debts before I even moved in, yet the landlord, who was never around, always insisted on rent payments. After months of receiving foreclosure notices without any court action, I finally contacted the mortgage company. They offered a $2800 relocation settlement, which I accepted. Although I felt I deserved more after five years of living there, I was exhausted by the careless landlord and the property's deteriorating state. It was time for a clean break and a significant change.

Amidst losing my job, car, and school income, I faced immense hardship. Unable to care for my son, I made the painful choice to entrust him to his father for his safety, a decision shaped by previous involvement with Child Protective Services concerning my second son. My intention was never to view his father as an unfit caregiver; he was his parent. Based on my past experiences with my other son's father, I didn't foresee a similar outcome. We agreed that he would return our son once I regained stability. Sadly, his assurances were false. Influenced by their greed and envy, his supportive family convinced him to keep our son for the financial advantages they gained. It took over a year and further struggles before I finally became stable again. During this time, I had to seek help from someone I considered a friend – one of the women my last son's father's friend dated and who had previously looked after my son. This also proved to be a negative experience. Because his father refused to care for him, I constantly struggled with childcare until he was about five, at which point I felt defeated. Even though I knew she was involved with a friend of my son's father, I didn't intervene and continued to let her watch my son at her boyfriend's home. I would drop him off, and either she or her boyfriend would handle pickups. I would then pick him up after work.

Losing my car led to rental expenses to maintain my job and residence at my aunt's. Despite this hardship, I was determined to manage. Eventually, I bought a new car. The childcare arrangement, however, became problematic. Despite providing adequate supplies, my son consistently developed diaper rash, necessitating frequent work absences for medical appointments. Unexpectedly, his caregiver quit due to a new job and suggested her retired godfather as a replacement, which I foresaw as another problem. After several months, I grew dissatisfied with the inadequate care and recurring diaper rashes. This situation worsened when I was laid off during the 2008 recession. Subsequently, the former caregiver's godfather attempted to have me fired for refusing to pay for a final week of care after my layoff. His harassment continued at my home, prompting me to obtain a restraining order in Upper Marlboro, MD. This marked the start of a turbulent and challenging period. I eventually recognized a pattern of repeated obstacles that would persist until I accepted a different path guided by a higher power's plan. True progress, similar to advancing in a video game, required overcoming these challenges without taking shortcuts.

While driving on Suitland Parkway, I noticed a daycare and enrolled my son. It was excellent until his father's erratic behavior—late pickups and the smell of alcohol and marijuana—ended the arrangement after a few months. He then attended a good daycare near Penn Station Mall in Forestville, MD, but my frequent hospitalizations and job instability made it unsustainable. My son eventually went to a daycare by the Addison Road metro. Overwhelmed by the constant struggles of managing work, hospital visits, finances for clothes, housing, and daycare, I decided his father needed to take responsibility. After enduring numerous car accidents, classes, visits, and court proceedings, it became too much. The day I dropped him off with his father was heartbreaking, especially hearing his plea, "Please don't leave me I will be good," but I felt I had no other choice.

Despite the potential for ridicule, my son's safety and security were paramount. Having no other means, I was forced to seek income through less conventional avenues. I contacted my son's former babysitter's boyfriend, knowing he had connections. With the few contacts I had, I managed to gather just enough money. I even gave him sixteen hundred dollars to invest, hoping to repair my roof and relocate. Instead, he bought a PlayStation 3 and spent lavishly on food, then falsely accused me of spending the money. My anticipated return of $600 was clearly a waste.

Today marked a significant turning point at TMH, strengthening my belief that my journey has a purpose. For the past year and a half, my focus was diverted by my therapist. Our professional relationship spanned seven years, and although I sensed an attraction, I never foresaw its development. In 2015, I was arrested for stabbing my second ex-husband during a blackout, triggered by being off medication and under the influence after he attacked me. This individual, whom I considered a friend, was irresponsible and expected others to handle his obligations. Despite his intelligence, he seemed naive and lacked ambition or future plans, a realization that came after the stabbing. We briefly lived together while he was supposed to be renovating my house in Capital Heights, Maryland. During this time, we became better acquainted, but his lack of direction ultimately led to my departure.

Following the incident, I was placed in a domestic violence intervention and re-entry program at a Silver Spring, Maryland hotel. This came after numerous stays in city shelters, each with time limits and specific criteria for mothers with children, leaving me feeling desperate as my time at The Savoy shelter on Oak Street, Southeast, neared its end. Exhausted from pursuing every available shelter, I finally found one for women experiencing mental illness without children. The combination of medication and the MKUltra program made me feel like I was losing my grip on reality.According to my records, I qualified for Calvary, which offered a comfortable, family-like atmosphere unlike the other shelters. Despite this, I still faced constant negativity and animosity. On my first night, feeling utterly hopeless, I attempted suicide. However, the director's unwavering support was crucial. She welcomed me back and provided what I had lacked for years: a way to address my hidden traumas. The program pushed me to confront these deeply rooted issues. It seemed that people judged me superficially, never understanding my internal battles. Through counseling and listening to others' experiences—some less severe, some similar, and some even more harrowing—I was able to face my darkest, most concealed thoughts and realize I wasn't alone in my struggles.

As I started to recover, I kept in contact with my second son. Unexpectedly, my first ex-husband, a truly awful individual, reached out. He explained that our son had questions and was unaware of what had happened to me. The shelter where I was staying had been featured on the news, and my face was shown. As a result, my son recognized me and reconnected through relatives. I began to notice a pattern in my life: problems appeared to coincide with the return of my sister, former partners, or son. At the time, I didn't see this trend and was oblivious to potential problems. He seemed genuine, and I've always been hopeful that people can change. My longing to see my son led to a meeting at Washington Hospital Center in DC. He claimed to have an appointment related to a past shooting injury that necessitated a colostomy bag. After faking a cancellation, we went to the cafeteria, where my son asked a challenging question. Although I wanted to be honest, I felt unable to share the entire truth, telling him I would explain when he was older and could understand. He was only fifteen. I was very aware that his father, a textbook narcissist, was ready to seize any weakness to hurt or abandon me. This was a pivotal moment where I started to think about the consequences of my choices, as my past impulsiveness had only led to bad results.

The pressing need to get back to the shelter before losing my spot was a major concern. I had been excited to begin my new job at SGT Technologies in Greenbelt, MD, a NASA contractor involved in the complex scheme that caused my initial illness. My ex-husband's infidelity with my coworker, and seemingly many others based on deceit and stolen appearances, was a tactic to monitor my every move along with my family. Unfortunately, this opportunity didn't last. An unexpected meeting with my uncle, another enemy connected to my mother, resulted in sickness and frequent hospital stays, preventing me from keeping my job and my shelter.

Driven by eagerness for the new job, I left for work too early, a mistake I didn't realize until arriving at Anacostia Station thirty minutes ahead of schedule. This oversight posed a problem with the shelter's pass system, which regulated leaving and returning within specific times. Despite the front desk attendant's false claim of ignorance about my early departure (even though the door required a buzz to enter and exit, implying her complicity), I faced the consequences alone. It seemed a shared responsibility, as she shouldn't have allowed me to leave at that hour. A condition causing me to involuntarily fall asleep and wake up in different places, akin to severe jet lag and stemming from a disrupted internal clock often due to sleep deprivation, severely impacted my mental and physical health. Ultimately, this led to my eviction from the shelter.

In desperation, I contacted my ex-husband. He picked me up and took me to his supposedly vacant, post-raid residence in Fort Washington, MD, a charade intended to make me believe he lived there. I spent the night with my son, went to work the next day, and found myself homeless once more. Due to my probation and a court-issued protection order, I returned to my aunt's residence. During this period, I underwent surgery for a dislocated shoulder. My therapist called to check on me and, upon learning about my lack of funds and medication, offered assistance. Suspicious and accustomed to independent problem-solving developed from navigating difficult situations without support—a surface-level self-reliance that often masked my intuition's warnings—I declined his offer. I was then residing at the North Capital St., NE shelter as part of a re-entry program following a stabbing incident and had only one week to secure housing before my sister volunteered for me to stay with her. While staying with her, a therapy session took an unexpected turn when I confided in my therapist about a challenging situation. He offered financial help, which I accepted. Upon collecting the money while he was away, he expressed concern for my well-being and reiterated his willingness to assist me.

Our relationship began with excitement – outings, casinos, shows, and shopping, where I enjoyed complete freedom. However, between April and March 2015, a shift occurred. He became insecure and distrustful, likely due to past hurts. His escalating accusations, stalking, and harassment mirrored the painful experiences with my jealous ex-husband, something I swore never to repeat. As a result, I withdrew socially and stopped asking for anything, asserting my self-respect and refusing mistreatment. Despite this, in February 2016, after an illness, he called to propose. In a vulnerable moment, hoping for change, I accepted. It was then I recognized a pattern from his past relationships. Initially, he had claimed his girlfriend was stalking him, going through his things, and neglecting him. Through our conversations, I realized I was again being manipulated. He even proposed, likely just for sex, as I had refused him due to his instability. He saw me as emotionally vulnerable and believed material possessions could win me over, failing to understand my desire for respect and unconditional love. That very night, he proposed, expecting me to leave my home, car, and everything familiar to move to Joppa, Maryland, for a man I barely knew, based solely on material things.

My vision of marriage involved a traditional church ceremony with a pastor's blessing and shared future plans, a stark contrast to a civil courthouse wedding. Life presents challenges that test our judgment, and this felt like another. Despite attempts to reconcile, his actions, like secretly saving numbers and contacting distant family as if married (discussed in our sessions), signaled the end. The world has hidden darkness, sometimes within families. His early behavior made me question a lifelong commitment. Observing him, I recognized issues with alcohol and drug use, leading to negative drunken monologues about the past and perceived mistakes in my life. Past experiences taught me the importance of careful evaluation before significant decisions. Ultimately, a future with him was untenable, especially given the significant age difference; he was nearly my stepfather's age. Although initial feelings existed, the situation soon felt familiar, and recognizing recurring patterns is crucial, as they persist until one aligns with their intended path. The men in my life have consistently caused pain, seemingly without remorse. This pattern contributes to my book's progress, which, after seven years, should be complete.

Despite personal struggles, my commitment to writing endures. Like many others, I've experienced significant emotional pain. It was my second ex-husband who recognized my lifelong tendency to observe, a skill developed from witnessing turbulent childhood events: my stepfather's eviction, my aunt's infidelity, and my grandparents' abusive and alcohol-fueled arguments. As a child, I learned to be quiet and adjust to instability.Although I've written throughout my life, many important stories have been lost. Now, I desire to possess something permanent: my own narrative. My primary motivation for writing is a deep-seated belief in my purpose. TMH has repeatedly intervened in my life, even when I resisted. TMH has indicated that I have a task to fulfill, which I now understand to be sharing my thoughts and experiences with the world. The quiet of my surroundings, punctuated only by the air conditioning and distant traffic, underscores my solitude. My attempt to persuade my son to visit has failed. His father likely considers me an inadequate parent due to my limited resources and activities. I have no money, no car, and have had no contact with him for five years—a situation beyond my control.

My youngest son's behavioral problems led him to live with his father, but these issues unfortunately worsened. While our custody shifted to weekdays with his stepfather and weekends with me, he increasingly skipped school to be with his father. Sadly, he began to emulate his father's criminal activities, including theft, robbery, drug dealing, and drug manufacturing, which ultimately resulted in a four-year prison term. He is scheduled for release on November 17th, and I am hopeful that he has gained insight from this experience.My eldest son continues to show disrespect towards me and our family. While I wish he would simply communicate that he is well, following him on social media is the only connection I have. Despite the challenging circumstances surrounding his birth and my mistakes with his father, I am happy with his growth and wish him well. His accomplishments are significant; he graduated high school at seventeen with honors and a scholarship, demonstrating his exceptional drive. He has consistently pursued and achieved his dreams, and I am proud of him. It is disheartening that despite my unwavering support and presence throughout his life, he was influenced to treat me poorly, like my other children. Although disappointing, witnessing his success is enough for me, and I believe TMH is aware of everything.

Diagnosed with Congestive Heart Failure, cysts, fibroids, gastroparesis, diabetes, and various mental health conditions following a period of declining health—conditions that resolved upon separating myself from certain external influences, I endured frequent hospitalizations and numerous medications. This difficult time was compounded by feelings of being misunderstood and unfairly labeled as manipulative and attention-seeking. A distressing experience with a psychotherapist, whose controlling and obsessive behavior led to stalking and harassment after I ended the relationship due to health issues, further complicated matters. His persistent pressure for me to live with him or stay overnight, even when I was ill, was deeply unsettling. It became clear that peace of mind returned only after ending this relationship, highlighting concerns that his continuous prescription of medication, particularly the excessive recommendation of Xanax (eerily reminiscent of my abusive ex-husband's possessiveness), was potentially exacerbating my condition.

Having survived significant abuse in my marriage, those memories remain too traumatic to recount. Throughout my life, I have consistently faced and overcome considerable adversity. Despite having spoken about these challenges over the years, I often felt unheard. I share my story now with the hope that it may connect with, provide solace to, or simply be acknowledged by someone who can identify with these experiences. If my story offers even a single person a sense of not being alone, then its telling will have been meaningful.

He intervened when he saw my ex-boyfriend abusing me, as I had no support system. He ensured I completed my education but believed having my second child would be detrimental. His interest in much younger women became apparent, signaling that we had grown apart. The loss of one of my twins and the subsequent adoption of the other stemmed from my inability to cope as a single parent, especially with his lack of support. I hoped my surviving son found a better life. Our relationship ended due to the immense pressures I faced: school, graduation, independent living, working, and traveling to the correctional facility in Lorton, VA, to visit him and manage his affairs. I used my earnings to support our child and encountered men who offered me material things in exchange for intimacy. My mother's advice about the power of withholding something valuable has always been a guiding principle for me.

Someone uncertain and wanting something badly might act desperately. Keeping them uncertain can be advantageous, as the mystery can motivate them to try harder and invest more. Initially, I helped him with money and gifts but was eventually deceived. He said he was returning home and could live in Maryland because his mother had an empty apartment and he wanted me to have it. My heart broke when I became pregnant again and found out he had a new girlfriend he was living with. I had already spent two years with him, and it was my first heartbreak, a deep, physical pain. I got through the relationship but also experienced the loss of two babies. By eighteen, I had lost four children. My twins were born prematurely and small, but I didn't hold them to avoid attachment, not realizing it would be the first of many losses. I continued working hard, juggling school and my job at Boston Market. Later, my son and I moved to a cockroach and rat-infested apartment on Third Street. The sounds of pests in the walls kept me awake despite my exhaustion. Often, I would spend the night at the neighboring hotel, walking the hallways and talking on the payphone until my money ran out. Sometimes, I would wander around Chinatown until morning, especially if my mother had dropped me off for the evening. She would usually pick us up in the morning. During the day, I spent time with my mother, my oldest child, and my newborn at my grandmother's house. My mother was always busy running errands for my grandparents, trying to please and help them.

My apartment, despite its lack of safety and a bulging ceiling the management neglected, was my sanctuary. For $225 a month, I controlled who entered our lives, focusing on my son and myself while others were absorbed in their own struggles. Eventually, the ceiling collapsed while I was cleaning, hitting me as I protected my son. The dangerous conditions and management's neglect forced us to move in with my sister on Nova Ave. Living with my alcoholic and volatile sister was harmful to my well-being. I never used alcohol or tobacco until after my mother died, and my sister introduced me to these habits. The deaths of my grandparents and then my mother left me feeling utterly alone and unsupported. My life has been chaotic, so please excuse any disjointedness in my writing, as I'm recalling events as they come to me. In 2005, Washington Hospital Center saved my life after a car accident. My son's father, my closest friend and a source of tough love, and I shared a deep love, but his struggles with addiction prevented us from being together. There comes a point where you have to recognize when enough is enough. He will always hold a special place in my heart. Regardless of any outward animosity, our love remained constant. He rescued me countless times, despite my attempts to push him away, driven by the fear and resentment I harbored from my first marriage. It took me time to understand that love is not painful; fear is. Abuse escalates, and leaving becomes increasingly difficult the longer one stays in that situation.

My son's father was my strength to leave my abusive marriage. Although we would break up, we always stayed in contact. When I finally couldn't endure the beatings anymore, he came to get me. Having never known love before, I struggled to accept the real love and family I had never experienced or imagined.After leaving, I went to stay with someone I thought was another friend in Southeast, Washington D.C., off Alabama Avenue. I didn't have money for my medication and began hallucinating, seeing star troopers from Star Wars around the building. There was talk of a black card and stolen money—a black card had been placed on the roof. I heard my son screaming, "Mommy, they're trying to kill me." Convinced it was another hallucination, I called the police and ran towards the alley, only to find my son wasn't there. The police escorted me back to my ex's, insisting I hadn't taken my medication. Later, I overheard my ex and his friends discussing stolen money. His strange behavior and the disappearance of my book startled me. I could hear them reading it through the vents and hallway, mocking my private thoughts. They used my book and my medical transcripts from my repeated social security applications (retrieved after my arrest for stabbing him while living there) to create a blueprint of my life, twisting my words to make me seem crazy through lies and deception. He had just betrayed me, and now this.

Living in a bed bug-infested apartment that I was constantly cleaning, my living situation worsened when he insisted I sleep on the equally infested couch, despite repeated spraying. The actual source, his old bed ("BOO BOO") from his youth stored at his uncle's, remained untouched. My time there was marked by turmoil, including stolen money and a night where, hallucinating about my son's release from jail, I overheard him reconciling with his children's mother. Confronting him led to a fight where he choked me and dislocated my shoulder. Overwhelmed by past trauma, I blacked out and stabbed him with a knife. Despite no need for stitches, he had me arrested, likely wanting to keep the incident discreet. That night in jail became a revelation, as TMH brought forth suppressed truths. Memories of the arrest and the police station flooded back. Surrounded by what felt like spirits, angels, and ancestors, I experienced vivid visions of my future and heard my son's voice, whom I thought was dead. It was an endless night of profound realization.

The officers, whom I recognized as my ex-partner's downstairs neighbor, appeared unaware of other activity and concentrated only on me. Following a doctor's examination and medication, I fell asleep. Instead of jail, I was taken by van to DC General Hospital. Disoriented and without sight, I overheard the officers discussing where to take me. After being discharged, I was transported to an unfamiliar part of the jail and put in a bleak, dark holding cell—a cement room with just a steel door and a small window. Despite prior arrests, I had never been held in this part of the jail before. I spent the entire night alone. Before I was moved, the front gate opened, and I recognized my youngest son's father's voice. My earlier call to him had been declined, so I felt relieved that he might have changed his mind. Shortly after, the jail psychiatrist came with my medication, and I was then moved to a cell across from other men. Three days later, I went to court. I felt hopeful when I heard my son's father again, assuming he was there to bail me out, but then he disappeared. They deny this ever occurred, but it did. I know it did. Although my thinking wasn't completely clear, I remember it. I'm uncertain if it was real, and you likely are too. To find out, you will need to continue reading. After my release back into the community under the re-entry program, I stayed in several shelters, eventually ending up at the Days Inn in Silver Spring, MD.

My relationship with the psychotherapist deteriorated after I sensed his biased attitude and condescending remarks, which seemed to stem from my sister's fabrications. This was yet another instance where my family's manipulations poisoned a relationship. His suggestion for a cheaper wedding gown, followed by the statement, "We're not spending a lot on this wedding. I've already spent too much on you anyway, what more do you want from me?" revealed his true motives. While marriage should be about love, he made it clear that he no longer valued me and was rushing the relationship.Having experienced a similar situation before, I tried to distance myself. He persisted by showing up unannounced and even waiting outside my house. Eventually, I had to threaten police intervention due to his stalking behavior. He even paid for my phone with the ulterior motive of accessing my contacts to undermine my relationships and spread falsehoods.

I am prioritizing my business and have zero tolerance for stalkers, as this triggers painful memories of my first ex-husband. I want no contact with my sister, her allies, or anyone who may have influenced him. My decision to end the relationship stemmed from a significant betrayal of trust: my psychotherapist, someone I had confided in for over two years, was communicating with, agreeing with, and possibly socializing with my family – an egregious violation.

Although I initially intended to extend wedding invitations to family out of courtesy, he exploited this by acting as if no invitations were ever sent. He became invasively involved, collecting contact information and sharing it with estranged individuals. Ironically, this situation led to a temporary reconciliation with my sister, as I had to stay with her until my apartment was ready. Absent these circumstances, we would never have reconnected, as there is no real affection between us. I should have been more aware, but I was oblivious to any government involvement. Having endured much darkness in my life, I've learned to seek brightness even in the darkest times, and this optimism has consistently sustained me. I believe TMH has always been there to support me, even when I had given up, reminding me that I am not alone.

For instance, early in our relationship, on St. Patrick's Day, I posted a picture of my drink on Facebook, which prompted negative, jealous comments from my son's father and his sister, accusing me of neglecting my child – a complete falsehood, as my children are my top priority. Following a heated exchange, and with my son's birthday approaching, I borrowed his car to deliver gifts to my son. However, he insisted on accompanying me, despite my illness and it being his car and his money. I drove to Clinton, dropped him off at a store, picked up my son, and took him to Dave & Buster's. Subsequently, I faced criticism for allowing my son to be around him, which was absurd. My son's father was a constant presence of drug use, drinking, and bringing women around our son; the situation was truly ludicrous.

People have always tried to control my life, seemingly unaware of my past experiences. My youngest son's father witnessed my difficult relationships with my ex-husbands, in fact, he was the reason for their demise. Regardless, we always moved forward, even without a sexual relationship. Although I could have ended things at any time, my lingering affection kept me in the relationship. He was clear about his refusal to marry me, and I accepted this. We successfully co-parented, but outside interference was constant. This interference was the reason I left: I was tired of a grown man being coddled like a child when his brother, a lazy and potentially dangerous individual obsessed with computers and children with no female partners, lived there. Their mother only appeared for financial reasons, neglecting her older children before having more. Even her sick husband was belittled. I left my previous social circle because they were hindering my progress, especially with my child support ending. After the separation, I focused on myself and moved. One day, I met a man cutting grass near my new home who was connected to my second son's father, known for attending Daddy Grace Church uptown, where this new acquaintance frequently took me. This initially reminded me of my second son's father, but this new man asked for my number and offered me an escape. He eventually convinced me to join him for a meal at a southern restaurant. We spent time together, and I returned home. The next morning, we had breakfast. I had a busy day, so he dropped me off, and we planned to meet later at his house. I was wary because of its proximity to my ex-boyfriend (later my second husband). He denied knowing my ex, but I would later discover his connections to my ex and my family—everyone was interconnected in ways I didn't yet understand. I had been celibate for about a year, even during an engagement with a man who had erectile dysfunction and tried to buy expensive pills. Despite our engagement, I had no interest in sex, and it wasn't part of our understanding. He was dishonest and sought control and sex, which I didn't want. That night, we were intimate, and it was surprisingly good because he was gentle and considerate. Despite this, I ended the relationship due to his constant excuses and dishonesty about having two sons.

During my recovery from a mysterious head wound, my second ex-husband, part of the group seeking to harm me, reappeared needing help. He pretended not to know how I was injured. At the emergency room, the doctor found my explanation of simply waking up hurt unlikely, suggesting I was hiding something. While we weren't typically physically violent, he once stole money and pushed me into a cement wall, fracturing my left ring finger, which remains crooked post-surgery. His eagerness for me to leave after his sister's supposed death, followed by a false story about his unharmed brother's car accident, made me suspicious. I later discovered his sister was alive in North Carolina and had stolen my identity and inherited property. I knew his account was untrue, having seen his brother the previous day, unharmed. Before this, he and his friends read my book aloud one night, trying to make me believe I was losing my mind. The pain from a previous incident, where I was pushed through a glass table causing severe nerve damage and severed wrist tendons in my left hand requiring extensive stitches, overshadowed my hand pain at the time. Despite this, I can still type and cope, unless death intervenes. It's disheartening how deceitful even close family can be, destroying relationships. Understandably, I didn't write much in 2019. I've decided to rewrite my book a third time with a new approach. My memory has been affected since a 2005 car accident, and I constantly try to piece things together despite significant memory loss. Some memories are unwanted. Forgetting this past year has been a relief. I'm currently employed and housed, and I've stopped seeing a psychotherapist and taking medication, which has cleared my head, though I still struggle with anxiety, PTSD, and occasional depression from the betrayal of those I cared about, including my children. I've tried to stay focused. I sense upcoming difficulties, likely because I've overextended myself trying to assist others again. I hope things improve after my upcoming marriage, as I've spent the year working and preparing.

The end of the year approaches, and though I yearn for peace and happiness, they feel unattainable. I am constantly supporting thankless individuals who manipulate, abuse, accuse, and exploit me. It feels as if everyone is intent on my destruction. Despite my efforts and sacrifices, they always find fault. I have resigned myself to caring only for myself. After entering a re-entry program and securing employment, I experienced housing instability, moving between shelters. When my time at Calvary concluded, I had no remaining options or family support. Before leaving Calvary, I reconnected with my third son. Knowing his father had instilled negativity in him, and wanting to spare him further trauma, I had previously refrained from contact. I suspected my ex-husband would use him as a tool to manipulate me, a tactic he had often employed, and I refused to endure that again. Our meetings took place at Hechinger Mall, and he typically requested money. He was not demanding but rather easygoing and reserved, like his brother. I had asked all my children if they ever felt unsafe and wanted to live with me, and they all declined. Perhaps due to their youth, they were unaware of the dangers I had witnessed. I regret not insisting they come with me. I love all my children deeply. My son began calling me frequently, and we were forming a bond, until one day.

While I was in Baltimore with the psychotherapist, my ex-husband contacted me from jail. He had been arrested and needed money for our son, who was alone due to a "weekend lockup." Unable to provide immediate assistance, I reached out to my sister, who lived near my ex-husband's mother's residence on Isherwood, NE, WDC, where he claimed they were now living.I sent money via MoneyGram and asked my sister to meet my son at Hechinger Mall. Aware of the potential negative consequences, I felt compelled to act. My son needed me, and I believed his father was using him to maintain control, a pattern reminiscent of my past experiences. Soon, he began manipulating our son into asking me for money, perpetuating the cycle of control and deceit. He proposed a meeting, and I agreed. He and another man picked me up, ostensibly to go to his mother's house to see my son and relax. Instead, we ended up on South Capital St. SE, across from the gas station on MLK Jr Ave SE. His friend departed, and he asked me to wait while he supposedly went to arrange a ride across the street. He mentioned needing to use the restroom, but I suspected he was assessing the surroundings. I gathered my belongings, prepared to leave. We then went to a woman's house, where he immediately commented on my appearance. He then made a remark to her, "I thought you said she was dead," which angered her and caused her to threaten me. I simply walked out, and he followed.

After calling for a ride, we went to his mother's house. About an hour passed while he walked around. When I asked about my son and what we were doing, his drug use was obvious; his lips were white, and his appearance and behavior were drastically different from my memory of him. He reminded me of Pookie from New Jack City, and all I wanted was my son.He then called the same woman we had just left, telling me she was upset that he had brought me to his mom's. He laughed, intending to scare me, but I had witnessed this behavior before and was unfazed. I started walking toward the bus stop to avoid the drama. He was just my son's father, my ex, and I was trying to co-parent. He hadn't brought my son and was clearly trying to get money from me by pretending to be unsuccessful. He had given me a Victoria's Secret nightgown, which was likely stolen and intended for later cash return. I assumed this was another attempt to appear important.

Surprisingly, his friend ended up walking with me and even got off the bus with me. I knew my ex had a history of trying to damage my reputation and create a false image of me, despite knowing the truth. Since we were no longer together, I was suspicious of his motives. His friend mentioned that my ex had asked him to come along because I had "that." When I inquired what "that" was, he asked me to wait while he called my ex. I didn't know this friend and don't even recall his name.Earlier, while we were hanging out and smoking, the topic of my ex came up. I shared my side of the story, including how he had talked about my son during breakfast. I showed him my scars and explained the plea deal. His friend seemed okay, but not enough to stay the night. As it got late, I told him he had to leave. He had been trying to get my ex to pick him up, but he never came. Before leaving, he directly asked if I would sleep with him, phrasing it as, "Can you have sex with me?" I told him he had to leave, and he did so respectfully.

Later, my ex called, angry as usual, demanding the nightgown back. I told him he wasn't getting anything back. I knew once I agreed to anything, he'd use it as an opportunity to abuse me. Even if he didn't, why did he think I'd entertain him? That night, I made it clear the old me was dead and gone. The new me wouldn't accept disrespect. I ended the call by saying I wasn't scared of him anymore. He couldn't hurt me anymore, and my son finally realized he knew me. That's all that mattered. I told him "FU" and hung up. As expected, the immature boy rushed to my house, throwing another tantrum and ready to fight. This time, I had the final word, and he knew he couldn't touch me. These events are part of my story, and eventually, you'll see how they all connect - every relationship, setback, and delay. I was the unexpected element. Once again, I was out of options, but it didn't matter. I was never meant to please anyone but TMH, which is why I'm still here and thriving. Despite feeling misled and manipulated from 2015 to 2018, and nearly dying from gastroparesis, I've overcome every challenge.

My second ex-husband approached me after we had a bad breakup. I was ill due to dark magic directed at me by him and my family, my first ex-husband, and the psychotherapist. They had joined forces to destroy and stop everything I had unknowingly started to build. The one link in all of this was my sister, another hater. So they sent in the fake landscaper and my second ex-husband to finish what they started; we were not yet married at that time.It began after the last incident when I cut off communication. I would receive calls at work asking for help with the lights at his home after the last incident where I overdosed. I was tired only to wake up in the hospital with no wallet, no phone, and no coat. I reached out to my cousin after all at the time I felt I could trust her being as I had taken care of her and her brothers for years when they're mother could give a damn making sure they were fed, head done, rests properly of school and always giving when I didn't have even as she was an adult as I said looked at her as a sister, because my aunt did not care I felt it was my duty to protect her especially since her father is the one that had molested me for years and eventually raping me I never wanted her to go through any of my pains I did that a lot for many. I selflessly endured hardship to help others, driven by compassion. I cared for them as if they were my own children. I remained in the relationship, awaiting my inevitable dismissal. He eventually revealed his ex-partner's mother had passed away. While I acknowledged the situation, I failed to heed the universe's warnings.

Meanwhile, his ex-partner's family squandered the inheritance from her mother. Amidst the chaos, my belongings—clothes, identification, phone, and money—were stolen and given away. He feigned ignorance. I later discovered he had moved his ex-partner and her family into his home after removing me. I helped him and we hooked up again. Just as my life was about to change for the better — I had a decent job, a stable residence, and was doing well after seventeen years of paying child support for a son who was taken from me in my previous marriage — my life changed for the worse. My son doesn't even know me at all except for pictures. His stepdad didn't bring him around me until he was fifteen years old on Mother's Day 2016, while I was in the shelter. It had been fifteen years since I last saw my son after he was taken from me one night after his father had abused me for the final time. He damn near put my eye out, but instead of jail, he got away with lies and a clear setup once again. The abuse resulted in nerve damage to my retina from having my face rubbed in the carpet. That was the night I left; my skin had been completely removed from my eye, and I had become tired of the abuse.After we were married, I returned with his so-called friend. He had previously denied any knowledge of what I was talking about, but I knew the truth. I excused his lies, hoping he had changed.

That same night, the police discovered he had been cheating with an ex-girlfriend from school who lived in the basement of our apartment complex on Kennebec Ave. The police were unable to help me get my baby back. Shortly after, I reached out to his father and his brother for help, but that was another disaster. I ended up leaving without my son after a fight with his father, who tried to spit on me as we left the parking lot. His father's girlfriend at the time and his mother used a plea I took against me in a previous case against me to keep my son from me. He was raised to believe his stepmother was his mother. I later filed charges and was granted custody of my son. How can you retrieve what's no longer there? He was gone. I did not abandon any of my children. Their fathers chose to take control of the situation. With my second son, the situation was out of control, and his father suggested he come stay with him so they could be close. During the raid on my home, my other two children were removed and taught horrible lies about me. I had to keep leaving or taking time off work. The moment my son received his social security card and birth certificate, it was all over. The government and my family took care of my second son, who learned so much "BOO BOO" during that time. I would soon regret that decision, as it was just the beginning of my troubles.

Then, around age twenty-three, I had my third son. His father had a plan from the start to ruin my life. I was just beginning to experience life and what it could be like without my crazy family, and everything was going well. His plan was to impregnate me, marry me, and then take my son once he didn't need me anymore. He used sympathy to gain assistance and housing, fabricating stories of my abandonment and wrong doing. He repeated history by taking my son from me to receive benefits, and his new mistress fraudulently used my child support payments for tax benefits. He presented himself as a loving and selfless man, while living with and supporting another family. Despite knowing this, my son's happiness was my priority. I offered to remove him from the situation, but he assured me he was okay. I've always maintained contact with my sons, ensuring they have my current information, even those who dislike me.They would undoubtedly cause trouble if necessary. When I asked, they all assured me they were safe and unharmed. My youngest son loves his father deeply, but his father resents me for choosing to keep him after multiple miscarriages. He wanted me to abort the pregnancy I didn't lose, but I discovered I was already two and a half months along. I had no choice but to leave my son with his father due to my second son's behavioral issues and his father's lack of support. Exhausted, scared, and fed up, I placed my son where I knew he'd be safe. Yes, his father has a drug problem, but I'm confident he wouldn't harm him. Unlike my other partners, he has a job and a loving family. At least, that's what I knew from living with him and his family. Unbeknownst to me, he had a different plan. Like the others, my family had manipulated and bribed him with lies, deception, and greed after my accident. I knew this had led him astray .I learned another valuable lesson: Don't share past experiences, as people often use them against you to elevate themselves.

One day, I returned home from work to find my second husband facing eviction by his mother. I offered him a place to stay with me if his plan to move in with his uncle fell through. I explained that I wasn't sure if I'd remain in my house due to an upcoming housing authority review triggered by my previous eviction and subsequent shelter stay.TMH will likely assess me on my ability to apply knowledge in new situations, rather than simply regurgitating memorized facts. I was too trusting and failed to recognize the warning signs, even when those I helped repeatedly wronged me.He seemed to believe that my past struggles were somehow a debt I owed him, as if my current success was due to his actions. He constantly used painful memories to manipulate me, assuming that I wouldn't have achieved anything without his interference, while conveniently forgetting the pain he caused.

My overly trusting nature continues to cause problems in my relationships. It's confusing that people criticize me, yet still seek my help and guidance when they're in trouble. I used to believe that those I helped had good intentions, but I now realize that they didn't truly care. Those who try to hurt me will have to answer to a higher power. I am a child of TMH, and I know I haven't come this far on my own. I know that every time I've fallen, TMH has reached out, caught me, and carried me to safety. I don't want to seem unreasonable or mean, but so many people have taken advantage of me that I can't trust anyone. People often engage in harmful behaviors like lying, stealing, cheating, and manipulation, causing significant distress to others. Even amidst such negativity, I have consistently endured hardship, not only for myself but also for the well-being of others. Through divine intervention, I have been granted the opportunity to reclaim what I have selflessly given away. My work, words, and ideas have been unjustly taken, but through my narrative, I will rightfully reap the rewards. I am profoundly grateful for this chance to finally share my perspective, which has long been ignored and dismissed. By telling my story, I hope to dispel the falsehoods that have been used to obstruct my path and hinder my destiny. Through divine grace and mercy, I stand tall, knowing that my destined path has unfolded through trials and tribulations. Though my journey was unique—with helpers removed and adversaries sent to disrupt—it was ultimately for my betterment. Every lesson learned, every obstacle overcome, has strengthened my resolve. While free will and choices may have delayed my destiny, unwavering effort and righteous choices have ensured its arrival.

I've been betrayed by the only two men I ever truly believed cared for me selflessly. The manipulation with my second ex-husband started when I was severely ill due to a curse I was unaware of, and he moved in with me. During my hospitalization, he feigned concern while secretly wishing for my death and conspiring with others against me. Severely ill, I remember him whispering "I love you" before leaving for the first time in fourteen years. He saw my vulnerability as an opportunity, which I allowed, ignoring my gut feeling. He constantly brought up the past and attributed my success to himself. I would temporarily cut him off for this, as he hadn't faced my struggles. He would apologize, claiming he didn't want to stay with his uncle. I later found out that the aunt he accused of advances was actually his stepsister, and his family had a history of incest. The sickness and dysfunction I sensed in them mirrored their own lives, which I had unknowingly adopted. This kept me from my own path and blocked my blessings, trapping me in a cycle of negativity, trauma, lies, abandonment, and betrayal. I felt alone, depressed, drugged, and broken. However, after TMH freed me from my traumas, addictions, and negative energies, things began to change. I recognized what TMH had been trying to show me my whole life, though they put many obstacles in my way: molestation, sexual assaults, domestic violence, accidents, and ongoing abuse. These illusions were designed to divert me, to maintain contact with what had been stolen, with a hidden agenda to control, isolate, destroy, prey on me, and force me to be someone I'm not.

After ending the relationship with the person practicing dark magic against me, I desperately needed help. Their actions were making me physically sick, causing days of vomiting that led to severe dehydration and vomiting blood, requiring hospitalization. Some days, I barely had the strength to function. This felt like the movie "The Witches of Eastwick," where they tried to destroy me indirectly by using others to poison me. Planning my dream wedding during the pandemic was challenging, but I managed while working, maintaining my home, caring for my children, and dealing with a jealous ex. Two days before the wedding, everything went wrong. After weeks of waiting, my sister finally brought my dress, but it wouldn't zip. I had already paid my aunt six hundred dollars for alterations, and this was another devastating setback, part of a larger scheme. He didn't even have money for his tuxedo, and the money for food would now go to the reception. The dress was ruined, taken apart at the seams beyond repair. Despite my aunt's excellent work on my other aunt's wedding dresses under pressure, this time was different. This was my final wedding, my special day, a once-in-a-lifetime event. I was determined not to change my mind.

The wedding planning process was incredibly stressful, particularly due to my parents' insistence on a split-cost warehouse reception and my sole responsibility for the flowers. The situation became so overwhelming that I regretted sending the invitations. In the end, my parents only paid for the flower arrangements and even expected us to wait an hour for them to prepare the venue. To make matters worse, pre-wedding rain threatened my dress, forcing me to borrow money from my sister for a replacement, as my credit was already ruined by others' past spending. Despite my efforts to repair it through debt repayment and hard work, my credit score never improved. The honeymoon was equally disastrous, beginning with a last-minute change in transportation. Instead of a limo to Fager's Island, we were dropped off at my sister's house to change, and she ended up driving us and picking us up. Following the terrible honeymoon, during which I engaged in partying and smoking, I failed a drug test at my new DOT job, despite having passed one just four months earlier. This failure was deliberately caused by my sister, who leveraged her past friendships with my co-workers. I was supposed to repay her from my first paycheck after the honeymoon, and she was determined to sabotage yet another good job, along with many childhood friendships. My entire life was being manipulated by my sister and family, as well as my exes – both one I was involved with and one I never pursued, but if they were in my contacts, they were enlisted to assist in my downfall.

Our honeymoon was far from ideal. We were confined to walking around the resort. A wedding gift of one hundred dollars from my nephew covered a single dinner and cigarettes. For the next few days, we ate wedding leftovers and, lacking transportation, remained at the resort. The long-awaited intimacy on our wedding night, after months of abstinence, was disappointing and brief. Wedding planning had left me utterly drained.Later, my sister dropped us at my place, and I received a perplexing message about a letter from housing at my aunt's. This made no sense as I was already housed. I suspected a family scheme to bring my husband to my aunt's, knowing his animosity towards my uncle, hoping to provoke a conflict and ruin me. I preempted a potential altercation and arrest by arranging for my cousin to receive the letter. This event was never mentioned again.I am now nearing the place where they plotted to steal my inheritance and property, presuming I would never return or uncover their deceit. However, their scheme was Divinely revealed, prompting me to share my story and expose the many involved, including my cousin's girlfriend, who mistakenly believed I was interested in a man she desired. My disinterest disrupted their plans.

Upon my return, I became the sole provider. I relied on DoorDash, Instacart, and Uber Eats for income as the pandemic lingered and my partner received no unemployment benefits. Our finances were dire, marked by DHS inquiries and a drastic rent increase from $168 to $1600. Despite earlier agreements, our reality was overwhelming. The more I worked, the more complicated our lives became. I was prioritizing everyone else's needs over my own.I came to the realization that I needed to release what was not meant for me. This was not part of some greater plan, and my partner was destroying the foundation I believed was built on struggle, loyalty, trust, and love – all of which proved to be illusions. A past remark from my partner during my previous marriage echoed in my mind: "Don't be a fool."

It was not apparent at the time, but the events unfolding were part of a deliberate and long-standing strategy aimed at my downfall. As has been the pattern, their goal was to dismantle everything I had built and keep me subjugated. The performance evaluation conducted after my hire was a pretense. The reality is that I have consistently been surrounded by envious individuals. Sadly, at this juncture, this includes everyone from family and friends to colleagues. I have relinquished this situation to TMH, a move that is detrimental as I disentangle myself from their manipulative projections. Their efforts to impede my progress will be futile; I desired change, and I have always been proactive in achieving my goals. I have never sought pity. I have embraced both successes and setbacks with equanimity, accepting them without assigning blame. In retrospect, I see that I inadvertently excused the malicious actions of others. My focus was solely on my personal growth and overcoming adversity. While I may have discussed past traumas extensively, it was not to elicit sympathy but because those experiences remained unresolved. For instance, I omitted the detail that my sister insisted on driving me to and from work for a fee of $165 per week while simultaneously plotting my termination. Furthermore, my co-workers often resented my perceived sophistication and individuality. Once again, my life has been subjected to sabotage. I have endured workplace harassment and judgment fueled by envy. My professional life has been characterized by a disheartening cycle: securing employment, my sister's unsolicited involvement, a decline in morale, and the onset of paranoia. Across numerous companies, I have contributed my skills in problem-solving and innovation, only to be dismissed after my ideas were exploited for their benefit. My broad experience across diverse sectors has made me a target; they recognize my ability to resolve their challenges and capitalize on my strategies after my departure. This is a cruel pattern that constitutes my reality. The root of this pattern lies in malevolent influences and family members who have been engaged in deception and obstruction since my childhood, concealing a secret designed to suppress me and elevate themselves.

Remarriage was a mistake I deeply regret. My spouse hadn't held a real job in years, despite their claims. They expected work to simply fall into their lap and made no effort to find any, nor did they help us prepare to move out of my house before the lease expired. Divorce became unavoidable; the situation was untenable. Their unemployment, constant negativity, and angry outbursts wouldn't change my decision. I initially wanted to help, but I refused to carry this burden. When the time came to move, I was going alone, unless they found employment. Even then, I intended to file for divorce immediately after the move. Life felt overwhelming with my job, a second job, and dealing with vehicle troubles. The desire to quit was strong. Having finally overcome past issues with self-esteem and self-sabotage that led to hospitalizations and illnesses, I knew I had to be strong and independent. This was the path for me, though I was unaware of the schemes against my spouse and family.I decided to move far away from everything familiar. This place holds nothing for me but painful memories represented by broken bones, bruises, and scars. Each scar tells a story of suffering: children taken, a son facing a potential HIV death due to family actions or sex rituals – the uncertainty is devastating. I never told my ex-husband about any of this after they received the money. I've always stayed out of everyone's lives, accepting everything without interference.

Life has presented significant challenges, and despite having many stories, my journey hasn't been easy. My stepfather's early advice about not letting others control my life, as I would bear the consequences, proved insightful. I learned that sharing my plans prematurely allowed others to undermine them. Those closest to me, and what I held dear, were used to sabotage my future. For years, my life was based on lies, misplaced trust, and unwavering belief in those nearest to me. Navigating the pandemic, marriage, work, and maintaining my mental well-being has been particularly hard recently. Moving forward, I need to separate myself from those with different aspirations and focus on preparing for Thanksgiving. It's crucial to remember the obstacles I've overcome to reach my present state. The lack of familial love and support has added to life's difficulties. My definition of family stems from my early childhood, marked by the painful loss of loved ones. I experienced genuine joy and the true meaning of family and love during my parents' marriage and with my grandparents. The 2005 car accident caused amnesia, and my happiest memories are from before that event. While I physically recovered, my memory remains affected. Although I had written three books previously, they were either lost or stolen. Following my release from jail for stabbing my second ex-husband, I faced homelessness. Initially, the thought of recalling everything felt insurmountable, and I considered giving up. However, the act of writing seemed to unlock my memories, both pleasant and painful.

The pandemic unexpectedly offered a chance for creative writing. Initially a little worried, I placed my faith in a divine plan. My work as an accountant and on various contracts, before, during, and after the pandemic, alongside additional employment, proved to be a fortunate and sustaining experience. I gradually recognized a pattern of overextending myself for individuals who showed a lack of respect and consideration for my well-being. Realizing this path was unsustainable, I made the difficult choice to distance myself from those who did not value me.My journey to this point involved significant adversity. I faced periods of homelessness, sleeping in public spaces for safety. This was compounded by the trauma of sexual assault and abuse. Driven by the necessity of self-reliance, I was determined to survive. For an extended period, I faced repeated denials of social security benefits for my health issues, a stark contrast to the ease with which others received them. Despite the frustration and injustice, I remained committed to moving forward.

Psalms 27/9-10 "Hide not thy face far from me, but not thy servant away in anger thou hast been my help, leave me not, neither forsake me, Oh Go my salvation. When my father and mother forsake me, then TMH will take me up."

I realize now that those around me from 2011 to 2021 were indifferent to my well-being. This isn't a new question; the lack of concern then explains the lack of genuine concern now. My 42 years have included significant trauma, and the pain from my broken relationship with my ex-husband persists. However, I refuse to be ruled by fear any longer. I feel that TMH is testing my resolve to stand up for myself and stop others from controlling and destroying my life. My patience has not yielded the results I had hoped for. My leaps of faith have consistently led to unexpected difficulties. Many would judge my decision to remarry the man who abandoned me during a pregnancy that ended in miscarriage. Despite this immense pain, my faith in TMH remained. After you had me arrested, I experienced homelessness. TMH believed in me when others had given up. When they faced their own hardships, they reached out, and I offered my assistance. They subsequently tried to make me feel indebted. My initial offer was simply to help, not to remarry and have my life systematically dismantled. I wanted to trust our relationship, but I cannot trust someone who lacked self belief.

Married life has been a struggle the past few months, leaving me feeling trapped and confined as I try to save TMH from closing. Despite my husband's assurances of support, I feel alone; his lack of ambition makes it hard to have faith, and my efforts to help feel futile. My upbringing instilled a strong work ethic, which clashes with the expectation of being provided for and assisted. Facing an uncertain future, I am no longer willing to tolerate instability. I regret allowing this situation to develop and will learn from this error in judgment, taking increased precautions moving forward. Regardless of what happens, I am determined to share my story. My next destination will determine whether things improve or worsen. Right now, an obstacle requires me to keep moving forward. Adding to the stress are my rude and disrespectful upstairs neighbors who blast music until 4:00 AM and let their children run around until 3:00 AM. While I can tolerate some noise, the lack of consideration during the pandemic is disheartening. I believe life as we know it will drastically change as rapidly advancing technology eventually replaces the need for human life. This is just the beginning.

A supportive husband prioritizes his wife above his own pride, family, and security. While future missteps are possible, their outcome remains to be seen. People frequently misjudge me, perceiving me as a young, gullible girl easily swayed and dominated. My presence is only acknowledged through loud and disruptive behavior, marked by dramatic outbursts and yelling. My quick temper has historically led to immediate incapacitation and isolation—a calculated tactic to paint me as volatile, irresponsible, and unstable, ultimately causing my loss of freedom. However, I am increasingly aware of these repeated patterns and recalling past solutions. I am now developing more effective ways to manage them.

Nine months into this ongoing pandemic, I was growing despondent due to a lack of stimulating activities. I am accustomed to working, and despite numerous pandemic-related opportunities, I have consistently been provided for, regardless of challenges. With the holidays approaching, this is the least opportune time for celebration. If anything, I have squandered time on trivial matters and could have progressed further in life by now. Despite my dedication to motherhood, I feel I have significantly failed. I do not hold my children responsible; they were merely instruments in a larger scheme. My relationships and children were negatively impacted by something whose origin remains unclear. While I can identify those involved, I can only speculate on their actions, which seemed boundless in their intent to suppress and belittle me, despite the contrary being true. I withdrew, seeking solitude, but a great deal is now becoming apparent, and I am dissatisfied. The central question is: how can I prove it?

Having surrendered to a higher power and trusting in its honesty, regardless of potential pain, my future path is mine to decide. Despite everything, I am grateful to be sharing my story today. A year has gone by, but my life feels stuck. Constant worry about the future and creating further problems consumes me. I feel trapped and see no way out. Reflecting on my journey, I recognize how far I've come through TMH's grace. The pandemic has been particularly challenging, as I am accustomed to work and activity, not idleness. My life's work feels insignificant, and my choices seem to have yielded no accomplishments. My adult children are distant and hold resentment. Securing permanent employment has been impossible due to the demands of raising children, navigating the legal system, and maintaining relationships. Prioritizing others has led to my current unstable living situation, and a planned move has not materialized. Trusting in TMH, I made the mistake of marrying last year. My unemployed, unambitious ex-husband was accustomed to being cared for, and our marriage only brought financial strain. I received no gifts for holidays. He only attempts to please me when divorce is mentioned. I had hoped he would change after the pandemic, but I am doubtful. His focus remains on video games, smoking, having guests over, infidelity in our bed, and drug use while I work tirelessly. I kept silent about my awareness of his behavior, preparing to leave. I anticipate happiness after the pandemic and am ready for a divorce.

This situation is unbearable; I couldn't continue living a false existence. It's upsetting that he doesn't appear to care about the disruption his actions have caused in my life. I am completely drained and long for a return to the peace I knew before I offered him assistance. The pain comes from feeling manipulated from the start. His initial lie about employment and the truth about his living situation—being evicted because his girlfriend, children, and himself were straining his mother's finances while he concealed it—are deeply hurtful. I regret opening my home; it wasn't my obligation. My previous help with the light bill and a TV I never used was clearly exploited when his girlfriend immediately returned upon payment. This echoes the patterns of my first marriage, a cycle that seems to repeat until I truly learn. My life has been marked by a pattern of welcoming deceitful and malicious people who feigned kindness. I consistently extend help to those in need, yet I yearn for a time when I will receive genuine care. I reflect on the abundant blessings I have received. My deepest desire is to be loved authentically, without any expectation of material gain, personal benefit, or hidden agendas.

My struggles center on love, not on wrongdoing, which comes naturally to me. I excel at being used, lusted after, and then disregarded. My desire is to be genuinely loved. Despite contributing significantly and enabling the success of others through my abilities, which were recognized early in life, my potential has been exploited for the benefit of others. Malevolent influences have consistently interfered, forging unhealthy connections (soul ties) with past partners, family, colleagues, and supporters to drain my energy and engage in harmful practices, a pattern that tragically affected my mother.A soul tie represents a profound emotional and spiritual link formed between individuals through various relationships. These bonds can be powerful and lasting. While some are positive, others result in detrimental attachments that impede personal development and healing. The idea of soul ties, originating in New Age philosophies and embraced by some Christian groups, became prominent in the early 2000s. It provided a framework for understanding and breaking free from damaging relationships, irrespective of spiritual or religious affiliations.

Astral projection, or projection, is presented as an intentional out-of-body experience based on the esoteric idea of an astral body. This subtle body allows consciousness to operate independently of the physical form and journey through the astral plane. Astral travel is described as an age-old practice across various cultures. The text warns that during astral travel, other souls, including negative entities seeking to evade judgment and cause harm, can enter one's physical body while awake. It suggests sensing these entities through music and advises resisting them by either simulating physical combat or overwhelming them with love and compassion, which can disorient and neutralize them. Conversely, angels are also said to use astral travel to convey messages.

When my parents separated when I was nine, my stepdad left me with my mom's family instead of taking me, and I never understood why, especially since I would have gone with him if he'd asked. My mom's family has always held my telling the truth about my aunt's husband's abuse against me, which uncovered even more secrets. While I want to believe my stepdad's family was always distant, I suspect things changed after my grandparents died and they became Jehovah's Witnesses, altering their family dynamics and values. I'm done with half-truths; it's time to share everything. Shame kept me silent before, but at 43, I felt it's necessary to be open. It's impossible to know what's right when you've been told something harmful is acceptable, especially by trusted family—my sister, an uncle by marriage, and other paid relatives—who deceptively called their actions love. Looking back, becoming a mother at 14 makes me question everything. My sister sexually abused all of us—me and my cousins, boys and girls—under the guise of exploration, claiming her involvement in prostitution and her being the oldest justified it, and since we were never caught between ages seven and thirteen, it was normalized. Initially, I was clueless about sexual acts until my uncle demonstrated penetration after years of molestation, culminating in him forcing himself on me when I was a thirteen-year-old virgin. The pain is all I remember.

Exposed to numerous inappropriate situations from a young age, I believe this delayed my ability to speak out. My family's skewed understanding of love inadvertently left me susceptible to predators, including the father of my oldest son and others who likely perceived such behavior as acceptable due to the absence of intervention or healthy relationship models. The question of accountability persists.I have persevered solely through the grace of TMH, the only one privy to the complete truth, and ultimately, His judgment is what I value most. The scripture, "Vengeance is the Lord's," and the promise that He will "make your enemy your footstool," has been a long-held conviction. However, the silence surrounding my narrative continues to trouble me, especially given that the only accounts shared have come from those who have harbored lifelong animosity, such as my sister, grandmother, and aunts, who consistently made their disapproval known.

My arrival was immediately met with my sister's predictable resentment, a reflection of her long-standing hostility towards my life choices, evident in how she treated my children, nieces, nephews, and cousins. Tired of the lies, projections, and delays, I am now ready to speak my truth. My aunts, driven by their own paths, have consistently shown hatred towards my mother and me for our achievements. My grandmother's bitterness, possibly stemming from her experiences with slavery, led her to despise my mother because of her skin color, appearance, and loving nature, even wishing to change her own skin. My grandmother has always called me evil while trying to steal the innate knowledge I've had since birth. She fears the exposure of deep secrets, including the deaths she orchestrated for insurance money.

Reflecting on my past, I've been judged in every way. I had a child at fourteen, which might have damaged the one child who loved me, all to save another. It's astonishing. My eldest son recently brought so much into my life – the one I conceived through sexual assault and had no intention of raising because at fourteen, I clearly had no choice; they wanted the money. Once he was born and my mother was murdered, I was no longer needed. They could then freely collect and create drama in my life while deceiving him. My second son was imprisoned for fifteen years. During this time, he contracted HIV from their sex rituals and destiny-swapping orgies. He might have been institutionalized, like I was, to silence him about what happened. The separation and supervision he endured might have prevented him from speaking out. I never suspected the foster care system or even my family could be involved until I learned about cults and societies, both dark and light. These forces have significantly delayed my life and contributed to my son's HIV diagnosis while in foster care, under the care of my sister, father, and the government. It makes sense now, remembering the Publishers Clearing House win and my son being in the dream I envisioned – that I spoke or will speak on this – TMH was in it. The vision showed my son having orgy parties, but I never paid attention to the faces. I think my son was part of something much bigger than I could even imagine: the FBI, feds, family, the bugging of my home, me seeing Beyoncé and other celebrities, and my ex outside my house – this really happened to me. I was being shown what has already happened; now what is really destroying him is that we have all seen the movies "Get Out," "Us," "Them" – they unalived my son, not physically but spiritually. He is not with the Feds or in jail; he has been cloned, from what I currently see, and the government and my family have been trying to silence me by making me seem unstable so this wouldn't come out. It looks like him, but it's not; they used my son to get close to me and spy, to keep me down. The drastic changes in my life, including my decision to cut all ties with him, were due to their manipulation. They used him to monitor and harm me. I repeatedly expressed my disbelief that this was the same child I had raised, unaware of how accurate my assessment was. The question then becomes: who is inhabiting his body to target me? Perhaps I should have left my eldest son wherever he was, but as a mother, that thought never crossed my mind. I love all my children equally and unconditionally.

My eldest child, despite his outward success, has been the most disappointing. I sacrificed and endured so much for him, opening my home and heart with unwavering support. Yet, the moment he turned seventeen and graduated (with my help, I should add), I lost my job driving him to Delaware for his first day of college. My sister was invited to see his dorm room, not me. I was simply the chauffeur, paid with stolen money that had also funded his graduation, prom, and countless other things. Throughout it all, he never acknowledged my sacrifices, which hurts deeply. I don't blame him; I blame those who brainwashed him, just as they once brainwashed me. He's another follower who believes without questioning, never researches or challenges, always taking the easy path, assuming they have his back. But the moment you don't let them control your life, the moment you're no longer useful, they'll turn on you. He will have to learn this on his own, as I tried to shield my children from my family. They set me up with that raid; my husband and my children's father were all part of the plan to destroy my life. This is the consequence of my non-compliance.

Life feels stagnant as the pandemic has disrupted the brief period of normalcy I experienced. The isolation has triggered feelings of depression and anger, making me want to give up. My life is changing gradually, and I long for a fresh start in a new place where I'm unknown, free from bad memories and a lack of hope. However, finding a job and a car while facing constant obstacles and uncertainty makes this seem impossible.I am weary of prioritizing others at the expense of my own well-being. My focus on solving other people's issues has left me feeling unfulfilled and insecure. Even though I was lucky to have a job during the pandemic, I question the risks involved. I crave stability and reliability, but I consistently face issues with employers and colleagues who underestimate my intelligence and try to exploit me. Ironically, my hard-earned intelligence and achievements appear to be the reason some people attempt to sabotage my reputation.

In 2022, seeking a fresh start, I made a pivotal decision. My life has been a constant struggle, with hardship and overcoming obstacles as my teachers. Despite persistent effort while battling health issues and frequent hospitalizations, success has felt out of reach. Consequently, I have chosen to leave behind everything, including those who were insincere and plotted against me, a situation in which I have been entangled for too long. I recognize the blessings in my life, particularly considering my circumstances. I do not seek pity, as I remain resilient. As a strong Black woman, survival is inherent to my being. My childhood was happy until my parents' separation at age nine, when my mother moved in with my grandmother. This marked a jarring shift, characterized by instability, arguments, infidelity, dishonesty, and malice. While I desired to support my mother, I was unaware she would permit such turmoil and devastation into our lives. We experienced a dramatic decline from abundance to destitution. I became the primary caregiver for younger siblings after my sister declined.

My upbringing was marked by my parents' struggles with alcohol, partying, and conflict, which remained a mystery to me until insights from deceased spirits revealed their underlying lack of control. This occurred against the backdrop of Project MKUltra, a top-secret CIA program initiated in 1953. Its aim was to develop mind-control techniques for interrogation and forced confessions through brainwashing and torture. Officially halted in 1973, MKUltra employed methods such as high doses of psychoactive drugs (notably LSD), electroshock, hypnosis, sensory deprivation, isolation, and verbal and sexual abuse.

The program continued under the new name Project Artichoke, managed by the CIA's Office of Scientific Intelligence and coordinated with the U.S. Army Biological Warfare Laboratories. Both MKUltra and Project Artichoke engaged in illegal activities and unethical experiments on unsuspecting U.S. and Canadian citizens. MKUltra's operations were far-reaching, disguised as research conducted across over 80 institutions, including universities, hospitals, prisons, and pharmaceutical companies, often utilizing front organizations to conceal CIA involvement. While some high-ranking officials within these organizations were aware of the CIA's role, the program remained hidden from the public until 1975. In that year, the Church Committee of the U.S. Congress and the Rockefeller Commission investigated and exposed the program's existence.

The investigations faced significant obstacles due to CIA Director Richard Helm's 1973 order to destroy all MKUltra files. Consequently, the Church Committee and the Rockefeller Commission had to rely on sworn testimony from direct participants and the limited number of documents that survived the destruction order. In 1977, a Freedom of Information Act request led to the discovery of 20,000 documents related to MKUltra, prompting Senate hearings. Some surviving information about MKUltra was declassified in 2001.

Throughout my life, I have faced a relentless barrage of significant challenges and hardships. Beginning in my early years, I experienced molestation, separation, sexual assault, early motherhood, institutionalization, near-death encounters, and a multitude of other adversities that have deeply influenced my perspective and strength. These trials have been consistently interwoven with manipulation, deceit, envy, and conflict, impeding my efforts to find love, stability, and advancement. Despite these ongoing difficulties, my resilience has never faltered. The recent pandemic has further tested my mental and emotional strength, yet I have continued to persevere, sustaining both my living and my sense of self amidst widespread turmoil. The last three years stand in sharp contrast to my earlier life, highlighting my personal development and capacity to adapt.

Life's journey, marked by both achievements and disappointments, has taught me the importance of balance. Though I lack definitive answers, I am gaining insight from my challenges. Each difficulty faced and lesson internalized signifies advancement in my spiritual development. Despite a life filled with remarkable events, I continue to steer my course, consciously opting for strength and development at every juncture. My core belief for attaining success is relentless perseverance until the precise result is achieved – not just any acceptable outcome, but the genuinely correct one. This conviction has motivated me to share my story, which began in 2005 after a major car accident caused total amnesia. I have no memory of the crash itself, but its physical effects endure: scars and nerve damage impacting the left side of my face. Thankfully, a talented surgeon significantly repaired the damage. The father of my youngest child was with me during the accident. I suffered critical injuries, remained unconscious for a week with extensive bruising, and was told I almost died twice. My sole recollection is waking up to my son's father holding my hand, telling me to be still, and then alerting the medical staff that I had regained consciousness. My son's father and his mother retrieved me from the hospital. Upon seeing myself, I had no feeling in my face. Remarkably, none of my own family members came to see me; in fact, many wished for my death in the accident.

I lived with my youngest son's father, who frequently drugged me and abused my prescriptions for his own high and that of his friends. Following my release from care, my memory was completely gone – names, birthdays, social security numbers, everything. The doctor suggested my memory might return as the brain swelling decreased. My first book became my lifeline, piecing together fragmented memories. This was lost when he discarded me like garbage after achieving his calculated goal of getting me pregnant, treating me as if I were a stranger. He also tried to murder me twice by sabotaging my car's brakes.

We haven't reached that part of my story yet, so remember this. It seems that my memory improves with each writing session, allowing me to build a coherent narrative. I suspect an ex-partner or family member hoped my amnesia would stop or delay me, but my memory was already gone. For some reason, TMH only intended for me to recall what he deemed important, both positive and negative. I needed to understand the purpose behind all of this. I would eventually learn that everything happened for a reason. There is life after death – he saved me, but his motives remain unclear. I now understand it wasn't accidental; I was meant to remember all the terrible things people have done and continue to do in my life. It's shocking that the police report for the accident has never been found, and why are all court documents and hospital records from 2001 to 2012 missing? The investigation was incomplete and poorly done. Throughout my difficult journey to get help while sick and vulnerable, meticulous records were kept. People acted without caution, unaware that their actions would lead to their ruin. As I've stated before, everything leaves a trace, digitally or physically. The truth will come to light.

Despite my post-surgery appearance, the father of my youngest child remained supportive. He was unique in allowing me to embrace my femininity. Once, we were an inseparable pair, like Bonnie and Clyde. However, our seemingly unbreakable connection fractured during my fourth pregnancy. Following a previous abortion in Florida and a devastating stillbirth, he doubted this pregnancy's success, despite my assurances of his equal involvement. Our relationship strained, and I endured several life-threatening incidents. As we drifted apart, I faced further difficulties due to family disputes and Child Protective Services. My attempts to support my sister were complicated by her lifelong jealousy. Initially, I mistook her actions as playful, but I eventually recognized her deep resentment. Her unhappiness stemmed from her relationship with a manipulative man who had previously been involved with our aunt and had observed us since childhood. Disturbingly, this type of behavior wasn't uncommon in our family. This same aunt had also been romantically involved with her cousin and had been unfaithful to her husband, leading to his suicide. I hope this narrative is clear, as these events are interconnected.

My sister's unexpected arrival, following a fight with her partner who discovered her infidelity, immediately burdened my already small apartment. Despite this, I offered her shelter, a pattern of familial accommodation I've always upheld. Almost instantly, she began pursuing my husband, our marriage still in its early stages. Her brazen attempt to seduce him in front of me at Anacostia Park ignited my fury, leading to a confrontation. Back home, an injury from the earlier fight required a hospital visit, one my husband and sister did not accompany me on. Instead, they returned to my apartment and slept together in my bed. This betrayal was the final straw; I evicted her and her children. In their departure, they stole my son's pet turtle, Squirtle, a creature known for its peculiar habit of following me to inhale smoke. This incident is emblematic of the years of pain my sister has inflicted, a pattern of behavior I can no longer excuse. The theft of Squirtle, who was somehow given to my sister only for her to feign finding him and then surrender him to a shelter, is but one example in a litany of her hurtful actions.

Beyond this personal betrayal, I've endured repeated identity theft, as have my neighbors, resulting in three police calls to my residence. The constant lack of support and active attempts to undermine me have left me exhausted. For seven years, I've been entangled in governmental bureaucracy marked by altered paperwork and false reports. During a period when my children were in her care, my sister lied to the court about my whereabouts for six months, despite my living with her to escape my ex-husband. She then disclosed my location to him, enabling him to force his way into her home and pursue me from her residence to the courthouse, where he attempted to strangle me. He was arrested for threats and attempted assault, while I was detained for missed urine tests resulting from his persistent harassment. He manipulated my assessment schedule, ensuring my results were consistently compromised. This resulted in false positives, fluctuating results, and inconclusive tests—all deliberately used to keep my children from me. It's crucial to remember that marijuana can remain in one's system for at least thirty days. The government's failure to protect me persisted even after I withdrew my plea. They allowed my abuser access to my statements and new address, despite my enrollment in the victim advocate program, leaving me vulnerable to further harm. This compounded the trauma of my already difficult childhood.

They initially offered information about my children's location in exchange for my cooperation following my arrest. However, this information was deliberately withheld until my sister intervened on my behalf, a step she hesitated to take due to her role as their informant. It is shocking that she, a mother herself, would betray me in this manner, presuming her involvement would remain hidden. The reasons behind their collective attempt on my life are still unknown. Various motives could be at play: financial gain, deception, incest, identity theft, forged signatures, false allegations, infidelity, or even murder all in an effort to conceal a network of lies. This was a carefully constructed trap, and my appeals were ignored. He was my first significant adult love, yet I was profoundly mistaken in believing him to be my soulmate. He completely disrupted my life, causing me to lose everything, including my sense of self, before vanishing after his release. I discovered that my cherished memories had been either stolen or destroyed, including my children's photo albums, wedding photographs, my wedding dress, and personal journals. These irreplaceable lifelong memories were callously taken, while he selectively kept items, purely to inflict pain.

Photographs, mere snapshots of fleeting moments, eventually lose their significance. However, the memories etched within my mind are permanent, impervious to theft or destruction. These memories, though the only remnants of a painful past filled with setbacks, are now viewed with a different perspective. I've come to realize that others can only affect me to the degree I allow. The power to accept or reject their actions resides within me. Consumed by love, I once believed I had control of my life. In my youthful naivety, as older people might say, I fell for a destructive man. He entered my life, inflicted whatever damage he could, and then left me to pick up the pieces. I met him in the summer of 1999, shortly after graduating from UDC and embracing a second chance at life. Following a difficult experience with a deceitful friend who was also a Metropolitan Police officer, I decided to establish an independent home for myself and my son. This officer offered assistance, surprisingly paying for a room uptown for my second son and me. While grateful, I made it clear that I don't accept financial favors with strings attached. If that was his intention, he might as well take me to a shelter. He provided keys, an envelope with two passes and $100, and told me to contact him if needed.

A few days later, as my hotel stay neared its end, I reached out for help. As a police officer, I hoped he could direct me to resources. He assured me not to worry about the next day and promised to call after work. Later, he called the hotel and waited for me outside. In his car, he handed me a lease and keys – in his name. Desperate, I accepted.This officer later revealed a corrupt and disturbing side; I discovered his involvement in the exploitation of young girls. I was fortunate, especially considering our sexual encounters, as he wrongly suspected me of infidelity within his own illicit activities. Eventually, enough was enough. One night, simply because I didn't answer my phone, he held a gun to my head. Looking him in the eyes, my only request was to move my son away so he wouldn't witness it. He laughed, calling me a "crazy bitch," but I remained unfazed. He left. The following morning, I visited the rental office, presenting the lease in his name along with my money order receipts. I explained my serious situation, and they agreed to transfer the lease to my name. This marks a fresh start for my baby and me, as it's my first time filing taxes and having my own apartment. Despite the day's challenges, I feel blessed. Having faced such trials before, I'm not as stressed. I simply wait for my blessings, trusting that TMH wouldn't bring me this far to abandon me now.

However, the more I hope for positive change, the more negativity seems to arise, with more detractors than supporters, including my own husband. I married to escape my family and so-called friends in DC, having never truly believed in friendship. I've come to understand that many people attempt to manipulate me, even strangers. It's astonishing how often I receive dismissive glances or harsh stares. I used to believe something was wrong with me, but now I realize I haven't done anything to warrant such treatment. People often involve me in their own confusion, blaming me for their life choices, even those who know me. I'm unsure if it's for a reaction or if everyone simply longs to be elsewhere. I felt a swift shift in people's attitudes when they realized I would offer genuine help rather than simply giving them exactly what they demanded.

Throughout my 44 years, I've grown tired of being exploited. My suffering has been immense, benefiting others due to my own allowance of such situations. I failed to take responsibility, relying instead on others. The hardships I've faced feel endless, and I now understand that TMH presents trials until the lesson is learned, urging us to pay attention. My greatest struggle was not prioritizing myself and breaking promises made to TMH. Looking back, my attempts to fit in were naive and foolish. I've always been on a solitary path, and I now recognize my self-reliance. I'm weary of defending myself against accusations of being crazy or a liar. Having been used and manipulated, I yearn for genuine connection. My mental and physical health is poor, yet I persevere, having overcome numerous challenges with TMH's support. I write to echo the sentiment of my adversaries: a lack of trust makes love nearly unattainable. My life has been marked by the jealousy and hatred of those who exploited me. Eventually, I became indifferent to others' opinions and withdrew, permitting further harm by dishonest individuals because I accepted it. People act within the boundaries we set. My ex-husband, like so many others, let our life disintegrate, despite my dependability.

In 2022, I am embarking on a new beginning, free from the weight of others' issues and financial obligations. I refuse to be a victim of illegal acts and will hold those responsible accountable as I rebuild with a strong sense of self. For the past 44 years, my life has been defined by selfless devotion—protecting, defending, covering up lies, and prioritizing others at my own expense. I believe truth is fundamental, and deceit only leads to more falsehoods. While truth stands alone, lies will eventually be exposed, revealing the dishonesty of those who spread them. My life has been challenging, marked by the untruths and assumptions of others. I have rarely known genuine honesty, and I have made mistakes and told lies that were subsequently concealed. I view these as "detours," each providing valuable life lessons. I never received guidance or warnings and was not allowed to fail. I was considered an adult when it was convenient for others, but after achieving success, I was treated like a child again. I have been independent since the age of fourteen, following the birth of my first son after years of enduring inappropriate touching that began when I was thirteen.

My mind is overwhelmed by recent events, and I anticipate more to come. My recent move was intended to bring peace, but it is disheartening to see how many people seemed to delight in my pain. I was unaware of the extent of opposition against me, with people feigning good intentions while harboring negative feelings. Shortly after discovering his mother was evicting him and his fabricated family—his children, their mother, and his nephews—I should have recognized the warning signs, but as I've learned, he is deceptive. I attempted to integrate my past with my present to build a future, but I now understand that it's best to leave the past behind. Foolishly, I brought what I believed to be the best part of my past into my present by marrying him. The marriage was troubled from the beginning due to his inability to maintain employment. My family's repeated concerns and requests for him to work were ignored, as usual. I often felt foolish when assured that everything was fine because he was supposedly employed.

My second marriage happened during the 2020 pandemic. It felt like a disastrous decision from the start, made when I was sick, vulnerable, and isolated. I even worried about who would bury me if I died, despite having insurance.My oldest son and I are estranged. My second son is serving a harsh 15-year prison sentence in Cumberland for car theft; he also contracted HIV in foster care. He was separated from his brother by my sister. This second son was raised by my mother until he was six and then returned to me after her death. Unable to care for him, I sent him to my cousin in Lacrosse, VA, temporarily, but he came back when he was around nine or ten. I have five sons total; one was secretly given up for adoption. I fear losing all my children, who are already scattered.People interfered, but I stopped them from taking another child. I pray for his safety, regretting some things but not preventing them from taking another child to use against me.

Soon after my first child, I got pregnant again. His father, wanting to portray me negatively, refused support and offered money for an abortion. Already struggling with our first son, I didn't go through with it. I had twins, but the girl died, and the boy survived. I never held him, giving him up for adoption for a better life, as I couldn't provide for him then. My aunt was charging me for everything, and his stepfather was in prison.For three years, I've experienced intermittent job losses, relying on unemployment. This contributed to my questioning things. Easy things are often undervalued. I should have been honest with myself but didn't want to seem crazy or foolish by calling off the marriage last minute in front of my family. I felt stuck because he falsely claimed to have a job.

Forgive any repetition as I struggle with memory loss, and my thoughts come in fragments, which I jot down as they surface. This man, along with his associate from the towing company who also participated in the schemes against me, was given the stolen phone I mentioned earlier. In return, he would supply the man with drugs or something similar because "BOO BOO" isn't paying any bills.I've been living a lie, clinging to false promises. Knowing my history and the pain I had caused him in the past due to my own betrayals, why would he seek me out? I now understand it was all about revenge, defiance, and deceit. My so-called husband was aware of his situation when he came to me, and I, in my naiveté and good intentions, always wanted to help or fix things. He remembered the traumas I had shared with him, stole my book, and weaponized those vulnerabilities against me.

I believe everything was meticulously planned, possibly starting with an incident when I missed a Xanax dose and experienced a bizarre episode at home. During this time, I vividly recall hearing and seeing my son being shot. I also had a delusion that I had won the Publishers Clearing House Sweepstakes. For some reason, despite my son's girlfriend being outside my home and acting disrespectfully, I went downstairs with a mini sledgehammer to confront her. The police arrived and questioned if I was on medication after multiple calls reporting people engaged in sexual activity in my yard and throwing rocks at my window. One night, I frantically called the police numerous times, but each time they arrived, no one was there. They warned me that continued calls would result in my arrest and commitment, before escorting the person off my property. I was indifferent to their warning, feeling numb and with a clouded perception. I was consumed by pain, and my life felt like it was collapsing. I was deeply unhappy but too impaired to fully grasp the extent of it.

Therapy with a psychotherapist and psychologist was sought as a safe space for open expression. Anger management and sessions with both were mandated to expunge a minor, non-stitch requiring stabbing incident from my record. For two years during probation, I confided in my therapist about my husband's betrayal and abandonment. My psychotherapist offered assistance during this time, though it differed from my expectations. His older age and neediness made me wary, despite his initial appeal as a source of support during a period of isolation. Aware of potential psychotherapist manipulations, I remained cautious but accepted his help, including a week's hotel stay. He later stated his goal was to rebuild my confidence. However, I felt his objectives were achieved through dishonesty and manipulation, a pain I shared with many others who had been similarly deceived.

My anxiety medication also contributed to my distorted perceptions. For instance, I experienced a hallucination of my second ex-husband and his former girlfriend outside my house, leading to a police call and warning. Subsequently, I became convinced my son was being released from prison and brought to me, fueled by a misinterpretation involving Publishers Clearing House. This was followed by a paranoid delusion of being targeted, believing the police were surrounding and listening to my house. In a state of terror, hiding in my closet, I attempted to unalive myself with my prescribed medication, feeling overwhelmed and exhausted. An associate, upon contact, initiated a welfare check. My survival was due to waking up in Prince George's Hospital on Memorial Day 2015 in the psychiatric ward, attended by a priest and a doctor. I felt I had lost my mind, fixated on getting to my son.

Upon discharge into my stepdad's care, our routine involved lunches at Cracker Barrel to discuss my experiences, followed by him giving me $200 and leaving. This, I came to believe, was another deceptive facade, mirroring his past actions with my mother. I was plagued by anxiety, convinced of my son's death, being followed, and my house being bugged. The near-fatal attempt stemmed from this overwhelming distress. In a moment of unawareness of a larger scheme, I contacted my second husband for temporary shelter, desperate not to be alone. Despite being labeled delusional and hallucinatory, I suspect this was a calculated manipulation to portray me as insane, perhaps even making me believe it, or maybe it was a reality occurring outside my immediate perception, akin to MK Ultra or a form of possession where I was not myself, a fact others were aware of.

I believe I was being manipulated towards self-destruction, imprisonment, or disappearance, all for others' gain, to seize what I believe is rightfully mine after the concealment of my heritage, inheritance, and past. I contend that my identity has been misrepresented, that I am younger than my birth certificate indicates. I believe circumstances were altered to my detriment from the start, with others unjustly benefiting while using malicious means to keep me impoverished. My strong work ethic, driven by a desire to escape, was also exploited. The underlying reasons for these actions remain unclear, though TMH once advised patience and observation, suggesting that their motives would eventually become apparent. It seems my life story has been repeatedly weaponized by others for their own benefit.

His controlling nature, driven by his own neediness and dependency, was immediately apparent. I have a fundamental belief in freedom and personal autonomy, and being manipulated into uncomfortable situations is something I find completely unacceptable. While I understand that everything has a cost, this doesn't excuse his attempts to control me. He mistakenly believed my youth and past hardships made me an easy target, using gifts of jewelry, money, and other material possessions as tests to see how far he could push my boundaries. He misjudged me. I have never been swayed by such tactics, despite numerous offers, some quite extravagant. Why would I compromise my self-respect in that way? Once lost, it's impossible to fully recover. Respect is earned, not freely given. It became clear that the situation was irreparable. Material possessions hold little significance for me; they are transient. Initially, he showered me with attention – dinners, outings, and gifts intended to cheer me up. However, the speed at which he offered a 2 1/2 carat ring raised a red flag, especially since it came with unspoken expectations. I had to remind myself to consider the true cost before committing to a lifestyle based on the same manipulative agenda. Suddenly, none of it seemed worthwhile, especially not at the expense of my peace of mind. When he proposed, a part of me hoped his intentions were genuine. However, his erectile dysfunction revealed that the relationship would lack intimacy, reducing me to little more than a social accessory. Knowing my vulnerabilities from our therapy sessions, I had always been wary of him. Ironically, learning about his ED was the first time I felt a slight sense of ease. Initially, things were pleasant; we traveled and attended events, and I enjoyed it while it lasted. But then, his behavior shifted. He began stalking me and fabricating accusations simply because I needed some personal space after a period marked by jail, probation, homelessness, and illness. All I wanted was to be alone in my own home, but our constant outings made that impossible. He acted as if his financial support and proposal entitled him to unrestricted access to my life. I quickly put an end to that. I refuse to allow any man to control my life to the point of discomfort; that is a guaranteed path to disaster.

Initially, our relationship was purely platonic and enjoyable. However, things changed when he claimed a costly doctor's visit, stating he waited an hour while I was absent. This wasn't the friendship agreement we had – one without sex. I wasn't fooled. He was around sixty, my stepdad's age. He had been a good friend, but that was over. His talk of wanting only friendship and companionship turned out to be false. I felt deceived again, though I recognized the signs early this time, preventing a bigger problem. I now realize he contributed to my Xanax issues, taking advantage of my clouded judgment. Although I may not always react immediately, I am perceptive and intuitive, eventually understanding situations. As I began to sense his controlling nature, I decided to create distance, having promised myself I wouldn't endure any more mistreatment. Around the same time, my second husband's life was in turmoil. After mistreating me, he moved his children's mother, their children, and nephews into his home. His mother, visiting from North Carolina, discovered this and demanded they all leave. He insisted he and the children's mother weren't in a relationship and hadn't been for three years, claiming it was solely for his children's sake, but this was untrue. They were both exploiting the situation, living off her deceased mother's money until it was depleted. Following his sister's death, which deeply affected him as she had always been supportive, he faced financial responsibilities. To support himself, he started selling drugs from his Southeast DC home, where he had an established operation. In a misguided attempt to regain financial stability, he moved his child's mother back in, thinking he could take advantage of her vulnerability after her mother's death and their prior connection. However, this plan failed, and he lost his home of over twenty-five years.

Later, I learned the truth: they had wasted their money and intended to marry and file joint taxes to clear his debts. He wanted me to shoulder his burdens, a "destiny swap." Realizing I was paying for something worthless that was hindering me, I quickly ended the situation. This was just one of many revelations as I connected the dots with information TMH was providing.

He manipulated her by making her believe she was the reason he was evicted and had nowhere else to go. This lie became evident after their marriage. I found this selfish; why would he burden me with his problems after what I had endured? When he returned to my life, I believed there was no deceit. I was trying to move forward and leave the past behind, but by letting him back in, I wasn't truly doing so. It was confusing, especially since he had initially stated that if I helped him, we wouldn't be in a relationship, and it would only be temporary.

I had intended to leave before he re-entered my life; I had even confided in my sister about my plans. One cannot force help upon everyone, especially those unwilling or unable to accept or comprehend it. My departure plan was formulated and awaiting execution, unbeknownst to him. This situation was already unfavorable, given his decade-long unemployment and self-destructive behavior, with no regard for the future. His mother's provision of his condo at age 21 enabled 30 years of stagnation, a disservice disguised as support. One cannot enable dependence for 46 years and then abruptly withdraw support without warning. The gravity of the situation only became apparent through his mother's intervention, a harsh awakening if true. My intuition signaled trouble, though its source remained elusive. Thirty years in the same environment cultivates complacency, particularly without external pressures. The core issue was the inability to demonstrate learned responsibility. I needed to escape the deceit and envy. His refusal to acknowledge his own culpability was the most frustrating aspect. He consistently criticized, lied, and deflected blame for his errors onto others. His frequent inaccuracy and unwillingness to own his actions generated turmoil. My perspective shifted after locating the address of his children's mother online and providing it to him. Despite his consistent child support payments, she had falsely claimed she would not pursue legal action. My intention in sharing the address was not malicious but to enable him to seek visitation. Funds were being deducted from his wages for her benefit. This only came to light during my separate tax filing, as our joint filing plans never materialized. She continued to receive payments, including stimulus funds, throughout our time together. Despite his pretense of caring for his children, his pursuit of visitation was merely a means to ensure the continuation of the garnished payments, a right he possessed. His feigned heartbreak and crocodile tears were another deception; I was deceived once more. I grew weary of his lies and infidelity. He mistakenly believed I was unaware of his affair. Our marital intimacy, our supposed honeymoon, was clearly over, though I hadn't yet grasped the full extent. He worked nights, while my schedule involved both day and night shifts. He claimed a chance encounter with a former flame led to a hotel job nearby his other workplace. He was involved with her. The distinct scent of another woman became noticeable on him, not perfume. As a woman, one instinctively recognizes such things; it was not my scent.

I initially gave him time to find a new place, letting him stay in my son's room temporarily. Eventually, it became necessary for him to leave, which wasn't contested since his disruptive and destructive behavior was escalating. He mistakenly believed I was the one who would move, and my awareness of his true intentions grew. I regret not realizing sooner his manipulative plan when he helped me move. He succeeded in making me ill and stealing my car keys while I slept. Using these copies, he later took my car from the parking lot, negatively impacting my income. His consistent aim was to disable me for his personal gain. I wrongly trusted someone who was actually an enemy, bitter about my choices and wanting me to suffer for his own failings. Spiritually, this relates to the concept of energy swapping, which I will explain further.

A peaceful walk in an unfamiliar area offered a much-needed change. The sky seemed exceptionally bright, and a stillness enveloped everything – the birds, crickets, and gently swaying trees. In that moment, I appreciated the beauty of a life free from chaos. I sat and meditated, savoring the tranquility of a beautiful summer day. The past three years have been a complete disaster. I've become attached to unsuitable people, partly due to family obligations, but this is about to end. I now understand the wisdom of loving some people from a distance. As always, I'm learning from my mistakes independently. I had hoped this time would be different, but the only change was the absence of physical abuse. The mental and verbal impact has been equally damaging. Despite my car being repossessed or stolen this morning, overdue bills with accumulating late fees, and being alone with TMH, I am surprisingly in good spirits. Perhaps this is why I feel unworried and undisturbed by the surrounding chaos. Life has taught me that anything freely given can easily be taken away. I always anticipated this outcome because it came without effort. I believed that hard-earned possessions would be lasting, but TMH removed them simply because of unequal investment and excluded me from the situation. Yes, I am favored.

My unwavering loyalty and determination have often led me down difficult paths, as I tend to persevere beyond my limits. This time, however, TMH intervened, preventing a recurrence of past experiences. It troubles me when individuals behave as if they are irreplaceable, failing to recognize the material and strategic nature of their roles, which inherently allows for substitution. I have consciously trained myself to avoid attachment to possessions or people, understanding that everything in life serves a purpose and has a limited duration. It often feels as though my gains coincide with others' losses, with the knowledge I share being disseminated elsewhere but not to me.

I have made a deliberate decision to redirect my life's course, guided solely by my faith and a sense of divine purpose. Today began with optimism and focus, an expectation of a positive day ahead, which the universe seemed to confirm through meaningful signs. During a walk on the trail behind my home, I found a charm hanging from a tree, inscribed with three words:

- Compassion: An excessive tendency towards sympathetic pity and concern for the suffering of others.
- Truthfulness: The state of being true, though its revelation can often be disruptive.
- Forbearance: Patience, self-control, restraint, and tolerance, qualities often mistaken for weakness.

I believe that faith, coupled with these principles, will enable me to achieve my aspirations. The charm also bore a link to a Feng Shui website. This ancient Chinese practice, rooted in Taoism and focused on harmonizing environments, has spread widely. I interpret this discovery as a significant sign. Reflecting on the inscribed words, I recognize my consistent demonstration of compassion and truthfulness, as well as my capacity for restraint and tolerance. However, I question my patience with others. The message I gleaned was to remain authentic, practice self-compassion, maintain inner stillness, and patiently navigate life's challenges, trusting in divine support. This moment marked the commencement of my journey of self-discovery.

Simultaneously, my ex-husband continued to visit, unbeknownst to me, with ulterior motives. He was secretly plotting against me, collaborating with my family and former partners. I began to notice a pattern of missing possessions whenever he was present. This realization prompted me to sever connections with anything detrimental to my well-being. Seeking to rebuild a relationship with my father after years of estrangement, I reached out, only to discover the painful truth. He was the orchestrator of the entire scheme, employing people from my past to inflict harm or incite self-destructive behavior, all in an attempt to keep me in a negative state. This was done to preserve a false image maintained by him, my stepmother, aunt, siblings, and other relatives. I would soon understand the reasons behind the hardships I had faced – including imprisonment, hospitalization, and defamation – which were the result of malevolence, greed, and dark practices.

Recent weeks have presented significant difficulties, with former allies now obstructing my advancement. I've regrettably returned to low-income housing, navigating bureaucratic complexities and forced to disclose private details—a situation I desperately wished to avoid. The difficult decision between unreturned affection and my ambitions was forced upon me. I am certain of achieving my objectives were it not for past burdens and the damaging effects of my initial marriage. It's a disheartening cycle: escaping one issue merely precipitates another with a similar result. Ultimately, I recognized a recurring pattern: these challenges consistently arise after each accomplishment. Progress is constant, and while circumstances may seem familiar, they can suddenly shift to prepare for subsequent trials. These hardships serve as tests. Have I truly learned and will I persevere with conviction, or will I revert to old patterns?

I often felt confined, lacking a comprehensive understanding of my circumstances. I struggled to reconcile learned principles with lived realities. It appeared as though there was an intention to keep me stagnant, to extinguish my aspirations. My choices were based on falsehoods, a source of current regret. I betrayed my own commitments, and the reasons remain unclear. I am experiencing pain and require healing. My deep desire is for serenity and a cessation of the discord, deception, manipulation, and untruths. I consistently recognized his limited viewpoint, shaped by his upbringing and associations. He exploited my experiences and empathy to exert control. This narrative was never his; it has always been mine.

From the start, I sensed our marriage was a mistake, my judgment impaired by illness and vulnerability. He presented a false narrative of supporting his mother and facing eviction after his sister's death. The truth was that his children's grandmother had died, and he took them in to prevent their homelessness – his daughter and granddaughter facing a women's shelter, and his son and nephews a men's shelter for three years. Subsequently, I became homeless, and he abandoned me in the hospital and jail, leaving me to die alone, revealing his complete disregard for me. I ignored my instincts and made a grave error in marrying him. I knew he was dishonest about his intentions, aiming to exploit her vulnerability after her mother's death. They falsely portrayed her as the abuser, while I actually helped him find her and witnessed his selfishness. He constantly expressed missing his children but did nothing beyond paying court-ordered child support, which had a valid basis.

Throughout our relationship, I felt used until I resolved not to endure it any longer. Despite past mistakes, I prepared myself for trouble in this second marriage. When I realized his destructive nature would bring me down, I refused. While he was deceitful and neglectful, disregarding the consequences of his unemployment and lies, I was secretly planning a move far away from his negativity. I had never encountered such darkness in a person, someone who saw no light except in me, with the goal of extinguishing it. Astonishingly, I fell for it again.

Our relationship intensified. Then, he claimed his mother was selling the condo, stating his kids' mother had intercepted the notification. He had to leave and lied again, saying she was staying there without helping, leaving his mother to handle everything. In reality, his mother likely realized they were all dependent on her and evicted them. Perhaps she had similar experiences, contributing to her dementia. These people are terrible, resorting to dark magic when things don't go their way, possibly the same tactics they used against me at the end of our sham marriage. The man I married had assumed his father's identity; our marriage was under a false name. I never saw his birth certificate, and despite his claim of needing his brother to verify his identity, I never saw that document either. The deception was extensive, involving family and the judicial system – more people than I could have imagined.

He had me arrested and put on probation for supposedly stabbing him in self-defense—an injury so minor he didn't even require stitches. His motivation was simply to discard me for another lover. It was during this time that I discovered a pattern: many of my past partners were also attracted to the same sex. Shortly after, this same individual needed a place to stay. Despite his past actions, I offered him temporary lodging in my son's room, under the strict conditions that he buy his own food and find employment within 30 days, as I was not in a position to support him. He agreed and moved in. While he did eventually meet these conditions, it came at a great personal cost, and his real intentions remained ambiguous. This relationship, like my marriage before it, was built on deceit and turmoil—experiences I had worked hard to overcome after a past marked by trauma and drug-induced confusion. With a clear mind, I gained a fresh outlook. I felt liberated, ready for change, and resolved not to let anyone hinder my progress. I had come too far to regress.

My path ahead is uncertain, yet my resolve to reach my goals remains strong. Freedom was the first step, and I trust that faith will lead me to a better future despite the inevitable hardships of life. Life's cyclical nature reminds me of washing clothes: a turbulent process that ultimately results in cleanliness and vibrancy. The rough and tumble within the machine mirrors life's struggles, but the outcome is renewal. Colors brighten, scents purify, and garments are refreshed. This illustrates that enduring life's trials will forge a stronger, more vibrant version of myself.

Do I desire love? Yes, but it feels unattainable for me now. Despite any loyalty, faithfulness, or honesty I might offer, it's simply not meant to be, at least not at this time. Too many adversaries lie in wait, ready to damage my reputation, infect me, or harm me. After all I've experienced and witnessed, I prioritize safety. I no longer blame myself; why should I diminish my worth for anyone else? I have dedicated my life to reaching this point. People often judge me quickly based on appearances and my guarded emotions, a defense I developed due to past pain. They don't see the struggles, sacrifices, and scars I bear with dignity. This inner strength is a gift from a Higher Power, as I've never been given anything freely. Everything I have has been earned through effort, and for that, I am grateful.

Having faced numerous challenges, I choose to reject negativity and move forward with the wisdom and blessings I've gained. My inherent optimism allows me to see good in everyone, even the deeply flawed. I inherited this trait from my mother, who consistently helped the deacon despite his struggles with addiction and his rigid religious demands. Tragically, he infected her with HIV, which progressed to AIDS and caused her death. This pattern of suffering has plagued my family for too long. My mother's health was already fragile due to diabetes, and when she started dialysis, a neck infection developed. The dialysis tube was moved to her arm, which was cited as the cause of death, though I suspect negligence played a significant role. In her final days, she was neglected and unloved; even the nurses seemed indifferent. She developed severe bedsores from immobility and was treated with disdain. Despite being a single mother of two at seventeen, I did what I could between school and work to care for her – washing her, talking to her, and combing her hair.

Her experiences echoed my own, as I too was shamed and made to feel worthless for speaking out about my uncle's abuse. He molested me from the age of nine until thirteen, robbed me of my innocence at thirteen, and led to me becoming a single mother at fourteen with someone I believed loved and cared for me. Similar to my situation, others made her feel ashamed and unloved, as if her visual impairment was her only defining characteristic. An unsettling incident occurred while I was collecting mail at my grandmother's house: I discovered a letter from the archdiocese addressed to my mother. My grandmother had forged my mother's signature, marking her as "do not resuscitate." This was a difficult situation for my mother, who was still weak after being taken off life support only a week prior, a situation she had miraculously survived.

My family seemed primarily concerned with financial gain and acquiring things without effort. Like my mother, I held the belief that if a higher power intended for me to have something, it would come to pass. Despite everyone else believing my mother was deceased, I knew she was alive. I refused to allow them to declare her dead, even after my aunt held a mirror to her nose, just as I had previously declared she was breathing independently. I faced shame and blame for the loss of my innocence, fueled by others' comments and their desire to undermine my self-esteem. I was once a carefree, feminine child who enjoyed tennis skirts and tube tops, before experiencing heartbreak and the threefold theft of my innocence – losses that can never be recovered, just as my mother cannot be brought back. My search for love led to numerous relationships and marriages, each ending in disappointment. However, each heartbreak brought valuable lessons and fostered personal growth. Despite financial fluctuations, I consistently managed to stay financially stable and maintain my mental well-being. My current pain resides solely in my heart, which is understandable. I feel isolated and unfulfilled unless I am providing for others, even in non-material ways. People value me for the love and support I offer, even when it's not reciprocated or acknowledged. I deeply miss my mother and grandparents, who were the only ones who truly cared for me.

Their guidance has been a constant throughout my life, enabling me to accept things as they come. I believe that destiny will deliver what is meant for an individual, whether good or bad, and that a higher power will ensure its arrival. I have been progressing well spiritually and must maintain focus on my path forward. Dwelling on the past or making impulsive decisions based on it will only impede my progress. I am actively working on overcoming my marijuana habit. My life has been marked by trauma and heartache, and the fear of failure is present. Past attempts to seek help from a psychologist resulted in medication rather than solutions, leading to further complications, delays, and setbacks. I became emotionally numb, unresponsive, and ultimately gave up, losing my sense of self and allowing manipulation due to another person's insecurities and neediness, all while they were in another relationship. I recall a night at home when I began hearing my incarcerated son calling for help, which caused me to lose touch with reality. Looking out the window, I hallucinated seeing him get shot. I ran outside, called 911, and the police arrived to tell me no one was there, escorting me back inside. On another occasion, overwhelmed, I took all my medication, mixed it with alcohol, and attempted to end my life, believing the FBI was surveilling my house because my ex-husband had lied to me. I was severely dehydrated and had been hiding in a closet for two days. When I finally went to the couch, my phone rang. It was a good friend. I answered, but then collapsed and lost consciousness. My friend, concerned, sent the police, who found me unconscious in my living room.

Waking up in the hospital was disorienting. The nurse expressed relief at my consciousness, noting the lack of emergency contact information. She cautioned me to take things slowly, emphasizing the severity of my condition and near-fatal state. My immediate concern was my son, who I believed had been shot. The nurse reassured me he was unharmed and attributed my confusion to an overdose, explaining my memory was unreliable. By day's end, I was moved to the psychiatric ward. Faced with this reality, the question of who I could depend on arose, and the answer, TMH, was undeniable. This experience forced a crucial reassessment. My attempts to control or manipulate situations had proven ineffective. I was left with no alternative but to place my faith in the one being who asked nothing of me but faith and love. He had consistently been my support, and I had to trust in His continued presence. Writing this book has brought new perspectives and understanding. I had been too preoccupied to see what was always there. Now, with clarity of heart and mind, my vision is sharp. I am actively shaping my life, refusing external control, and accepting ultimate responsibility for my choices.

For 44 years, I had allowed others to dictate my life, beginning with my grandmother, aunt, and other relatives. Their actions, though they believed them justifiable, were not acceptable to me. I am ready for change and anticipate the future. They were all united in the belief that my accounts of molestation and sexual assault were fabricated, suggesting I desired and deserved the abuse. Consequently, I was forced to keep my son, a situation that has tragically led him to believe I never loved him. This is a lie, a consequence of what was forced upon me. However, this doesn't excuse my son's behavior as a tool of manipulation, marked by disrespect stemming from lies and deceit. Unaware of his role as a pawn, he is vulnerable to attack when he is no longer useful or begins to question the established narrative. In such times, one tends to gravitate towards those with shared experiences. The truth is, they prepared for life in their own way. Life is impartial, offering neither love nor concern—a harsh reality I have come to understand. Following my sexual assault and subsequent arrest, my mother abandoned me, deeming me too troublesome. Her boyfriend rejected me, and no one else intervened. I became a ward of the state. I recall informing the prosecutor that there was no one to contact; my family claimed my stepfather had moved on and no longer cared. I had always known my mother's family was estranged due to revenge and hatred. He was kept away by my mother and her family's delusions, not by his own choice. As expected, I was prepared to go to Mt. Olivet receiving home after an overnight stay at the youth center lockup. The next morning, I was taken to CCB and then to court. I was surprised to see my father there, unaware that the attorney had located him. When my case was called, the judge spoke briefly, and I only remember her saying, "I release you to your father," adding that she couldn't disclose something. I was escorted back and released to him.

Considering past unfair experiences with my sister, whose poor judgment unfairly affected me, I question a recent decision. The first night, he picked me up, and I stayed with my aunt. The next morning, my stepfather took me to a place on Georgia Ave NW where he obtained keys. Afterwards, we went to the bank, marking the start of another cycle of setups, cover-ups, and distractions.

Perhaps it's just me, conditioned to expect everything to fall apart when one thing does. I refuse to fall again—no more shelters or pain; that's my firm stance. However, I've learned resilience: even if I stumble, I'll emerge stronger. I deserve respect, love, and care in all aspects, mirroring what I offer others. The balance has been off; I've mostly been the protector, provider, and acceptor without reciprocation. My priority now is self-love, understanding its necessity before extending it to others.

Though it may seem something is wrong, the truth is more a painful awareness. I've learned that even those closest can be less kind than strangers. Someone I thought cared has proven otherwise, confirming my long-held suspicion of a lack of genuine connection and revealing a deeply dysfunctional dynamic. My initial excitement about the move has waned, overshadowed by the realization that my sister's contact is limited to attempts at manipulation, financial exploitation, or fueling her need for gossip and validation. Two months have passed since I moved, and there have been no calls or visits, leading me to believe any future contact would be self-serving. My new address is deliberately kept private. This won't be my last move; I intend to become untraceable due to repeated betrayals. I am exhausted by the constant dishonesty and manipulation. I value honesty and direct communication, believing in saying what I mean and meaning what I say. It's disheartening to think others might see me as naive, and I often doubt the sincerity of their words and actions. I have no patience for insincerity or irrationality. If you can't be genuine, I prefer no interaction at all.

The people around me are primarily interested in gossip, lacking genuine care for my well-being. I deeply miss the few people with whom I could have truly meaningful conversations. I long for the comforting presence of my grandmother – the simple act of resting my head in her lap and talking, or her reassuring smile, is something I dearly miss. I've been told my feelings and relationships are false. I settled for inauthentic affection when I yearned for true love. Now, I choose self-love, which I believe is the most reliable form of love, requiring only my own approval and that from a higher power. My desires are simple: happiness, freedom, peace, and relaxation. To achieve these, I need to maintain my independence and find contentment within myself. I hope to find a partner who offers equal effort in a relationship. While my current situation isn't ideal, it's not unexpected. Each move brings significant life changes, requiring effort to rebuild my previous stability. I recognize that different communities offer different structures, order, and senses of community, inevitably leading to changes in lifestyle.

Despite encountering constant temptation to abandon my faith in TMH, my resolve remains firm. He has repeatedly rescued me from evil, and turning back would be a grave mistake, leading to inevitable failure after the lessons I've learned. My understanding of right and wrong is now clear. The stark contrast between my neighborhood, marked by negativity, and other areas filled with love highlights the destructive nature of anger. Although I was once part of both worlds, I am determined to escape the pervasive negativity, a significant challenge in my daily environment. Each morning brought a feeling of paralysis. I recognized the need for balance, even if it meant ending my marriage. Hoping for my second husband's understanding proved futile; expecting different outcomes from the same actions is foolish. He never grasped my perspective and consistently treated me like a fool. While the prospect of being alone was unwelcome, I yearned for genuine love and a partner who matched my energy. This elusive connection left me feeling trapped and attracting the very negativity I wished to avoid. Having strayed far from my true self, change is necessary, but the path forward is unclear. I am learning that the universe responds to our thoughts, bringing new insights and unexpected opportunities. This journey of self-discovery is exciting, like solving a puzzle that reveals hidden truths. The difficulties have passed, and I feel a renewed sense of hope. I am now considering my next steps, knowing my current situation is unsustainable due to a lack of privacy and constant intrusion. My inner peace requires solitude, as being around unbalanced energy drains me. This energy depletion might stem from others' connections, underscoring the reality of energy transfer. I have chosen solitude to protect my energy, recognizing how easily we absorb the energy of those around us. This awareness has led to a withdrawal from social interactions, as I have witnessed deception even from seemingly supportive individuals, who ultimately caused harm.

Deception can be present even when things appear peaceful. Despite contributing over $3,000 to housing, through my own money or assistance, respect isn't guaranteed. Instead, I'm constantly aware that this isn't truly my permanent home and that external factors can control my life. While renters have the same rights as homeowners, and I am responsible for property upkeep once the lease is signed (which is why I prefer owning), my experience here has been marked by manipulation from someone connected to my family who shouldn't be involved. This person continues to interfere with my employment despite my attempts to leave the situation. My landlord also failed to disclose crucial information before the lease agreement, specifically the 11 pm to 8 am quiet hours and my responsibility for emptying the dehumidifier on weekends. While I don't object to these tasks themselves, I believe they should have been communicated upfront. Ultimately, I desire peace and to be left alone. A temporary setback caused by my dishonest husband complicated my plans, but I've begun a new chapter, even though the path forward isn't yet clear. I believe only TMH can resolve this situation and help me recover.

My grandmother's adage, "people will talk until you die; it's up to you to prove them wrong," deeply resonates with me. I believe that as others witness their error in judgment, TMH's favor upon me will become undeniable. I trust in His power to bring my adversaries to submission. My life has been consistently guided by the principles of "Vengeance is the TMH's," "be careful what you say and do, you never know when you're entertaining an angel," and "you reap what you sow." These core beliefs have enabled me to accept the various circumstances life has presented. I have faith that everyone will ultimately receive their due, and TMH will ensure I receive what is intended for me, be it positive or negative. My personal journey with TMH has been a positive and supportive one. Consequently, I am consciously avoiding drastic alterations and choosing not to fixate on past events. Furthermore, I acknowledge the necessity of ceasing marijuana use and am actively working towards this goal. Life has presented considerable difficulty and pain, and the fear of failure remains a significant concern. There's also an underlying fear of losing my sense of self by relinquishing control. However, I find solace in knowing that TMH's support is unwavering. I am in the process of learning to place my trust in TMH rather than attempting to independently resolve situations, which has historically exacerbated them. At this juncture, my faith in and love for TMH constitute my sole reliance. He has consistently stood by me and will continue to do so. The process of writing my book is affording me fresh perspectives on aspects of life that were always present but previously obscured by distractions. I now possess clarity of both heart and mind and will no longer permit external forces to dictate my life's course. Ultimately, I recognize that I am the one accountable for my actions. I have a strong intuition that a significant and positive transformation is imminent. Having endured a prolonged period of external control, my paramount desire is now to attain happiness. My relationship with TMH has always been a deeply personal and solitary one, and I recognize this as the only element I require for success. It is my unwavering faith in Him that has brought me to this point.

We often have faith in things without realizing it, until it appears. TMH rewards faithfulness. We must do the work, but when we combine that work with faith and prayer, we activate a power within ourselves we never knew existed, leading to many other blessings and realizations.It was a quiet, peaceful day with bright sunshine, though it's been hot - ninety degrees for the past few days. I've embraced the peace and quiet, and in doing so, I've found myself and realized many things that were right in front of me all along. I was too distracted to see them before.

It's perplexing that despite my repeated statements that our relationship is over, my ex-husbands persist in contacting me. Perhaps they lack other support systems and are only now recognizing my worth. For an extended period, I enabled their deceit through my acceptance of their lies, excuses, and manipulation. Dishonesty is inherent, and familial estrangement indicates a significant issue. Acknowledging the uniqueness of family dynamics, I should have been more discerning. The turning point was realizing the foundation of this situation lay in my own narrative. I possessed more agency than I recognized; I simply needed to recall my story and adhere to the established pattern of my life.

Today, I felt a shift in my energy upon encountering another falsehood in his message. He must underestimate my intelligence if he believes his fabrications will deceive me. I am thankful for the gifts I've received, though my past low vibrations and habits have obscured and hindered their use. Doubts lingered about whether ending my vows a second time was the correct course. My first husband's warning, "Don't be a fool," echoed in my thoughts, and its significance is now clear. When your intuition signals something is amiss, it's imperative to withdraw. Something has been overlooked. Examine the situation dispassionately, without heightened emotion, and the concealed truth will be revealed. My past habit of suppressing my genuine feelings and thoughts often culminated in volatile outbursts. While anticipated, my learned composure still caught others off guard. His text evoked indifference, leading me to silence his notifications. Despite consistent prayers for his reformation, his deceitful nature remains unchanged. Regardless of the turmoil, I am prioritizing peace and progressing forward.

Misery does indeed love company, and my initial instincts were correct, though someone convinced me otherwise. Problems stemmed from numerous sources: him, his family, my family, former partners, and many others. Love's blindness led me to make foolish choices based on belief. Heartbreak became unavoidable. Both husbands isolated me entirely. My friends and family, due to my husbands' contrasting personalities, rarely saw them and perhaps missed the signs that something was wrong. Both relationships were uniquely destructive. My first husband was abusive, possessive, and seemingly my worst nightmare, until my last relationship proved equally damaging.

Like my second husband, my first was primarily after my money, and his proposal remains a mystery. Initially, things were pleasant despite his frequent arrests for simple assault. I was young and naive, especially after a difficult relationship with a police officer who was later arrested and publicized for running a prostitution ring, though he never involved me directly; he was, however, deceitful and manipulative.

A disturbing pattern emerged: all my relationships ended up in the news. This was no accident. These individuals, with their criminal pasts or mental instability, were deliberately sent to disrupt my life, aiming to drive me mad, kill me, or push me to suicide. Yet, they never succeeded; a higher power always intervened. I have triumphed over all the unjust hardships I faced.

Despite my hardships, I've finally found peace. I am grateful for this chance to breathe, heal, and focus on my long-term aspirations, which have been repeatedly thwarted and even stolen. However, the truth remains, known fully only by those who lived it. As divinely instructed, I am writing this. I will persevere, and everything will be alright.For years, others have presented their versions of events, but my perspective has never been sought. I don't know why my side has been deemed unimportant, but my silence ends now. Though I've tried to move forward, others continue to attack my character. Therefore, I am sharing my story and revealing previously concealed crucial facts. I've now defined the direction of my current writing and feel ready to share my experiences.

My life was so tumultuous that I never paused for reflection. Many things became normal until I was guided to recount my story and clear the names of myself and others. Perhaps my isolation stemmed from the absence of family, friends, and love, leading me to believe life wasn't for me. After multiple suicide attempts due to depression, TMH showed me love, recognized my worth, and helped me move forward without past burdens.I have faced significant difficulties yet remain unbroken. I am thankful to TMH that these experiences haven't scarred me. I have much to be grateful for; I want to believe this, though I'm unsure how long it will take. He stayed when others left, even when I couldn't stay for myself. Briefly, I was angry and had much to say. Feeling misunderstood and alone, I fell for a deceitful person with ulterior motives. I was vulnerable, sick, and isolated, making decisions under the influence of pain and medication, with no support. I believed I was alone, but someone was always there, repeatedly saving me. I was saved because I always prioritized others, and because many individuals created chaos in my life while watching me struggle, never grasping the extent of their impact. Yet, I continued to overcome. I am still processing everything. TMH has witnessed everything, and consequences will follow. This is not only redirecting their malice but also guiding me towards a different life path – one I have long prayed for. This journey has been chaotic, but I know I will triumph because it is all happening in divine timing.

I have decided to keep a journal to see how things unfold. Interestingly, I reconnected with someone I used to talk to before my marriage. Our relationship ended primarily due to my heartbreak and hopelessness, not because of him. I've been reminiscing about past happiness and the person I shared it with. He was constantly in my thoughts; every moment felt deeply connected, even without physical intimacy. Fear caused me to withdraw, and we both ended up blaming each other. Now that we've reconnected, I recall the reason for my fear: it seemed too good to be true.

He admitted his desire for revenge and his resentment after I ended contact and moved on, even though he never tried to reconcile. He assumed our connection was purely sexual, and I subsequently married someone else. When we reconnected, he didn't mention that he had separated from his partner and was undecided, expecting me to wait for him to make up his mind. Knowing my own nature, I wouldn't be able to hold back if I were truly invested, so that wasn't a viable option.

Reconnecting with him reminded me of the reasons for our initial disconnection: as always, he shifted the blame onto me. The men I encounter often fail to take responsibility for their actions, projecting their insecurities onto me and misinterpreting my independence as neediness. When they realize I am not dependent on them, they become fixated on disrupting my life. However, I have moved past these experiences and released these individuals, allowing them to continue their self-destructive paths without my involvement. I refuse to be a secondary option; I seek a committed relationship, not a casual encounter. If that's not possible, then there is nothing to pursue. My self-respect and self-worth prevent me from settling for less. Given the risks involved in casual encounters, I choose a different path. My belief is in mutual progress, shared growth, and achieving goals together. Togetherness is paramount. Individualism within a partnership often indicates a power imbalance, which is not what I desire. Collaboration in any relationship—whether personal or professional—builds a strong and resilient foundation. Without trust, honesty, and respect as the basis, instability and conflict will inevitably arise.

Despite a small hiccup recently, my general outlook remains positive. It's uncanny how one situation ends and another immediately begins, leaving me feeling vulnerable to manipulation and heartbreak. My deepest desire is for peace and serenity, yet it feels perpetually out of reach. Already disheartened, the world seems intent on further isolating me, unnecessarily exacerbating my pain.In my previous marriage, I even referred to myself as the "minimum bitch" due to feeling undervalued. It felt as though my partners would become overly comfortable, prioritizing staying in over shared experiences, effectively confining me to a domestic role without my consent. While I allowed this dynamic, its abrupt end was imminent, mirroring the unexpected surprises I had experienced.

Though I possess a resilient exterior and can be perceived as strong, my femininity is something I primarily express in intimate settings. Intimacy requires a genuine connection and time; it's not something I engage in casually. I often find myself carrying the weight of responsibilities in relationships, while my partners passively reap the rewards of my efforts. This pattern echoes my ex-husbands' deceptive proposals, where they sought to exploit my resources based on false pretenses. I am weary of these games.Today, the new man I'm seeing has been occupied. When I suggested we spend time together, he informed me early this morning that he had to cancel last night's plans because he spent the entire previous day cutting grass. Although I'm also busy with my entrepreneurial pursuits and was available a few days ago, I sense that something is amiss.

He FaceTimed me from a store, looking for a blue and silver gift for his aunt. After disappearing for hours, he called again from another store, buying gum and water, making me suspicious he was freshening up after seeing someone else, though I didn't say anything. When he finally contacted me later, I told him everyone would be gone. He was dressed up, clearly drunk, and grinning foolishly. I desire a genuine, drama-free relationship, and his actions were the opposite. Given the world's chaos and my awareness of men's behavior, this was not it. He kept calling, trying to convince me he had changed, but I knew he was just trying to justify his behavior because he realized I wasn't fooled. He expected me to feed him despite his lies. I refused, reminding him of the imbalance in our efforts, with me always cooking and him rarely reciprocating. I'm tired of the one-sided financial burden. I'm questioning the worth of giving love and support without getting anything back. I'm always the giver, never the receiver, due to how I was raised. I don't experience being spoiled or taken on dates; I only get visits. I give love without expecting it, but I want and deserve more than just self-love. Real love feels unattainable this decade. I'm losing hope as I face financial difficulties and the need to sell my belongings, even my sense of happiness.

My sister's visit today was quite an experience. It's interesting to observe the insincere people in my life, many of whom will eventually face consequences. He will bring my adversaries under his control. Despite her seemingly genuine behavior, I'm aware of the covert actions taken against me by many within my circle, including her, my niece and nephews, and other family members from both sides. Their aim has been to drain my energy and imitate me after ridiculing me, subsequent to her involvement in stealing my inheritance to uphold a certain image. Much has been disclosed, and even though she assisted me today, I still sensed the envy and deceit. Nothing she possesses is truly hers; in fact, it was stolen from me, although I currently lack concrete proof. However, I will await TMH's intervention to expose all those involved, revealing their true nature and hidden secrets, so they may experience the same hardships I endured for years. During that time, others stood by and watched me suffer through trauma and trials, having made their choice, and now TMH will decide their punishment for the repeated betrayals. The animosity directed towards me remains unclear; perhaps it stems from a fear of the truths within my story, truths that have been deflected onto me for years, with others complicit due to their own embarrassment and pretense. While they may point fingers, only TMH will reveal everything in due time, and I anticipate their attempt to prove him false. The lies of my former husband, both spoken and written, have only reinforced my suspicions, much like finding the condom at my new friend's car door. With TMH's unwavering support, I've chosen to navigate this path alone, recognizing that venturing outside my comfort zone has consistently led to disappointment. Despite my silence, there is a limit to my endurance, and I will not be perpetually provoked. Eventually, everything will be revealed. I believe the time is now, after the persistent betrayals have become evident. Blood ties no longer hold significance given the extent of the harm inflicted upon me by so-called family driven by greed and jealousy. Ultimately, TMH will restore divine order, ensuring everyone finds their rightful place according to destiny. This includes in-laws, so-called friends, acquaintances, neighbors, and strangers, as well as all those involved in the payment plan. The most prudent action is to prepare for this inevitable outcome. The specifics of the plan remain unknown. You believed you understood, but he is about to unveil the truth. I am no longer withholding anything; whatever is destined to occur will happen according to His will. TMH's retribution will befall those who doubted and disbelieved.

I've spent the night reflecting, proofreading, and looking back. This morning, I even found myself laughing and smiling as I recalled love and happier times. Last night, I severed ties with yet another deceitful individual. My friend, with excessive confidence, called and acted as if nothing had occurred. He wanted to proceed as though my feelings were insignificant. I perceived only more manipulation and a lack of genuine effort to communicate or make progress. This negatively affected my mood, so I ended the interaction. I am confident I will recover; I desire to be left alone. Currently, my focus is on achieving the goals I set three years ago, before my entanglement with the adversary who was then unknown to me. It was becoming increasingly clear who was behind my setbacks, and I was unwilling to reinvest time in understanding anyone new; there were already too many conflicting personalities in my life.

Today I'm aiming for an even better day than yesterday. Despite a packed schedule, I'm determined to complete all my tasks independently. While I'll need to catch up later, I'm prepared to do so. I've been practicing patience, as waiting is inevitable. The past couple of days have been tough, yet surprisingly, I've maintained my inner peace. It feels like negative influences target me through love, exploiting my unconditional and non-judgmental nature. I give people chances, but I need to stop this pattern. I should only change for myself. I've been hurt before: I allowed past experiences to create self-doubt, even when my intuition was correct. I try to leave situations without bitterness, but it never works out. My lack of self-belief stemmed from a desire for more, a yearning to avoid repeating painful situations. I simply wanted someone to love me exclusively – nothing more, nothing less. No transactional aspects, just pure love. My understanding of true love is questionable, given my history of poor relationship choices. Now, I feel apathetic. My only real desire is to leave DC. My destination is unknown, as I've never ventured outside the 495 loop due to constant demands on my time. People consistently deplete my resources, which go towards children, bills, and caring for others. I question why I remain in this cycle. Deception and manipulation have become familiar. Why am I burdened with these responsibilities while others are not? Every attempt to break free leaves me in a worse situation. Why can't I find peace in solitude? I'm accustomed to being alone and self-sufficient. I know there's a valid reason for my current unavailability, but I'm struggling. It feels like I've lost everything I've worked for, while others have been allowed to stay and thrive. Despite being falsely accused of using someone, I now only want to live authentically. The circumstances prevent me from having a job or a family, and I find myself at TMH again. I trust TMH will support me, but I'm not used to this extended period of inactivity. I feel a strong need to be productive.

My recent disappointments have dredged up past hurts, leaving me feeling angry, frustrated, and betrayed by the deceitful and lazy people I keep encountering. I'm weary of these letdowns and have realized that my urge to constantly help and fix others is part of the problem. It's time to prioritize self-love, as I've been freely giving my heart to those who don't value it. I've questioned my worth, but now understand that I need to shift my perspective and demand more from others to receive more in return.My withdrawal from everyone wasn't driven by a desire to be alone, sad, or angry, but by a lack of trust. Despite my kindness, it feels like everyone is against me. I was caught in a lonely and depressing cycle, weighed down by others' expectations and assumptions, which left me feeling powerless to control my own life.

I've embarked on a path of self-reflection and healing, seeking happiness amidst the turmoil. My uninterested response to my persistent ex-husband reflects my understanding that anyone who wants to be in my life needs to actively seek me out. I tend to attract those needing assistance, carrying their emotional baggage until they move on, often taking my happiness with them and leaving me alone. Despite investing in others' growth, I consistently end up isolated. I'm desperate to leave the past behind and embrace what lies ahead. Quitting smoking marked a positive step towards change. I'm tired of broken promises, shattered dreams, and heartache. I'm determined to escape my current circumstances and break this relentless cycle, clinging to the hope of a better future, however distant it may seem.

Exhausted but resolute, I will continue independently, seeking guidance and trusting in a higher power's constant strength. I need to adjust my approach and patiently await the opportune moment. My investigation into my name revealed that a former psychotherapist has been misusing my identity, a discovery that likely extends to others in the medical field who have access to confidential information like NPI numbers. This pattern of others easily obtaining things under my name while I struggle despite my own efforts has been ongoing for years and is inexplicable. The only initial clue was the unexpected connection to my stepfather's name when I looked up an address, along with a disturbingly familiar image. This exploitation needs to stop.

Further unsettling discoveries arose online. My sister's Ancestry page indicated a supposed death in 2021. Subsequently, a police call prompted me to file a report. My sister and niece then appeared, seemingly to gauge my awareness of their clandestine activities. I feigned ignorance during their visit, during which they inadvertently disclosed certain information. It's noteworthy that their visits are typically event-driven.

My sister tried to justify her need for a place to stay by blaming her past actions, using me as a shield while projecting her problems onto me and neglecting me during my own crisis. Even after leaving Sheriff RD's residence, she again sought shelter. I was unsure of her intentions – whether they were genuine or a trick to infiltrate my home with harmful intentions – so I was initially hesitant. However, TMH confirmed her involvement in schemes against me, including theft and potential physical harm, which led me to completely cut ties with her and others involved. My close circle has shrunk to four people, and TMH was about to reveal the true characters of those motivated by greed and envy, including my father and sons. While the disclosure of these things wasn't my primary concern, it was important to TMH. I had a good day, unaware that my sister had created an online death page for me on Ancestry. They were all plotting to kill me, knowing how much time and money she had invested in Ancestry, and pointing out things to me that I never knew. She also revealed that my uncle, the oldest son, was my grandmother's first husband's child, not my grandfather's; he was adopted. She also mentioned that I was aware my grandmother, my mother's mother, bleached her skin.

All of this would eventually make sense, but at the time, I didn't understand why these things were being brought up. Our relationship as siblings had always been poor, and I would eventually understand why this family is known for hiding secrets and lying, which is why nothing has ever been resolved. My sister has always hated me, but I haven't reached that point in the story yet; everything is just starting to become clear. I simply acted as if I was unaware to see how long everyone would continue the lies and who the real instigators of the setups in my life were, and I was consistently astonished. The next revelation came through a phone call from my father. I was instructed not to answer, as doing so would expose the truth. By not answering, I would receive a voicemail message, which said, "Yeah, this is Dad. Just checking to see if you're still alive! I've been tied up trying to do everyday things. I think I've been forgotten about. I'm all messed up, okay? Call me."

It might sound strange, but my stepdad's calls were a tactic. He never initiated contact; I always did. They started calling to see if I'd survived their dark magic attacks—projected spells. Since he couldn't send minions anymore, he had to check himself. Sending dark magic has consequences, especially against lightworkers. He was getting sick and scared of the truth about their involvement in theft and murder. I later found out they were bringing in immigrants for arranged marriages for money. My cousins and brother were involved, and I wanted no part of it. They also planned to kill me for an insurance payout I never agreed to, looking back at invites to meet with him and an insurance agent. I was only sixteen when my mother died and refused to give my information in court, even though my father took me there. Being a minor, my consent apparently didn't matter. I pray for them. I remember childhood jokes about my stepdad being an atheist, which I didn't believe because my grandparents were Catholic. It was all unexpectedly connecting; those I once admired were the ones I now disliked. My extended family on both sides—aunts, uncles, and cousins—were all after me, for no reason I understood. I didn't know I'd inherited anything after family deaths. They were determined I wouldn't. From childhood, I possessed a unique ability to communicate with TMH and angels, identifying as one of the 144,000. This drew unwanted attention, fueled by greed, theft, and murder, leading to personal targeting. Had communication been chosen instead, I would have been generous. TMH allowed these hardships, knowing my heart and that the betrayal would have been worse had I not been protected from greater exploitation.

Despite facing potential death, TMH intervened, revealing malicious plans by removing life-long blockages. During periods of stillness and isolation, I was vulnerable, unaware of being manipulated. However, TMH had a grander plan for my return, using me to expose long-hidden truths. My sister and others attempted to manipulate me through my niece, instructing her to falsely claim discomfort due to a mentioned man's presence, hoping for a reaction. This tactic failed. For years, I was entangled in their dramas, facing consequences alone while they moved on. This pattern has ended. I have endured enough suffering from their actions, including experiences with jail cells and psych wards, and I refuse further involvement in their contrived situations. Their issues are their own. I am increasingly aware of their attempts to suppress me and trap me in a poverty mindset, and I will no longer accept their projections. Despite it being my mother's birthday, I am at peace because my true love supported me unexpectedly after a simple request. He is my trusted confidant, steadfast partner, and loves me unconditionally. Despite disagreements, we always reconcile due to our profound connection, which is palpable to others.

Despite familial issues, my ex-partner and I maintain a supportive co-parenting relationship, a stark contrast to my experiences with my own family. His recent visit provided closure, even though he expressed a desire to reconcile, a path I've closed due to broken trust. The visit was peaceful; we talked openly, and I retrieved my TV. I'm confident he will eventually understand the truth surrounding his other relationship, just as I did. That chapter is over for me. If I hadn't confronted his deception, the pretense would likely have continued. My stepdad taught me well; in this situation, it was checkmate, a quiet resolution without animosity. He seemed to expect a dramatic reaction after removing his ring and leaving, but I had already mentally ended the relationship. Though I still have feelings, he revealed he went to his stepmother's, where he was involved with both his mistress and stepsister, giving the mistress gifts for arbitrary reasons – what I call "BOO BOO." He was unhappy there. Sensing trouble, I refused to let him stay, preventing further complications. I felt equipped to handle any resulting negativity independently. His presence was a harbinger of chaos and illness, a symptom of a toxic soul tie formed through our marriage, friendship, and sexual intimacy. His negative karma was affecting me, and I couldn't allow it to continue. My concern diminished further when my car mysteriously disappeared. My sister's contrived "rescue" was another manipulative tactic in their plot against me. Their aim was to make me appear insane and incapable while concealing their own involvement in my difficulties. Regardless of their efforts, I persevered, using the principles instilled in me since childhood, my resolve only wavering at my mother's passing. This situation also brought TMH's revelation that neither those who left nor He were to blame; they were victims of a setup. I owed TMH an apology for my anger and frustration, stemming from the loss of those I found love with. Initially, I viewed any involvement of church, religion, or TMH as malicious, as if the purest-hearted were being used to rectify others' wrongdoings – a concept akin to sacrifices prevalent in various industries, but unexpectedly present in everyday life. I've come to realize the world around us holds far more potential for discovery than I ever imagined. As a child, I was deliberately shielded from knowledge of physics, religion, talismans, symbols, and other subjects, out of fear that my understanding would expose the falsehoods underpinning my life and ancestral energy. They knew I inherited gifts from my grandmother and sought to prevent my enlightenment. This explains why I often sat with her instead of playing with other children and why I was known for completing my sister's homework in fifth grade, while also tackling seventh-grade material. My life has been marked by achievements, despite any attempts to suggest otherwise. Despite their lack of direct involvement, they inflicted significant trauma upon me from childhood into adulthood, fueled by intense hatred and a desire to end my life and assume my identity. However, TMH intervened and prevented this.

My father told me I didn't need to buy a bed, so I needed to arrange transport. He said he'd be home if it rained, so I planned to ask my son's father and others for help then. The delay was frustrating, and I regretted moving my son's bed if I'd known. Not having eaten and feeling unwell, I ordered a sandwich. I dislike dishonesty; it's better to be upfront about limitations so alternative solutions can be found. People's indirectness is puzzling, and a storm seems imminent. For now, I'll wait for my food. Later, a friend I'd contacted about the bed called, ready to help since he had work nearby the next day. Picking up the bed involved another issue. My stepdad and my friend seemed to have some unspoken history, as my stepdad was unusually quiet and withdrawn. Additionally, the bed had a bloody pillow top, which felt disrespectful. However, I needed the bed for my son, as we were finally close to living together again after years. He was happy and didn't want to leave his quiet space. I didn't mind the pillow top since the mattress was clean. Things were fine until I spoke with my sister, which, as usual, led to changed plans. I'm realizing that anything I tell her tends to be altered, delayed, or stopped. This was the start of a developing situation. I began to wonder how long this had been happening and if my focus on work and illness had made me oblivious to betrayals by those closest to me.

News of my son wanting to spend more time with me had, of course, reached his father. Around that time, having bought a phone to better connect with my son, I also began to notice suspicious activity. My phone, connected to a network under my email, was being tracked, and my privacy was being invaded. This intrusion contributed to the loss of my side business due to numerous complaints about undelivered orders. Furthermore, my emails and contacts were being accessed, and attempts were being made to damage my reputation with potential employers and other important connections. When I raised these issues with my son's father, it quickly escalated into an argument. It wasn't until I pieced everything together that I realized they were all collaborating and that he was involved in an affair with my cousin. He became angry after I mentioned that his friend and I had slept together following a night out we all shared. I didn't consider it significant, as we hadn't been in a relationship for over three years, and he was treating me poorly. This period coincided with my earlier struggles and suicidal thoughts in 2015. A mutual friend, who was also my marijuana source at the time, was a supportive figure. One evening, while I was particularly down and intoxicated, we kissed. It was unplanned and unexpected; I was hurting, and he had offered comfort on multiple occasions, which eventually led to that moment. This continued for some time. After I moved to Southview, near my cousins on Barnaby Road, SE, WDC, he would visit her secretly. I suspect he had a feeling and saw his friend's car outside. Despite his own actions with my family, he was concerned about what I was doing. I didn't see our interactions as cheating or deceit; it felt like none of their business. We would meet occasionally to smoke, and we supported each other for a while. We grew very close, and I ended things because I felt we were becoming too involved, and I worried someone would discover our connection. While I personally didn't care, I didn't want to be the reason their friendship was ruined, so I stopped all contact.

After relocating to Sheriff Rd., NE, we reconnected. At that time, I faced unemployment and delays in my school checks. Foreclosure forced me to leave Capitol Heights, MD, and move to Southview after briefly staying with my aunt, where I sold items at a yard sale until my house check arrived. During the yard sale, a member of Rayful Edmund's crew bought a freezer and patio set, a red flag I ignored at the time. He worked in maintenance at Southview and offered to help me get a place, surprisingly putting the lease solely in his name. This proved disastrous as he overcharged me. I recalled his nickname and his unsavory associates, including my first husband. Visiting him one evening, I discovered he lived three doors down from my youngest son's father.I realized then that people had been manipulating my life through a larger network than I understood, and I had been naive to their control. My time at Southview ended violently when he repeatedly punched me in the eye, worsening previous damage. I defended myself with a knife and ordered him to leave. I later called the police as the situation escalated; he would enter my apartment without permission and had other maintenance workers spying on me, despite us not being in a relationship as agreed upon. I pressed charges in PG County, transferred the lease to my name, and moved back in with my second husband in Fairfax Village, SE, WDC—a place I didn't want to be. They all tried to keep me trapped, but I was determined to escape.

My sister's involvement was significant. She stole my resume, secured a job nearby, and offered assistance contingent on my help. Desperate due to illness, awaiting disability approval, and facing eviction, I reluctantly agreed, unaware of the potential exploitation. Her plan involved accumulating overtime and filing taxes, leaving me with minimal earnings after considerable work. Subsequently, she intended to establish two households and purchase a new vehicle, continuing her pattern of taking advantage. I was compelled to seek financial assistance from my stepdad for rent, providing a temporary reprieve from impending homelessness. Meanwhile, my sister received support from other family members, while I was consistently excluded, facing dire circumstances that had previously led to incarceration and shelter stays.

I've recently recognized that certain relationships were manipulated to control and harm me. Despite this, I've remained strong against the deceit of those who underestimated my resilience. Throughout periods of homelessness and imprisonment, my faith has been my anchor. To protect myself, I've made the painful decision to distance myself from my entire past, including my children. By the grace of TMH, I survived these hardships and was finally finding closure. Despite numerous attempts to rebuild my life, I often made missteps. It's disheartening that others fail to consider my experiences. Despite appearing outwardly fine, I feel profound inner loneliness. I unknowingly kept harmful individuals close. Since my move, no one has shown genuine care. I've come to the stark realization that those closest to me were my greatest adversaries, profiting from the chaos they instigated for years. This prolonged situation has become tiresome and repetitive.

Past events no longer concern me. I now understand that rejection has been a form of divine protection. Men have treated me as dispensable, only seeking me out when they needed something. I believe this underlies much of what I've endured. With him gone from my life, I sense impending danger or unease. My sister and family persist in their insincere gestures, feigning concern when I know I am the last person they genuinely wish to help or see happy. This has been a long-standing issue, but my breaking point occurred when my sister selfishly took my children. Instead of offering support during a crisis, she betrayed me and inflicted immense pain. My children were taken during a raid and remained in foster care for seven and a half years. During that time, I learned my second son was assaulted as retaliation for my sister's inability to break me. She allied herself with jealous and resentful individuals. Eventually, I demanded they leave me alone, recognizing their own denial of their struggles and their choice to uphold false appearances while attempting to destroy me.

The fundamental issue has consistently been about money. Everyone involved has engaged in deceit and theft to obtain it, or they have stolen and attempted to conceal it, myself included. My help was exploited. When I ceased enabling them, they resented me for no longer bearing their burdens. Even though I had already suffered, they expected me to continually steal and succeed, despite their own dishonesty. They would offload their problems onto me – the person who consistently provided support, maintained peace, and cared for everyone, even when my own children were used against me. I should have disengaged long ago. While a mother's love is inherently unconditional, this sentiment was not reciprocated. I understand that TMH uses trials to strengthen and rebuild, a process that can be distressing. Although overwhelming, it's essential to trust in a larger divine plan. This process is akin to laundry, where items are agitated to emerge clean and renewed.

Facing setbacks has taught me that difficult times prepare us for growth, just as rain precedes sunshine. My recent job interview, sought after a long period of unemployment and feeling isolated even from my children, caused me significant anxiety. This solitude has highlighted the need to reassess my social connections. I yearn for simple joys. Today, I nearly let overthinking and the urge to control things beyond my reach ruin my peace, until I was reminded that I am not alone. Having been surrounded by insincere people, I'm determined to restore my mental, physical, emotional, spiritual, and personal strength. Accustomed to self-reliance after thirty years, this unprecedented quiet in my life feels like a never-ending cycle of unhappiness. Today, I consciously choose to break free and move forward, trusting in support that has always been present, especially when others have let me down.

August eighth marked what would have been my second wedding anniversary with someone unsuited for me, a relationship that ended prematurely, much like a past one. My father, stepmother, and aunt were the architects of this situation. My sister and niece visited recently, a reminder of recurring family patterns. Disturbingly, my niece shared that my grandmother's boyfriend's inappropriate attention made her uncomfortable, stirring up painful memories of a childhood marked by neglect and a toxic family dynamic. I could never accept the incestuous relationships prevalent among relatives, where my objections were dismissed. I distanced myself years ago, recognizing this as wrong. The underlying issue was the exploitation of children within the family for twisted purposes, leading to generations potentially affected by disabilities. Their casual acceptance of this continues to anger me, especially imagining any harm coming to my niece. The innocence stolen through such acts can never be recovered. At 46, I still grapple with how different my life could have been without such trauma. My niece's continued exposure is concerning, even a seemingly harmless interaction with an old man reminds me of past experiences, though one felt playful, the other unsettling. The old vet, who later moved in with my grandmother, was never disrespectful, unlike the accusations my grandfather made against my grandmother with his own father.

As I explained earlier, my family has always been about money, and he had a disability and was a veteran. Again, I ask, at what cost? It's never really been about the checks, but about how much personal information can be obtained to claim benefits later for policies. I truly hope nothing happens to anyone undeserving. I promise it won't be swept under the rug like mine. In fact, that's why I feel it's necessary to share my story. I won't go to jail because they're still using the excuse that he goes to the park during the day to watch kids. I had to stop and ask, if you know this, why would you even have her near her?

Then my sister had the audacity to confess in front of my niece that she witnessed my uncle try. It's amusing that no one will ever hear her admit she knew the truth all along but let others spread lies about me. She and my aunt, her partner in crime, had an image to uphold. They think they've outsmarted TMH, but they are mistaken and will ultimately pay for their actions. Their lies and dishonesty have been deeply damaging, and they will be held responsible. I will simply observe their inevitable downfall. When TMH comes, I will not help them, as they have only ever brought negativity and deceit into my life and never offered me any assistance.

Many have tried to sabotage me and the plans TMH has for me. However, I am confident that no weapon formed against me will succeed because TMH has always been with me and will not abandon me now. Throughout my life, I have been repeatedly betrayed and wronged. It has all been a fabrication—my relationships, marriages, jobs, the abuse, everything was deliberately orchestrated from the moment I was born to steal my money.Each day feels increasingly drawn out. I desperately need a car due to the sheer volume of tasks I have. It's revolting how people only offer help when it serves their own interests. The ongoing madness persists. TMH is the only family I've ever truly had. It has been a long and arduous journey, but I am still here to share my experiences. I awoke with a sense of refreshment and happiness, accompanied by a sudden surge of energy. This is because I have finally released all the negative individuals from my life who constantly tried to impose their issues on me, as if I were responsible for the consequences of their choices. The truth is, they created their own problems and then immediately expected me to solve them.

At this time, my focus has been on myself; if I do not learn to love myself first, no one else will. I miss my son as I have not seen or heard from him after disconnecting his phone due to the deception from his father's other daughter, her mother, and others in the circle. If only I had a way to see him, it would be great. However, his stepdad will not make the same effort as me to make sure we see each other. But it is okay; it will work out in time. This time is for me to prepare not just for myself but as well all my children/adults who have all been removed and placed with others to benefit from all my pains and labor. I'm going for a walk in nature today.

Lately, I've realized that people keep interfering with me. I'm not sure why they can't just leave me alone and focus on themselves. They seem too focused on what I'm doing and need to redirect their thoughts to themselves. I'm tired of people trying to destroy things before they're even presented, which is why I've distanced myself. People usually forget about those who are out of sight and out of mind, but these people continue to harass me even before I have a chance to live my life. They want to keep me trapped in a cycle of confusion and distrust. Currently, I can't trust anyone except my family. Even F.A.N.S. are considered enemies until proven otherwise. I wonder why I'm a target. If people truly understood my struggles, they wouldn't treat me this way. Appearances can be deceiving. Despite my numerous challenges, I remain strong and resilient, ready for whatever comes my way. I patiently and silently wait for TMH's help.

Embarking on a new career path signals a significant and positive life transition. I've intentionally released past burdens that were no longer beneficial, realizing how many there truly were. Past disappointments evoke not sadness, but a sense of bewilderment. I'm learning the importance of discerning the complete picture for true understanding, as appearances can be deceptive, and truth requires time, patience, and thorough examination.

Reflecting on past relationships with men, particularly those ending in hurt, has been a source of pain. I now recognize a pattern originating in my youth and extending into adulthood, even involving men introduced by my father and stepmother. Often, these men carried their own past traumas, unresolved maternal issues, confusion about sexuality, or the impact of assault. While women frequently feel isolated in their experiences, this understanding has been helpful. My inherent optimism has always led me to believe in everyone's potential, irrespective of their history, and to strive for genuine perception. Despite encountering numerous challenges, my resilience has never wavered. In retrospect, those I allowed into my life as friends or romantic partners were insincere, intentionally placed to undermine my progress, a consequence of my own unresolved issues.

Despite enduring past pain, I remain hopeful for genuine love and support. I am actively working on forgiveness, trusting that I have been divinely protected from those with harmful intentions and believing that better times lie ahead. My determination to thrive persists. I have made the decision to embrace solitude. It has been over six months since my last social interaction, a state that does not particularly trouble me. Throughout my life, even within relationships and marriages, I have often felt alone. Reflecting on the past, it's clear that true familial love and care were absent. My mother's inability to love me authentically was due to external forces. It is deeply regrettable that my mother was killed, my children were harmed, and I experienced theft and broken relationships, only to then become a target myself. My profound sense of isolation led me to find solace and healing. In hindsight, remarrying was a mistake in every sense. Both of my husbands proved to be deceitful, unfaithful, and manipulative from the start. I later discovered the second husband's living situation was not as presented, adding to the deception. Recently, I've come to the realization that I may have been involved with someone insincere, possibly a temporary substitute related to his past relationships. Seeking clarity, I've turned to tarot to better understand the trajectory of my life and pinpoint where I consistently encountered flawed individuals— those I perceive as opportunistic, immature, narcissistic, and simply foolish. It's disheartening how often people feign agreement only to betray me when I deviate from their expectations. I am weary of the persistent drama, dishonesty, and failures in my relationships. I had hoped to find a soulmate, but he is younger and not ready for commitment. Although a strong connection existed, I now suspect he is navigating similar painful experiences I have already overcome. The pain inflicted by someone deeply loved can be profoundly numbing. My last marriage was exceptionally draining. For three years, I was the sole support for my ex-husband through his health issues, transportation problems, and general instability. I independently managed all aspects of life, both positive and negative, constantly struggling to maintain stability.

Despite past betrayals, I offered him friendship and a fresh start when he claimed his mother had kicked him out and sold their home. I believed his story and tried to help, but he destroyed everything I had worked for. He even had me arrested for allegedly stabbing him, though he didn't require stitches. He is malicious, like my other former partners. People may change their appearance, but their true nature remains constant. His intentions regarding his child's mother became apparent after the death of his sister and her mother. They lived lavishly for three years while I was rebuilding my life. Then, he contacted me because his utilities were shut off. He complained that she broke his TV and ate in front of him without acknowledging his own faults. My initial response was to tell him he was an adult and she wasn't obligated to feed him. He insisted it wasn't about that; since he allowed her and her nephews to stay with him and their children, he felt she should share. This suddenly reminded me of the pain of being hungry and watching others eat when I had nothing, especially with children present. I assisted him when I should have ended the conversation. However, knowing my compassion for children and my inability to ignore their suffering, I couldn't refuse. He initially acted as if my financial help was sufficient, but now he accuses me of being the one he depended on.

Feeling incredibly alone and unsupported, I was weighed down by frustration. I've always valued directness and honesty, believing that true loyalty means offering candid feedback, even if it's difficult to hear. While some might see my outspoken nature as harsh, I see it as a vital part of genuine friendship. Unfortunately, not everyone appreciates such candor, especially those hurt by past deceptions. My own heart has known its share of pain, often compounded by avoidance rather than direct confrontation. Despite this isolation and feeling trapped, I persevered. Thankfully, having my car allowed me escapes to parks and malls for some much-needed air. This forced solitude became a period of intense self-reflection, a time to face and conquer my inner struggles. As I've done many times before, I resolved to be independent and blessed. When they tried to undermine me by taking away my side hustle, my lifeline between jobs, they underestimated my resilience. Whether it's cooking a meal or styling hair, my ability to hustle has always been unwavering, and it's this very drive that has brought me to where I am today. I have never resorted to dishonesty, devalued my worth as a woman, or taken anything for granted. I've come to understand that my inherent value is immeasurable.

I learned long ago the futility of giving up on my aspirations when hard work can pave the way for achievement. The details of who did what and why remain unknown, and ultimately, it's not my concern. It's perplexing to encounter individuals who seem to harbor baseless animosity towards me. It's a recurring pattern: everything is amicable until they attempt to exploit my generosity, ideas, or finances. Declarations of love and affection quickly turn to hostility the moment I assert a boundary.Consequently, I've relinquished the hope of traditional love and family. My true support system lies with my F.A.N.S. and TMH, with TMH consistently bringing me joy. A past connection with my stepfather dissolved when I recognized the insincerity of him and my stepmother, a sentiment that extends to the rest of my family. It feels as though they've been actively working against me since I turned eighteen, creating persistent obstacles in my life. Sadly, every man in my life, including my own children, feels like they were influenced against me. A sense of being cursed has overshadowed the past thirty-six years. This journey has been profoundly humbling and transformative, and I'm uncertain of my capacity to endure much more.

My capacity to give, though heartfelt, has limits. I've come to understand that not everyone welcomes help; many are settled in their familiar realities, even if untrue. They resist change, hindering their growth and accepting only what they expect. My own path has shown me the value of risk and exceeding perceived boundaries. Even in unfavorable outcomes, the effort itself is worthwhile. The only true failure is not trying at all. I must now prioritize my well-being and heal. I've consistently placed others first, my efforts often unappreciated and reciprocation conditional, ultimately costing me dearly. I mistakenly believed an older, seemingly stable partner would be different. This pattern of attracting the wrong people stems from focusing on their potential rather than their present reality. I need to recognize their self-perception, as projecting my aspirations onto those who don't share them is futile. Their mindset was fixed, lacking a desire for personal growth or alternative paths. They didn't grasp life's varied opportunities and the diverse ways to achieve success. Ultimately, survival instincts drive us to overcome challenges, regardless of circumstances. Each day requires stepping outside your comfort zone to discover and embrace your purpose, leading to unimaginable possibilities that only taking a leap of faith can reveal. It may be challenging, but perseverance will make it natural.

My heart is heavy; I've been unable to sleep or eat for days. Others seem much happier. There was a gathering at my stepdad's, to which I wasn't invited. My sister's invitation seemed motivated by a desire to show off and for family to pry into my life, so I declined. To them, I've only ever been a source of amusement, financial gain, and a drain on their energy—someone to gossip about and onto whom they project their own lives. Relationships follow a similar pattern: money, sex, solutions, and absorbing others' problems. I feel seen for little else. I need respite because my ex manipulated me into believing a friend was stalking me when, in fact, it was many within my circle, including mutual friends. I've endured constant lies, betrayal, and rejection from those I trusted, including my own family, who, along with my exes, children's fathers, ex-husbands, childhood friends, and even strangers, have been actively conspiring against me. The relentless blame has been exhausting, and my yearning for a soulmate has only resulted in pain and betrayal. My life's goals are clear, yet the potential attention they may attract is daunting. The discovery of the widespread deception against me has been devastating. To think that someone used my own iPhone, given to them by my ex, to spread hate and negativity about me to my family and childhood F.A.N.S. is almost unbearable. I never thought I could withstand such a targeted attack, but it has shown me how strong I can be. Sleepless nights and a restless mind are my constant companions. My life has been turned upside down in recent months - relationships, finances, and housing have all changed. I miss falling asleep talking to someone and being held. TMH is always there to talk, but nights are still lonely. Daytime is manageable, but nights are unbearable. Maybe it's because I quit smoking. People assume I smoke to get high, but it was to cope with PTSD and anxiety. Medication is not an option due to my gastroparesis, caused by black magic and too many prescribed drugs. It destroyed my stomach lining, and the dark magic caused constant vomiting.

This temporary setback will be overcome, as I have faced and conquered challenges before. My body is adjusting to the detox, and I expect to resume my normal routine within days. For years, my schedule has been a rigid one: rising at 4:30 a.m., leaving by 6:00 a.m., arriving at work by 7:00 a.m., and a late return home. This has been a difficult period, realizing that family and others have sought unearned benefits from me, including money, influence, and fame. The recognition of having many adversaries has been hard to accept. Deep down, a feeling of solitude has always been present, and recent events have illuminated the reasons for this.

Looking back, I suspect TMH may have deliberately caused my amnesia after the 2005 car accident, during which I briefly died but was saved by TMH. Throughout my week-long coma, none of my family members visited, to my knowledge. Upon regaining consciousness, covered in stitches and bruises, only my youngest son's father and his family were there. My recovery is an ongoing process. I hold no bitterness, but I am trying to understand my life's trajectory. It is ironic that I face such hostility for living authentically, a way of life others actively try to undermine. If they directed that energy inward, they might experience similar personal growth. I am preparing for work tomorrow, hoping transportation is on time, as I need to be at the courthouse early to file divorce papers. My seven months of solitude have brought clarity: TMH is my only true constant. He has validated my thoughts, leading to a rediscovery of my true self. I had lost sight of my identity by focusing on distractions and other people. I had ambitious goals but never finalized them.

Having become aware of the superficiality surrounding me, I consciously focused on identifying genuine connections and find peace in this realization. My mistakes have been valuable teachers, emphasizing the need for thorough investigation before placing trust, as betrayal can originate from those closest to you. Prioritizing self-love and resisting the urge to change for others have been the most significant lessons. Because people often present deceptive facades, it's essential to heed what TMH reveals, even subtle clues, as the answers are often apparent.

In my pursuit of true love, I now believe it may only exist according to TMH's will. For the present, TMH's love suffices. Though I've sought tangible affection, the difficulty of trusting anyone has led me to rely on TMH for comfort and protection while awaiting a love that is sincere, authentic, and divinely ordained. My days have become monotonous—a cycle of work and home, lacking meaningful conversation. Writing has become my outlet for expressing emotions, preventing them from being suppressed. While work can be draining, each new level presents fresh challenges, though my co-workers seem to harbor dislike towards me. I fail to comprehend what makes me intimidating. Like everyone else, I am here to earn a living, not to create conflict or supplant anyone. This is a direct company hire, and I hold no animosity. Having worked on contracts previously, I understand that successes and setbacks are part of the process, a pattern of constant giving without reciprocation in my case. It feels unjust to face disadvantages in life due to outward appearances. We are all human, and superficial traits should not be the primary basis for judgment. I intend no harm; I experience the full spectrum of emotions and life's changes. While my expression may differ, I have learned from my experiences. When faced with failure, I seek alternative approaches, remembering the childhood adage, "Try, try again." Nothing is insurmountable with effort. I am striving to navigate these challenges, and my faith in TMH sustains me. I believe that all things are possible through Him; He remains steadfast. Through heartbreak, disappointment, and numerous setbacks, He has always been my protector. Despite my many falls, His love has always been sufficient to lift me. Following my car accident, I initially desired to recall my past, but I now understand that significant memories will surface when the time is right.

My intuition was correct; life is gradually returning, and while the memories are not always pleasant, confronting and processing the pain is necessary for healing and progress. I am learning that growth requires releasing and healing past hurts; otherwise, one remains stagnant.

After a severe car accident that left me comatose and severely injured, requiring facial plastic surgery that still affects my nerves, I began writing a book to recover my memory. Although successful, my ex-partner's family stole it. My life has been marked by constant upheaval, both as a child and an adult, moving between jail, relationships, and a fruitless search for love. I never experienced the love of a mother or stepfather and have always been alone. While solitude is often painful, I have found peace in it, and peace of mind is invaluable.

This newfound peace is the driving force behind my current divorce. I initiated the proceedings, and our court date is set for January 23, 2023. It's ironic how similar my experiences are across all aspects of life – relationships, work, and general existence. It seems I must leave a situation to be valued. For instance, my son is used to exclude me. Despite three years of relentless work with minimal support, my husband was willing to let us become homeless – specifically me. If we separated now, he would leave me to face being alone, a fate I've always anticipated. I've long understood the impermanence of things and the importance of not becoming too attached. As my situation has become clearer, I've gained the resolve to develop a plan to protect myself. The moment I told him to leave, I knew I wanted a divorce and that I would move on. My life began in solitude, and I expect it to continue that way. His sudden concern is a familiar temporary facade, but this time, it won't work. It's truly over.

I'm leaving for a place I should have reached years ago, and now he pretends he wants to fix things. Sadly, he thinks I'm stupid and naive. I'm not sure how he kept his job at the hotel for so long, given his lack of cleanliness. What's done in the dark will eventually come to light. My assumption is that he was sleeping with the boss, because there's no way an average employer would have kept him around - he was always dirty. He fooled me with all his "sweet talk."We are talking about a grown ass man who I had to tell to take a shower and brush his teeth. I used to think it was because of his living conditions, but now he is just nasty and then I wonder why I do not want him touching me. I hate my optimism. Sometimes I thought he did not shower much because his bathroom used to be messed up, but that never stopped me when I stayed with him. I have lived in some of the most unconditional circumstance I mean disgusting but in life I learned you make do with what you have and just maybe if you do it and go through it at the end of the day you will never have to go through it again passing test of strength and faith perception plays a big part things are as you want them to appear so view them how you want them to appear and suddenly they will   without any limitations be ready at any time for anything can change , you may have to readjust at any moment. My job is the same now . I am a contractor, so I expect things to end whenever. Only there is a difference . When someone is being just an A-Hole then there is a problem. You see, I intimidate my coworkers and do not want to be a supervisor. I am not fading. I did not sign up for drama, I just came to do my job. My contract was to end before Thanksgiving Day. I received a call saying they wanted me to return the following Monday. Someone was supposed to start and did not show. I started to say hell no, as usual why not? I needed the money, and it gave me something to do. I felt a little disrespected; if I wasn't good enough for the position, why call me back at all? And then they expected me to write out notes on how to do a job when the previous supervisor had only shown me once. I'm not sure if that's good or bad, but to me, it was insult to injury. Still, I completed the contract in good standing.

They called me back after hiring someone who didn't even show up and then bombarded me with all the things they didn't want to do or understand. I'll have to check with TMH, but I believe Friday will be my last day with this company. To be honest, I don't see growth; I'm just working hard to make someone else's job easier. This wouldn't be the first company to take advantage of me, and I'm sure it won't be the last.

I wish those against me would leave me alone. I am better off and less stressed by myself. While I sometimes chat with one or two people or my children, I'm mostly alone. Years of solitary holidays, with no family or friends, have changed my perspective. Even my children don't call or visit. I've never expected or received anything. Since my children aren't with me, I decided to still celebrate holidays, though I cook less now. I was always alone for years until just before my marriage, when I would visit my stepfather. Currently, I'm not speaking to any other family members and don't really trust anyone. They seem to only care about keeping you in debt and love to gossip, especially my deceitful siblings who are afraid of me exposing their secrets and have long been jealous. My sister's behavior dates back to childhood; her actions then could be described as playing with, fondling, or even molestation. I was around seven. Given her promiscuous past and issues with alcohol, she'll never admit the truth. She'll never acknowledge how many times I helped her, including when her children lived with me, ensuring they got to school on time to avoid fines and completing her work assignments because she couldn't. They never valued my originality; I am genuine, unique, and unforgettable, and everything I do is heartfelt. She repeatedly betrayed me by taking my children and lying, all for money. Getting a job would have been easier than her pretense. I've earned everything; nothing was ever given to me. In fact, she and her allies took everything from me. I am authentic, while she is fake, hiding behind a false smile. Eventually, her wrongdoings will be revealed. Tomorrow is a new day with a brighter future, and I find peace in letting go, even if I don't fully understand everything.

I'm ready for a strong finish and a graceful transition, but I need closure. I want this divorce finalized and to be free from my enemies. I'm weary of the chaos, struggle, disrespect, and envy. Today, I'm trying to quit smoking weed again (LOL), and I hope it sticks this time. Usually, I only feel the need to smoke when stressed or recreationally in social settings. It helps me stay calm and out of trouble. I've endured so much that seems endless. I'm done with relationships, friendships, family, and work – everything. I can't trust anyone with my feelings, not even a psychiatrist, so I turn to substances to cope. I've decided to directly confront my deep-seated issues and every trauma, regardless of the pain. In the past, I've trusted the wrong people and avoided my pain by ignoring, replacing, or misdirecting my anger. I'm determined to break this cycle and no longer live in heartache or agony.

Feeling overwhelmed and misunderstood, I've always prioritized others, often at the expense of my own well-being. Now, realizing the extent of the opposition I face, I'm entrusting TMH to guide me, as I can no longer navigate this alone. I feel trapped and need TMH's intervention to find a resolution, just as in the past. My desire is to break free from this negativity and the people who wish me harm. Despite my constant efforts to help, I'm bewildered by the animosity directed towards me.The time has come for this to end, and I believe the answers lie within me. I'm no longer interested in excuses; this entire experience has been confusing and chaotic. My focus is on moving forward, trusting that TMH will determine the right time, place, and individuals. With faith in divine timing, I will patiently wait for everything to align. My deepest longing is for peace and happiness, and I trust that I will eventually find the clarity I seek. Weary of the struggle and the search for genuine people, I yearn for reassurance and tranquility, finding solace in the words, "Be still and know that I am TMH."

Today, I've made the conscious decision to prioritize myself after a lifetime of trying to please others. While financial wealth may elude me, I've finally found inner peace. Despite the pull to go to work, I chose to stay home, acknowledging feelings of being used and exploited. It's become clear that my kindness has been mistaken for weakness by many. Others have moved on, leaving me to deal with the aftermath for their replacements. This recurring pattern of being used and criticized, despite my essential contributions, has been a constant in my personal and professional life. Recognizing these parallels across different areas of life is crucial for understanding the root issues. I'm tired of being taken for granted, always the last resort, only needed when things go wrong. This cycle in life, work, and relationships – where I give endlessly and am then used and abused – has to stop. Once others are stable again, I'm discarded until their next crisis, and then I'm blamed for my anger when I finally reach my limit.

Yearning for a complete reinvention, I desire a new job, a different place to live, a fresh romantic connection, and ultimately, a new sense of self. The outward persona I present doesn't reflect who I truly am inside. The authentic me has always existed, yet remains unseen, as others only perceive superficialities. My sense of not belonging stems from a fundamental difference; I am meant to be distinctive and a leader, unlike those who have unjustly adopted aspects of my identity – be it my name, my style, or my character. Their attempts at imitation are incomplete, for my true essence is irreplaceable. Though they may overlook me, their attempts to erase and supplant me reveal that they recognize my significance.

While the path forward is unclear, I trust that a higher power will not burden us beyond our capacity to endure, even when our own vision is clouded. Despite feeling defeated by obstacles, I believe justice will eventually prevail. This difficult period will also come to an end. My faith in this higher power is unwavering; past experiences have shown consistent support. The timing may not always align with our desires, but it is always perfect. It's important to recognize that challenges are not solely indicators of sorrow or disappointment; they can also signify progress in an unexpected direction, as life rarely unfolds exactly as planned. Ultimately, everything aligns with a greater design.

It is remarkable how this higher power intervenes in countless ways during times of need, often in surprising manners. Today has been a source of joy, and I am grateful for taking this day for myself. I have reached a point where a long-held aspiration has been realized. Writing by the water has always been a dream, and I am filled with happiness for making it a reality. Initial concerns about the weather proved unfounded. After a lengthy walk, a perfect spot appeared – beneath a tree, complete with three chairs and a table, situated directly overlooking the water. The table manifested precisely when needed; a request fulfilled. This serene scene was accompanied by the sweet songs of birds and the sounds of life. I sense that a significant event is approaching, and until then, I will remain attentive to the guidance from unseen forces. As the temperature begins to drop, I will continue these reflections once I am home.

This morning, after a peaceful day, I returned the car and am fervently wishing for my own vehicle soon. However, saving for the necessary lump sum feels impossible given the current high cost of living and my financial stress. The cold weather exacerbates my physical limitations due to age and anemia, causing body aches. I'm also facing potential health concerns, as I recently learned I might have sickle cell, pending confirmation. Adding to my worries, I've discovered possible tampering with my medical records, which is perplexing. Given that neither of my parents, to my knowledge, carries the sickle cell trait, its potential origin is unclear. Over the years, many things have been revealed and concealed. My feelings about this are more curiosity and a sense of acceptance rather than sadness. Regardless of any connections, those I held dear, beyond family ties, are no longer present. The relatives who remain have always been distant and critical of my success. Despite any perceived potential for failure, I am determined to persevere.

Work has been surprisingly positive. Despite underlying negativity from some, I've made a significant impact. I've noticed considerable envy, with others imitating my appearance, speech, and demeanor. My need for a car is pressing, but my lack of funds is a major obstacle. Owning a car would bring peace of mind, knowing I wouldn't have to worry about affording basic safety, comfort, and warmth. Despite my profession as an accountant, my credit score hasn't improved enough to allow a car purchase, even after 25 years. Contrary to expectations, negative items haven't been removed from my credit report after the standard seven-year period. While I can manage without a car, it would undoubtedly improve my relationships. I believe my hopes for better connections are being answered.

I'm beginning to realize that my desire to love and help everyone isn't always reciprocated. I remain hopeful that someone significant will enter my life soon. I've grown too comfortable in my solitude; it's not painful, and I don't object to it. I am thankful for TMH's support during another challenging time. I've prayed for the release of love in my life, as I feel lonely and desire affection. I plan to take a walk and reflect on this. Feeling confined and lonely at home, I trust in TMH's timing. I am asking for love to find me. The recent days have been emotionally turbulent. Another weekend has passed, intensifying my feelings of loneliness and isolation. The lack of a car contributes significantly to this feeling of being trapped. Without a car, sufficient funds, or close friends, prayer is my primary recourse for a change in circumstances. Life's difficulties can be overwhelming, leading to tears and a yearning for the escape of sleep. Time seems to be passing quickly, and I feel stuck in a cycle of despair. Moments of feeling unlovable and unworthy occur, but I hold onto the belief that I will find my way forward. My life's journey has been marked by unforeseen changes that have brought me to my current situation. Through the process of letting go, I've learned that life continues even after heartbreak. Lately, I've felt somewhat down without a clear reason. Perhaps it was simply another disappointment, another promise unfulfilled. It's now time to move forward with focus.

I've been praying for divine intervention to remove negativity and bring inner peace. People who wrongly believe I need them are trying to block my path, but I am learning stillness and surrendering to the protection of my ancestors and angels. This situation is painful and confusing, yet I know I am blessed, loved, and grateful for divine love. Despite betrayal from family and friends, I continue to grow, move forward with focus and determination, trusting that my needs will be met and my enemies' actions will be revealed with their consequences. I have learned from my mistakes and am tired of waiting for positive change; I want the negativity and drama to end, trusting TMH for justice and resolution. Even after experiencing betrayal, I ask for grace, mercy, and forgiveness, while also seeking accountability for those responsible. The countdown to my birthday and other events seems to align with TMH's plan. While I've asked for everything to be revealed in divine timing, I long for an end to the delays. Now that I realize TMH has always been the only one truly on my side, I am ready to move forward. I see there is nothing to lose but those who have seemingly hated me since birth and intended to destroy what I built after taking what was mine. I look forward to the future and choose to trust no one from my past, knowing this difficult time will pass.

Recently, I spent 24 hours helping others, only to be left alone with my own growing problems. Others have taken everything I've built, leaving me with their burdens. This is the result of harmful soul ties, highlighting the importance of recognizing how others affect one's life and blessings. Though I know I'm not alone, I am losing hope and faith, weary of constant betrayal and hurt that allows others to prosper while I am destroyed. I am stuck rebuilding while they feel nothing, and I am tired of this injustice. It is emotionally draining to see my ideas and teachings repeatedly exploited without consequence. They thrive while I remain stagnant despite my hard work and dedication. My efforts are acknowledged, yet nothing changes; I am trapped in a cycle of labor, only to have my achievements stolen and my life disrupted. I demand justice for all who have wronged me and the return of my stolen possessions without further delay. Countless individuals must be involved in these situations. How can irregularities like forged signatures, false accounts, false warrants, and children entering the system be allowed in a marriage when checks are supposed to be in place? Judges and many others are complicit, and the sheer number of people involved is overwhelming.

Despite my impending divorce, the thought of solitude brings a twinge of sadness. Yet, I'm reminded of my recent self-imposed isolation, which now feels like a necessary preparation. My tendency to withdraw served to keep unworthy individuals at bay.Someone has captured my attention, and the feeling is reciprocated. I'm cautious due to our age difference and worry I might have unintentionally created distance. He intrigues me – ambitious, driven, and reminiscent of a past version of myself, which I find alluring.I'm learning to be more mindful of my energy and approach life with greater deliberation. This newfound freedom feels right, and inexplicably, I feel a deep sense of loyalty towards him. Our connection seems effortless and unspoken, though I recently felt awkward due to my hiatus from dating. After a period of isolation from men, compounded by abuse and illness, I've forgotten how to enjoy casual dating. He could be the one to reignite that spark.

Our communication is easy but infrequent; our last conversation might have continued if I hadn't ended it. We need to find a comfortable, public meeting place to avoid any misinterpretations or the impression of ulterior motives. While we both possess street smarts, he's unaware of my past. Our initial meeting happened shortly after my release from jail and while I was living in a shelter. This experience underscores the importance of not judging appearances, as reality is often more complex, and everyone carries their own story. I've always been authentic, simply mirroring the energy I receive, which others sometimes mistake for insincerity or arrogance. I am now open to a submissive dynamic with a responsible partner, someone who would appreciate the chance to indulge and enjoy life without negative repercussions.Trust is a significant issue for me, and I need him to be more forthcoming rather than expecting vulnerability solely from my side. I'm uncertain why my intuition is hesitant about this relationship, but I need to pay closer attention to those feelings. I'm weary of initiating contact. I am attracted to him and have been fantasizing about him since our initial encounter. I hope my instincts are correct this time, unlike in the past when my judgment was clouded by apathy and anger. Now, I'm better at recognizing deception.

Today has been difficult – a stomachache and my paycheck vanished instantly. Being cut off financially for two consecutive periods is disheartening, but I accept it as a necessary setback before improvement. This situation tests my trust, faith, and belief in a higher power. I pray for those who wish me harm. My lack of funds is concerning, yet I trust that a greater plan is unfolding for me. I've asked for divine protection on my journey. I believe that significant challenges precede greater triumphs and deeper understanding.I'm increasingly frustrated, not just by who took it, but also by their reason and the fact that people have been taking from me for as long as I can remember. Now, I want it all back immediately. If it were meant for them, it would have been addressed to them. I don't care anymore about the punishment for their wrongdoings, as if I haven't been through enough. The funny thing is, everyone thinks I'm hurt, but I'm not. You can't miss what you never had. Today, I only have what I've earned, not what was given.

Remember this: TMH will ensure everyone bows before me and becomes my footstool as I achieve my goal to succeed above all those who have tried to keep me down. Their actions only made me stronger. I have always been blessed. TMH loved me when no one cared. I am highly favored and blessed because I have always loved Him first! When no one else thought I was worthy, He already knew and waited while He strengthened me from the wounds inflicted to stop me. Instead of fixing me and blocking those who came for me, He allowed me to go through it to understand how it could be, all by choice. Then, He gave me something no one ever has: an option.I used to be so angry and focused on revenge. I wanted to change and fix everything on my own. I was so consumed by proving myself to others that I couldn't see what was right in front of me.Having sought external validation and affection, I eventually realized that self-love was the missing piece. Prayer became my anchor, guiding me to discover this inner love when I felt lost. I am eternally grateful to TMH for their constant presence, even during times when my own pain and anger deafened me to guidance. Despite my struggles, that unwavering presence and love never ceased, answering my prayers and directing my path.

Meanwhile, my second ex-husband resumed his relationships with his wife, his stepsister mistress (residing with his stepmother), other casual partners, and family members. His motivation was revenge for my attempts to assist him, a scheme supposedly devised by his wife or a coworker (possibly one and the the same) who falsely claimed pregnancy. This elaborate deception involved a fabricated trip to North Carolina to see his mother, which never occurred. Instead, he attended to obligations under the direction of his mother and aunt. His constant lies, potentially in collaboration with his stepmother, extended to a possible plot against his mother and me. His obsessive viewing of Eastern Star, Masonic, and similar society activities was not random; it indicated his family's deep involvement. It is with profound dismay that I acknowledge my entire life and everyone connected to it appear to have been orchestrated. The genesis of this is still under investigation, but it seems I was sold to a cult as an infant by the parents I believed loved me – a truth that has since been revealed through further shocking secrets. This is a conspiracy of unimaginable scale, involving false identities, stolen destinies, murder, life insurance fraud, government complicity, and black magic. In the name of TMH, I implore justice, protection, and peace.

Despite a lifelong history of independence and competence since age fourteen, my siblings, family, and associates conspired to manipulate the court into declaring me incompetent and unstable. Their aim was to strip me of my ability to care for myself. The hypocrisy is evident: if I were truly incompetent, how could they have obtained a PPP loan, and whose account did they exploit to steal those funds? These individuals are not incompetent or insane; they are profoundly foolish criminals who have relentlessly tried to silence my truthful account. After a long and difficult struggle, I now stand on equal ground. My truthful narrative will empower others to form their own judgments, free from the fabricated web of lies. They possessed intimate knowledge of my life story long before I did, having accessed my akashic records and plagiarized my writings. This stolen information fueled their plot to steal my intellectual property, destroy my reputation, and ultimately, eliminate me. Throughout this time, he remained married to his child's mother (never divorced) and was involved with another woman he married in another state – a chaotic and drug-fueled entanglement with individuals driven by greed and resentment towards any affection shown to me. Their strategy involved marrying me solely to obtain a marriage certificate with my name, followed by orchestrating a divorce through blatant infidelity in my own home and vehicle while I worked three jobs. He had already sabotaged one of my side businesses by stealing my car, acting on lies fabricated by my own sister and family.

I accidentally answered his phone and spoke with a woman from an insurance agency who was discussing plans with him, assuming I was already aware. This sparked my suspicion, so I checked his phone. I found messages with his children's mother that contradicted their public animosity. There were also numerous nude pictures from websites and, I assume, past or current sexual partners. I pretended not to know anything while I formulated my response. Days later, while cleaning, I discovered a machete hidden under my pillow. He claimed it was for protection, but I knew he was lying. He also pretended to keep a gun under the bed, but I only ever saw it when he was leaving with a large, black tote bag containing unknown items.

I was finally seeing the truth that had been hidden for years by distractions designed to keep me vulnerable to their attacks, projections, and manipulations. They had maintained an elaborate lie since my childhood for their own benefit. Although I wanted to react, I remained calm, determined to uncover everyone involved.Amidst all this, my youngest son's father betrayed my family by having a child with one of them. I even wrote a letter releasing him from child support so he could be with this pregnant person, possibly my sister or cousin—they are all F.A.N.S. Who knows? He was still sleeping with his first child's mother, who has been using black magic against my son and me with his other children, one of whom isn't even his biological daughter. They all think I'm naive, but I already know about the stolen money, houses, cars, sex rituals, and inheritance. The TMH boats, all stolen, all purchased at the cost of my suffering, are the ultimate proof. Even though I haven't received what was rightfully mine, I trust in divine timing. Everything will be revealed and returned, and those who have lied, stolen, and accused will face judgment from TMH, whose authority is absolute. Military and official ranks mean nothing; no one is above TMH.

It's absurd to think I'd be harmed by my children inheriting what I leave behind. They are grown, the youngest being sixteen. This won't hurt me; they will eventually understand my reasons. I have consistently provided for them, including a son who barely knows me, and continued to support them in times of need for over eighteen years. They have filed taxes for years, while I haven't. Every dollar I spent was earned, yet they believe my reduced income will destroy me. I will adapt, as I've been navigating this for years and learning. They intended to use my appearance against me, but they only made me stronger, underestimating my inner resilience. I'm thankful my outward appearance doesn't betray my experiences; it was deliberately designed that way. I believe in directness, and I raised my children with the same honesty, always caring for them and being truthful about life's realities. The world is harsh, and I wanted them prepared, unlike my own difficult learning experiences. I did my best to equip them for life's challenges, even when it was tough. I was raised with tough love, and that was all I knew to give. Though female, I was raised as a boy. Thankfully, I have only sons, and I hope they will be different from their fathers.

Love is complicated, and at this stage, I have no interest in revisiting past relationships. They were all insincere and ultimately betrayed me for various reasons. Their fear, misunderstanding, intimidation, and weakness prevented genuine love. They were all attempts to manipulate me, create drama, and shift blame. It's a small world, and connections are often surprising, even through forgotten acquaintances. But TMH has a way of revealing things. My life has been about survival and overcoming obstacles. I was trapped in a cycle of questioning coincidences, only to find they were orchestrated by interconnected groups led by a single individual with blind followers. I have never been part of this, even before I was aware of it. While imperfect, I've always known when to leave. This has caused resentment from those who may have controlled me when I was vulnerable. Even then, I knew my boundaries. My detractors tried to pull me down, but they couldn't control me. They resorted to group tactics and rituals to harm me, yet they still failed. TMH has the ultimate authority.

The truth will always come out, and The Most High (TMH) guides you to your authentic self. A pivotal lesson I learned is that "TMH cannot bless a mess," a realization that changed my life. He respects boundaries and won't interfere where unwelcome. Often, we impede our own blessings by seeking the approval of others and taking shortcuts. It's crucial to act with integrity, trust in divine timing, and maintain faith – this waiting period is sometimes the true test. Hold onto your belief and proceed with caution. Always trust your initial instinct; it is invariably correct. Believe in your aspirations, and they will be realized. It has been a long time since I've dated; I've been preoccupied with dealing with detractors and focusing on everyone else. I now see that the government, my family, and even my F.A.N.S. have betrayed me. While I am disappointed, I am not angry, as I allowed it to happen during a period of personal confusion. I nearly lost my life due to jealousy, deceit, cover-ups, and theft. I am unique, and while there will be forgiveness, these actions will not be forgotten. People are not to be trusted.

My court date is set for January 23rd, and I am anticipating it. I resumed writing nine months ago, and everything is now clear. The illness, stress, depression, and loss were all forms of manipulation. They do not want my happiness or success, yet they fail to grasp the ultimate judgment that awaits. I am surrendering and allowing TMH to handle this, as I have done numerous times before. I know He will intervene once I release control.They exploited, used, and discarded me, yet they never truly let go. They held onto connections that I severed the moment their lack of love was apparent – or at least, that was the facade they presented. They never genuinely loved or cared; their only aim was to exploit my energy and gifts for their own protection and advancement under false pretenses. My heart, body, and mind became so desensitized to this that TMH intervened. I was becoming indifferent to the negativity, and TMH wanted me to recognize the truth to prevent a recurrence of past errors. Now, I am working and content, grateful, and feel that many of my questions have been answered. I feel a sense of lightness and closeness to TMH, and I give thanks to Him, my ancestors, guides, angels, and my heavenly family for saving me from myself and those who sought to harm me. My learning continues, but I am blessed to maintain stability as I adapt to this newfound understanding.

My divorce was finalized today. The outcome wasn't what I desired, but I'm relieved to be free. I'm unhappy with my life; everything feels hopeless and irreversible. Time is irreplaceable, and I need to pray for forgiveness for allowing negativity to impact my happiness and peace. I've been dreaming and wishing, but now I'm ready to take action. Life is chaotic and misdirected by others; true happiness can only be found through spiritual and religious connection, not physical or mental suffering. I'm separating myself to be with TMH. I realize now that the childhood lesson of "blood is thicker than water" was taught by people with the wrong mindset, who were unhappy and driven by greed. Love was meant for me, but they wanted me to believe otherwise, that I was destined for a life of pain.The pain I've experienced feels like punishment for something I did in a past life, meant to make me feel inferior. My family excludes me, and it hurts deeply.

I no longer wish to participate in their fabricated reality. I need to distance myself from those who have never wished me well. I am exhausted from a lifelong struggle that began in my childhood and have no more energy or time to dwell on the past. Both my expectations and the expectations of others have become overwhelming. This was manageable until I began exploring tarot and reading, which revealed the extent of others' animosity towards me. I felt the universe communicating through my phone, confirming that I am indeed loved and that releasing unfulfilling relationships and situations would open my life to unforeseen hope and possibilities. I understood that I am worthy of love, even if unrequited. I was making positive progress with my career, divorce, and new beginnings, realizing that the universe intended for me to recognize my self-worth and that I deserve more than what was being presented and communicated to others.

However, an adverse force was intent on undermining my life and self-belief. For nine months, I was deceived by illusions and false hope, irrationally believing in someone's genuine care and potential for emotional and financial compatibility. I was mistaken and am now accepting the reality of my life: hard work and giving love without expecting anything in return. I recognize that their underlying goal has been to erode my self-esteem; I am not angry, merely more aware.I long to escape this nightmare born from the deceptions of others and malevolent influence. I must rectify the fantasy I have constructed. I resigned from my job and relinquished my car, trusting in the universe's provision. Consequently, I now face overdue bills and lack the means to pay them. Today, I had to pawn my possessions for food, having been subsisting on expired items. I understand the error in my belief in illusions and accept responsibility for this setback. Nevertheless, I am learning from my errors more swiftly than before, enabling me to correct them before they escalate.

I need to be more guarded about my personal life, even with seemingly caring individuals. Their intentions might not be genuine, and they could be waiting for my downfall. I must accept the current situation, acknowledge my limitations, and strive to learn from this. Time, options, and finances are dwindling, and I'm hoping for a positive change. It's imperative that I quit smoking and actively pursue the transformation I need and desire. Smoking is a deceptive habit that harms individuals while benefiting the government – another method of control. The truth is, the government exploits what it can profit from, legalizing and taxing harmful substances, mirroring a system of control like the prison system. It's ironic how people claim slavery is over. Is it truly over when we work tirelessly daily, allowing others to capitalize on our ideas and labor? As workers, we perform the bulk of the work for minimal pay, only to return a significant portion to the government through taxes with a minimal return. In the current economy, a fair exchange rarely exists due to intermediaries, and even direct transactions are subject to taxes. Consider stimulus checks, unemployment increases, pandemic scares, and foreign conflicts – are these truly for the benefit of society or primarily economic maneuvers? Many will simply spend this money on non-essential items like electronics and vehicles, contributing to a system of surveillance and societal control. Yes, we are being monitored through our purchases and accounts. Slavery and imprisonment exist in disguised forms, perpetuated by ingrained beliefs. Stop being passive; conduct your own research and be observant. Things are rarely as they are presented. Break free and have faith. The government, like many forms of evil, demands a price for status, even if it costs one's life. Despite feeling exhausted and abandoned, I must advocate for myself. No one will rescue me; I am responsible for my own liberation. If there are repercussions for standing up, then at least I will have stood for something. I will no longer tolerate feeling worthless or insignificant. I refuse to be manipulated into silence. I will overcome this betrayal and speak my truth, and no one will silence me. My words have the potential to heal and awaken those silenced by fear and illusions. If you trust in the Most High, I believe protection will be granted. New and unexpected paths will open; with faith, anything is possible.

Each day remains unchanged, marked by the continued negative influence of the same individuals on my diminished life. My certainty in feelings and trust has eroded, leaving only TMH as a reliable presence in dire situations. Past experiences have extinguished my belief in positive change. This time, I have established firm boundaries to prevent further manipulation. My aspirations, creditworthiness, public image, and professional life were abruptly ruined. Choosing TMH meant severing ties with my children due to their negative influences, a painful but necessary decision. Although accustomed to solitude, the weight of having nothing and no one is still deeply felt. I suspect a deliberate effort to dismantle my life to seize the rewards of my three decades of relentless, joyless work. The outcome is devastating: damaged credit, estranged children, and the loss of my vehicle and home. This engineered downfall was meant to obscure their exploitation, but I now see their deception. I am in the process of restoring my reputation, and this ordeal is nearing its conclusion. My past blindness has given way to clarity. While uncertain of TMH's plans for me in this life or the next, I believe it entails more than my current suffering. Despite a strong desire for immediate escape, fear of a worse afterlife prevents me from ending my life, as previous attempts have failed, with TMH intervening. This ongoing torment and confusion are overwhelming. I am currently unable to manage basic needs like eating, paying bills, or even leaving my residence.

I've faced recurring disruptions, but I'm growing resilient. These challenges are teaching me valuable lessons, showing me where not to invest my energy. I now prioritize what truly benefits me. If giving consistently depletes you, it's time for a change. Seek a fresh outlook. What once felt familiar has become unproductive, either unsatisfying or overwhelming. It's important to keep searching for the right fit, even if solitude is necessary temporarily. Reflection will guide you. I once prioritized others' happiness over my own, leading to feelings of stagnation and pain while witnessing others thrive through my efforts.

No longer bound by past expectations, I recognize the disparity between my genuine love and feelings of loneliness. This realization, while tinged with sadness, fuels my personal growth and self-love, including accepting solitude. Past experiences, though unforgettable, now serve as stepping stones. The recent clarity, though initially sad, prepares me for future revelations. I anticipate further disappointments, but repeated exposure has lessened their impact, perhaps a lesson in vulnerability. Instead of processing past traumas, I suppressed emotions and pushed forward. I now understand the importance of acknowledging feelings without becoming trapped by them. Recent discoveries of disturbing situations, even from trusted individuals, confirm a long-standing pattern.

Despite enduring attempts on my life fueled by lies, hate, jealousy, greed, and the concealment of wrongdoing, I survived through my resilience and divine grace. Their efforts to harm me, even through unknowing others, ultimately failed, as truth always prevails. While these trials were unjustly directed at me, the hardships and those who inadvertently contributed to them prepared me for life's challenges. Remarkably, I maintained love and understanding, transcending their negativity by holding onto a belief in unconditional higher love. Unlike them, who thrived on my energy and blessings without confronting reality or learning from life's lessons, I faced my trials head-on. Their lack of growth will make the inevitable consequences more severe. These experiences, though painful – marked by abuse, misuse, judgment, and hate – have equipped me with invaluable lessons, enabling me to stand strong and move forward.

Having navigated my necessary lessons without seeking shortcuts or resorting to deception, I am now ready to receive my rightful blessings. My past failures have forged my strength, validating my pain. With newfound knowledge and understanding, I will await divine intervention, whether it brings my enemies to submission or grants me the respect and apologies I deserve. I will accept either outcome with forgiveness and without resentment, hoping they too find wisdom in their errors. Divine mercy is for the deserving, while divine retribution awaits those who are not. Having learned to let go of past hurts, I am prepared to start anew, guided by the lessons of my past, and confident in facing the next chapter.

Exhausted from constant betrayal and the indifference of those around me, I can no longer remain silent. They carry on without guilt, seemingly unaffected by the devastation they've caused. Trapped and suffocated within these walls, I'm choosing to step forward, even without resources, driven by a desperate need to escape the endless cycle of deceit that has shattered my life. The persistent drama orchestrated by others only intensifies my despair, leaving me feeling worthless and utterly alone, with no hope for the future. For too long, I've been overlooked while others prospered at my expense. That ends now. I refuse to be silenced any longer. My priority is to break free from this oppressive environment and pursue happiness. The pervasive sadness and lack of support have left me isolated, with nothing left to hold onto here. I must leave.

I am being subjected to ongoing harassment and spying, evidenced by repeated police visits to my home that disrupt my community. My private activities within my residence are my own concern. As an adult, I reject these attempts to entrap me and falsely portray me as unstable. These actions, which I refer to as "BOO BOO," are intended to intimidate me and facilitate the misappropriation of my social security, unemployment, or other assistance benefits.For the past five to seven years, my accounts have been compromised. Initially, I addressed the resulting debts and allowed the situation to persist. However, I realized this only enabled the perpetrator to continue these crimes under my identity, negatively impacting my life. My hospital records, email, phone, and bank accounts have been hacked. My mail has been forwarded to an unknown address, and I haven't received any for the last three years. Despite changing my email address twenty-eight times and consistently reporting the account hacking, these issues continue.

I was forced to delete cherished digital memories of my children, retaining only mental recollections of significant events like my mother's wedding and graduations. This occurred after giving my son a phone to maintain contact, which was then hacked by his uncle, who possesses IT skills and engages in hacking. The uncle's brother, a police officer, facilitated the exploitation of this situation by everyone except my son. They undermined our relationship, stole money to keep us apart, and concealed their deceit and theft. These individuals, including high-ranking military Master Chiefs within both their family and mine, are all complicit. My brother, a PG County police officer, is also involved.This corruption, which has persisted for over seventeen years, remains unaddressed. I am speaking out to demand that it cease.

After needing time for self-care and gaining perspective, I am starting a new job at a local law firm on Tuesday at 10 AM. I am grateful for the financial security this new chapter provides. Although I anticipate a stressful initial two weeks, I am prepared to handle it differently based on past experiences. My taxes are filed, and I look forward to moving forward. Recently, someone attempted to provoke me by opening an account under my first married name, Mitchell, a name that usually evokes anger. However, I recognized this as a manipulative tactic intended to disturb my peace and affirmed my faith in continued support, knowing that past experiences are behind me.

Despite ongoing slander and mistreatment from my son's father and others, who are attempting to involve my past relationships, I remain indifferent to their actions, which seem to reflect their own preoccupation. While they have tried to manipulate my children against me, I refuse to engage in such tactics, having dealt with this before. I am hopeful that this challenging period will soon end, and I will experience joy, finding strength even in small signs of hope as I await the overwhelming happiness I have prayed for.I am determined to leave the past behind, releasing the anger and pain associated with past traumas, and move towards a peaceful and hopeful future. The experiences of abuse, drugs, and theft are behind me. The time when I was severely ill and those around me, despite feigning concern, were toxic and exhausting me is over. Although my desire for peace led me to move, my problems persisted and have unfortunately worsened.

Feeling trapped and increasingly lonely after a divorce, I long for a fresh start, leaving the past behind. Love feels unattainable, and isolation seems inevitable, a familiar pattern. Despite repeated disappointments with men, I recognize it's not my place to change them. My purpose, I believe, is to offer the love I've never truly received, but I'm currently too drained for relationships, focusing instead on work and home.The situation with my children is heartbreaking. My son's father concealed the birth of another child, impacting my son deeply as they try to maintain their image and exploit him. Helpless, I can only pray and trust that a higher power will intervene and resolve this. I've surrendered this situation, believing that in time, things will change, and I will regain a peaceful life, free from romantic entanglements and unnecessary drama, prioritizing inner peace.

Despite feeling moments of despair and believing I am only meant to give love, I recognize these as negative thoughts. I am resilient, a survivor who has overcome significant challenges, and I possess the strength to persevere.It is disheartening that those I have helped have often betrayed or abandoned me. I maintain a strong facade only through the grace and mercy of TMH, for whom I am grateful for my life and love, accepting all that comes. If my path is to be alone, I accept it. Any deviation from this path is my personal journey, requiring understanding only from myself and TMH. Leaving Sheriff Rd, which I hoped would be a new beginning, has instead been a repetitive cycle, akin to Groundhog Day, marked by the same issues and individuals employing different deceptive tactics. The past seven to eight months have been an emotional rollercoaster – experiencing periods of being unpaid, depressed, happy, and sad. Despite my faith and inner strength, my thoughts remain confused and empty.

I have come to the stark realization that my entire life has been built on lies, and I have been isolated and disliked by most of my family and F.A.N.S. This is why TMH has become my unwavering support and protector, a truth I've subconsciously known but resisted believing. I harbor no anger or hurt, only a slight disappointment, which will not deter me. I am moving forward resolutely, leaving the past behind. I am relinquishing control and entrusting everything to TMH, confident that the truth will be revealed. I will observe and allow events to unfold, knowing that hidden actions will eventually come to light.I am returning to work tomorrow, but I am already formulating my plan to leave this situation permanently. My priority is to save money and escape. I foresee no positive developments in my future here, and everything feels contrived and insincere.

My oldest child attempted to kill me, and my second child is incarcerated in maximum security for a 15-year term while living with HIV. They view me solely as a source of money and are unaware of the difficulties their actions have caused. I am uncertain of my third child's whereabouts, with their father suggesting military enrollment, though I lack confirmation. My youngest child has sought to avoid the family turmoil, and I have been unable to see them since the car was taken. Continuing my visits, which had been a positive bonding experience, was deemed detrimental to their well-being. Furthermore, my ex-partner was a constant source of irritation.Life sometimes necessitates difficult choices to maintain equilibrium and shield what is most important from negativity, potentially involving personal sacrifices and strained relationships, even with one's children. I fear my youngest son's innocence is at risk from the surrounding chaos and negativity, akin to how pure individuals can be corrupted by addiction and turmoil. This individual (TMH) is easily agitated. I have always believed that positive and destined things will eventually return. I will continue to work tirelessly, even for minimal earnings.

Exhausted by everything and everyone, I previously considered ending my life. Although I experienced insomnia and delusional thoughts, I understood their absurdity. At forty-five, feeling as if my youth is almost over and I have nothing and no one, I recognize this is fictional. Believing I will receive what I am owed in a future life, I have no intention of committing suicide now. Condemnation may follow regardless of one's actions, so it's best to disregard unsupportive people.I am attracted to my friend but fear making the first move. He has options, and I don't want to be just a fling. I am usually busy and defensive, but not with him. I confronted the devil about his lies, though he continues to act innocent; they all play a part. I pray that TMH will reveal the truth and those who hate will fall. I hope my tax refund arrives soon so I can travel, buy a car, and move. I trust this will all happen in divine timing; what TMH has put together, man shall not destroy.

Having endured deep hurt, I sought divine help to transform my life. Despite my consistent efforts to assist those in need, I am aware of intense dislike directed towards me. While solitude offers me peace, I long for genuine connection, as I perceive that others' affection is merely for personal gain. My belief in mutual love and support has been shattered; I now understand that self-love is paramount and true external love will manifest without pursuit.

Having navigated life's challenges with strength, weakness, boldness, bravery, and success, I feel I have reached a point where I have nothing further to lose. I was once lost and confused, questioning my purpose and life's expectations. The relentless hate and threats against my life were perplexing, as I believed I had done nothing to warrant such negativity, especially after past wrongs against me had been revealed, and I had offered forgiveness. Yet, attempts to steal from me and endanger my life persisted.My past and its inhabitants no longer hold significance for me; they are as if dead to me. Relying on my enduring faith, I will continue to stand alone, as has been my pattern. The resurgence of past issues following my separation from my ex-husband, after two decades of letting them go, was unsettling, yet familiar. It is crucial for individuals to mature and cease harmful behavior before serious consequences arise.

It would be unwise to change my loyalties now. Life has taught me that true care is scarce, a lesson reinforced by a thirty-year illusion of divine protection that paradoxically allowed me to survive even great losses. Despite this, I now struggle with growing insecurity, lovelessness, and distrust. My progress is hindered by the demonization of a past influence that remains a part of me, much to my frustration. For over three decades, I have fought against hate, deceit, envy, and greed— qualities I do not possess. My consistent efforts to help others lead me to question why I face continuous hardship, disappointment, and setbacks. My belief in mutual love and protection is challenged by the apparent contingency of affection on material offering. I strive to support others, even children I rarely see, facilitating their success while I remain stagnant. Perhaps assigning blame is pointless, and I must accept my part in allowing false narratives to endure. Now that they are gone, I am back where I began. Maybe this was always my destined path.

Recent events, though chaotic, align with my long-held understanding of life, shaped by experiences others seem oblivious to. What others find shocking is my normal. This perspective once made me feel flawed, but I now realize my family and friends have been the ones acting unusually. My definition of success has evolved; it's no longer the ultimate goal.A significant issue within Afro-American culture is the pervasive infighting and competition that hinders collective progress. Instead of uniting and supporting each other's advancement, there's a tendency to undermine one another, ensuring no one rises. This contrasts with other cultures where unity and shared progress are prioritized, driven by understanding rather than greed. Within our culture, envy prevents mutual support, regardless of shared background.Love and knowledge transcend race and structure. Knowledge empowers, which is why there are attempts to limit access to it, maintaining a control that is ultimately illusory. We are often only taught what others deem appropriate. True understanding requires independent research and critical thinking, moving beyond blindly accepting narratives.

Human beings are born with innate knowledge, talents, and intuition that should cultivate our individuality and create unity through diversity. It is essential to recognize this reality and actively pursue understanding. True evaluation lies in common sense and love, not superficial traits like skin color, as we are all essentially the same. Thought, the foundation of comprehension, requires only a grasp of truth, irrespective of financial status or appearance. Accepting this reality equips us to overcome the unknown by making it manageable Throughout my life, I have experienced envy and greed, leading to the sabotage of my opportunities. My only respite seemed to occur during periods of illness, incarceration, homelessness, or drug use. My family was also unsupportive, collectively working against me. The depth of their resentment became evident when my children were taken away. The extent of the hate, the orchestrated schemes, and even threats of violence were shocking revelations. A supportive family is a true gift, something I have never known within my own. Despite being labeled as "ghetto," I am living authentically. My struggles are genuine, and I am thankful to have something worth fighting for. The intense hatred directed towards me, seemingly for simply being myself, feels like a crime in their eyes. Financial pressures forced me to temporarily cease writing, as my unemployment and other support have been repeatedly obstructed or stolen, a concerning pattern. The whereabouts of my mail have also become uncertain.

It has been ten months since I first reported these issues, yet no action has been taken. Consequently, I am unable to access necessary resources due to not receiving my mail, and all my support has been discontinued. Despite having been in this situation before, my personal information is being reassessed. I will endure, as I always have, sustained by my faith in The Most High (TMH) and the protection of my angels. Without TMH, I would have nothing. My life has been characterized by solitude, save for the hostility of enemies and deceitful individuals intent on my destruction through illness and fabricated scenarios designed to humiliate or kill me, mirroring the fate of my mother. My mother did not contract HIV/AIDS accidentally; she was intentionally harmed out of jealousy and a desire for her insurance money for superficial purposes, building upon years of misrepresented images. Now, they are attempting the same against me, having replaced me with my sister and brainwashing my eldest son to take my place – a plan he was aware of for years. Unbeknownst to them, he has always been ashamed of his association with our troubled family, a family he never should have belonged to. While he lacks complete knowledge of the situation, he trusts the full truth will emerge. His lifelong desire to escape has been realized. Despite their attempts to perpetuate their lies by pursuing him, no harm will come to either of us; this ordeal too shall pass.

Despite enduring significant hardship and a previous attempt to share my experiences through writing that resulted in theft and a security breach, I remain determined to tell my story. After seven years of effort, I am now hopeful that my narrative can finally be revealed without fear of loss or suppression. Moreover, I possess additional shocking information, including factual testimony that those involved believed I would not survive to disclose, thus evading accountability. Their attempts to manipulate my story will be overshadowed by the emergence of truth.Surprisingly, my faith has remained steadfast. I vowed to the TMH that any conflict between my authentic self and prevailing opinions would become evident. Instead, my journey has been amplified globally through calls for investment and further investigation into long-hidden truths. I have come to understand the crucial role of discernment in choosing whom to trust, as words can deceive, but actions always expose true motives. Relying on one's instincts and observations is essential. Ultimately, every experience, good or bad, contributes to our ability to navigate future challenges.

Recent upsetting discoveries about family, friends, and romantic partners have left me emotionally numb after 30 years of poor treatment. Despite choosing solitude, they remained preoccupied with me, though never positively. Contrary to their judgment that I'm conceited, my self-reliance stems from a lifelong lack of consistent support, except from TMH. TMH has been my constant through loneliness, challenges, and crises, representing my joy, grace, mercy, and remaining capacity for sincere love. My faith in TMH assures me that everything will ultimately resolve itself in due time; He is omniscient and unfailing. Anything contrary would be malevolent. I pray for TMH's guidance to understand these burdens, which are physically and mentally exhausting, leaving me with only my story and TMH to confide in.

I am experiencing deep frustration due to persistent drama in my life, despite my efforts to isolate myself. This ongoing hardship has left me exhausted and considering giving up on this cycle. It's apparent that some challenges are insurmountable, and a romantic relationship is not worth this struggle. My current priorities are relocating, finances, acquiring a car, and achieving greater stability – goals I have been working on for the past five to six years with TMH's assistance.Regarding a separate issue, I intend to call the Mayor Control Center tomorrow morning to inquire about the lack of action on a matter discovered in May 2021 and reported in July 2022. Despite filing police reports and notifying supervisors, I have received no response. Given the lack of progress and the potential for a conspiracy and unlawful activity (related to uncollected funds since sixteen years ago, except for the initial pandemic year), I am prepared to escalate this by contacting higher authorities.

My visits to the courthouse and probate court uncovered troubling inconsistencies. Property records for my grandparents displayed different typed names compared to earlier entries, and I was denied access to criminal case files. This suggests a potential "inside job" involving either errors or deliberate misconduct, which I intend to investigate further at the probate court tomorrow morning. I am confident that the truth will eventually come to light.Guided by my faith, I am actively pursuing this matter. I believe what is rightfully mine will be returned, as I have always been provided for. With my computer now repaired after being hacked multiple times (this is my fourth attempt at writing my story), I am resuming my work. While the expense of replacing phones, laptops, and computers to share my story is significant, I believe it will ultimately be worthwhile.

After my family attempted to take my life, I asked my youngest son's father to repair my car's brakes as a cost-saving measure. On Valentine's Day 2023, while driving to meet my second husband for a trip to Atlantic City, the brakes failed, resulting in an accident and a delay. The following morning, my face was significantly swollen, resembling the aftermath of a stroke. TMH treated the injury, which remains noticeable. My son's father reacted with indifference and a lack of surprise when I contacted him.A few days later, my ex-husband mentioned needing to visit his mother in North Carolina due to her dementia. Subsequently, the insurance company contacted me about my husband's policy. Upon his return, I questioned him about this. He claimed they contacted him after his return and that he intended to discuss the policy with me. However, I had previously stated that his return was contingent on his complete commitment to our future.

The situation evokes the fable of the industrious squirrel preparing for winter while the idle go without. Those who neglect to invest effort, time, or resources will not share in the rewards and will be left wanting; one must earn their way, as nothing is free. The calculated actions of my family and F.A.N.S. to deprive me of my inheritance are deeply disturbing. Driven by envy and jealousy, they have stolen my earnings and possessions, continuing a lifelong pattern of exploitation. Their aim is to silence me before I can reveal their long history of misconduct. Simultaneously, my sisters, cousins, ex-partners giving their girlfriends and friends – essentially anyone they could buy – have been giving away my identity to steal my hard work through identity theft, causing chaos in my life and spreading lies to inflict harm. Others were manipulated with information about my inheritance and encouraged to cause my death out of greed. Furthermore, my ex-husband, my children's fathers, my former partners, and their entire network, including family and F.A.N.S., have collectively sought to overwhelm me with stress, hoping I would take my own life, die, or be killed by the diseased men and hitmen they sent – each with their own motives. TMH initiated a campaign of deception against me, which included creating false police reports and policies, hiring a hitman, and embezzling my inheritance. Their efforts have escalated to falsely declaring me deceased, misleading courts into believing I am either dead or unidentified. Beyond seeking control through SSI and power of attorney by falsely claiming my incompetence, they have extensively manipulated my identity and life story, obscuring the truth To uncover the truth and resolve this situation, forensic investigation, DNA testing, and fingerprinting are likely necessary. These measures are crucial to expose the deception and identify those requiring the missing information. Although the identities of these individuals and the best way to reach them are unknown, there is trust that TMH will resolve this matter in due time.

This situation involves the use of a falsified death certificate with altered dates following my mother's murder. My accounts were hacked, and my ex-husband was coerced into marrying me to gain entry to my home, obtain personal information, acquire a life insurance policy, and create false identification in my name. Simultaneously, his mistress was brought into my home to poison my food, and diseased individuals were paid to infect me, creating the illusion of recklessness. Their lives were projected onto me, intending for me to bear their karmic burden, believing it was "my turn." However, they underestimated my ability to see through their deception. While I may not have been fully aware initially, TMH has revealed enough for me to recall my own experiences and the fates of others murdered through food poisoning, black magic, or direct killing. Their objective was to seize the assets others had rightfully earned.

Ironically, despite fighting for our people to rise above negative stereotypes, they succumbed to the very traits they sought to prevent: sneakiness, conniving behavior, and deceit. They resorted to murder and theft, not for basic necessities, but for material wealth to display and create a false image. They employed various methods, including black magic and MK Ultra, to control the situation and conceal years of their crimes against others. This involved repeatedly making me sick, causing disappearances into mental institutions or jail, and feigning illness to cover up diseases spread through sex rituals and other practices. Their plan was poorly conceived and executed, leaving a clear trail of paperwork and documentation for every transaction, making it impossible to hide receipts or withdrawals, particularly given their complacency. TMH's aim was to create the illusion of my death while fraudulently collecting benefits on behalf of a deceased and incapacitated person.

Betrayal and false accusations have strengthened my resolve, proving their attempts at manipulation to be futile. I seek justice and inner peace, knowing vengeance belongs to a higher power. While acknowledging my imperfections, my honesty with myself, the Divine, and others remains unwavering. Others sought to undermine my integrity. Divine intervention revealed that my experiences are not random but a hereditary gift. I am among "The Chosen" mentioned in Revelations 14:1-20.My prolonged suffering might stem from alterations to my birth certificate and identity. My life, as I know it, may be fabricated, a staged existence orchestrated from birth with my early death anticipated. My survival and transcendence are unexpected, fueled by transferable energy, a reality paralleled by mind control – the means behind years of illusions designed to make me appear insane and be institutionalized, preventing my truth from being revealed. They hoped I would revert to my old self and act alone.

Witchcraft, though encompassing both good and bad, is fundamentally malevolent and can be deadly without righteousness. Prayer provides the sole defense against evil, including threats from family and past relationships. I believe I am fighting a supernatural evil aiming for my soul, a claim God will deny. I feel compelled to share how divine and angelic intervention saved me from myself and others. My trials were educational, preparing me to navigate future difficulties by discerning good from bad and protecting me from ancestral injustices. These events were a form of preventative justice.Ultimately, justice will be served, and I will find peace. Their attempts at manipulation are futile and only reinforce my strength. I have been betrayed and falsely accused to damage my reputation, but vengeance belongs to God. While I am imperfect, I strive for honesty with myself, God, and others. Despite my acknowledgement of flaws, some have sought to portray me negatively. God's intervention revealed that my experiences were not random but a hereditary gift. I am not alone in possessing such abilities, as the Bible mentions "The Chosen" in Revelations 14:1-20.

My birth certificate, birthday, and even my name were altered, creating a fabricated life designed to end prematurely. Surviving this staged existence, which was meant to keep me from revealing the truth, was unexpected. They attempted to make me appear insane and be institutionalized to prevent exposure. Mind control and energy transfer were used to create years of illusions.Witchcraft is inherently malevolent and dangerous. Protection can only come from prayer against evil forces, including my family and past acquaintances. I believe I am opposed by demonic forces seeking my soul, but it belongs to the Most High. Compelled to share my story of salvation, I will recount my experiences with the guidance of my angels and the Higher Power. The hardships I endured were intended as lessons and preparation, guiding me on what to accept and reject, ultimately safeguarding me from repeating past injustices. These were preventative measures.Unresolved issues can prevent souls from moving on, though they may choose to remain as spirits. Everyone has a story, both good and bad, and the realities depicted in media are genuine and understandable through direct experience. We were programmed to deny these truths and forbidden to discuss them after a shift, as it would harm those who were seemingly victorious. However, our victory was an illusion; we were defeated by our own internal conflicts and cover-ups of potentially grave errors. This pattern of blame and deflection must end. We need to mature and accept responsibility for our actions.

Betrayed by intimates and grappling with resultant emptiness, my faith in TMH persists. Despite a life marked by loyalty, obedience, and patience yielding continuous hardship and dashed hopes, I believe divine justice will ultimately rectify all wrongs, even as I feel isolated and disillusioned. At 45, I am weary of deceit and appeasement. My conviction that righteousness would bring positive results has only led to isolation and dissatisfaction. Though burdened by hardship and heartache, my faith in TMH's guidance remains firm; I trust that my time will arrive despite present heaviness. Looking back, my path has been obstructed by those desiring my failure. For five years, I endured illness and stress, oblivious to the sabotage of trusted individuals who rejoiced in my difficulties for resisting their control. Despite their malice, I never succumbed to despair, choosing to leave behind the detrimental environment of my past, including its betrayals, abuse, solitude, and incarcerations which felt inescapable. Instead, I dedicated myself to a higher power. Even amidst hatred, TMH consistently guided me from darkness. Although I sometimes wished harm upon my wrongdoers, my ultimate desire was justice. Through my darkest times, TMH offered solace and strength, leading me toward a future where my adversaries would be revealed and defeated.

Through unwavering faith, I was protected during difficult times, finding refuge in various places while experiencing homelessness. While grateful for past support, I now recognize divine intervention in my survival. Others were divinely observing and waiting to guide me.As it is written, taking the first step allows divine guidance. Though my upbringing was a form of guidance, it was only the beginning. A Higher Power operates on divine timing, revealing truths in my life. Having endured numerous hardships, including homelessness and loss, I share my story to offer hope and affirm the reality of a Higher Power's saving presence, even in the face of violation and near-death experiences. Trusting your intuition is crucial, as those closest can cause the deepest pain. Remember, no matter the difficulty, others have faced similar or worse challenges. Everything can change at any moment; it's not over until declared so. By trusting your intuition, you can begin a path of self-improvement and a better future.

Despite loving my family unconditionally, they have repeatedly tried to kill me due to envy and resentment. My life has been blessed by TMH, my angels, and my ancestors, and I have survived theft, betrayal, and attempts on my life. As a realist and warrior, I fought for the survival of others who were ultimately defeated by black magic, age, poison, or lack of support. Their beliefs were labeled as insanity, and they were discredited and silenced, their stories untold. However, I witnessed everything and have known for years that I am the Chosen One. My family understood that I must share their experiences, allowing them to happen so their voices could be heard through me. I will ensure they receive the recognition they always deserved. Death only occurs after an act of pure evil, leading to banishment. Until then, spirits transition between realms, their purpose continuing through others. Everyone has a twin in some realm, and death represents a spirit's transfer to a new vessel for a chance to return. Some restless spirits seeking justice remain ethereal and communicate through me, hoping to use TMH – seemingly insignificant, yet meaningful – to achieve their aims by "Giving thanks to TMH."

My grandparents experienced injustice, but ultimately justice was served. My belief in a spiritual afterlife, supported by the Bible and Quran, leads me to believe the deceased remain present in spirit. I am committed to uncovering the truth and achieving justice for the wrongs they suffered. This experience has brought me clarity and revealed those who oppose me. Consequently, I now reject earthly love, viewing it as lustful, deceptive, conditional, and self-serving. Those who offer such love are unworthy. I now seek only divine love.I long for stability in my personal and professional life and hope for understanding regarding my past. My life feels unbalanced: employment lacks transportation, transportation lacks funds, and employment lacks transportation. Men have appeared during times of struggle, not independence. I am weary of being judged superficially and desire to be loved beyond appearance, sex, or money. Constant disappointment and insincere words have taken their toll. I am tired of manipulation and control tactics. Others have exploited my experiences and actively obstructed my progress. Therefore, I choose solitude and have no interest in relationships, perceiving others as wanting to control my hard-earned achievements.

I am finished with the hexes, curses, and blockages that have been placed upon me and the resulting delays. Despite promises of a brighter future, it seems unattainable. The expectations placed upon me are overwhelming. Although I maintain faith, I am still waiting for positive change. My positivity is met with active harm and attempts to impede my progress. My faith and prayers continue, yet I struggle to understand why these harmful actions are allowed to persist. I long for support. I have consistently been fair and open-minded, especially towards those I do not know well. I have moved past my history and refuse to engage in negativity or deceit. My trust lies solely in TMH, and I remain guarded against everyone else.

For a significant period, I have been celibate due to various circumstances, including incarceration, infidelity, and failed relationships. My last marriage, like those before it, may have been intentionally sabotaged. The motivation extended beyond love and involved financial gain. It appears that money often drives people to commit evil acts, with some boasting about their wealth instead of using it for good. Everyone has their own story, and mine includes the murder of my elders, a consequence of greed and methods that have been used for decades. They were weakened and made vulnerable to the malicious actions of others.

I write this with the hope that it reaches someone who will finally listen and put an end to these injustices. These deaths were driven by nothing more than greed. It makes one wonder how much wealth is truly needed, especially when used to maintain a false image. I suspect there is a list of targets. Currently, someone is supposedly assisting her ex-husband's best friend's blind sister, who owns a sex toy shop, while simultaneously exposing my niece to these matters under the guise of help. I have a strong feeling that my niece will be the next victim, and tragically, I fear I will not be alive to witness it. My prayers are for my niece's safety, as she is also a Capricorn G.O.A.T. She has already made observations and comments that remind this person of me, and I fear she is being taught destructive things. My niece is intelligent, and I worry about a repeat of the past.

I pray for justice and ask TMH to protect my niece and my youngest son, whose father, my sister, and cousins are all involved in this. They seem to be connected through stolen books and phones over the years and have cultivated a network that leaves me unable to trust anyone. They may have contacted and corrupted others. I suspect they are the type to orchestrate harm through others while feigning ignorance. A mug I once saw comes to mind: "I will put you in my trunk and help others look for you." This aptly describes the kind of people involved.In the name of TMH, I reject all childhood traumas inflicted upon me. I implore TMH to remove any burdens placed upon me through these traumas, which were intended for my future ruin.

My life has been marked by significant challenges since childhood, including recurring illnesses like nosebleeds, ear infections, and strep throat, which resulted in the removal of my tonsils and adenoids. Abnormally large adenoids obstructed my breathing and increased my health risks. A temporary separation of my parents coincided with a pause in what I believe was the practice of black magic, which had been present throughout my life. However, my teenage years and adulthood were subsequently filled with chaos and confusion after my mother's departure.Reflecting on past failures, it seems my life was destined for destruction and death. Despite this, I maintain hope for change. I have faced numerous obstacles, including drug addiction, imprisonment, psychiatric hospitalization, and abuse, overcoming them through hard work and faith. I believe TMH recognized my value and allowed me to confront these destructive forces, fostering resilience in the absence of guidance, support, or love. Tragically, my family, who should have been my strongest supporters, have instead been my greatest adversaries, betraying me repeatedly.

My family's portrayal of me as helpless and incapable stemmed from their desire for financial control, disregarding my well-being and aiming to deprive me of everything I valued. They opposed my success, love, and happiness, wanting me to have nothing. Despite their harshness, my love and respect for my grandparents sustained me, and I hoped for better times. While the definition of love remains unclear, I learned difficult lessons. Around 2007-2008, during Adrian Fenty's campaign, my sister's manipulative and dishonest actions became apparent. She falsified transcripts, exaggerated information, used her political connections to influence judges, and even attended the Inauguration Ball. My father inexplicably allowed her to reside in my home after she missed a North Carolina court appearance related to federal embezzlement charges. This was consistent with her history of financial misconduct, including a citation for tax evasion and embezzlement at Rosenthal for unauthorized credit card charges. She had also engaged in similar behavior at an employment training program on Q St NW.

She stole my resume to get a job and then made me do her work. Although she promised to help me while I waited for my social security decision, she instead took credit for my work, kept my overtime pay, and gave me only a small amount of money at tax time. This forced me to ask my stepdad for money, making me appear irresponsible. Their theft of my money led to my poverty. They are also using my stolen resume to discredit me by providing incomplete information.NCFN used deception to help her move from a shelter to public housing, while I received no help getting housing to regain custody of my children. Fifteen years later, I finally received a voucher, but now they are trying to evict me because she can no longer receive housing due to her lies and deceit. She may still have a voucher because of her connections with the staff. She also had support from politically connected family members who are former judges, lawyers, law enforcement, and military personnel. Despite a history of stealing from companies, she remained employed. I always knew she had access to resources through these connections. While I have known about this for a long time, my children were always my priority.

Powerful individuals secretly manipulated and defrauded me, fully aware of my knowledge of their actions. Though they now feel shame, their continued surveillance and attempts to harm me are of no concern. Despite their theft, I have rebuilt my life and am grateful for the ensuing publicity, confident that this situation will also pass. While I would not have chosen this experience, I accept that I cannot change the past and instead choose to learn from it and create something positive. Their attempts to make my life a futile struggle, hoping for my downfall, will not succeed. I am a resilient fighter and survivor, contrary to their attempts to portray me as a victim of manipulation and abuse by those closest to me. They believed these tactics were necessary to get close, but the truth will be revealed.

Separately, my sister orchestrated a calculated plan to take my children. Exploiting the court system and manipulating it with biased narratives favoring my children's godfather, she secured housing vouchers while my pleas and concerns were ignored. My children were used as pawns in this scheme, with collaborators joining in. Driven by hate and fully aware of my history of abuse, their goal was to destroy me, steal my children, and shatter my life. I felt trapped and isolated, with everyone around me seemingly acting against my interests. Despite these overwhelming odds, my resolve remained strong; my children needed me, and I refused to give up on them. I still need to address the initial situation that was ongoing while this plan to ruin my life and cover up past abuse and deaths was being formulated. My mentally unwell family recently discovered this history on both sides. Knowing this, they joined forces and resorted to immature, indirect tactics like rituals instead of confronting me directly. They fight in secret, but TMH is aware of everything. My ancestral gifts allow me to see and communicate with those who have passed. They tried to block this gift by traumatizing me and denying my ancestors, especially TMH, but TMH intervened.

My biological parents concealed a profound secret: a special gift I shared with TMH. They were not my true parents. Tragically, my grandparents were murdered because of their own gifts. TMH revealed this truth to me during a particularly vulnerable period, empowering me to confront my deceptive "parents" – a deep betrayal after their long-term efforts to sabotage me. I was unaware of any theft or related notifications. They exploited my life, a fact that became starkly evident when I turned eighteen and started my own life with my son. Subsequently, they relentlessly sent hardship my way: abuse, infidelity, involving my children, and even orchestrating my incarceration. When I escaped that cycle, they intensified their attempts to destabilize me, determined to ensure my failure. For a time, I achieved a better life than my tormentor had envisioned for herself. Unable to surpass me, she instead focused on dismantling everything I had built for my family and me.

Despite becoming a mother at thirteen and raising my son independently from fourteen, I never engaged in the behaviors I am now accused of. Had circumstances been different, my life's path might have been different. While I cannot change the past, I have fundamentally reshaped my future – a significant accomplishment given the relentless torment and discord inflicted upon me by her and her allies, without any regard for the harm caused. She orchestrated a raid on my home, leading to the removal of my children. For seven and a half years, I fought her in court as she relentlessly tried to keep my children from me, regardless of my compliance. I was consistently defeated because she presented herself as a caring aunt and sister, despite her financial impropriety and manipulation of the system. My children never benefited from the funds she received; she prioritized her own indulgences while pretending to help with what she had taken from me. She even used my children to escape a low-income housing program and obtain foster care licenses, all while I worked tirelessly to reunite with my family. Her focus was on personal gain and outdoing me, not on my children's well-being. Ultimately, she succeeded in taking control of my life through the complicity of individuals within the judicial and other systems, including workers and anyone susceptible to manipulation, all aimed at my destruction

Fleeing an abusive arranged marriage orchestrated to ruin my life, I continued working and visited my children weekly. Despite a lack of protection from family and law enforcement, I persevered, praying for exposure of those involved. My voice was finally heard when my son was abused in foster care, placed there by my sister. Recognizing his resemblance to me and his strong will, she separated my children, contradicting my initial plea for them to remain together. She kept my eldest, who was already being indoctrinated into their lifestyle and was non-verbal. My second son, however, fiercely defended me against her and his father's affair and conspiracy with my childhood friends to harm me. My second son became dispensable after they obtained his social security and birth certificates, essentially viewing him as a means to an end. He was sexually assaulted and returned to me. Unable to provide constant supervision due to work, I asked his stepfather for help. Tragically, he also abused my son, exploiting his acting out – which stemmed from the abuse he suffered while living near my sister and his father – for late-night encounters and, unbeknownst to me, participation in sex rituals.

Driven by motives of future chaos, manipulated destinies, and exploiting my children for tax benefits and energy harvesting, my ex-partners exhibited a recurring pattern. These individuals, averse to work for years, learned about Earned Income Tax Credits (EITC) through me. While not my primary reason for having children, EITC offered a way to recover the time and financial investment in their upbringing, particularly given the initial lack of support from their stepfathers, which I later demanded. This also enabled us to acquire new vehicles and enjoy outings. My sister sought to undermine this stability, including our trips to parks and arcades.My family intentionally isolated me until my children were removed. Our independent and happy life contradicted their values. They neglected their own children and responsibilities, prioritizing substance abuse and shallow relationships maintained by lavish spending. Possessing my children's information, they could fraudulently file for benefits, ignoring the certainty of audits. Unlike them, I consistently refused to file false claims. They lacked the foresight to understand the inevitability of audits and that children grow up, eventually leading to the cessation of benefits and the exposure of secrets. Their attempts to exploit the system for personal gain were ultimately unsuccessful.

Despite significant hardship, my faith provided strength. A period of peace followed, but behavioral issues arose in my son when he perceived unequal treatment among his siblings. This resentment grew due to perceived unfairness and hurtful actions, leading him to repeatedly run away and eventually be incarcerated. While others viewed his imprisonment as a success, I have faith in divine intervention and his grandmother's protection. I believe in his inherent goodness and ask for prayers as he faces negative influences.Concurrently, efforts to destroy everything I had built were underway. My primary focus was regaining custody of my children, a process that lasted seven and a half years. It only ended after my son was assaulted. Following these events, I implored the judge for help in caring for my son and addressing his trauma upon his release, but my request was denied. My eldest son, who had been shy and withdrawn, graduated early at seventeen with a scholarship and moved to Delaware on his own, a significant change. During a visit, I advised my children that if they ever struggled to express themselves verbally, they should try writing down their thoughts. He took my advice, a decision I later regretted. While living with my sister, he wrote to express his unhappiness. I encouraged him to voice his concerns, as I had always ensured my children's needs were met. However, despite providing numerous receipts and complaints, these were dismissed in court. I was declared an unfit parent, and the legal battle ended.

My son's trauma led to defiance, and sending him to his father only worsened things, though he always returned to me. I also raised another son alone. Securing child support from my third son's father was necessary. This third son was manipulated by his father's mistress in a scheme involving false adoptions and marriage to portray me as unfit for financial gain through child support, tax evasion, and other illegal means. They suggested I relinquish my parental rights to avoid child support, which I refused. I paid to protect my son from further trauma, unwilling to lose more after already losing everything due to a fake marriage. After hiding my son for thirteen years, his father reappeared, adding to the pain and now demanding I sign away my rights. They placed me in a shelter for selfish reasons, feigning care and a change of heart, which I didn't believe. My love for my children prevented me from giving in to their manipulations.

I later learned his mistress worked with my aunt and the childhood friend he robbed at Rosenthal, suggesting their possible involvement. Having already lost everything, they sought to destroy me, blaming me for their own failures.Meanwhile, the father of my fourth son battled a severe cocaine addiction, openly flaunting it due to perceived untouchability from military and law enforcement ties. He was constantly pursuing other women, echoing past relationship patterns where promising starts ended after a family death on his side. Encounters with drug-using cousins (cocaine) explained his ability to help me quit while supplying my incarcerated ex-husband. His family had a history of addiction. I noticed his changes and anticipated another abandonment. True to form, he left during each pregnancy's later stages – five and a half, seven and a half, and ten and a half years – after the initial demanding years of childcare. Despite their flaws, I always spoke respectfully of their fathers to my children. This respect was never returned. I fully committed to each relationship, but their aim was exploitation and inflicting misery.

The father of my second son was twice imprisoned for smuggling and other illegal activities. During his first sentence, at 17 and pregnant, I regularly visited him in Lorton, VA, and worked at Boston Market for support. During his second sentence, again pregnant, I maintained our connection. I observed that men were only respectful when pursuing intimacy. Upon his release, I became pregnant again. He offered money for an abortion, which I refused. He was incarcerated again while I was struggling to support our first son, so I kept the money and the baby and arranged an adoption. The rumor about me and nearby ninjas was started by three spiteful women I had cut off long before their setup at the hotel, as they always resented me.

Having endured significant family hardships, I sought to distance myself from unnecessary drama by the time I finished high school. This decision was met with disapproval from certain family members who, despite their own issues, seemed intent on undermining me. This included someone who had been involved with my second son's father and harbored resentment towards me during his incarceration. At that time, I was living with an acquaintance of my step-stepfather's family. My son's father would call me collect from Lorton, assuming I could afford the calls despite being a sixteen-year-old working at my first job, Ma's Place. This job had been secured for me by my stepdad immediately after he picked me up from jail. He provided me with an ATM card, checkbook, and keys before leaving me on my own until he brought my sister and her children to my house unexpectedly one night.

During this tumultuous period, while pregnant, I overheard a disturbing conversation where this family member told my son's father that he didn't need me because I was too young. Exhausted by the constant conflict, I resolved to end the cycle. Shortly thereafter, I returned home to discover my checkbooks missing and my belongings thrown onto the street.Prior to this, my father had involved the FBI in investigating the Fort Dupont rapist, identifying me as a key witness. Despite my age, I was determined to pursue justice and felt immense relief when my account was finally believed.Earlier, my aunt had physically attacked me for speaking out, attempting to dislocate my jaw and hitting me. Despite this violence, I remained resolute and left to rebuild my life at Ma's Place. Starting in entry-level positions, I advanced to become a server, using my earnings to secure temporary housing. This became unsustainable when the restaurant relocated. Additionally, there was considerable conflict involving individuals I was loosely associated with, none of which I participated in. My past experiences with incarceration have taught me the value of avoiding such situations, something those with supportive families might not fully grasp.Despite any mischaracterizations, I am resourceful and determined. While I engaged with individuals who offered assistance based on potential, these arrangements were ultimately used to support my son's father, covering expenses like babysitting and rent. Losing this support was a significant personal setback.

After our relationship ended, he returned home and showed affection to everyone except me, offering no help with our son. He had been dishonest with our son, who eventually discovered the truth himself. While the revelation was upsetting, his father made that choice, regardless of our relationship. He ended things, stating he didn't want to hinder me, despite my move from Maryland to DC at his request due to his parole restrictions in DC. He provided my mother's rental company's contact information, which I used.Despite this upheaval, my sister helped me find a job at Rosenthal Chevrolet Jeep in Virginia, where she was a cashier, my aunt was a title clerk, and I worked as an accounting clerk. However, I lost this job because I couldn't afford a babysitter after moving. When I asked my son's father to watch him while I worked, as my aunt required $165 upfront, he refused, citing his own need to earn money. This led to my eviction and job loss. A police officer who had previously flirted with me noticed my eviction and offered help. With nowhere to go, I accepted. He paid for a week's stay in a room for my son and me, after which we moved to Sixteenth St., NE, where I met my first husband, the father of my third son. He was deceptive, and I was unaware of his true nature. Be cautious; appearances can be deceiving and align with your desires rather than reality. The devil can exploit your wants, and God may allow it. Blaming God for the consequences of your choices, made despite warnings, is unwarranted. Pay attention.

Initially hesitant due to a recent painful breakup and his seemingly hustling demeanor, I resisted my future second husband's advances. My emotional guard was up, and I wasn't looking for a new relationship. However, when my son's babysitter was unexpectedly evicted, leaving me panicked about his whereabouts, he offered comfort. He contacted the babysitter, who promised to return my son later. During this anxious wait, he asked me out. I realized I hadn't paid him much attention before. Soon after we became involved, everyone in our building moved out, except for a woman downstairs whose daughter was friends with my son. This woman began appearing frequently at the shelter shortly after we did. Despite these strange circumstances, I continued to reject the officer's advances, determined to avoid further heartbreak.

Over time, we began talking and spending more time together. We were staying in an apartment under his name, for which I paid the rent. We had sex a couple of times, but our physical intimacy was limited, lacking much kissing. He was constantly busy with work calls. A few weeks after we broke up, I saw him on the news – a fourth district police officer arrested for identity theft, impersonating an officer, and running an illegal prostitution ring.Our relationship ended before his arrest because he discovered my past marriage and became angry. I was on a train and didn't see his reaction until I got home with my son. He was there, and once inside, he acknowledged that I wasn't promiscuous. He offered his help, noting that I paid my own bills. Then, he put a gun to my head, threatening to kill me. I looked him in the eye and calmly suggested either he or I take my son across the hall so he wouldn't witness it. He looked at me, called me crazy, laughed, lowered the gun, and left. I knew things would likely escalate. That very night, my first husband came by, and we made love. It was the most intimate experience because we were so alike, he brought out a wild side of me, and I felt safe with him.

As tax season approached, and facing potential homelessness due to a previous eviction, I sought a new apartment. At Barac Company in Takoma Park, MD, I inquired about vacancies and found one in my building, across from the evicted babysitter.

Amidst this, my ex-husband tried to make his son's mother jealous by driving past her house with me. Her reaction was to ram his car and attempt to run him over. Consequently, he and his son arrived at my door seeking shelter due to his car being wrecked. After putting his son to bed, we talked. He expressed a desire to keep his son, but I refused to be involved and insisted he return the child to his mother. He complied, and I didn't hear from him for several weeks before he reappeared. I considered our interactions casual, not a relationship.

My second son's father had previously taught me a harsh lesson about the fragility of connections. I had resolved not to become deeply involved again, yet he charmed me with material gestures and social outings. We were constantly together, oblivious to his deception. The truth emerged at work when I received a call about my rent money order, which I had entrusted to him; he had cashed it and kept the funds. My preoccupation had blinded me to his deceit. He then revealed he had been selling drugs from my home while I was at work. Despite knowing he was involved in illicit activities, I was unaware it was happening under my roof. I was furious. He stated he had already rented a U-Haul, packed his belongings, and found a new place for himself and friends, initiating another period of instability for me. My efforts to secure housing for my children were once again disrupted. Prioritizing their safety became a struggle due to conflicting opinions and external pressures. It felt as though everyone was working against me, leading to repeated setbacks. We ended up in a Travel Lodge in Bladensburg for about two weeks. I retained the U-Haul, learning to drive it, as our primary mode of transportation for the children.

Further complicating matters, he was arrested for assaulting his aunt. His explanation resonated with my own family experiences, leading me to believe him. Following his court appearance, I was left to care for our children, return the U-Haul, and cover the mounting hotel expenses, which shifted to weekly payments. While he was incarcerated, I secured a new residence. I maintained daily visits and correspondence, ensuring his needs were met. Unknowingly, this marked the beginning of another detrimental cycle. I've come to realize that I've been alone all along. People judge me without truly knowing me or understanding my struggles. I'm okay with that, as no one could love the real me beyond superficial reasons like money, sex, or looks. I'm more than meets the eye, and I've worked hard to overcome my past and let go of negativity, including fake relationships and even my most cherished possessions - my children. Though it pains me deeply, I know I must trust in a higher power and surrender control, especially since most of my children are adults now. They've been turned against me and brainwashed, just as I once was. I must pray and let go, focusing on saving myself and all that I've worked for.

Despite a friend's disinterest, possibly due to age or a lack of romantic feelings, I remain optimistic and focused on the future. I feel closer to achieving personal freedom, experiencing a sense of lightness. While saving for a car is challenging due to necessary home repairs from suspected landlord negligence and general living expenses, I trust in a higher power to provide, as always. I am grateful for the peace and solitude I've sought and the blessings I have. My prayers are for a quiet writing space free from negativity, peace, respect, a home, a car, and a loving family. I believe my blessings are near and am thankful things aren't worse. I also pray for a change of heart in those who wish me ill. A minor setback with misplaced keys didn't disrupt my day; I continued with my routine, confident that things would resolve. I have faith that my prayers for a house, car, autonomous management position, loving partner, family, strength to finish my book, a fresh start, financial abundance, freedom from struggles, victory over enemies, elevation, and escape from poverty will be answered. Hope and faith are essential for realizing our desires, and blessings can be easily missed if we aren't attentive. Even unexpected answers are still responses to our prayers. I believe in daily gratitude for everything, including the simple acts of life.

Recognizing the profound energy exchange in sexual connections, I am choosing to isolate myself to protect my personal energy, which I believe others have unknowingly exploited. I am aware of the duality of good and evil, light and darkness, and suspect some individuals attempt to gain positive karma by draining others' energy through harmful actions.

My intuition tells me that my biological family may not be my true family and has deceived me, a realization that explains a persistent feeling of despair and suggests my entire life may have been manipulated. I trust the truth will eventually be revealed.

Despite feeling like nothing has changed and my efforts are futile, an experience this past year renewed my faith and determination, teaching me to persevere through unforeseen obstacles. I am exhausted from an erratic sleep schedule that allows only a few hours of rest each night, and despite my desire for change, I am beginning to lose hope. My faith is wavering, my appetite and sleep are gone, and I am weary of others interfering in my life. While I am imperfect, I do not intentionally harm others and constantly struggle with a lack of peace and deep isolation. Regarding the LGBTQ+ community, I want to be clear: I harbor no hatred, only love, despite the cruelty I have experienced. Rumors and lies are circulating about my past experimentation with bisexuality in my youth. I unconditionally love my son, even though we are currently estranged. I recently learned he may have undergone a gender-affirming procedure. The last time I saw him online, he was showcasing his achievements, and I saw pictures with new physical features, the authenticity of which I couldn't determine. I do not perceive gender, as I believe everything is energy. Considering past lives and other realms, who knows who anyone truly was? Therefore, I do not judge; it is not the person but the energy transferred to another vessel. This is my personal perspective, and I respect everyone's right to their own beliefs.

I disagree with reinterpretations that change the names Adam and Eve, as the original text specifically mentions them. My accountability lies solely in my own actions and beliefs. Recognizing the deceptiveness of appearances, I believe in individual autonomy and freedom of choice, without judgment or attempts to manipulate emotions. Each person's path is distinct, and I extend wishes for love and respect to all.My experiences have taught me that individuals I've known, including former partners, were either consistently dishonest or changed over time. They are aware of my current understanding, and I recognize their actions as premeditated and driven by financial gain. Their lack of genuine interest in exclusively female relationships has been the fundamental issue, not any personal failing of mine. They maintained a false pretense to hide their sexual preferences, involvement in orgies, and their receipt of payment.Like everyone, I have a personal history that includes youthful experiences and adventures undertaken without guidance. However, I have consciously chosen a different direction, one that diverges from constant partying and drug use. There is an appropriate context for all things, and sexuality is not a defining characteristic of a person's worth. While others may not approve, my choices are my own. Everyone possesses the liberty to reshape their lives as they see fit, and I have found contentment in solitude, free from the pressures of relationships. My past remains in the past, and my focus is on moving forward. The compulsion to force relationships is perplexing, given that free will is inherent to us all.

Life presents choices, and it moves forward regardless of what we decide. Forcing someone to stay in an incompatible relationship prevents happiness. Perhaps this is Satan's aim: to keep you trapped in harmful situations like abuse, drug use, energy manipulation, or anything your conscience tells you is wrong. Free yourself; the Most High hears you. With time and effort, He will liberate you, and things will improve.This is the root of the confusion: I do not agree with threesomes, orgies, swingers clubs, or similar activities that go against established standards. I believe in following TMH's instructions without changing them to please others. Your thoughts are important, and TMH cares for everyone. Ultimately, faith and belief are necessary for success. Without them, challenges will continue, and goals will be hard to reach. Remember, life has many aspects, from recreation to education. Life can be misleading, and things are not always as they seem. Instead of harming me, I hope people will focus on loving themselves and looking inward.Your beliefs shape who you are, and your self-image can either help or hurt your life. As you progress, you will gain achievements and recognition, leading to new opportunities. In the afterlife, all spirits are equal, so judgment should not depend on gender. How someone looks now might differ from their past life. Instead of creating trouble to mask your own inner struggles, return what you have taken.I have asked TMH for either peace or freedom because there is little goodness left in this greed and envy. This situation took three years to develop, so I have waited three years to leave, and I am weary from trying. I have grown and understand my purpose and why TMH continues to protect me.

This current existence feels like an eternal punishment, yet perhaps it holds a higher purpose. Though my strength wanes, my faith endures. I am committed to persevering through this difficult period until I can return to my heavenly home and family. Love is absent here, and I am isolated. While I once longed for love, I now see it as a distraction that hinders my progress. My time is short, and I am withdrawing from others. Although I believe TMH is concerned, I will remain questioning even if my prayers are answered swiftly.The past three years have been turbulent, marked by a divorce. These experiences have revealed that negativity directed at others inevitably rebounds. At the shelter, we learned that our self-perception influences how others view us, and we were encouraged to engage in self-reflection and personal improvement.

Recently, there appears to be a decline in personal care regarding appearance. Many seem indifferent to their attire, haphazardly choosing clothes without looking in a mirror. This lack of self-presentation may contribute to low self-esteem, which some might consider a trend, but it is detrimental. If you don't present yourself well, you won't be taken seriously.The perceptions of others matter, which is why previous generations emphasized dressing well. Pride in one's appearance reflects self-respect and influences how others regard us. This contrasts with the contemporary notion that dressing well indicates a lack of ambition.Ultimately, we are accountable for our energy and actions, as they mold our reality in this life and beyond. Self-love and personal development are paramount, while seeking external validation is less significant. Self-respect impacts all aspects of our lives, and by transforming our thoughts and beliefs, we can shift our energy and reshape our experiences.The universe responds to our intentions and actions, so mindfulness is key to avoiding unintended consequences. While my desire to help others is strong, it can be draining to assist everyone. Consequently, I must be discerning about who I help and who I distance myself from. Though challenging at first, I now recognize that I am on a divine path, free from unnecessary obstacles. Even when my faith has wavered, it has always been there to sustain me.

Throughout my life, my children have been my priority, and I would have sacrificed everything for them. Recently, I faced immense pain. Despite this, my devotion to TMH remains absolute; pleasing him is my deepest desire. He has repeatedly saved me and continues to bless me, even when I have made mistakes. Reflecting on the past, I see a family history of mental illness and recognize betrayals from those I once helped. This was confusing, as I harbor no ill will. I pray for those against me, trusting in TMH's greater plan. Enemies surround me, both within and outside my family. My only option is to surrender this situation to a higher power. I am thankful for the understanding that this is beyond my control and pray for healing, peace, and protection from evil.

My unwavering faith in TMH has sustained me through every hardship. He has always been there, even when others tried to take what was mine and exclude me. But TMH intervened. I wait patiently for His guidance, trusting in His timing. With His grace, I am ready to fulfill His will.I have reached a point where I no longer seek or expect love or friendships. For reasons unknown to me, TMH has chosen for me to be alone.The kind of love I witnessed in my grandparents' relationship seems to have vanished. Their love profoundly impacted me. I am grateful for our ancestors' struggles for today's freedoms and rights, facing inhumane treatment through marches and protests.Years ago, society failed by allowing racial animosity to escalate. Prejudice and self-hate exist within all races. We must look beyond skin color and see our shared humanity. Our ancestors fought against slavery and oppression, preserving their dignity to achieve the impossible. It is crucial to remember their sacrifices by striving for greatness and maintaining self-respect. The destructive use of resources questions the true purpose, as it was never part of the intended plan.

Worthless feelings like jealousy, envy, and greed undermine work, respect, esteem, and honor. Our ancestors, united in purpose, understood the importance of our actions. They valued freedom of speech, peace, and mutual love and respect. However, their achievements have been diminished by internal violence. To build a brighter future, we must remember the power of unity and teamwork. While many seek divine intervention, collective effort is the key to eventual success, acknowledging that progress takes time. Love was a fundamental aspect of my upbringing. While striving for better relationships is common, personal growth and well-being are essential. Remember that each person has their own unique destiny to fulfill. Trying to follow another's path, despite initial appearances, will ultimately fail. Achieving your life goals requires personal effort; no one can do it for you. This principle applies to those committed to TMH's path and their true purpose, not to those seeking fleeting connections. I still hope TMH will bring me a meaningful relationship, but instead, I encounter dishonesty, hate, and lovelessness. My experiences are filled with illusions, lust, and circumstances that lead to my ruin. I have been left to navigate this alone. I would leave this world with anger at life's choices, as they seem to stem from the devil, not TMH. My attempts to leave have been repeatedly prevented. I continue to write, but past failures have extinguished my enthusiasm. Yet, I believe this time will be different, although the constant reliving of past traumas and the awareness of how others' perceptions have defined my life have deeply affected me.

Life feels like a constant struggle against hidden forces and intentional sabotage. Despite persistent efforts through prayer, meditation, faith, and hope, progress remains elusive, marked by repeated setbacks. Weariness sets in from the endless cycle of waiting and hoping for change. Navigating life feels precarious, driven by the need to make the right decisions and honor what I believe in, while diligently avoiding unnecessary obstacles and seeking divine guidance. Yet, despite adapting and striving, the universe offers no clear response, leaving me to rely solely on unwavering faith.

My desire is simple: a genuine partnership built on love and friendship. However, seeking answers through external sources like tarot readings has only led to confusion and regret, obscuring my path further. There's a sense that something significant remains hidden from me, a truth I believe is deeply personal. Years of solitude, surrounded by untrustworthy individuals and unable to find peace even in work, have taken their toll. The feeling of being constantly watched, harassed, and disliked, without the support of friends or family, is overwhelming. Hope for love, both familial and romantic, has faded, leading to a bleak outlook on the world. My present longing is for stability: secure employment, a stable home, consistent income, and perhaps a glimmer of optimism.

There was a time when I underestimated the extent of intentional harm directed my way, attributing my difficulties to close acquaintances and family. I now understand the depth of their actions – compromising my accounts, manipulating my relationships, and fostering negativity. It feels as though they seek to diminish my self-worth. My one remaining unhealthy habit, smoking, ironically provides a form of solace. I have accepted solitude and am ready to move forward independently. Celibacy has been a conscious choice, a way to avoid the risks and negativity associated with relationships. It's clear that jealousy fuels the desire of others to see me fail. Nevertheless, my determination to persevere remains strong, anchored in my faith. My trust has been broken, and I now suspect that others are actively trying to undermine my efforts and steal what I have worked for. I will not allow my hard work to be taken. Disruptions aimed at disturbing my peace and hindering my work-from-home situation are constant reminders of the violation of my privacy, a pattern that stretches back to my childhood. The aim seems to be control and misrepresentation, but I am responsible for my own life and refuse to be defined by their actions.

I am weary of deception and uncertainty, tired of the constant shifting of reality. The weight of the unknown is heavy. Anger simmers over the irresponsibility and lack of vision from family, who now seem to expect me to bear the consequences of their actions. The stagnation of my credit over decades is another source of frustration. The estrangement from my children is a deep pain. Despite years of dedicated effort, permanent employment remains elusive, often sabotaged by false narratives intended to ruin my reputation and end contracts. These individuals, marked by their own lack of achievement, seem to find solace in the misery of others. Yet, I will not be deterred by their negativity and will continue on my path, guided by my beliefs. Negativity is pervasive, stemming from various close relationships, creating a suffocating web. Despite deliberate attempts to undermine me, my commitment to my goals endures. Currently overworked, underpaid, and lacking reliable transportation, I still dedicate myself fully to every endeavor, believing in the power of a positive impression. However, the prevalence of malicious intent creates significant obstacles. Dissatisfaction with my current situation and a longing for change are constant. For three long years, I have felt trapped in an undesirable environment, surrounded by negativity and stagnation.

My sense of purpose and existence is increasingly unclear. Despite significant dedication and love invested in various endeavors, my efforts have been unappreciated, and personal development has been neglected in pursuit of achievements. I feel as though I am merely existing. My acts of service have consistently led to exploitation, necessitating continuous rebuilding. While I long for an escape from this pattern, I realize it is not feasible. My inherent talents and abilities compel me to follow the path that TMH has set for me. I believe that if this destiny were meant for someone else, TMH would demand the same commitment and effort that I have applied to become one of the Chosen, a 144,000 Earth Angel.

For 42 years, I have dedicated myself to being the ideal child, family member, wife, friend, and mother. Yet, despite this relentless effort, I feel I have gained nothing. My struggles have been ignored, and my endeavors seem to be mocked. At 45 years old, I refuse to continue this way. Everything I have accomplished has been through sheer hard work and perseverance; nothing has been freely given. Maintaining a positive outlook is difficult now that the truth has been revealed and my beliefs have been shattered. I yearn for peace and rest, but it appears that these may only be attainable after death, as they seem unlikely in this lifetime.

Moving forward with a renewed sense of hope, I've decided to release the past and embrace a fresh start, stepping out in faith to face the future. I've resolved to resign from my job upon my supervisor's return. I am no longer willing to tolerate disrespect and interference in my personal and professional life and insist on being treated with respect. Having learned from past experiences, I will no longer succumb to manipulation, disrespect, or foolishness. I am weary of ongoing changes and difficulties and hope my next endeavor will be my last and most fulfilling. I am praying for positive developments in my life and echo Mary J. Blige's sentiment of "No More Drama." Over time, one tires of constant struggles, chaos, and envy, and it often feels as though conflict follows me. It appears many lack the self-awareness and drive to better themselves, instead choosing to exploit others' successes. I have experienced numerous manipulative situations and setups related to past relationships.

It would have been helpful to understand the evolving gender roles in society, where women are increasingly taking on traditionally male responsibilities. While I don't favor either extreme, a balanced sharing of roles would be preferable. Genuine and responsible men seem to be dwindling, often replaced by those who engage in gossip, scheming, and expect women to shoulder all burdens. It seems some women enable this for material gain, losing sight of their responsibilities to their children, prioritizing superficial things, drugs, or sex. The world is full of complexities. People permit outsiders to cause problems and then blame their partners. Ultimately, these issues are interconnected, as people only behave in ways that are allowed.

I am choosing to release myself from the dishonesty, manipulation, and chaos that surrounds me. My desire is for freedom and peace, and to achieve this, I must let go of everything. Trust has become impossible; family and so-called friends have proven toxic, intending to harm and exploit me. I deserve respect and pray that TMH will eradicate the malice and deceit in my life. My faith lies in TMH, where truth and justice prevail, and there is no room for stress, dishonesty, failure, or disappointment, only everlasting joy. All praise to TMH, my ultimate father and reality. Simple things, like not having a car, weigh on me, especially on difficult days. While I plan to rest and then venture out for fresh air, my focus remains on cleaning and my writing. I anticipate potential interference from those I consider malicious, who have been attempting to sabotage my life and online access in hopes of my surrender. However, I will not give up. I am determined to achieve justice, having lost faith in the legal system and the trustworthiness of others. Standing with TMH, I believe this adversity will soon end. I am committed to moving forward without distractions, trusting in divine timing.

After what feels like four or more lonely years filled with heartache and confusion, I realize the pursuit of romantic love is not for me and breeds anger. Despite my willingness to be accepting, forgiving, and unconditionally loving, I've concluded that true love no longer exists. Instead, I witness only addiction, lust, and irresponsibility. My aspiration for a fulfilling life in D.C. remains, yet the path forward is unclear. My attempts to find peace and happiness through various avenues have been unsuccessful. Despite a long history of work, I've lacked proper guidance, or perhaps my vision of fulfillment is unattainable in my current circumstances. My fundamental desires have always been peace, happiness, and love. The irony is stark: I offer much but receive only heartache, emptiness, and betrayal. I am weary of making misguided decisions based on past experiences. Trusting my intuition has led to my aspirations being stolen and exploited. While I strive for positivity and to lead with my heart, maintaining balance is a constant struggle. My desire for a simple life is complicated by family conflict and failed attempts at reconciliation. It feels as though I am trapped in a never-ending cycle of hardship. I face unwarranted animosity, constant solitude, and financial instability, finding success solely through the grace and mercy of TMH. Others are unaware of the significant challenges I've overcome. I present an outward appearance of ease, concealing my struggles and conserving my energy by addressing each situation as it arises.

The holiday season brings a familiar sense of isolation, a stark contrast to cherished childhood memories. I long for the warmth of family gatherings filled with the aromas of my grandfather's cooking: his famous rolls with grape jelly, collard greens, mac and cheese, fried fish, chicken or roast, and sweet potato and old-fashioned yam pies. Laughter and prayer accompanied these feasts, washed down with fresh lemonade, a tradition lost since Christmas 2000 on Queen Street. Though a traumatic event disrupted that holiday, I ensured my children experienced a magical Christmas beforehand. My children have always been my priority, their safety and well-being unwavering, regardless of my circumstances. It's a poignant irony that despite consistently caring for younger relatives, often more responsibly than their own parents who engaged in neglectful behavior I witnessed in my youth, I was unfairly judged. Unlike them, I chose a different path for my children.

My upbringing was marked by unsettling realities, including news of violence against a relative and a family history intertwined with St. Elizabeth's hospital and potentially exploitative practices. I recall my great-grandmother's aneurysm, my mother's defense of my abused cousin, and the overall instability. While youthful anger once consumed me, I discovered strength in faith and truth as a young adult. I believe in a higher power's ultimate justice. Today feels different, and I have a date tonight, a step I hope isn't a mistake. He seems genuine, but I'm apprehensive due to the intense energy and my prolonged absence from dating. I yearn for sincere love and peace, hoping this isn't another failed attempt. I want to be loved for who I truly am.

I eagerly await the end of this difficult journey, feeling the weight of constant battles and repeated betrayals despite my efforts to help others. As I prepare for my date, I hope for the best and trust in divine protection. My words may be veiled, but I believe I am safe. My last work environment was incredibly toxic and chaotic from the start. Despite the initial chaos, a surprisingly smooth transition occurred after I took a leap of faith and quit. The job was a nightmare marked by manipulation and underestimation. The receptionist and her assistant were incompetent and unpleasant. HR was unprofessional, and IT suffered from substance abuse and theft. Many employees lacked ambition, focusing solely on their paychecks and engaging in time theft and manipulation. The older female employees were overly protective of the men in IT. The entire workplace was poorly managed, with an abusive VP and a lazy, dishonest, and incompetent supervisor who even practiced witchcraft and tried to sabotage my work. Many colleagues were unprofessional, unreliable, and often intoxicated at work, leading to constant issues.

I was hired because my supervisor, the Contract Assistant Controller, was unqualified and intended to rely entirely on my work. When her spells failed, she collaborated with others to sabotage me, hoping to create a false impression of my work. The receptionist also had grievances about the unprofessionalism and inexperience of most staff. Ultimately, their goal was my termination, but I resigned first. HR advised against it, but the next morning, I learned the easily influenced CFO didn't want me back, which I saw as a blessing. I suspected something was amiss there all along.

Following my departure from a previous employer, a coworker's invitation led to the discovery of his duplicity, including involvement in suspected prostitution possibly involving my son. I also experienced what I believe were attempts at energy harvesting and destiny swapping, potentially affecting family and past acquaintances. This individual led a double life and was connected to the same cult/coven as my family. He also installed spyware on my devices. Additionally, my stored DocuSign signature was misused to create fraudulent documents and alter hospital records, implicating cousins and lovers in the medical field, although I lack concrete evidence.I sought assistance from TMH, whom I initially trusted but later found to be disingenuous. Before my exit, they intentionally used my paid time off and failed to inform me about my expiring metro benefits, resulting in a $300 loss. Despite promises, I never received my remaining wages. While I choose not to focus on this now, I intend to file a report eventually. I am committed to asserting myself, particularly given my history of being underpaid and overworked, often enduring extreme hours without proper compensation or breaks.In my personal life, past hurts have made me cautious in new relationships. My current involvement with someone younger creates some unease, though I appreciate that he is not a gigolo. His intentions remain unclear, and as I seek exclusivity, the relationship may not last if his feelings are otherwise.

A recent outing to a club with him was a significant error. He apparently drugged my drink, leading to illness. His dismissive behavior afterward, rushing me out of his house and only contacting me a week later to see if his plan had worked, was deeply troubling. I spent a night in the ER but thankfully recovered quickly. I have been recuperating for about a week, during which I have received numerous interview opportunities – three promising and two possible. However, my previous employer, the corrupt company linked to my family, is hindering my job search by providing negative references. I trust that TMH will ensure my continued success and that those who plotted to delay my progress, cause distress, breed envy, and harbor hate due to their own guilt and shame will face judgment and that truth and justice will prevail. I suspect another setup orchestrated by my ex, who was apparently collaborating with others. I question if anyone is not attempting to harm me for financial gain or to sabotage me despite my leaving toxic situations. The incident where I was poisoned during excessive partying, seemingly for payment, suggests they preferred to portray me negatively rather than kill me, likely to continue exploiting my energy through harmful rituals. It was time for me to end these associations. The participants in these activities risk serious health consequences. They seem to treat this as a game, but the potential harm is real, and I will not participate. Furthermore, there was an attempt to manipulate my sexual orientation and project their own issues onto me, sending someone to drain my energy through what I recall as energy transfer. I believe that no harmful intentions against me will succeed, and TMH is in control. I am moving forward. I learned the importance of detaching from detrimental influences. Unbeknownst to me, someone was married and having an affair with my former deceitful boss and her associates. I felt sympathy for his wife, who I suspect may be connected to my family or past acquaintances. They believed they had manipulated me, but TMH had other plans.

Since leaving my previous job, I have started working for a reputable non-profit organization downtown. Despite the thirty-minute commute, my presence still seems to bother individuals connected to those who harbor ill will towards me. This experience has reinforced my belief that my positive energy is unsettling to those with negative intentions. Leaving my accounting career of 24 years to pursue writing my book feels like the only true justice I will experience. This endeavor is mine alone and cannot be tainted. I am grateful for another year and spent my first completely solitary Thanksgiving in 45 years. Despite past difficult holidays and illnesses, I am content with my food, shelter, and freedom, and I feel optimistic. Although there have been setbacks, I remain resilient. Even though I recently quit my job and continue to experience mail theft, I believe these challenges will pass.

For the past three years, I've felt stagnant, with the exception of a new friendship. While we connect well, our slightly off communication makes me uneasy. His mirroring behavior causes us to alternate roles. If he is truly my match, why are our lifestyles so different? As an introvert, I clash with his preference for partying, though he often claims to be busy. My intuition suggests he's hiding something, and I believe the truth will eventually surface. Recently, I've felt balanced, leading me to question if our relationship will ever progress beyond its current hidden state. Realistically, I doubt it will work due to our contrasting lifestyles. While I value fun, I also believe in boundaries and the importance of growth and discernment. Therefore, I haven't made a definitive decision. Although past experiences have led me to overthink, I am now relying on my gut feeling. I believe our intuition, a gift, guides us towards truth, even though not every decision will be perfect due to free will. I have finished writing my books and am now focused on the editing process, aiming for completion and copyright by my birthday this year. I am currently taking a break from romantic relationships due to the associated risks. Having come this far, I refuse to jeopardize my progress by repeating old patterns or returning to my past. The potential for fleeting pleasure is not worth the risk, especially given my past experiences. He and I both work, and I am against his avoidance of staying over, as I am not interested in a casual arrangement. I intend to address my feelings and accept the outcome, whether it's acceptance or rejection.

Experiencing a familiar lack of care and feeling used, reminiscent of past relationships, raises concerns about the current connection. While uncertain, intuition suggests a recurring pattern, possibly involving manipulation or energy drain. Despite advice to drop defenses, the truth will emerge over time. Thanksgiving was a positive experience spent with someone genuinely caring. A brief call from F.A.N.S. felt more like a schedule clearing than a heartfelt greeting, requiring further consideration. The lack of consistent communication, distance, and the feeling that the relationship is reduced to infrequent late-night sexual encounters highlight its fundamental issues. More than just sex, a need for attention and presence is unmet due to suspected partying and infidelity, indicating a manipulative dynamic and a waste of effort. Current experiences suggest love is tainted by greed and disloyalty, although this belief is being challenged.

To ensure financial stability, I am prioritizing a break from romantic relationships. Securing a car is an immediate need, but requires employment for loan approval. To address this situation and counter the misrepresentations damaging my reputation, I've decided to publish my personal narrative for clarity and a fresh start.I learned that a former coworker was instructed to discourage my progress. It seems others don't understand that my past depression stemmed from the difficulties of raising children and enduring abuse—circumstances some have tried to continue. However, this will no longer affect me, as I have let go of guilt, hate, worry, and sadness, placing my trust in a higher power for things beyond my control. Honestly, I am growing tired and frustrated, wishing someone would simply explain what is happening. My life is filled with too many games and conflicts, and clarity has always been absent. I had hoped to be retired and relaxed on a beach by now, but instead, things have worsened. Just as I begin to understand what has been happening behind my back, more trouble arises.

Reviewing ancestry records, I realized frequent name combinations within my family likely caused confusion and facilitated years of deception using false documents and previous names. I recall my last son's father mentioning a reason for naming him after himself, and knowing his birth certificate was altered, his birth name differed from the one he used. I long for the truth so we can move forward to where we belong, trusting in divine timing. Ironically, I've spent this time not in sadness, but constructively understanding the past and present. They want me to give up, but I won't. I tried that, and they responded with attempts to harm and defame me. They may have won a battle, but I am determined to win the war. This is my promise.

As 2025 ends and 2026 approaches, I'm reflecting on my progress and goals. My primary goal is to honor my ancestors by publishing my book by my grandmother's birthday. Reviewing and editing my writing, I am pleased by my ability to recall significant details. This memory and ability to fill in gaps were my initial motivation for writing the book. It has helped me see what I missed and recognize my abilities. I can now express my words and emotions more openly, based on facts, not just thoughts. Everything I write is verifiable. This book has allowed me to share my truth without interruption, judgment, or labels, freeing my mind from forced lies and negativity designed to make me feel inadequate and insane. These falsehoods were based on projections and misinterpretations of my life and others'. Now, I can finally share my side, supported by evidence and "Big Facts."

I have always been a crucial missing piece, but I was silenced. Now, I am back to expose lies and reveal the truth. Through my writing, I have freed myself from bondage, guilt, and the burden of hidden truths. Truth has always been my path, regardless of expectations or potential shame and guilt. I've navigated life's challenges without guidance, experiencing both trauma and triumph. By speaking my truth, I break the cycle of slander and lies, liberating myself from guilt and loneliness. With faith in a higher power, I move forward, embracing life's uncertainties and trusting divine guidance. I have chosen to remain single because I am tired of being put on hold and used for others' convenience while being left alone. I have been alone for too long and refuse to waste time on unequal relationships where my feelings are often disregarded and ignored.

Considering celibacy until marriage due to repeated experiences of being wanted solely for sex and money, I am seeking genuine connection rather than superficial encounters. Tired of manipulation, games, betrayal, and control, I refuse to compromise myself for conditional love based on external factors. I desire to be loved for my true self. I have encountered individuals who attempt to diminish others' achievements out of their own unhappiness and low self-esteem. I believe in karma and hope for their eventual understanding. Despite the harm caused, I extend love and wish them well. I have prioritized myself, especially after discovering spyware on my phone, a result of manipulated trust. This necessitates purchasing yet another phone, highlighting ongoing safety concerns. However, I maintain faith that genuine connections and opportunities will come to me in time.

Currently focused on my book and adapting to life changes, I am prioritizing rest, balance, and identifying my true values. A recent realization about a untrustworthy individual has reinforced the importance of discerning genuine relationships. My future will be built on actions, not words, with no room for forced or pressured connections, as true love should be effortless.Reflecting on another challenging year, I feel resilient and protective of my hard-earned peace. This difficult journey has been meaningful, and I now seek solitude to continue writing. As I return to editing my book, I recognize the abundance of grace and favor in my life.

Despite facing constant opposition and attempts on my life, TMH has consistently protected and guided me, preparing me for a brighter future where I can break free from long-standing personal and familial burdens. My aspirations include helping others through various means, and I envision expanding this book as I achieve my goals. My unwavering commitment remains to positively impact at least one person, which would bring me profound peace. Having endured relentless negativity and numerous betrayals, I find myself resilient. These repeated trials orchestrated by TMH have served as crucial lessons. I pray that I have finally absorbed these lessons and that the right opportunities will soon present themselves.

Recent emotional turmoil gave way to catharsis today, a release I hadn't experienced in three and a half years, culminating in a moment of genuine happiness sparked by a new connection. While we both navigate post-divorce life as friends, I sense a fundamental difference in our current paths. We are both seeking new beginnings, but our approaches differ. He appears to embrace his newfound freedom more openly, while I am cautiously exploring new possibilities after past disappointments. I don't believe there was any exploitation involved; rather, we were two independent individuals. My current priorities lie in my book, establishing stability, and securing my finances. While I am open to love, it is not my primary pursuit.

The extent of past and ongoing betrayals continues to surprise me. I struggle to comprehend why some individuals seek to inflate their self-worth at the expense of others, failing to take personal responsibility for their own self-esteem. It's a reminder that boundaries are essential. I have always been self-reliant and my own greatest advocate, which has been instrumental in my journey. True self-confidence comes from within, and external validation is unnecessary. The only acceptance that truly matters is divine acceptance, found through prayer. This realization is key to inner peace. The person who compromised my phone, motivated by jealousy and a desire to conceal their lifestyle, including multiple partners and orgies, contacted me. This incident reinforces my cautious approach to relationships, prioritizing safety over fleeting encounters.

Experiencing a recent communication lapse, the individual who compromised my phone contacted me with disingenuous apologies and terms of endearment, anticipating a different response. I have firmly established that I am not a temporary option. It has become apparent that some men expect me to overlook their periods of absence and subsequent returns as if nothing transpired. I have unequivocally communicated that I have moved beyond such patterns of dishonesty. These individuals often create their own difficulties and then avoid taking responsibility. As Martin stated in "Welcome Home Roscoe Jenkins," I am now prioritizing my own well-being. My commitment is to put the past behind me and enter 2024 free from stress and negativity. Despite significant losses in recent years, I am resolved not to repeat past mistakes, particularly in toxic relationships. Having successfully rebuilt my life previously, I am confident in my ability to do so again. Starting anew can be a liberating experience, offering fresh perspectives and opportunities for personal development, which is a necessary step forward. While everyone encounters adversity, the critical factor lies in making sound decisions in the future. My focus is now solely on myself. If others do not align with this, they need to move aside. Life holds vast potential, and I am beginning to recognize the possibilities, both appealing and unappealing, understanding that they are all part of life's journey.

During the editing of my book and in preparation for writing the final chapter, I reflected on my life and the numerous challenges I have overcome. Surprisingly, I feel no anger, sadness, or disappointment. Life has presented me with many obstacles, yet I have managed to conquer each one with the support of my angels, ancestors, and TMH. There have been unexpected deviations and delays, and my story continues to unfold. I continue to add chapters, hoping that one day I will reach the conclusion of my seemingly endless narrative. Will it ever end? Or is there more to come? It is possible that I may need to begin another book, as my journey continues.Throughout this seemingly unending and arduous journey, I have discovered countless hidden truths and secrets. Remarkably, I have become desensitized to these revelations; nothing surprises me anymore. Despite the difficulties, I have persevered and achieved many things. This experience has reinforced my awareness of my capabilities, and with faith and trust in TMH, I have been able to navigate through it all with patience and time.

I am no longer disturbed by insignificant matters that require little effort or time. My focus remains simple, recognizing that I am often a secondary consideration in the narratives of others. People will only act according to what you permit, and some will even test those boundaries. The question is whether you will accept this. I have chosen to prioritize myself because without self-love and faith, true love does not exist—only negativity and hate from those who attempt to lower you to their level. I have changed and grown; the person I once was is gone and will not return. I acknowledge my imperfections and choose to work on them, striving to become better and wiser. I am ready to embrace the abundance that life offers when you step back and appreciate the opportunities presented. Remember, you must take that initial step before TMH can meet you and elevate you. Are you ready?

For years, the holiday season has been a source of loneliness rather than joy. Unlike my sister, whose birthday celebrations were a yearly event, mine was always overshadowed by Christmas. As my family grew distant, holidays became a stark reminder of my solitude. For 45 years, I've navigated birthdays and holidays without contact or gifts from family or the children I raised, a consequence of past relationships built on exploitation. My son's stolen future is a heavy weight, leaving me with little to show for my struggles. The inherent contradiction of being created to give love without receiving it fuels my loneliness. Despite being favored, I struggle to understand why I'm perceived as loving. A predicted blessing has materialized into a successful year at work, marked by a full year of employment and new friendships, albeit some flawed. My tendency to give more than I receive has led to a New Year's resolution focused on self-love. It's ironic how much I do for others, yet I continue, guided by an external request. Despite betrayals, I hold onto the belief that everything happens for a reason.

The universe's plan for me remains unclear, marked by silence. I question the apparent disinterest of others in my life. Hoping for a shift during the holidays, I've planned a solo birthday trip, wishing for an unforgettable and deserved celebration. Despite feeling alone, my hope for 2024 is a year overflowing with happiness, love, wealth, and justice. Another challenging year has passed, ending with my approaching birthday and a sense of disappointment and directionlessness. My efforts seem futile, leading nowhere.I've resolved to leave my past behind, a life marked by obstacles, envy, and slow progress despite my efforts and beliefs. The constant mixed signals and the failure of simply going with the flow have led me to silence and prayer, trusting that things will resolve themselves. Help may not arrive immediately, but it will be timely. I'm finished with superficial connections, prioritizing my significant and successful life. I must now rely on myself. Whether a deliberate hardening of my heart, intended to prioritize self-care, I must trust the process, though I feel close to giving up. Despite my struggles, I'm often perceived as privileged. My inner self remains untouched.The longing for my grandmother is profound. Her love, understanding, and solutions offered true comfort. Though I connect with her in spirit, only her physical presence would bring real solace.

Another difficult year has passed, bringing further understanding of myself and my upbringing, often revealing surprising secrets and their impact. Remaining calm amidst daily disappointments and lows has been my way forward. Approaching my forty-sixth birthday without plans, I'm grateful for the resources to manage unexpected expenses. I'm consciously shifting my perspective, choosing to see the positive and praying for peace and abundance. Work is stable, and though still alone, I've found peace and can finally breathe freely again.Many obstacles have been placed in my path, but I'm no longer dwelling on them. Life's challenges have taught me resilience; I take the hits, recover, and keep trying until

I succeed. I realize now that I should have expressed my feelings during those difficult times, but I was solely focused on finding solutions.

Life feels like an immense, confusing jigsaw puzzle where the right pieces are only discovered through experimentation. Despite the arrival of a new year and the fulfillment of past predictions, my circumstances remain frustratingly stagnant. Though doubt creeps in, I know this reality is not imagined; I've experienced this before. For over forty years, I've maintained faith that TMH will intervene at the appropriate time. Perhaps this current struggle is that time, regardless of my missteps. I believe TMH sustains me and sees a purpose in my continued existence. I yearn for progress and trust that TMH will prevent my ultimate downfall and loneliness, for I believe I deserve love. Yet, my efforts yield only heartache. This turmoil feels contrary to TMH's plan. I am losing clarity on my emotions and beginning to question my worth, influenced by negative external forces. I believe my purpose lies in loving and sharing my struggles through storytelling, hoping this will lead to a better situation. Having lived in D.C. my entire life, I am weary of hurt and betrayal. Recently, my sister's so-called wellness check by the police, despite years of family neglect, exemplifies this. Knowing my address, their choice to involve the police felt like a deliberate act, especially considering their past attempts to harm and defraud me. During the police interaction, where body cameras were present, I articulated their motives clearly, questioning why they would send the police when they knew my location, highlighting their pretense of concern and their attempts to portray me as incapable after stealing my inheritance and leaving me impoverished. The police officer even echoed my question to my sister. Their actions continuously expose their ill intentions. Despite facing animosity and threats, I remain unharmed, blessed, and highly favored.

Life experiences have led to the conclusion that love is nonexistent. Therefore, I have chosen to emotionally close myself off and prioritize my well-being. I will reserve my feelings for those who truly deserve them. For the time being, I am content with being single and focusing on healing. I trust that TMH will reward me in the future. I remain hopeful and will continue to pray for the right person to enter my life at the appropriate time. My current focus is on achieving significant goals related to my finances and mental health. I recognize that certain individuals and situations are not divinely intended for me and will patiently await what is meant to be. Wasting further time on unproductive interactions will only lead to anger, which seems to be the desired outcome of others. While occasional disappointment is inevitable, past experiences have taught me that perceived setbacks often serve to prevent greater future pain, as TMH has a complete perspective. My disappointment stems from understanding the reasons behind the withholding of love. Others have reacted negatively to the love and indifference I have shown in the past, and my withdrawal of affection has created conflict. I will no longer engage with these individuals, as any attention will only encourage the continuation of their harmful behavior, which I will not allow. My sole focus is now on myself and the will of TMH. Anyone who disagrees can address their concerns directly to him.

I have been praying for my wishes to be fulfilled, and despite the waiting period, I acknowledge my blessings. Everything worthwhile requires effort. Distractions, such as internet issues, have impeded my progress, but I will not be deterred. The anger I once held has lessened through expression, allowing happiness to return. I recognize that simply existing is not my ultimate purpose. Persistent obstacles continue to disrupt my plans, but I anticipate greater happiness once justice prevails. My goals include publishing my book, relocating, distancing myself from negative influences, and investing in personal growth without looking back. I welcome quiet days for reflection on past hurts and those who caused them. Constant disruptions and delays are a significant source of frustration. Repetitive negative situations have become tiresome and pointless. My patience has run thin, and I am prepared to make drastic changes to escape harassment and stalking, trusting that TMH will guide my heart. While not violent, I will protect myself and have made a conscious decision to change my approach to life. The irony of those who claim violence while frequently seeking external drama and exhibiting harmful behaviors themselves is not lost on me.

I have been praying for a new beginning, including a new home, family, friends, and lasting stability. I am determined to replace negativity with positivity and embrace what I believe is my destined path. Despite external opinions, I am resolved to release the past and move forward. True healing requires letting go, and I am willing to start anew, even if it involves loss. I am weary of constant upheaval and desire stability. My life has been marked by instability since my parents' separation in 1989. Despite overcoming numerous challenges, I continue to face negativity and attempts to undermine me. I have learned that negative influences can come from anyone, not just close relations. My past belief in the inherent goodness of people has been shattered by betrayals from various sources, highlighting the unfortunate reality of evil in the world. Some individuals react with anger and seek to harm when their demands are not met, revealing their own unhappiness.

Despite feeling incomplete, I am grateful for my blessings and trust in divine timing for peace. I believe those who have harmed me will face consequences, but I choose to respond with love and prayers, recognizing their ignorance. My past experiences have taught me the destructiveness of hate, a path I refuse to revisit. I am committed to my goals, understanding perseverance makes anything possible, and I will hold onto my remaining faith and peace. Resisting retaliation has been difficult, as it would only validate my offenders and give them victory. Instead, I choose to disengage and not be drawn into their negativity. I belong to TMH and will avoid their traps. Past challenges have resurfaced, and my response remains, "This too shall pass" and "Vengeance is TMH's." I have faced painful truths about the people in my life, feeling hated, harmed, used, or abused by almost everyone I've encountered. Reaching my limit of mistreatment from loved ones, I've chosen to walk away instead of fighting and compromising my values. I allow others their assumptions and the consequences of their actions. Their hatred seemed to emerge only when I ceased to enable them through lies, projection, support, or care, as if it had always existed and I had merely revealed it. Despite my consistent efforts to help everyone, regardless of their treatment, I felt I never truly mattered. My love and generosity were twisted into a perception that I believed myself superior or that I didn't need their help. I never intended to offend; honesty was my way of showing love and loyalty. To witness wrongdoing and not offer help, knowing how to correct it, is not love but rather hate and indifference disguised. I never anticipated that extending help to so many would create such turmoil. My kindness was met with betrayal from those I assisted, including ex-partners, my sister, and cousins whom I supported emotionally, financially, and with food throughout their lives.

My actions were simply offering the help I never received, driven by a desire to see everyone succeed. I opened my home, provided food, and gave generously, even when lacking myself. The betrayal and lies were particularly hurtful given my underlying fear of failure, which unfortunately materialized in experiences with the psyche ward, jail, and homelessness. Yet, even during these hardships, I continued to help others. Those who hurt me most have not diminished my capacity for love, but they have reduced my willingness to give as I did in the past. Their attempts to harm me are noted. While their approval is not required, a higher power has witnessed everything. I harbor no grudges or resentment toward those who plotted my downfall and caused daily suffering, including former recipients of my help and their new allies. My love and compassion remain steadfast despite countless betrayals and attacks fueled by their poor choices and misfortunes, which they project onto me. Ultimately, their identities are insignificant compared to my unwavering commitment to peace and kindness.

I chose a different path from my family due to their "craziness," seeking to distance myself from them as soon as possible. Money played a significant role, with them using it for greed and evil. Their misdeeds will eventually be revealed. While not innocent myself, I have changed. Raised in negativity and taught immoral values, I realized that imitation wasn't mandatory; I could transcend my environment. I sought knowledge to break free from those limitations. The belief that one is bound by their upbringing is false, as many have overcome their circumstances by choosing change and rejecting confusion, low self-esteem, and poverty. People face harsh judgment, and it's vital to rise above negativity and disregard others' opinions. One can choose to participate in negativity or move forward. Malicious intent is the only guarantee of stagnation. The negativity projected onto others, especially those striving for positive change, will be reciprocated. Opportunities should be based on current efforts, not on others' judgments of worthiness. Bad choices are a personal responsibility. While not everyone is malicious, those consumed by hate and destructive urges should seek professional help.

I've learned that dwelling on the past hinders progress and exacerbates problems. Instead, I choose to trust in a Higher Power's superior ability to handle situations. Had I been in control, I believe I would likely be in jail or worse. I have come too far to regress. Reflecting on my book edits, I see a past dominated by traumatic events, revealing repetitive, unlearned lessons. Around 2022, this pattern shifted, marking my ability to recognize and value life's positive aspects. My journey lacked external guidance, relying instead on faith and a Higher Power, teaching me self-reliance. My upbringing didn't provide these lessons; they were taught by the universe and TMH—a trustworthy teacher. I recognize the divine orchestration of my life and am grateful for the lessons learned in every relationship, good or bad. Surviving these experiences is a precious gift.

I've accepted my differences and the inevitability of some people's disapproval. Life involves both teaching and learning through seasonal connections. I've learned to release what TMH has removed, understanding it as protection, not harm. Clinging to the past only hurts me. Each seemingly insignificant lesson has contributed to my growth, overseen by TMH and divine beings. Karma observes all and eventually delivers consequences. I no longer seek revenge, understanding that it belongs to TMH, my constant judge, protector, and healer. His grace sustains me, making all things possible. In His time, truth and justice will prevail.

I've moved beyond negativity, finding peace and refusing to regress despite lingering shadows. My past trials have proven my strength. I patiently await the revelation of past mysteries, trusting they will restore hope. Our beliefs powerfully shape our reality; wish fulfillment hinges on them. The universe responds to our convictions, so re-evaluate before dismissing possibilities. Despite life's obstacles, illusions, and deceptions, I stand victorious, ready to share my story. Life's unexpected turns can erode our innate innocence and strength, often normalized by society. Without these societal influences, guided by pure intuition, our paths might be different. Knowledge and history help balance intuition with experience. Control underlies much of what we are taught, diverting us from our true purpose. While learning has value, preconceived notions obscured the truth and concealed evil. My family's control attempts involved withholding and then removing what little they provided, leading to interference with my creations and children, ultimately resulting in their destruction when control failed. I have always been an observer, awakening from past pain to share my resilience. Despite recognizing and being trapped in repetitive trauma, I sought understanding and the removal of internal blocks.

The revelation of enemies and their motives stung, reminding me that I am not heartless, but rather numb from the repeated blows. In this moment of vulnerability, the devil seeks my soul, but it belongs to a higher power. Regardless of my past suffering, I remain grateful and continue to praise. The suffering and lost experiences I've endured can never be truly repaid. However, I trust that TMH will provide restitution and, through him, all will be restored. I believe my life will change when TMH deems it appropriate. I know good things are coming; any delays are for my protection. I dream of someday driving my favorite sports car—a BMW i5, i7, or i4, a Porsche, or a Lexus—and enjoying the rewards I've worked so hard for. I've been wronged and taken advantage of many times, but soon it will be my turn to have some well-deserved fun.I long to escape to the beach, arriving at sunrise to watch the sun ascend over the water. As the gentle breeze blows and my feet sink into the sand, I'll wait for restaurants to open and enjoy a hot meal without the fear of poisoning. I yearn to explore new sights and escape the lies, envy, destruction, and jealousy of my current life.

I know TMH has someone special for me, a true love to share my life with. We will cuddle, cook, dance, make love, and support each other through all of life's joys. Everything is happening in divine timing; I can feel it deep in my soul that I will soon be free.I believe that I will be announcing the release of my book soon. I know from past disappointments that "this too shall pass." The sun shines brighter in the morning after many sleepless, restless nights. I can feel that help is on its way.The past three days have been interesting since my contract ended last week. It's amusing how I've adapted to certain life patterns that were ultimately illusions and lies. I consistently maintained employment and remained a dedicated worker throughout the pandemic, never neglecting my duties or slacking off. However, each contract typically soured a week before its end. In the past, it was worse because I would often become ill and be hospitalized for weeks right as I was ready to finalize a contract, forfeiting all my hard work and innovative ideas for companies that only made me feel used and insignificant.This experience is another sign from TMH that I need to let go and become my own boss. By working for myself, I won't allow others to dictate my life's purpose or control me through finances. If I don't comply with those in power, they may try to remove me and force me into poverty, but I refuse to give them that much power.

This is my path to success, built on unique projects, thoughts, and inherent gifts. Attempts to control me financially will fail. Though facing setbacks, my effort and faith will ensure nothing stops me. By writing my own narrative, I've already gained an advantage, and I alone will benefit.My life has been a carefully constructed deception, orchestrated for my downfall while others unjustly profit from my hard work. Despite tireless effort, I remain weary, with no progress or reward. For over thirty years, my credit score has stagnated despite consistent hard work and on-time payments, leading me to question the value of my labor, which seems only to benefit the undeserving. My credit report is filled with debts incurred in my name, debts I've been forced to pay through voluntary payments, wage garnishment, and taxes, trapping me in a cycle of debt while others accumulate wealth at my expense. Numerous complaints to government agencies have been ignored, dismissed as fabrications to avoid payment. These individuals, accustomed to crime and exploitation, lack empathy for my situation. I will only work for TMH, as only he can offer opportunities beyond a mere paycheck. Constantly repaying unknown debts is another reason for this writing. Everything I've achieved has been through my own effort, free from bosses or judgments. I plan to leave this area, where my credit, reputation, and work-life are ruined and where I am widely known, but not before clearing my name.

In the past, I've left situations unresolved. This time, this chapter will be complete, delivering a clear message: "I AM NOT A VICTIM, AND I AM INNOCENT." I am starting a new life of peace and unconditional love, trusting in a higher power as my only means of proof. They assumed I would simply walk away, but I believe in a higher authority that sees all, always, everywhere, beyond any court, and I have faith. I deserve the good that is coming, and everything will ultimately work out. Despite tireless work and a lack of love in my life, unnoticed by others, people who have tried to sabotage me no longer matter. What is destined cannot be changed or stopped.

Having consistently offered love and protection to those who only valued me for what I could provide, I was always the protector, a truth TMH recognized. Their recent distancing revealed greed, lust, envy, and jealousy. They wrongly believed I didn't deserve my blessings, considered themselves superior, and attempted to portray me as a failure, a bad parent, and mentally unstable. Throughout my life, I have fought for survival, enduring betrayal, lies, and the loss of my family, with everything being taken from me. I have survived assault, homelessness, and false accusations, yet I remain. My hard work has resulted in significant achievements that are mine alone. I have been used as a disguise, forced to appear inferior to those I am better than. Ultimately, TMH has the final authority, and I trust in this, waiting to see what will happen.

My day took an unusual turn with an aimless drive to Dulles, a search for escape. A meal at Cracker Barrel preceded a return home for a nap. Later, a spontaneous haircut resulted in a shorter style than my recent trim. With my grandmother's birthday nearing on March 3rd and being currently unemployed, I had the time to visit the cemetery, leaving flowers for my great-grandmother, grandparents, and mother. After the haircut, I drove to the park and discovered a new, secluded meditation spot closer to home by taking a different route. The remainder of the day was spent driving and enjoying the scenery, a departure from my usual hurried pace with a set destination, instead embracing the sights and the simple feeling of being.

As spring approaches, I feel a sense of renewal and anticipate a fresh start, reflecting on my life and uncovering painful truths of deceit and betrayal. My life's path seems intentionally difficult, echoing the experiences of my ancestors. Ironically, this realization brings a sense of solace, confirming my alienation from this deceitful world. The cruelty inflicted upon family is deeply disturbing, as if my struggles and sacrifices were exploited for the benefit of others. Memories resurface of being excluded while others enjoyed lavish vacations and celebrations. I was left to deal with the consequences of their actions, including a fabricated marriage and attempts to profit from stolen land. I endured homelessness and unemployment, resorting to drinking rainwater and sleeping on the streets. Each morning, I sought refuge at a nearby restaurant, grocery store, or gas station to prepare for another workday. For a time, my son shared this hardship, but eventually, I had to leave him. Relying on buses after my cars were stolen and repossessed due to unemployment, I still managed to save enough money to move.

I've consistently faced obstacles and delays, which I now understand were intentional efforts to keep me impoverished while others profited from my work and stolen possessions. Since 2021, someone has fraudulently filed for unemployment in my name, preventing me from doing so. Despite reporting this, I'm forced to work and pay fines for money I never received. The joint account with my supposed husband was also part of this. My attempts to seek help from various organizations were futile; without concrete proof, no one would investigate or offer support, despite my strong intuition about who was responsible. It's disheartening that the legal system, meant to protect victims, seems to prioritize financial gain instead. Frustrated and resigned, I've decided to entrust this to a higher power and await a response.

After twenty-five years of perfect attendance at work, I've chosen a different path. Tired of constant job changes and setbacks hindering my true aspirations, I'm now dedicating myself entirely to finishing my book – writing, editing, proofreading, and securing copyright. Throughout my life, I've learned to avoid attachment, except to my children, who were once my sole focus. However, my desperation inadvertently alienated them, revealing the potent force of jealousy. I now understand the danger of trusting those motivated by money or impulsivity, as they are likely to betray you. My loyalty to others, even those lacking self-belief, was ultimately wasted effort. I'm moving forward, leaving the past behind, confident that my value and positive impact will eventually be recognized. Despite significant suffering and being underestimated, I've persevered. The unwavering support of TMH has provided strength, balance, and protection, fostering resilience and the ability to withstand adversity. Challenges and adversaries have only strengthened my resolve. Assumptions and judgments have been proven wrong, as I continue to rise above. My past is simply that – the past. I've grown and moved on to a higher level. While others may dwell on my history, I don't need external validation, especially after repeated exclusion. I stand by my reasons for severing ties with most people and remain authentic. My family instilled in me the need to lie for protection, but I've learned that honesty is freeing. Unfortunately, I perpetuated this cycle of deceit. Instead of nurturing our natural talents, they emphasized rote memorization, creating illusions that have permeated our lives.

My life and finances have been treated like a game, but those responsible will now face the consequences. They've left a substantial paper trail, and in this technological age, they cannot hide. Technological advancements will reveal everything. Despite thinking they are unnoticed, they are being watched. Instead of harboring anger, I'm grateful for the knowledge and experience gained from those who deceived me. This has equipped me for future challenges. I've endured immense hardship and deceit, feeling trapped in a cycle of wrongdoing and dishonesty. People avoid doing what's right, and no one shows their true colors.I question whether the suffering they inflicted by concealing the truth was worth it. Their eventual punishment will be insignificant compared to the duration of their actions. By the time they are sentenced, they will have lived full lives, while mine has barely begun. Yet, despite their attempts to break me, I remain hopeful.

Having lived in DC my entire life, I yearn for a change of scenery, a chance to breathe. The idea of escaping to the mountains to scream freely is appealing. I dream of a cozy cabin, companionship with a kind man by a fire under the stars, grilling, listening to nature, and relaxing. These are my hopes and prayers for a positive transformation. My life has been stagnant for over thirty years – the jobs and people may change, but the routine remains the same. Therefore, I've quit my job to create change. As a single person without children, family, or friends, I am finally prioritizing myself, the one I've neglected for so long. This is a new chapter, a new me, blessed and favored. Much love and respect to TMH. Thank you

I've distanced myself from negativity and deceit, recognizing that inaction contributes to problems. I consciously removed myself from detrimental situations that misrepresented me. The truth always emerges; you cannot force someone to be false. Be authentic and define yourself. Embrace your worth; no one can derail your destiny. Life is a game of choices; your next move determines the outcome. I've progressed, leaving behind those who weren't meant to stay. While taught to avoid grudges, my different perspective led to negative labels, often projections of others' issues. They tried to redefine me and burden me with their problems, but I recognized the potential consequences were not worth it. My family, F.A.N.S., and colleagues attributed my struggles to my choices, but my inner work revealed the truth: they didn't expect my success.

Metaphorically abandoned with few resources, I defied their expectations and thrived. I'm grateful for their minimal support, as it forced me to find a new path, not back, but forward. I mistakenly believed helping others wouldn't harm me, but it did. Now, I'm finished with that. Despite years of betrayal and adversity, I focused on uplifting others. I refused to let past traumas hinder my progress.Rising above imprisonment, mental health struggles, abusive relationships, and poverty, I aimed high. My grandmother's words resonated: "Show them, no conversation; only action speaks louder." Despite warnings, I persisted in seeing the good in everyone. My efforts to help ultimately depleted me. My optimism, though unwavering, led to my downfall. Despite repeated abandonment and lack of true reciprocation, I persevered, always starting anew. Now, I prioritize self-love and my personal journey. My children were used as leverage, shielding me like chess pieces protect the queen. These relationships were manipulated to obstruct and defend. They believed that overcoming these protective barriers would lead to my defeat. However, my withdrawal surprised them and ensured my self-preservation. They were fighting themselves, not me. I learned valuable lessons from my hardships. Their perceived torture was my normal, given my past. I adapted to their foolishness and am grateful for it. Thank you for the abandonment and mistreatment; it revealed my inner strength. You tried to dim my light but only exhausted yourselves. I emerge refined and successful, a testament to resilience. I rise.

Life's frustrations led to a realization: this isn't just about my happiness. Editing my book, I saw that my story, connected to my past and losses, also belongs to others. They are communicating through me, allowing me to tell both our stories. This hidden truth, that I can communicate with those pasts, and the wrongs done to them, is why they want me silenced. My initial confusion about being punished as an outcast has clarified. This began before I discovered my parents' and grandparents' involvement in MK Ultra and their use as sacrifices. Do you believe in magic? Despite the confusion, remember that death is a journey to another realm where we may meet familiar souls.

Shows like "The Reading" and "Ghost" explore the idea of spirits remaining on Earth after unjust deaths, seeking justice by revealing the truth. This resonates with my family's long history of insurance-related deaths, something I understood only later. My mother was always strangely controlled, reminiscent of people being auctioned off during slavery. I suspect she was either kidnapped or went through something similar, possibly involving MK Ultra mind control in DC, which might explain her programmed interactions with me. Her jealous sisters and even her own mother resented her skin color and hair. A childhood story about a stolen white baby now makes me wonder if it was about her. I had attributed my grandmother's skin bleaching to a white or very light-skinned ancestor, possibly due to assault. This family history warrants further investigation. Unknowingly, I repeated my mother's patterns, marrying young to escape trauma only to enter an abusive relationship with my father. This could explain the disbelief I faced when I spoke out about assaults by my sister, uncle, and others. I remember telling my mother about her uncle's inappropriate behavior and her near-accident fleeing him. I suspect more happened. I was raised to be silent, echoing, "What goes on in this house stays in this house." Incest was prevalent in my family, likely causing the many disabilities and learning difficulties. My mother was exploited and controlled, used and discarded like I was, her life manipulated and ultimately ended when she was no longer controllable.

They tried to replicate this with me, sending infected men to perpetuate lies and conceal secrets of death, disease from sexual rituals, body and energy swapping, and mind control. They succeeded with my mother because, like me, she loved deeply and had no frame of reference for their projections. My parents' frequent clinic visits for my father's STIs were suspicious, but my sister dismissed my concerns about their HIV status and infidelity. Their attempts to discredit me only strengthened my resolve to uncover the truth behind numerous orchestrated deaths, including my mother's. I recall seemingly healthy people suddenly dying, a damn shame, and I pray for TMH to have mercy but also deliver justice for these long-unpunished acts. Ironically, their targeting me awakened me to the truth through TMH and angels, sparing me their fate. Stories circulate about orchestrated deaths on my father's side, concealed by the "dark witches"—my grandmothers and aunt. They devalued us, seeing us only for exploitation, providing only the bare minimum. Their mind control, black magic, and group tactics countered our inherent strength, not from magic but from our profound, even if unrequited, love. Our true wealth was spiritual, beyond their comprehension, making us untouchable. My aunts were also malicious, envious of my mother's ability to attract love and possessions. One aunt was trapped in a miserable marriage and squalid living conditions due to her choices, while her sister exploited government programs, enabling her children's criminal behavior. Now, they have united to harm me. I have been exploited by family, those in power within the judicial system, law enforcement, social services, and close associates, manipulated for their selfish gain. Those with addiction and greed were particularly susceptible to their influence. I was even kept from the truth of my grandfather's death. I know why he was killed and why my grandmother fraudulently collected disability payments for him. He was a gravedigger and later a painter who, unable to read or write, relied on others, explaining our bond through my reading and writing for him. Soon after his death, she replaced him with an alcoholic veteran. Their plans, my aunts' and their husbands', included the uncle who sexually assaulted me, echoing my mother's experience. It was always about money, never love, a truly heartless existence.

My stepdad's family has a history of service members, politicians, and law officials. I've heard stories suggesting my grandfather's death wasn't from cancer but black magic. Following his death, my aunt allegedly abused my grandmother, adding substances to her food to hasten her demise for inheritance purposes. This side of the family disliked my uncle, who ultimately inherited everything, possibly because he was the eldest or for other reasons. Despite this, they felt foul play was involved in my grandfather's death and that the inheritance wasn't what they expected. They suspected poisoning or black magic, believing those responsible feigned care to gain assets. They didn't consider our inherent worthiness of the inheritance, assuming I was undeserving due to not being blood related. However, our connection was deeper – a soul connection based on unconditional love, not material expectations. I'm still uncovering the full truth with divine guidance.

My sister, whom I see as a destructive force, believes she is entitled. I recall a late-night visit from a neighbor seeking my stepdad for an exorcism for his possessed daughter, a visit that now seems significant. Around 2019, I began to see my sister's decline, though I was reluctant to accept it. Hidden truths are now emerging, and her involvement will be her downfall. I remember her overspending with an ex-husband (the one whose children were taken away while he was drinking). After their divorce, he returned to North Carolina and reconnected with family, which upset my sister, even though she was receiving support from my niece's godfather and his mother – another situation heading for trouble. I've noticed a pattern of deaths occurring in close succession. Magic, when performed without protection or awareness, can lead to death, with individuals becoming sacrifices to elevate secret societies and corrupt establishments. This has been happening for years within my stepdad's family and my mother's side, with my grandfather, uncles, and others suddenly passing away. My uncle's brother recently had a stroke, and to conceal my aunt's affair and child with the neighbor, we've kept him isolated and unable to communicate verbally. He remains at home, receiving veteran's benefits, while we figure out a long-term solution.

The next-door neighbor's family, including his wife (my aunt) and trained daughters, are witches who initially practiced magic on him and later on me after I discovered the men sent to harm me were involved with my married cousin. After these deaths, I reflected on events involving my sister. Were they coincidences or planned? It started with her ex-boyfriend (before she lived with me), a family friend of my uncle and also my aunt's former boyfriend. He died suddenly with no apparent cause, though excessive drinking was mentioned. Given his past relationships with both my aunt and sister, I suspect they used magic for revenge, resulting in his death. Later, I noticed her ex-husband, who was once large, became very thin and died unexpectedly. She attended his funeral in North Carolina and visited his mother, with whom she was close. There had been a property dispute between her and his children's mother in North Carolina.

The pattern of greed and deception continued after his mother's death. My niece's godfather, a heavy man who enjoyed food and whom she cooked for, suffered a stroke and was found dead at home, having become thin. This sequence – stroke, thinness, heart attack, death – seems deliberate. She had gained his trust and personal information, likely hoping for insurance benefits or inheritance, wrongly believing she would be a beneficiary. Despite her schemes, she wasn't the intended recipient. The notary created fake online businesses (Red Flag Financial Forensics in 2020, later Veri Account in 2021) and fabricated documents for fraudulent purposes. I discovered this after calling her number and investigating online. It seems someone saw through her plan and left the inheritance to someone else, leading her to these illegal acts. She was supposed to receive ten thousand dollars after handling her mother-in-law's medical bills and start a business (Red Flag Recovery), which I suspected was also a fabrication. I didn't interfere directly, focusing instead on the negative energy she directed at me. I believe the deaths I've witnessed throughout my life, including my aunt's affair partner who shot himself, and the aunt who committed suicide, were not coincidences but results of mind control, possession, and illusions orchestrated by hitmen within my family. These events were planned to maintain undeserved positions and eliminate anyone who was vulnerable, ignorant, or opposed to their actions, including myself, blinded by love and preventing the truth from emerging.

My aunt's actions were deeply disturbing. Beyond leaving me as bait the night of the incident with the rapist's husband, the man who stayed in her basement, for whom she once slapped me, also died under suspicious circumstances. I believe she profited from these deaths and others through insurance fraud, living off these schemes for years. It's infuriating to see such blatant deceit and theft. One of her most heinous acts was sacrificing her own child. My cousin's murder was unexpected, a direct result of my aunt allowing dangerous influences into her home. After a raid, she became an informant and soon after, the individual involved was killed. She then moved from the projects to Fort Washington, MD, using insurance money and relocation funds. This family's behavior is truly awful.

I'm also concerned about my sister's claims regarding an older man from my grandmother's neighborhood. They're trying to fabricate a story involving old tapes with child pornography, suggesting he was watching children at the park and even my niece. This doesn't align with my memories of him as a child; he was always kind and playful. When I questioned my aunt about turning him in and the existence of these tapes, she resisted involving the police. My priority was my niece's safety. I warned her that even strong people can be broken by fear and that she should always speak up if anyone ever hurt her, explaining how our family might try to cover it up. My sister confirmed my own childhood assaults in front of my niece, which was important for her to hear, but she never acknowledged it otherwise. It became clear they were trying to indoctrinate my niece with their beliefs.

Later, a seemingly innocent gift from my second husband, an amethyst crystal from a 7-Eleven, felt sinister. I sensed a negative energy or spell attached to it and discarded it. I also had a troubling dream involving my father, uncles, aunts, and siblings participating in the sacrifice of women in an underground location. When I shared this dream with my sister, I felt a divine intervention, a prompting to stop speaking about it. Shortly before this, I found a large cockroach in my new home, which I interpreted as a sign of a monitoring spirit. It disappeared when I struck it, leaving me uneasy.

During my conversation with my sister about the dream, my niece somehow knew details I hadn't told her, creating an unsettling connection despite the distance between us. Suddenly, a storm erupted where I was, but my niece insisted it was sunny at her location, even sending a picture. I saw this as a divine message to be silent and disconnect, though I didn't understand it fully at the time. Looking back, I realize the extent to which my father, siblings, and former partners have all contributed to my current situation. The full picture was still unclear, but the pieces were beginning to fall into place. Shortly before contacting my sister, I had argued with my youngest son's father after I shared my spiritual beliefs and my suspicion that his friends and my ex-husband were casting spells on me. He reacted explosively, blaming me for everything.

Experiencing a pattern of betrayal and manipulation by my family, including hacking my son's phone to track me, has led me to sever ties with them. Their motives appear rooted in jealousy and a sense of entitlement. A stolen diary from my youth provided them with leverage, which they have used to contact individuals from my past. Despite a difficult and concealed childhood shaped by these experiences, I am now focused on the future and will no longer be silenced by their tactics. I am determined to share my truth, regardless of ongoing harassment. I believe in a higher power that supports me. My decision to distance myself was driven by a need for genuine connection, contrasting with the betrayal I experienced from my father and stepmother, who manipulated my children for financial gain. Prayer offered solace during this isolation and inspired me to share my story in hopes of helping others.

I seek justice for my ancestors who were victims of greed. I believe my mother's death involved foul play, suggesting a repeated pattern of harm through poisoning and disease. I suspect my stepfather may have intentionally infected her. The truth surrounding her death has been obscured by silence and manipulation, possibly linked to ritualistic acts and the involvement of others.I believe my uncle, a veteran, was also a victim, his inheritance stolen under suspicious circumstances. This theft appears to be part of a lifelong pattern of attempts to defraud me, including through life insurance policies. My family's aim is to keep these truths hidden. I am grateful for surviving numerous challenges through divine grace.

Although my present circumstances may seem overwhelming, I recognize this as another illusion created by negative forces. Having faced similar situations before, I am not afraid of loss, trusting that I will be supported and strengthened. Difficult times have ultimately made me stronger.

Uncovering hidden truths and forgotten memories has deepened my understanding of my family's past harmful actions and systemic injustices. My ancestors urge me to speak against these wrongdoings, even those shielded by family ties and the legal system. The illusions many live under, potentially stemming from childhood programs and MK Ultra, contributed to my mother's isolation and harm when she resisted, perpetuating a cycle of suffering in my life. It is time for change, justice, and the exposure of fraudulent official documents dating back to the nineties, a period of lax verification exploited for activities like PPP loans during the pandemic. This corruption, involving long-standing individuals and possibly secret societies, has enabled RICO crimes, gang stalking, hacking, and identity fraud. The shared names across my family generations do not guarantee blood relations, necessitating DNA testing to uncover the truth mirroring their deceptions. They have consistently tried to destroy my life, even manipulating my mother's death certificate by altering my birthdate to match her death date. The name and birthdate I've used are not my original ones, both having been changed. I advise against giving children identical names to close relatives, as it can indicate fabrication. While my relationship with my parents is accurately mother and stepfather, official records have been falsified. Naming me after my mother appears premeditated. I also recall a childhood rumor of a twin who died at birth, an unverified detail amidst recovered and suppressed memories, possibly influenced by hypnosis and trauma. Recent rumors suggest my stepmother assumed my mother's identity, while my sister and niece are using mine. I am aware many others possess my personal information, and investigations are underway. Additionally, my brother's wife allegedly used my identity for immigration through a sham marriage for financial gain, a family pattern.

I believe many were harmed or killed to suppress the truth. Documents were altered for personal gain, resulting in my inheritance being stolen and leaving me financially vulnerable, receiving only occasional, manipulative support from my stepfather. Even funds from my sister were ultimately mine. They have essentially lived my life while keeping me deprived. Throughout my life, inheritances were passed down through generations, including my grandparents. My uncle, not my grandfather's son, was jealous and opposed his inheritance due to their life choices. They never wanted my success or fulfillment, yet they never truly stopped me. My current position is due to hard work, struggles, and resilience, and I am moving towards a brighter future, never looking back or quitting, trusting that TMH will eventually intervene, with karma assisting in the interim.

My family history is marked by loss and betrayal. Following my grandparents' deaths, my uncle inherited everything but allowed my aunt to remain in our family home. Tragically, his will and trust were exploited during his illness by a deceitful individual. While other relatives prioritized their own families, my aunt and her drug-addicted husband stayed in the house, a situation that significantly contributed to my current poverty. The childhood home, or the rental property they supposedly offered, could have provided financial stability. Instead, I was left in despair, while they feigned innocence and, I believe, maliciously tried to portray me as unstable. This is evidenced by my aunt's institutionalization and her granddaughter's deafness, outcomes that I see as karmic reflections of their actions. Many past illnesses and unexplained events now make sense within this context.

My grandparents' house, a family establishment in uptown NW, was remodeled by my aunt and her husband. The addition of fish ponds in the front yard was a deceptive attempt to project success and respectability, masking their true nature. Their actions illustrate the consequences of negative intentions, particularly towards the undeserving. The entire situation was amplified and irreparable. After the deaths of those who once protected me, I became the target of relentless attacks against myself and my family. Energies were manipulated, my children and other innocent individuals were drawn into these schemes, and my relationships, friendships, and employment were sabotaged. There were even attempts to erase me, based on the false assumption that I lacked support. They were unaware of the divine protection I believe I have had since birth, as one of the 144,000. They underestimated my resilience, hoping their manufactured crisis would confine me, but divine intervention saved me.

Like many others before me, I was targeted and now serve as a vessel to share our stories—a secret concealed for decades after my parents were killed and I was adopted to steal my inheritance. Initially, they attempted to force me into a false marriage, followed by introducing a fabricated online lover. Their aims were to infect me with diseases, ruin my accomplishments, and discard me, a fate I suspect my biological mother suffered years prior. My cousin experienced a similar tragedy. In my childhood, my stepdad often saw her begging on South Capitol Street after her mother's death. The accepted story was that my great-aunt left her money, which she wasted on drugs—another life derailed. I now believe the truth is that individuals presumed dead are not necessarily so.

From a young age, I learned that appearances can be deceiving. This realization, around seven years old in Anacostia, may have been the genesis of my resilience, a "TMH"-guided ability to endure hardships like those before me. My life experiences were targeted for exploitation; others repeatedly stole and published my stories and poems, feigning understanding while failing to grasp the pain of fabricated relationships designed to pilfer my work. They viewed my life as a blueprint to undermine my resilience. For years, writing was my refuge. They underestimated my capacity to defend against lies and false narratives. Despite memory loss and the theft of my work, I've found a stronger voice than ever. They never anticipated that "TMH" would reveal the horrific behind-the-scenes actions. My early, emotionally charged writings were intentionally erased through orchestrated car accidents and abuse leading to head injuries. However, this time, a divine intervention, guided by my ancestors, unveiled betrayals and saved me. Now, I can share my story, expressing gratitude for this second chance at life and this book.

My deceitful family and their associates, along with their many manipulated allies, were the primary orchestrators of this exploitation. This includes my hateful stepmother, aunts (whom I suspect murdered my grandparents), and my wicked sister (who, with my aunt and grandmother, I believe killed our mother). Cousins stole inheritances and attempted to manipulate destinies by sending lovers to have sex with me for selfish energy exchanges, aiming for my infection and social isolation. They intended to deceive my partners into sexual activity, hoping I would become involved and appear to be the carrier, turning many against me. However, I choose not to dwell on the past, focusing instead on my future, as revisiting what was removed has proven detrimental. It is disheartening but true that my family and exes conspired to steal from me and my children. I have also been repeatedly exploited by others seeking personal advancement through illusions presented to the government to harm me. This involved my last son's father, my stepbrother and brother (a PG county police officer who collaborated with a childhood friend from PG county). This friend experienced a devastating betrayal and physical abuse around seventeen, which may have influenced her career choice. It seemed that greed and power motivated everyone around me, a blatant disregard for true authority and justice that originates from a higher power, "TMH." They all acted as if they were above the law.

Despite facing numerous obstacles, including addiction and homelessness, I persevered. When others had lost hope, I found strength and clarity through faith, enabling me to recognize the truth and break free from the surrounding deception. By walking by faith, I have overcome countless challenges. Throughout this journey, "TMH" has patiently guided me to safety. Even in my instability, I held the belief that enduring each trial and completing this story would lead me away from poverty and ensure justice. I have risen above illusions, addictions, lies, and failures, learned from my past mistakes, and offered prayers for everyone, even those who doubted and wished me harm. I persevered, and I will shine.In school, I learned that cheating undermines genuine learning. Ultimately, persistence is essential; never give up. You have the right to clear your name and free your heart and mind.

To my readers, I urge you to address your issues; you are not alone. Remember that every struggle has significance. Unresolved matters, even within family, will ultimately face justice if meant to. Trust in this. Often, the question is: who remains present? Frequently, those closest inflict the deepest wounds. If you stumble, do not despair. Revisit a time of happiness and begin anew. If that fails, start removing the people, places, and things that do not serve your best interests. Distractions often arise when you are nearing a breakthrough. It is okay to falter; everything can be forgiven through prayer and change. Begin again as often as needed, but only with belief and effort. Faith without action is ineffective. Life involves a process, and healing is crucial for completing your journey. True feeling requires healing. Be honest with yourself. Enjoyment and celebration are fine, but differentiate between healthy fun and excessive indulgence used to mask pain. If you are hurting, talk about it, regardless of potential consequences. Any pain experienced may be necessary. If your situation holds truth, simply share your story; "TMH" will handle the rest. I am living proof that betrayals can become blessings. What is lost is gone; the past cannot be changed, but you have full control over your future. Even when feeling unsupported, "TMH" sees and hears everything and acknowledges every thought. Be mindful of your powerful words; ask, and you shall receive. Your angels and intuition are always with you. I am a witness to all of this, having survived numerous attempts on my life to share my story. I hope it helps many, if not all of you.

Reflecting on the past ten years and the revelations I've received while listening to the peaceful sounds of nature, I've finally pieced my story together. The trials and tribulations I faced were necessary steps on the path to my destiny, guided by "TMH." Life requires overcoming obstacles to progress, much like video games. Today, closure is often equated with ending relationships and holding onto resentment. However, I've learned that not everyone can let go easily. I don't expect others to be like me; I reciprocate energy, not necessarily thoughts. Thoughts manifest based on what you dwell on, good or bad, so retain what you need and release the rest. I have endured much and reached my limit of being ridiculed, stolen from, lied to, and manipulated. I initially considered lowering my standards to help others who have never offered me anything but now realize I need to stand firm and not return to that cycle. This current movement forward is a result of releasing it all. My perspective on desiring a life of sufficiency has shifted after reflecting on my extensive hardships. These trials have forged resilience and unwavering resolve. I refuse to lower my standards to assist those who have only offered deceit and exploitation. For too long, I have faced ridicule, theft, lies, and manipulation, yet I remained steadfast. Finally, there is hope—a testament to my perseverance.

Everything will soon make sense. I had to experience the complete narrative to grasp the lessons, blessings, and setbacks that were all part of "TMH's" plan. I possess unique abilities that grant me a different perspective. Initially, my story was confusing, and I couldn't understand the sudden animosity from so many. Was it due to my ability to expose everyone's deepest secrets? I've always been outspoken, often to my detriment. I was raised to distrust religious and spiritual practices, which were labeled as evil and used against me to conceal my gifts. Despite studying many religions, I do not discriminate. Ultimately, there is only one higher power, the same across different cultures. It is remarkable how everything connects to the same figure, yet the world is filled with hate, not because of the core message, but due to cultural traditions. I've been reconstructing my life, and the pieces are falling into place: the accidents, memory loss, harassment, and abuse. The suitors sent by my father-uncle and family to exploit, disgrace, and shame me, as if I am not already familiar with such abuse.

I don't care what's been recorded and released without my consent. I know my self-worth, and anything said or seen doesn't matter. The truth requires an argument and back and forth not a lie so I choose not to entertain the chaos and lies.

Whatever it was done in the privacy of my own space or with someone I trusted as an adult that was clearly still in adolescence mode to do such a thing out of envy, and pay back because someone chooses not to entertain the "BOO BOO". Despite attempts by family members, both known and unknown, to distance me from my loved ones who have passed, I remain resilient. I am prepared to confront any challenge, refusing to succumb to shame, fear, or guilt - these are the true demons. The only guilt I carry is that which was projected onto me, a burden I never deserved. They believed it would break me, but it only fueled my determination to expose their true faces, hidden behind the masks they wished me to wear. They are afraid of their own lives and seek to destroy mine to conceal their own truths and face fear. I will refuse their labels, but I will embrace the precious gifts TMH has given me to unmask them. I have been, and will continue to be, blessed and highly favored.

My family, bound by blood but not by loyalty, was a source of profound betrayal. I discovered a lineage of liars, murderers, and thieves who inflicted unforgettable harm upon me. Their actions included attempts to destroy me through fabricated stories, false reports, forged signatures, and the theft of my properties and identity. They manipulated my children, corrupted law enforcement, and engaged in fraudulent activities under my stolen name, even entering into a sham marriage. Inheritance was stolen and squandered, all part of a plan conceived before the night I defended myself against abuse.

My life irrevocably changed that night. My sister resented my independence, and she, along with my stepmother-aunt and others, perpetuated chaos and dysfunction to undermine me. They sought to silence me, fearing my escape from their predetermined fate. Having witnessed too much as a child, I refused to follow their path of government dependence and a poverty mindset. I was determined to break the cycle of limitations, unlike those who comfortably repeated harmful patterns instead of seeking their own truths. My choice was to rise above their influence. Their attempts to imprison me failed. Many who were part of my upbringing were not genuinely familiar with true hardship. While they pursued fleeting pleasures, I focused on survival and protecting my son. My outward appearance of being privileged was a facade instilled to mask my inner struggles. This led to misjudgments based on appearances, with those who benefited from my support later betraying me. Despite their actions, I emerged stronger, learning and moving forward. They underestimated me, unaware of my inner strength. My success only amplified their resentment, a reflection of their own unmet ambitions.

This taught me the deceptive nature of appearances and the enduring power of inner strength, sustained by divine protection. I recall a time on Sheriff Rd, reflecting on my life and the manipulations intended to make me appear unwell. The lies about STDs contrasted with the reality of multiple sexual assaults, events I had previously silenced due to feeling unheard. I have come to understand that life presents choices, and many avoid accountability. I, however, have learned to confront truth, realizing that my earlier beliefs were shaped by ingrained patterns. I believe in individual agency. Blessed to have avoided diseases, a past relationship brought a temporary infection, leading to separation and self-discovery.

This was not coincidence but a sustained effort to keep me impoverished and unhappy, a pattern of harassment ongoing since at least 2008. This mirrors experiences with past ex-husbands, highlighting a calculated plan to control me. Forced therapy and the subsequent heavy medication left me incapacitated. The psycho-therapist was complicit, if not the originator, of this scheme, stemming from my first ex-husband and family after I ended his engagement with another woman. I reported his unethical behavior to the medical board without response. My writing serves as a pursuit of justice for the orchestrated injustices aimed at driving me to despair and dependence. I refuse to regress, having learned that people rarely change their true nature. He repeatedly violated professional boundaries, exploiting my vulnerabilities disclosed in therapy, a clear breach of my rights. Having received no help, this is my recourse. The situation was a web of resentment involving numerous individuals connected to my first ex-husband. Unable to pinpoint the exact source, my strategy was to adapt and consider everyone a potential threat. As I detached myself, I began to perceive the manipulations of TMII, initially veiled by intentional illusions. Having recognized it as evil, I rejected it entirely. Growing up, excessive television viewing instilled programming, creating false beliefs. Many fictional works have roots in reality, requiring lived experience or deep understanding.

They temporarily succeeded in causing me immense distress, including suicidal thoughts, manipulation of my perceptions, relationships, and health. But TMH revealed their motives. Karma will now take its course. Life is not trivial; magic, both dark and light, exists. My false marriage to someone already wed was a trap laden with their negative intentions and voodoo. My exes and family enlisted those I once feared, aiming to eliminate me after stealing my identity, a crime reported to the police who dismissed it due to the perpetrator's connections. My family was easily swayed by their pre-existing hatred and envy. My ex-husband exploited information from my therapy sessions. He and others subjected me to countless violations, forging signatures and stealing my assets. He currently resides in my house with a mistress. Despite rumors of renting and arson, I remain detached, having grown accustomed to the abuse. I have reached a point of no return, proudly reclaiming my life and success, which cannot be taken away. They placed liabilities in my name while I struggled, but I trust TMH's greater plan. Though I may stumble, TMH, my ancestors, and angels ensure I will rise stronger. Accuracy is crucial to avoid misjudging those who were merely caught in life's lessons. There are degrees of culpability, and some will face the consequences of their actions.

They wished me dead, resulting in multiple car crashes, one causing permanent nerve damage. My mobility declined, and I often lacked basic transportation, relying on public transit and sleeping on park benches while maintaining a facade for work. I accept my role in all situations. My health deteriorated after sharing my marriage proposal, a deliberate part of their scheme, involving my sister and the psycho-therapist. My family members had ulterior motives. My sister impersonated me unsuccessfully. Aunts and cousins misused my check. My step-family resorted to theft. Their actions stemmed from a desire to maintain social standing, leading them to recruit others and ruin their lives. We all have unique paths; they chose poorly despite having advantages. My sister had stability and opportunities I lacked. I now suspect my birth date was altered, making me younger than believed, intensifying the impact of early life events. I have felt alone for a lifetime, enduring poverty and hardship, only to be resurrected by TMH. I have a story to tell and a purpose, yet face constant obstacles. Their relentless attacks prove TMH's intervention in my survival.

They underestimated the resilient child they abandoned. I have found my voice and will expose their years of evil. My mission is to share my truth, hoping for justice or at least inner peace and to help others who have endured similar experiences. Many are silenced and manipulated. I will recount everything, the good and the bad. People, including the government, have attempted to kill me for financial gain. I was unaware until revelations from deceased loved ones and TMH exposed the theft, lies, and life insurance policies taken out on me. They sought my death, but I survived. I have endured immense suffering, but I trust TMH will restore everything. Those who have passed revealed the truth of their deaths and the plots against me. Retribution will come. I pray my story reaches and helps someone. Touching one life is significant. I desire companionship but prioritize my own healing and progress. No more delays or turning back.

My sister was not alone in her attempts to harm me. My stepmother and father contributed to my mother's death for insurance money. This family requires prayer and healing. They left me in poverty, expecting my failure, believing they had cursed me from birth with black magic. Unaware of their hatred, which had nothing to do with me, I continue to uncover the truth at forty-six. I intend to address the theft and murders through ongoing research. My father's refusal to escort me at my second wedding and my aunt's suggestion to ask a harmful cousin were pivotal moments. This cousin's father had included me in his inheritance. They orchestrated the theft of my belongings and invaded my privacy to manipulate perceptions of my sanity, exploiting my trauma.

I am shifting focus from designing my book cover to publishing my story by next week. I need to devise a presentation for viewers and readers. Facing financial hardship, including garnished unemployment benefits, I reflect on the knowledge I freely shared with others. Ultimately, only TMH and self matter. No one has truly supported me except TMH, for which I am grateful. My journey of the past five years, or perhaps my entire illusory life, compels me to share my story. I question if more is required and trust in divine timing. I remain alone and safe after the latest attempt on my life. I have harmed no one, yet endured much. TMH's unseen intervention sustains me. Weary but resolute, I harbor no ill will, wishing they would move on. It is telling how quickly alliances shift when one asserts oneself. I sought only peace, but their exploitation led me to reciprocate their energy. If they cannot engage with respect, I choose detachment. I hope TMH has the final say. I have an inspection this week, and regardless of the outcome, I am ready to leave this situation for a better future.

Daily, I improve. Facing potential pawn shop visits for survival, I prioritize food. I plan to visit the food bank and hope for housing assistance. Constant harassment, phone changes, mail theft, and stalking have been exhausting. My family's continued animosity fuels my desire to leave. I walk in faith, trusting TMH's timing. Despite two months with no income, I have managed through divine guidance. Prayer and patience are my achievements.My days have been productive, completing my book cover and final edits. I will pawn items for publishing funds, sensing an imminent breakthrough. I am grateful for TMH's provision, remembering that resilience comes from focusing on the larger picture. Setbacks only strengthen my resolve.I prefer order, and TMH's disruptions are frustrating. Little fazes me now. Mother's Day holds little significance, as my children have always been my greatest gifts. Life is about learning and moving forward, even if it means letting go of loved ones who were manipulated into deception. I must maintain distance while continuing to love and pray for them. My well-being comes first.I now view everyone differently, aware of their self-serving actions

Memorial Day brings reflection on loved ones both present and passed. As my story nears its end, I uncover more hidden truths. I realize that anyone from my past has been shut out because my life was manipulated and driven by greed – which is absurd. If the situation were reversed, I'd choose loyalty over anything, since money ultimately holds no enduring value.Loyalty from a friend is far more valuable than money. Money is fleeting and meant to be shared, not hoarded. Unfortunately, this perspective is often absent in the minds of those around me. Co-workers and F.A.N.S. alike have consistently attempted to undermine my destiny, as ordained by TMH. While they may have temporarily stolen what was meant for me, they should prepare to witness TMH's divine intervention. Everything will be restored in due time.They tried to poison me on my last encounter with another one of their minions to try to shut me down and up from telling the truth. All that have betrayed me will have to answer TMH's wrath and that has nothing to do with me. On my last encounter, I decided to go and seek what my delays were and evaluate the waters to draw out the snakes remaining in my life to change the wheel of destiny. Their goal was to stop, kill, or destroy what TMH has in store for my journey. Despite what appears to be a lack of awareness, I have consistently received blessings, obstacles, and protection, regardless of the challenges and schemes that have come my way. The statement "NO," as declared by TMH, stands, and I advise those involved to cease their actions before they are forced to stop. My former colleagues engaged in fraudulent activities by utilizing forged signatures and establishing fictitious accounts to engage in theft, espionage, and defamation attempts against me. Their ongoing efforts aim to dismantle everything I have built over decades of arduous work and perseverance, which have led me to my current position in life..I have continuously overcome all obstacles in my path. This perseverance is for the sake of others who are destined for destruction. Reality and karma are undeniable forces; karma never fails to reach its target. TMH is infallible in his judgment. If you have been judged, be prepared to account for all your actions. They attempted to poison me to manipulate my sleep and prayer. Swift changes occur without any misjudgment upon me, only upon those who wished and projected ill will. The landlord continues to instill fear and doubt, which is unsuccessful. I haven't forgotten the showerhead incident when I moved in. She claimed ignorance about the water damage in my ceiling before I moved in, despite the neighbor confirming the entire building has this issue. These leaks were known beforehand. They believe I care about their secret surveillance between my last residence and here with hidden cameras. I've decided not to allow anyone in my house for any reason unless absolutely necessary. I simply request that they give me the money they made from using my likeness and thank them for the free advertising. They have exploited and violated me for as long as I can remember. My neighbors have listened through the vents and used constant scare tactics that have never worked. From the day my sister was contacted by my landlord shortly after moving in, they have allowed her to pay another minion to add to the chaos and stress me out. It has never worked out the way they imagined; I have too much on my plate to even entertain their "boogeyman."

The individuals, including my fake ex-husband, who were paid to disrupt my life wasted my time, money, and peace for another's benefit. While they may blame the pandemic, it did not impact any policies or procedures in my life. This was all under the table and cooperation of crooked officials not all but the crooked ones without the law. Not anything mentioned in this story could have even been done without the help of the law, spiritual law that is what made it so. While I know that not all laws are corrupt and not all people are bad, I'm choosing to play it safe and stay alone. Jealousy and greed have killed teamwork and trust. People don't want to work together, they just want to take what I have. I've closed myself off to relationships because love doesn't seem to exist anymore. Many individuals, motivated by greed and a lack of work ethic, have attempted to exploit my efforts and ideas. These people, including F.A.N.S., family members, and former partners, have tried to attain positions they are not qualified for and maintain unearned reputations. I have chosen a different path, and I will not revisit any relationships with those who exhibit negativity, deceit, or violence. I hope those who have caused harm will face the consequences of their actions and be eternally punished. My trust lies in a higher power, who provides for me and guides my path. This higher power sees and hears all, and those who attempt to deceive or harm others will ultimately be exposed.

Revelation 14" There before the lamb, the 144,000 who had his name and his father's name written of their forehead and I heard a voice from heaven like the roar of many waters and like the vow or many waters and of thunder the voice heard was like the sound of harpist playing on harps, and singing a new song before the thorn and the four living creatures and before elders. No one could learn the song except 144,000 who had redeemed from the earth. It is who defined themselves as women; they are virgins. It is those who follow the lamb wherever he goes. These have been redeemed from humanity as first fruits of TMH and the lamb, and their mouth no lie was found, for she is blameless."

All that I have written can be verified through the courts and other resources. Some information has been destroyed or misplaced, but that doesn't matter when you have True Memory Help (TMH). I hope that the future will uncover the truths that have been hidden for so long. I hope my story can point in the right direction, reveal the truth, and expose those involved.As I approach the end of my journey, I pray for swift justice for all involved. Recently, I uncovered a disturbing truth about a psychotherapist I was involved with in 2015. He led me to believe he was separated from his wife, who was a stalker. In reality, he was still married and had plans to entrap me. When his plans failed, he used those close to me to destroy my life. This experience reinforces my reluctance to share my personal problems, as those I confide in often use my vulnerabilities against me.Those who have sworn oaths seem to be withholding their promises. When I discovered his actions, I left him immediately. Before I left, he paid a practitioner to destroy everything I had built. I had confided my deepest secrets in him, secrets that my family had been desperately trying to uncover for years. He exposed my enemies and rallied them against me; they were too weak to face me as an adult and were trying to protect their secrets, deceit, and betrayals from being revealed. They sought to keep my name from being cleared once and for all. I have endured lies and deception throughout my life, but I have too much to be thankful for to give up on life and dreams, as those who wished ill of me have done. I have never given up and never willI have adapted and persevered through all of life's challenges, choosing to stand, move forward, and pray for guidance. If my path is unclear, I reassess and adjust until I find the right direction. By overcoming doubt, guilt, and negativity, I am nearing a breakthrough. I am aware that some still seek to hinder my progress and silence my truth, but I trust that a higher power is at work, removing obstacles and guiding me toward greatness. I have chosen isolation to avoid distractions and delays, hoping to fall off the radar and prevent further detours in my life. I am determined to stay focused and avoid the negative influences that have hindered me in the past.

The world is a cruel place, and TMH is displeased. Why do people insist on invading my peace and privacy when I'm not bothering anyone? Someone has placed a listening or monitoring device in my home to spy on me, simply because I exposed and removed the listening devices from my phone. I needed the money from selling my phone to buy necessities, and I knew they were using it to spy on me as I no longer have the possession of any old phones. I will not tolerate being monitored and have removed anything that could be used to listen to or watch me including televisions and clocks. I've subscribed to off-brand companies for years, contrary to popular belief. People often create personas based on material possessions and brands, but in my world, names don't matter. I haven't always been successful; my journey has been filled with difficulties that taught me how to adapt. I've had to juggle ups and downs, subject to change at any moment, so I've learned to adjust to any situation. Despite attempts to portray me as a victim, I have emerged as a survivor. My strength comes not from others, but from the grace of TMH. While I may not have reached my desired goals, I remain hopeful, grateful, and open to change. I sense that change is coming; the demanding work must eventually cease. It's disheartening to discover how many have conspired against me for financial gain. We all worship a higher power, regardless of the name. Religion was absent in my early years; I attended Catholic school due to my grandparents' influence. Later, my mother and a deacon briefly introduced me to the Baptist faith. I explored Islam/ Muslim beliefs through relationships with my former partners, and then briefly experienced Pentecostal and AME faiths during my second marriage. I've explored and appreciated many religions, including Hinduism and Buddhism. Ultimately, I found they all convey the same message with varying beliefs—it's about personal preference. These preferences are based on beliefs, not religion; religion remains constant while beliefs differ.

Because of this, I chose not to adhere to a specific religion and instead embraced both spirituality and religion without discrimination, appreciating all faiths. My understanding comes from self-directed learning and personal reflection, not from indoctrination.I believe in praising a higher power in any religion and following its teachings, as there is only one supreme being I respect in beliefs but it's about what makes you comfortable, who cares what others think.. Due to the failures of earthly justice and laws, I choose to place my faith in the universe, without discrimination or specific beliefs. I follow TMH, which can be explained on its own. Others may judge me, but their hate doesn't matter. In the end, their beliefs and praises are no different from mine. We all have free will and can agree to disagree. Gang stalking and other negativity will not alter my path; they will only strengthen my faith as TMH continues to bless me. Through praise, faith, and flowing with life, I maintain my beliefs.I choose to forge my own path, as I need no one to feel complete. Many oppose me for various reasons, hoping to drive me to insanity and lock me away. This would allow them to assume my identity and steal my success. They question why I strive to be someone I supposedly hate, yet I excel based on the challenges I've been given. They would like to perceive me as a quieter Budda quote "knowing when it is enough is not quitting" in fact it is common sense you can lead but you cannot force and all that is meant no matter how many times someone may attempt to destroy it. Don't be deceived, it can only be delayed and detoured upon your discretion that is free will.

When my failure wasn't an option, they sought to destroy everything I built and steal my accomplishments. They spread lies to make themselves appear as me, the one they label as "evil." It's all nonsensical. I never expected to come this far and achieve so much. My unexpected success has caused them to unite against me, unaware that my support surpasses any belief or authority man made. I will continue to be blessed and highly favored. While others may choose hate, I choose faith, hope, and love. Some may try to deceive and destroy, believing themselves superior, but they will ultimately fail. Their attempts to provoke me will be unsuccessful. Despite their efforts to disrupt my life by interfering with my internet and mail, I remain informed and will continue to share my story as instructed. I will not be deterred and will continue to protect myself, guided by signs from the universe and my faith. My fate and destiny are clear, and I move forward on the correct path with confidence and unwavering focus on success.

They have begun to send in their minions as I complete my final edit. My landlord was sent to gather information, so I acted as usual, knowing her true purpose. Like others before, she feigned concern while attempting to access my accounts. I changed all my passwords and disabled my Wi-Fi before her arrival. She played her expected role, assuming she had the correct user, and gave a performance of despair, complete with tears.The same people who have been trying to destroy me are also one who even stated the same as my sister about sending the police for welfare checks . And she also slipped and said a few other things like who was going to play a part in my movie for my story being seeking information and spying to let me know they all were working together, and she was sent into a spy. I believe TMH taught me best when he said if you are silent long enough, they will tell on themselves.

Although my back has been hurting, I feigned additional pain and cried to buy myself more time - a tactic I've been using successfully throughout this ordeal. I even managed to get a meal out of it. I let her know that I was aware of her intentions; she'll undoubtedly report back to the others that I plan to finish the final draft tonight and publish it by tomorrow. She probably thinks she can check in on me every day and disrupt my progress so she can inform her co-conspirators. This isn't a friendship; she was only allowed in because they needed to bleed the radiators. People should really keep track of their lies, since they tend to incriminate themselves.. I am so ready to go, and they are for sure scared now trying to end me in any way and I fear no man TMH will not do any harm to me. I also noticed she took my keys to my house they can try it if they wish only if they knew what I knew they would have a seat "This too shall pass" I know they are for sure they are scared trying to save themselves by finding any way possible to sabotage or prevent me telling my story only more things done the more is revealed and remembered hoping I don't reveal it all especially the most recent of how discovered during the last gathering that my family has been marrying immigrants for money and possibly unalived someone and tried to frame me. They think I don't know as said before should have stopped poking the bear. I was hibernating and now I am awake. I want to know where they ever taught you should not throw stones when you live in a glass house be quiet and never go against anyone now, I love all but it's time to take your bow and exit stage left while you they are still able to fall upon knees pray forgiveness for your battle is no longer mines it belongs to TMH.

I remain faithful and hopeful despite the tiresome replays and obstacles in my life. Although everything I've learned has been extremely trying, things are slowly clearing up. I have so much going on in my life right now, but I trust that TMH will show up on time. My life has been a crazy jigsaw puzzle.I'm yearning for resolution. This journey has been arduous, and I refuse to endure another day of turmoil. I've resorted to pawning my belongings while malevolent forces close in. The landlord is scheming to evict me, despite the fact that the ceiling was damaged before I moved in (I have emails as proof), and the kitchen sink faucet needs replacing. I've applied for assistance, which led me to pawn valuables to afford food. I'm reluctant to leave my home, fearing they'll intrude and rummage through my possessions. My privacy is constantly violated; I can't even find solace in meditation or a bath. It's uncomfortable here, but I must trust in divine timing and wait for help to arrive.

I miss working, if only to afford a car and escape this community. My phone and laptop accounts are persistently hacked, forcing me to buy new phones, switch internet providers, and change usernames and passwords daily. They wanted me to give up out of fear, but they don't understand that I've been through this many times before. My faith does not contain fear; my heart and soul are devoted to a higher power. Peace, respect, and distance from these people and these places is all I desire. Their attempts to bring me down will fail; I've been saved too many times and have been in this situation too many times. I'm unaffected by their scare tactics; I've been here before—jobless, nearly homeless, and without end.

I am attempting to isolate myself and I am grateful to them because their past actions have only made me stronger and wiser. I've endured abuse, neglect, and rejection my whole life; one more day won't kill me. My fate rests with a higher power. Everyone has a path in life - choose one. If you fall, keep going. TMH forgives, so you can correct your mistakes. The problem is, people have become accustomed to using others instead of working hard to achieve their goals. Instead of putting energy into trying to intercept and destroy others, take that energy and put it into yourself and shine. It's about greed, and many expected me to crumble and fall. They didn't expect me to stand and keep going through faith and prayer. I say try it and see the sun instead of hiding in the darkness with secrets. Considering starting a new story due to concerns about plagiarism and sabotage, which I believe involves my ex-partner and a former coworker using blueprints from my past work. This follows a disturbing pattern over the last year, including alleged poisoning, identity theft, hacking, digital signature theft, and emotional distress. An individual I was interested in may also be involved, possibly in energy harvesting. As a result, I need to distance myself from everyone until their trustworthiness is proven and will no longer tolerate gaslighting or mind games. Regarding a recent interaction, my silence is not an invitation to manipulate me. I have healed and am not influenced by past dynamics. I ended contact after a concerning encounter where boundaries were disregarded. Although initially willing to offer support as a friend, persistent manipulative behavior and lack of accountability have ended that possibility. This situation reflects a broader issue I see in the world: an overemphasis on sex and sexuality rather than personal and societal growth. I value genuine connection, southern hospitality (even if not sincere), and respectful behavior.

I am not looking for casual encounters but a genuine, supportive partner. My priorities have shifted to my own happiness, and I will recognize those who have not been true friends. Having overcome significant challenges, I am focused on the future. Attempts to distract and harm me, potentially involving energy manipulation, have also occurred, possibly orchestrated by family members seeking to undermine my self-esteem. These attempts at sabotage have been relentless, even involving people from my own neighborhood.Consequently, I am accepting solitude for now, as my communication channels have been compromised. The pursuit of wealth and power has led many to betrayal and deceit. While these individuals prioritize personal gain, their actions are unsustainable and will ultimately fail. Despite their manipulations, their true intentions are known, and their defeat is inevitable through divine intervention.

I am exhausted by the ongoing hacking and harassment, despite reporting it to authorities who have dismissed my concerns due to lack of evidence. Attempts to delete my work online have increased my frustration and vulnerability. I have been a target of gang stalking and continuous violations aimed at silencing me. My pleas for help to reveal the truth have been answered by divine protection. I am witnessing negative influences being removed and trust that justice will prevail. My landlord's helpful demeanor appears to be a facade, as I believe many are conspiring against me. I am nearing a breaking point.

The confirmation of widespread conspiracy against me, involving multiple families, friends, and associates, to steal from me physically and energetically will not succeed in causing mental distress, as I have overcome numerous obstacles. Attempts to harm, institutionalize, and exploit me have been met with my resistance, and such behavior will no longer be tolerated. I believe divine justice will soon bring this to an end, as much has been revealed. The person I was interested in was using me. Policies used against me have been traced back to various individuals, including a former roommate, contributing to the theft of my assets. The individuals involved are from diverse backgrounds and have united to undermine my progress. I believe divine intervention is at work to restore justice for myself and the world. I am hopeful for the end of this journey and the realization of my dreams.

Assumptions were made about me, and my situation was exploited. My true nature was deliberately concealed, allowing their manipulations to continue. With my story finalized and the truth revealed, I am ready to move forward. Sharing my experiences and hidden truths will help others who may feel alone, as I once did. My trials have taught me that I am not alone and that encouragement is vital.

Through faith, I have learned that anything is possible, and obstacles can be overcome with belief. My journey has been challenging, but I have persevered. Like in the poem "Footprints," when I was struggling, I was carried and guided. Divine love has always been present, offering support and opening doors to guidance from loved ones.

Footprints

One night I dreamed a dream

As I was walking along the beach with TMH

Across the dark sky flashed scenes from my life

For each scene, I noticed two sets of footprints in the sand

One belonging to me and one to TMH

After the last scene of my life flashed before me,

I looked back at the footprints in the sand.

I noticed that at many times along the path of my life,

Especially at the very lowest and saddest times,

There was only one set of footprints

This troubled me, so I asked the TMH about it

"You said once I decided to follow you,

You'd walk with me all the way

But I noticed that during the saddest and most troublesome

times of my life, there was one

Set of footprints. I don't understand why when

I needed you most, you would leave me

He whispered "My precious child, I love you and never will

Leave you. Never during your trials and tests

When you saw truly one set of footprints

It was then that I carried you"

Recently, I've been seeing angel numbers, which I believe are significant signs offering guidance. This has reassured me as I work to finish my conclusion by the end of June 2024. I am determined to complete this, hoping it will bring relief from my current financial struggles. I feel a sense of peace as things become clearer, with confirmations that I attribute to TMH. I now understand who has opposed and harmed me, though one disappointing aspect remains unclear. My full story is extensive, revealed to me gradually as needed. This understanding helps me avoid past mistakes and prepare for the future.

The contrast between being celebrated on Father's Day and ignored on Mother's Day highlights inconsistencies in my treatment. These experiences have shown me who my true allies and enemies are, and I will act accordingly. I am eager to move forward, especially since neighbors who previously seemed to work against me are now feigning concern. I prefer to keep to myself, aware that TMH has already revealed their true intentions. I also seem to attract people struggling with alcohol, which appears to be a recurring theme in my journey, potentially as a trigger. I am focused on identifying and addressing important issues, drawing strength from recent lessons, some of which required revisiting for better understanding. I am grateful for all my experiences, both positive and negative, as they demonstrate TMH's unwavering love and have led me to a point of no return.

Yesterday, an encounter reminded me that I am often underestimated. A meeting with a former associate at the Wharf took an unexpected turn when I realized I was being watched. The person observing me was the sister of one of my son's father's associates, someone who had previously offered support but was clearly monitoring me and reporting back to them. TMH also revealed the true nature of another individual involved with my son's father and a group intending me harm. They underestimated me, believing they were deceiving me. These individuals were in my life for a reason, and TMH used them to assist me unknowingly. Understanding the situation, I gracefully distanced myself. This taught me the importance of discernment and allowing people's true nature to be revealed.

I am aware of negative influences but trust in the protection of secret knowledge given by TMH. I will continue to share my story carefully, revealing only my struggles for now. As one chapter closes and another begins, hidden truths will emerge. I am documenting those who have helped or harmed me, including my landlord, neighbor, and associates, who are unaware of my knowledge of their actions. Their sudden pretense of concern will be met with a plan that will surprise them. I will attribute my knowledge to faith and answered prayers. Despite efforts to stop me, my story is already becoming known, and it is time for its full release.

Hollow Love

My heart and soul are in despair, empty and alone.

I feel lost and abandoned, as if there's no hope left.

The pursuit of eternal happiness to conquer loneliness has left me feeling empty. My mind is blank, my heart is hollow, and my soul is vacant.

He told me not to be shy or stray from my true feelings. They may be hidden, but they are not unseen — just blinded to myself. As I sit still, waiting for Him to hear my cry and respond.

The love you give yourself is the best love, because even though you feel empty inside, it can be seen by everyone around you.

I am unsure if it is good or bad to feel empty. I pray for guidance and support. However, I also see the good in emptiness, as I discover my true self and worth.

My heart is full of love, despite all the hate against me.

It only strengthens me and allows me to share my love with others.

Their hearts are not empty; they are simply waiting to be filled with love.

My love is not empty; it is overflowing and ready to be shared.

The absence of love was merely a figment of the imagination.

Grateful for divine guidance and strength, I face persistent life challenges that feel like an endless, joyless cycle despite my prayers. Unhappiness from past experiences continues to affect me, including recent financial burdens caused by others. My desire is for self-sufficient happiness, as I've known only hurt and deceit, resolving now to distrust superficial appearances and seek justice.Completing my book sequel hasn't altered my circumstances. Despite attempts at isolation, my connections remain. Amidst ongoing hot weather, I've focused on publishing.

Life feels monotonous with its routine of work and prayer, lacking amusement and true companionship. Though financially strained and physically alone this summer, I won't complain. Hesitation kept me from recent opportunities that strayed from my plans. Debt collectors persist despite my writing. My current difficulties include overdue bills, inability to rent a car, and lack of funds and privacy. The uncertain future weighs heavily on me as I pray for divine intervention. I maintain faith in my progress and will continue writing to share my story. I understand that releasing negativity will bring clarity, leading to simultaneous improvement and worsening of my situation. Growth requires struggle. Others' actions no longer affect me; they've done their worst. Despite my efforts, I feel stuck while those who wronged me face no consequences, leaving me to depend on divine justice. The truth about my family's harmful actions has emerged: using their government connections, my parents exploited me for personal gain, causing enduring hardship. They manipulated my life, leading to poverty despite my hard work and eventual success, which was then taken away. Now awake, I'm reclaiming control, surrendering to a Higher Power to fight for me and restore what was lost, patiently awaiting His decision.

Internet attacks previously disrupted my writing, but I now manage them better. My family and associates remain critical and hostile, blaming me for their problems. Their negativity is perplexing. Their hateful actions—projections, cover-ups of serious crimes, and attempts to harm me—reveal their true nature despite their efforts to appear otherwise. I observe, trusting that their actions will have consequences, as divine justice prevails. Publishing my book today brings relief, though I'm mindful of potential errors, but not of the truth. They tried to silence and shame me, but I've risen above their attempts. I will continue my spiritual practices, trusting in divine timing. An interview is scheduled for tomorrow morning, followed by printing my book cover at the library. The book will be available soon, and I plan extensive promotion.

This project aims to offer understanding of my experiences and break down barriers to open communication. I am resuming my efforts to speak out against betrayal and deceit from those who are harmful. Silence and excuses for others' behavior will cease. A new phone symbolizes positive change as I begin to recover what was unjustly taken from me. My extended family and past partners, themselves dishonest, are aligned against me. They can have what remains of those who appear successful, as they are merely benefiting from what is rightfully mine. I recognize their dependency and my past choices in relationships, where I consistently ended up with less despite my contributions. My experiences in marriage and relationships taught me the risks of financial control by untrustworthy partners, leading to significant loss upon their departure.

I also love to shop, not just for clothes but for whatever I like. Thankfully, God provides for my needs, and I save for what I want. Yes, I used to be very stylish, but when you live in a family that steals and sells everything, as well as constantly moves residences, you learn not to get attached to anything. I've never been materialistic; I used to just charge it to the game and assumed whoever took it may have needed it more. I consider it a gift, as I know it will be returned, maybe not in the same way, but in another form that TMH sees fit.

The landlord believes they can manipulate and intimidate me, but I am no longer afraid. I know that TMH will intervene and that things will not go as planned. To protect my work from hacking and deception, I took control by publishing my e-book on Amazon today, even if it is unfinished. I refuse to let another book be stolen or lost. They may have silenced me temporarily, but destiny dictates that this time, my work will last forever. This is my testimony; we all have our own. No one can rewrite or create what you went through; they may speak it, but only you can feel it and tell it from your heart and soul. Anyone can plagiarize, just like in school you can copy off someone's paper, but if a question is asked, will you be able to answer it?

I will continue to circulate more copies tomorrow, both online and in person. Today, I went to the library and printed more advertisements for tomorrow's distribution. I also reserved a study room at the library for quiet and free internet access.I'm still living off the land, and it's free, which helps as I try to conserve mobile data on my phone. Things are looking up, and I feel less isolated and caged now that my book has been released. It's crazy, but I'd really like to see the expressions on the faces of those who expected me to fail and the haters who supported them. I know not everyone will agree with my book, but it doesn't matter as long as TMH supports me the rest will follow.

My landlord attempted to provoke me today, but I stood my ground and refused to be manipulated. I'm done with betrayal, and sadness has been replaced by love and fighting spirit from TMH. Releasing my book was a bit nerve-wracking, but I had to question my fears. This is simply who I am; people can take it or leave it. Their opinions no longer affect me. With the support of my angels and guidance from TMH, I will continue to write and move forward.

The past two days have been quite interesting. As I've been advertising and networking my book, I've encountered many people who are interested in my story more than expected. I need to start planning book signings with local stores, but I'm taking it one step at a time. I have faith in my leap and understand that it all takes time - I'm ready and patiently waiting. It's ironic how people can unknowingly help you, even when they're focused on their own agendas. My stepmother constantly preached patience, and ironically, her words ignited my meditation practice. Our adversaries can inadvertently provide the keys to our success, even while trying to bring us down.My father advised against applying for social security benefits due to my poor health. I followed his advice, proving that I had been listening all along. The answers were always present; I just hadn't been aware enough to recognize them. Life has taught me to make the best of any situation, even when it's initially difficult. My vision is now clear, and the sweetness is evident.The answer lies in our thoughts. If you believe something is a figment of your imagination, it will manifest as such. Do we truly need to eat, or is it merely a programmed behavior? We were taught to eat three meals a day, but who says we have to follow those rules? As we grow, we can change our patterns and reprogram our minds to align with our happiness, rather than adhering to routines.Organization is necessary, but things don't always go according to plan. When things don't go our way, we get criticized because it's expected. Perhaps we should just go with the flow of life and not stress about things that are beyond our control.

With five months left in the year, life is becoming more balanced. Recent events include reconnecting with an old friend and attending a job interview with high hopes. Possessions are being cleared out, with a TV already sold and the rest slated for donation or online sale to create space for new experiences. Solitude, while sometimes lonely, is valued for the peace and clarity it brings, a necessary contrast to stagnant or unsupportive relationships. The focus is firmly on the future, letting go of the past and actively removing anything hindering personal growth.The job interview felt adequate, a reminder of the importance of attention to detail after a period away from work. Alone time is precious, fostering a focus on justice and truth in a flawed world. A greater understanding of people is developing, looking beyond superficial appearances. While enjoying outings, a preference exists for less crowded, more remote locations. The pursuit of deeper truths and a refusal to accept things at face value are central to this forward movement. Despite current comfort, anticipation for brighter times and future plans remains strong, suggesting a period of calm before significant change. A three-day limit is now in place for online item sales before donation. The priority is to shed the old and welcome the new.

The stress of promoting the book has subsided, replaced by the ease of Independence Day. This recent respite was welcome, though anticipation for the book's final outcome is growing impatient. While eager for completion, the present situation and the necessary wait are accepted. Despite current stress and heartache, maintaining a positive attitude is a struggle, with peace and closure deeply desired. The loss of possessions is less significant than concerns about reputation and the feeling that hard work has been undervalued. A lifelong sense of being an outsider with a unique path is acknowledged, trusting in a larger plan despite current temporary difficulties that will lead to a distinct future.

The pain endured has been challenging yet ultimately beneficial, fostering strength. Despite occasional urges to surrender and weep, perseverance is recognized as the only path forward. Acknowledging imperfection, breaks are taken as needed, and finances are managed carefully. Hope for a brighter future is maintained through prayer, with the understanding that change is imminent – a calm before the storm. For now, the present peace is cherished, with prayers for more. Exhaustion stems from a cycle of constant restarts and recurring challenges. Despite diligent efforts to rebuild, there's a feeling of being trapped in the same starting point. Life has become a monotonous cycle of work devoid of joy. While material possessions, even the pawned bag that funded the first book, are replaceable, patience is tested. Prayer and self-reassurance are necessary to stay grounded and trust the process. With summer ending and another year nearing its close, the mid-year mark has passed with no change in circumstances.

Weariness comes from persistent drama and numerous attempts at sabotage. Despite adhering to TMH's guidance, there is no fear, only reverence for TMH, who oversees all. Frankly, the entire situation has become tedious. Success has been hard-earned, overcoming many obstacles independently. Others have wrongly perceived this success and tried to undermine it through slander, financial manipulation, and even malicious intent. Defeat has been refused. These individuals require healing and forgiveness through prayer. Exhaustion is overwhelming, and the need for rest is critical, yet escaping this perilous situation makes it nearly impossible. Maintaining composure is increasingly difficult, patience is waning, and a breaking point feels near. Despite not causing harm to anyone, constant attempts to hack systems persist, evidenced by verification codes. This immaturity must cease; individuals need to mature and accept responsibility for their actions. Attempts to destroy will not improve their lives; true healing and self-confrontation will provide the answers they seek. Genuine healing necessitates introspection and action; stagnation will persist otherwise. Self-love and acceptance are paramount. Personal flaws must be identified and addressed honestly, not concealed. Temporary solutions only mask underlying problems; true resolution requires addressing the root causes. Focus should be on personal growth, not hindering the progress of others.

The Facebook page was temporarily deactivated again to minimize distractions and prioritize work. Initially created solely for book promotion, renewed contact with a former associate led to drama when old acquaintances and family mistakenly believed a non-existent past relationship would be rekindled. Conversations resumed briefly last summer but quickly ended. It soon became apparent that his intentions were opportunistic and non-committal. He attempted to re-enter life, likely to exploit success or undermine achievements. It was discovered that he was also trying to create a harmful connection and had been sent by family with harmful intentions. His behavior suggested he was either another stalker or handler. Engagement was refused. His attempts at seduction through projected desperation were dismissed. It was clarified that the store visit was solely to inquire about posting a flyer, with no interest in his advances or claims of management. Misrepresenting oneself to appear important is unimpressive. Financial independence is maintained, and the affairs of others are irrelevant. Exploitation will no longer be tolerated, especially knowing his collaboration with adversaries. This was yet another act of cowardice. If a past connection did not succeed initially, it was not meant to be and ended for a reason. Revisiting it beyond a casual friendship or conversation is unnecessary. Past betrayal indicates future betrayal.

My book and accounts keep getting hacked, and I'm not seeing any sales. I don't have the funds to promote my book effectively without a job. I have one last job interview next week. I've already claimed the blessings and opportunities that TMH has lined up for me. I know TMH will intervene and elevate me, but until then, I'm hopeful for improvements soon. I need basic necessities and pray for a quick resolution. Despite ongoing harassment and attempts to harm me, I trust that TMH will provide. I'm tired of the court delays and the attempts to frame me with

STDs or worse. They even tried to steal my story, "BOO BOO," which I wrote based on my own experiences. Three stolen books preceded the one filled with lies, and they served as a catalyst for my determination. Rather than driving me to insanity and alienating loved ones, the trials and tribulations fueled my resolve. They inadvertently pushed me to work harder, unveiling the truth and clearing my name amidst the deceit.I am grateful for the strength I have found to recognize my self-worth and prioritize my own well-being. While some may persist in spreading falsehoods and negativity, they cannot alter my destiny or take away my accomplishments; this is an unwavering universal truth. I refuse to participate in their games anymore. The past is behind me, and I will no longer turn a blind eye to harmful behavior. I welcome friendships, but I will not tolerate those who only seek lust, steal my time and energy, or attempt to blame me for their mistakes. This is a deliberate and malicious plan.

The father of my youngest son contracted an STD from his stepdaughter, who may also be sleeping with his cousin or the mother of his other child, as at least one of them is pregnant by him. This situation involves his extended family, and all I can do is pray for them. Furthermore, there's a question of which man – my son's father or my husband – is involved with these individuals who seem to be part of a misogynistic group. Considering everything, these events now make sense to me, especially the fact that they had a child together. They are fraudulently claiming my son on their taxes to obtain benefits and are attempting to frame me. Their efforts will fail because I am celibate and not in any relationships. My focus is on rebuilding my life and uncovering my hidden and stolen identity. My investigation has revealed significant concealed information that I am determined to expose. My silence has ended, as detailed in my first book, and this is a continuation due to others stealing my work. They cannot comprehend my life experiences, including incarceration, psychiatric hospitalizations, homelessness, and the grief of losing my children through their brainwashing and false adoptions. Their sheltered lives prevent them from understanding my hardships. This is not arrogance but truth. Extensive research can reveal the truth, so their lies are unnecessary. My experiences have been profoundly difficult, and I speak from a place of deep pain. While I don't seek pity, I desperately desire justice and peace. I understand this will take time, but I long for peace throughout this process, as these individuals have caused me ongoing distress.

I confronted the associate who was stalking, lying, accusing, and trying to set me up. He feigned innocence and pretended he wasn't involved in the situation, but TMH revealed his true intentions. He then tried to raise his voice and claim it was his cookies, but I laughed and showed him the door. I've worked too hard to endure any more unnecessary drama, and this isn't the place for it. I attempted to extend friendship, but it was not reciprocated. Arrogance often masks a deeper insecurity, and I refuse to engage with it. My family has taken something that belongs to me - my book and the royalties it has earned. Despite this injustice, I remain at peace. I trust in a higher power; I believe that I will continue to be provided for, and that everything that is rightfully mine will be returned to me.

The landlord is using deceitful tactics, including misleading letters and manipulative three-way calls, to intrude into my private life and gather information about me, specifically regarding CC's email correspondence, to share with others. This is despite my clear statement that this information is private and for my worker only. I will not be manipulated or forced into unwanted relationships. This pattern of behavior is familiar, and I am prepared regardless of any recordings or notes taken. I have recently discovered that numerous individuals are colluding against me. I am also writing to report the imminent collapse of my ceiling, a repair already known to the housing specialist and detailed in a previous email. To prevent further damage, I am using a dehumidifier, which requires frequent emptying, and running the air conditioner constantly.

The housing specialist is being dishonest by feigning ignorance of this situation, mirroring the behavior of others following a disingenuous inspection in May 2024 where I was given 28 days to make repairs. I should not have to request payment for these known and required repairs.

Furthermore, it has been recently discovered that DCHA and DHS have compromised DCHA by diverting rental payments to themselves in collusion with landlords and a DHS worker with past connections, orchestrated by my family and the government. This appears to be a large conspiracy targeting me for decades, recruiting others in the process. Despite multiple attempts to contact the inspector, I have received no response. I have attached my email and photographic evidence of the urgent need for ceiling repair and request that this matter be reopened with a different inspector. Immediate action is needed to address this safety hazard. My landlord and others are colluding to evict me through intimidation and threats, but I am aware of my rights and will defend myself, having provided evidence of their illegal actions to access my private information and conceal their wrongdoings.Regarding TMH matters, I have been completely honest and believe in the possibility of success according to His plan. I am hopeful the men I met at the park will contact me, though I am unsure if they purchased my book. Managing electronics while dealing with my current situation is challenging, but I will continue promoting my book with limited resources.

Despite desiring change, I need faith and patience as I depend on TMH and live off the land. Some individuals want me to revert to past behaviors. My priority is basic necessities like shelter and food. I wish to relocate but lack transportation funds and continue to pray for a vehicle, understanding there may be a reason for this. Some have expressed ill will towards my travels. Thank TMH for protecting me and revealing their plots. I pray someone will understand my story.

There is a great deal happening without my knowledge, including the fact that my last son's father has been involved with his stepdaughter (also his second and first cousin, a minor), with her mother's awareness and her subsequent pregnancy by him at sixteen. This includes a hidden birth and possible illegal adoption of our son for financial gain and to conceal incest, confused sexuality, drugs, rituals, identity theft, and fraud. I demand my son back and want no further involvement in their actions and diseases. They also stole my identity to access money, open bank accounts, cover up incest, and falsely claim my death for their benefit. They should tell the truth instead of keeping it a secret. His mother's behavior stems from her own difficult past. There was a group effort to have me evicted for revealing too much truth, fueled by his drunkenness, cocaine use, and lust, which she used against him. We separated when our son was two, and he kicked me out after his stepdaughter became pregnant and had an abortion, which I exposed. They conspired against our relationship through what seems like black magic, influenced by his other children's mother. I could not reconcile with such behavior. While I forgive him, our relationship is over. He falsely accused me of infidelity with a friend, which occurred years later after he offered support, and our relationship eventually ended. He manipulated my emotions, lied to future partners, and had affairs with my family. He has also had inappropriate relationships within his own family. I have moved on from the past.However, I'm still struggling to maintain my sense of self amidst the ongoing conspiracy against me by numerous individuals, both past and present majority recruited by him.My parents colluded with my exes and sibling to destroy my life. They shared my personal information, enabling them to file child support, false adoptions, and insurance policies. They hoped these actions would lead to my demise, allowing them to steal and keep my possessions, acquire luxury cars, and engage in sex rituals and spell work. I pray they lose everything they gained in the same way they obtained it.

Having processed past hurts and external projections, I am now embracing a future filled with loyalty, laughter, joy, travel, and genuine love. Free from past falsehoods and illusions, I have deliberately sought closure to ensure a fresh start. Those who have wronged me have had their opportunities and forfeited them; there will be no second chances. My focus now lies ahead, following my own guidance.Despite being surrounded by dishonest individuals, I trust in a higher judgment. The betrayal of my children, including theft and forgery by one, has been deeply painful, but I am resolved to leave this behind. I no longer dwell on the actions of those who seek to harm me through malicious gossip, rituals, and illegal acts for their own gain. If things are meant to be resolved, they will. I seek a new life, untouched by those who try to profit from my potential demise through deceit and corruption. I am weary of these ongoing battles. Those I once considered family have repeatedly betrayed my trust. Their attempts at control and manipulation no longer hold power over me. They have stolen from me, inflicted immense suffering, and even contributed to the loss of loved ones. My survival and success are a testament to my own resilience and determination, not their nonexistent support. Despite their efforts to suppress me, I have risen above their treachery. My achievements are solely mine, and I will continue to flourish independently. Drawing strength from the wisdom of Ms. B and Meg, I declare "NO MORE." I release these individuals to continue their chosen paths without involving or projecting onto me. Wasn't this their desire all along?

The hidden truth about my youngest cousin's parentage, concealed by my aunt and cousins, is known to me. The neighbor's death to protect this secret is a possibility.

Their resentment stems from their failed attempt to compromise me with hidden cameras, a plan that backfired, leading to a relationship. Their indignation at the outcome of their own scheme is irrelevant to me. I have no interest in their compromised lives and entanglements. Their patterns of seeking "leftovers," mirroring my mother's, are something I actively reject. I value freshness and integrity. They are welcome to what I no longer desire. The woman who betrayed me and her accomplice believed themselves superior, attempting to usurp my life through their involvement with my ex-husband. Their circumstances were not a choice, but a consequence. My child support was solely for my son's well-being, ending my obligation. This situation may have contributed to harm befalling one of my children.

They may believe their actions will escape consequence, but divine justice will prevail. Their theft, deceit, and lies will be revealed. Their attempts to exploit my work and identity will fail. The harm they have caused on a larger scale will be addressed. My current journey is one of self-discovery and profound learning. The power of "no," recently realized, has been a transformative lesson, taught by an associate who entered my life for this very purpose. My past fear of the negative repercussions of saying "no," particularly in relation to sex, stemmed from traumatic experiences. I had internalized a belief that my "no" would be disregarded. For too long, I endured disrespect out of fear of abuse. I have now shed this fear, embracing the empowering strength of setting boundaries. Overcoming this obstacle, along with the associated illusions and trauma, marks a significant triumph. I am no longer afraid and am grateful for this newfound clarity. This closed chapter signifies a commitment to my own well-being and autonomy. I refuse to be controlled, objectified, or treated as someone's possession. My feelings are valid.

I am deeply grateful for the awareness and strength to heal provided. My journey of self-discovery and truth continues. I recognize that my kindness has been exploited by some whom I have helped and empowered, only to face their attempts to undermine me. Their efforts will not succeed. I am a perpetual learner, embracing life's challenges and moving forward, releasing anything that impedes my progress toward fulfilling my destiny. Confirmation has finally arrived: I was switched at birth and raised by my aunt and uncle, who are not my biological parents. My biological father, whom I believed to be my uncle, was murdered by the man I thought was my father. My stepmother is, in fact, my aunt, and the woman who raised me is not my birth mother. I am the product of an affair between my biological father and my aunt. I was taken from my birth mother, who was married to a wealthy man unaware I was not his biological child. When the truth threatened to surface, he was killed, unknowingly leaving me in his will. My biological father was unloved by both my stepmother and my birth mother at the time of his death, which occurred after the truth of his affair and my parentage was revealed. My stepfather left me an inheritance, which my uncle-stepfather, his wife, and family stole, along with my rightful place, and they continue to benefit from it while orchestrating attempts on my life to conceal their crimes. Immediately following my father's death, I became their target. During this time in Capitol Heights, I experienced visions. Believing my home was bugged, I suspected government agencies were monitoring me and had sent assassins. These experiences, initially dismissed as medication-induced, were actually my biological father communicating past and future events, a realization that predated my acknowledgment of my own gifts, which were suppressed through enforced silence and abuse. They always intended to eliminate me to gain access to the inheritance, especially after my use of black magic and spell work. My father, ironically nicknamed "Rolling Stone," was likely my grandfather's sole remaining heir. I have a sister who passed away in 2012, though her passing may have been faked. She and my brother, a post office supervisor, would explain the intercepted mail. These individuals have engaged in extensive fraud, including faking deaths, stealing policies, and committing murder.

Suspicious activity occurs around my residence between midnight and 5 AM, prompting me to adjust my sleep schedule for vigilance. Attempts to tamper with my email throughout the night indicate a persistent effort to compromise my accounts. Despite this, I will only change my passwords, knowing my communications are monitored, including by federal authorities. I trust in divine intervention for a resolution. While I recognize that not all law enforcement is corrupt, my experiences necessitate caution. This situation must change.

For the past several months, I have endured relentless attacks, financial hardship, and numerous attempts to silence me through harmful actions. These attacks are designed to break my spirit, but despite obstacles such as blocked income and hacked emails preventing job opportunities, I remain steadfast. Even the potential income from my book is being sabotaged. Despite everything, I trust that a higher power is aware of these injustices and will intervene. Awake early, awaiting the arrival of donation services, I am surprisingly energized and determined to expose all those involved. While they may disrupt my online communication, they cannot silence me physically, even as I am being followed. I am under attack by a large group, each with their own motivations, stemming from my refusal to be controlled and their past offenses: taking out loans in my name, stealing my children, misappropriating my benefits and child support, and more. My family stole the inheritance left to me after they murdered my father and mother. My son's father and his family orchestrated fake adoptions and stole the settlement from my 2005 accident, as well as a donation left for me. The accident itself caused memory loss, a coma, nerve damage, and facial surgery, and related documents have vanished, along with records of other criminal and neglect cases they sought to conceal.

I have done nothing to warrant this treatment; I simply removed myself from their lives. I have never sought revenge, only offered prayers, yet their ultimate aim is my death. I write daily in the hope that my words will reveal the truth if harm comes to me. I do not feel safe, but I trust in protection, which has never failed me before. I have survived previous attempts on my life and continue to tell my story.The attempts to destroy me extend far beyond my immediate surroundings, even reaching behind bars and overseas. The father of my second son orchestrated a murder attempt, and they have tried to frame me by planting drugs and weapons—tools of their own criminal activities—in my home. My incarcerated son, driven by anger and extortion, is complicit in their schemes.

Around 2015-2016, I welcomed my second son back into my life after his release from prison, a decision I now regret, recalling an incident shortly after my own release from probation. My hopes for a positive outcome were once again dashed.My second son was arrested the day before my birthday for vehicle theft and a subsequent gas station robbery after dropping my ex-husband off in the stolen vehicle. He is currently incarcerated for these crimes. While grocery shopping with my sister, my son's frightened friend arrived at my house. I had recently asked my son to leave for breaking my rules, which included respecting my home by not coming and going at late hours, not stealing, and adhering to my commitment to no sales from my residence while on probation. The day his friend arrived, he was visibly scared. When questioned, he denied any wrongdoing, but I knew he was lying. Earlier, my sister and I had noticed a suspicious van outside my home, prompting her to comment on potential trouble. My son had also seen someone taking pictures outside, but I hadn't thought much of it at the time.

My son was arrested days later for again driving the stolen car. The day before my birthday, police raided my home. Suspecting a setup, I demanded a warrant before they searched. They presented one, but as I anticipated, it was unsigned. Although they had already entered, I prevented them from touching anything. During the raid, the psycho-psychotherapist argued with an officer after lighting a cigarette. Despite the sub-zero temperatures and open windows, officers demanded he extinguish it, overstepping their authority. He left, and I waited over an hour and a half for a signed warrant. Simultaneously, PG County was called for a separate robbery in Maryland. Once the signed warrant arrived, they searched and found a gun, stolen IDs, and credit cards under my son's mattress. After reviewing the events, it appears the search was illegal, as DC's warrant wasn't signed, and PG County never provided one. It seems my son was also set up. This feels like retaliation for the pain I endured, but he is young. It's as if they aimed to destroy our lives, reminiscent of fictional cult plots with twin powers. This was our reality.Everything now became clear; they were trying to entrap me once again, under the false presumption that I was still on probation. I had completed my probation less than a week before the raid. Had I still been on probation, it would have resulted in my immediate arrest. They had already apprehended him earlier, and they believed I would soon follow.

The reason for PG's presence at my residence was the stolen vehicle. He had robbed an individual who was connected to a homicide that occurred on New Year's Day. My son, while intoxicated, confessed to me that he planned to retaliate against some individuals over a trivial Obama phone and a cheap (Under Armor) coat. He recounted how he had gone into a gas station and upon his return, the guy had left. He was determined to seek revenge, but I advised him against it, emphasizing that it wasn't worth it. Due to black magic and spell work being directed at me, I was unwell and my finances were precarious. He was impatient, but I was doing my best under the circumstances. While I was out of town with the psycho for New Year's, he called to tell me he was going to the club with his friend. My son was later charged with robbery, stolen vehicle, and accessory after being caught near my house. He was sentenced to fifteen years in Maryland, where he had just been released from federal prison. My ex husband paid him to set me and my son up, just as they had paid others. This is all becoming clear as my memory slowly returns.

I have endured many hardships without recognizing the hidden dangers around me. My ex-partner likely provided the weapon to the individual who used it against me, while my sister, following our usual pattern, called the police in an attempt to have me arrested. I had recently experienced homelessness and was attending classes related to a self-defense incident, ultimately accepting a plea bargain on the advice of my public defender. The day following the raid, the father of my youngest son appeared at my residence unannounced, under the pretense of allowing me to spend time with my child. This occurred annually on my birthday, as they consistently devised ways to disrupt my happiness during holidays.

I went to his father's house in Temple Hills, MD. Before this, I hadn't realized they were deliberately sabotaging me, especially during holidays or whenever I was ready to move forward with my life. These distractions all served to keep me from exposing the truth about their betrayals. I had experienced so many setups and betrayals that I had blocked some of them from my memory, not wanting to face who the real culprits were. As the mentally unstable individual continued their prying and accusations, trying to provoke me, TMH intervened to protect me once more. With the help of the shelter and the counseling I received there, I was able to remain calm despite the raid and my ex-husband's subsequent actions. I knew I was innocent and had nothing to fear.

However, my ex-husband tried to harm me after the raid. He deceived me into going to the south side of town, to a girl's house off South Capital St, SE, WDC, and MLK Ave SE, by promising that I could see my son. He tried to start a fight by claiming having the girl start out with "she is pretty", then expressing confusion and anger, suggesting she thought i was dead. As the girl's anger escalated, I left and we went back to his mother's house near the Pennacles. I've always disliked that area due to my childhood experiences, and now I suspect it was a trap. He then sent his associate, to whom he had lied, and we ended up talking and spending time together. Subsequently, he would cut off communication with my son and attempt to intimidate me by coming to my house, which didn't work as I was no longer afraid. Following their disconnection, they sent another hitman who was pretending to be interested in the lawn guy. I later cut him off due to his lies and inconsistency. He was married and temporarily separated without acknowledging it. Finally, they decided to send in my second husband to end it all.

I've had a good and peaceful day, but I'm waiting for a change. Even though I continue to face more enemies and feel like the world is against me, I trust that TMH will restore everything. Unfortunately, a group of DL men and others, including my exes, have become my enemies. It's disheartening that they have so much time to create conflict. So many people are unhappy, and it seems like everyone has a secret motive. I'm discovering hidden truths about relationships, both past and present, within my family and beyond. As they say, misery loves company. The truth will be revealed eventually. I don't know what the future holds, but I feel that once everything comes to light, it will be something big and something good. I'm ready to move away from all the destruction, delays, cover-ups, crimes, lies, and jealousy. None of it makes any sense. Life can be unpredictable, but I'm staying positive and trying to see things in a new way. My book sales may not have brought in a lot of money, but if I can help or inspire even one person, then it's worth more than money.

My landlord's demands have become unreasonable, so I've had to set boundaries with them. I haven't received a response to my message yet, which is unusual. Despite the ongoing issues behind the scenes, I'm staying focused on my happiness and freedom and continuing to work on my book. I have an interview tomorrow, but I'm still struggling financially and hoping for more profit from my book. I'm determined to find a way forward. I'm growing every day, and I pray that everything connected to me grows as well. I'm focusing on the important things in my life. My days can feel overwhelming, but I'm praying for a new vehicle so I can expand my marketing efforts. I trust in TMH's plan for me, even in the face of negativity. I'm thinking about changing the prices for my paperback and hardcover books and removing my eBook from Amazon because of their high profit margins. My romantic life continues to be unfulfilling, and every option seems motivated by negativity. After years of disappointment, even while in relationships, I have given up on love. I put my trust in TMH. If He intends for me to find someone, I will have faith and continue to pray that TMH will provide for my daily needs as He always has. My home is my sanctuary, despite the persistent surveillance and efforts to undermine my work. The individuals threatened by my success and determined to derail my journey with TMH have only made me more resolute. I will not abandon my path; I am too far along to turn back now. I have devised alternative strategies to share my story across multiple platforms and connect with a broader audience.

I've disconnected my phone and am moving forward with unwavering faith, trusting that the universe will guide and protect me if I continue to pursue my life's purposeI never fail or give up because I am always driven to reach my full potential, and TMH never allows me to truly fall. I always rise higher when presented with new opportunities, and amazing things happen when I turn negative situations into positive ones. I never know where I will end up, but that's what faith is all about. I was once bewildered by the expectations of those who saw potential in me that I couldn't see. Now, I realize how blessed and fortunate I am. With TMH's guidance, I know I won't fall too far, and I understand that others may view my struggles as a test of faith. I've learned that challenges are opportunities for growth and change, and that things aren't always what they seem. I remain patient and faithful, awaiting my turn in life, knowing that I'm on the verge of a breakthrough. Even when things seem difficult, I remind myself that troubles are temporary and that "this too shall pass." Everything will happen in its own time.

The memories I've suppressed, possibly due to retrograde amnesia or the stress of my book release, are resurfacing. I remember meeting a man around 2008, after my youngest son's father left and I was staying with my aunt in Fort Washington, MD. We met at a 7-Eleven, and although our relationship was casual, he was always there when I needed help or someone to talk to. Our relationship was based on friendship, not sex. We only slept together a few times during a difficult period in my life. Despite periods of disconnection, we always found our way back to each other. There were no expectations; we were simply content with our independent lives and the natural flow of our connection. He was always reliable and supportive, unlike other men I'd known. When I got engaged, I promised my ex-husband to cut ties with my past. We were both supposed to delete all contacts, but he secretly kept his, including explicit content of his mistresses, which I discovered after we were married. He was an independent contractor with a heart of gold and plenty of ambition. I was an accountant who moved around a lot. We connected and spent some time together, but he was younger than me and probably had other options. I think he realized I was married and moved on. I tried to find him on Facebook after my divorce, but he was rarely active on social media, and I couldn't remember his phone number. After doing further research, I discovered he was another paid handler who became disgruntled after being in contact with my ex-husbands and family. He was sent in to distract, attack, and destroy. I would discover that this group is made up of haters and hurt people who had trauma bonds and were deceiving me once more to continue stealing as they have done for years.

Due to head injuries and my family's involvement in black magic, I've lost many memories. Every time I've found happiness, it's been disrupted by illness or other setbacks. I'm looking for a fresh start somewhere new, where I can find happiness and build a deep connection with someone.I yearn for passionate romance, excitement, and enduring joy to compensate for the time I've missed. I aspire to create authentic memories with someone as extraordinary as myself, someone who complements my energy. I often fantasize about intimate nights under the stars, making love until sunrise by the water's edge.

Meanwhile, I have a job interview approaching, and I'm feeling incredibly anxious. My schedule has been chaotic lately, so I've been writing to occupy my time while I try to reorganize my life—discarding what doesn't fit and assembling what does. It's like having five puzzles mixed up in one box; it's a gradual process. I'm taking it one day at a time, and things are slowly becoming clearer. The truth about my parents remains a mystery, and I'm slowly piecing together the fragments. I know there's a connection underlying everything, but only time will reveal it.

The motivation behind destructive behavior baffles me. Money holds immense power, capable of both corruption and devastation. Greed, gluttony, and envy are considered deadly sins, yet they're foreign to me. I've always held the belief that what's meant for you will find its way, and if not, you must strive to achieve it. This concept of hard work seems alien to those who resort to theft and murder.

I have helped countless people throughout my life, offering my resume and schoolbooks to aid their job searches and educational pursuits. I have supported them through their struggles and encouraged their independence, yet they rarely acknowledge my assistance. Life has a way of humbling you when you disagree, and people are quick to use, abuse, steal from, and manipulate you. As soon as you put a stop to it, they try to destroy everything you've built, oblivious to the struggles you've endured to reach your breaking point. I harbor no anger towards them; I simply pray they find healing for the pain they're hiding. Even those who were absent during my struggles try to insert themselves for attention, attempting to fit in while harboring their own deep troubles.

A change of scenery would offer me a fresh start and a renewed focus. My landlord's actions, such as cutting into my ceiling to check the pipes and leaving a tarp up until next week, are intentionally making things difficult. If repairs must be completed by the 29th, they should be done all at once instead of causing me discomfort. I'm tired of "Boo Boo's" constant texts and repetitive questions. I ignored her this time. She's still invading my space, asking about my medical insurance. I think she wants to change or snoop in my records again. First, she tried to sabotage my housing, and now she's after my insurance forms. It's none of her business; it's my personal information. They expect me to be quiet and allow these invasions, or live in fear, but I'm not afraid.

I've been making positive changes and growing. Unfortunately, people consistently misunderstand my intentions and spread rumors, regardless of my actions. This behavior only exacerbates the situation and has negative consequences for them.Over the past few months, I've had to establish boundaries with many people. I've realized that some people misinterpret my kindness as weakness and attempt to take advantage. In the past, I wouldn't have hesitated to fight back, often without considering the consequences. Strong emotions can cloud judgment and lead to poor decisions, so I've learned to pause and reflect before acting. I also understand that substance abuse only exacerbates the situation. Life experiences, maturity, and time can have a transformative effect if we're receptive to them. In my past, anger and resentment fueled my reckless and uncaring behavior. I felt isolated and believed that the only way to be heard was through disruptive actions. I've realized that harming others is not productive, and silence can be a powerful tool for prompting introspection and revealing someone's true character. I've learned to prioritize my own well-being by disengaging from ego-driven interactions and distancing myself from triggers. While substance use can temporarily numb emotional pain, true healing involves addressing the underlying issue, often through prayer or spiritual practices.

Even in places we consider safe and sacred, like churches and families, I've personally experienced the negative influence of those around us. The devil often resides in our comfort zones. If you doubt this, try stepping away and observe the reactions of those around you. Will they support you or try to keep you trapped in destructive patterns? They may even use your deepest fears against you, all while claiming to be your friends and family. Your enemy has been influencing you negatively, leading you down a path of self-destruction filled with substance abuse and procrastination. It's time to break free from their grasp and embrace self-love and acceptance. Recognizing your true allies and adversaries is crucial for personal growth.

As I continue on my journey of self-discovery, I have come across another unexpected and disturbing revelation. When my mother was transitioning, she was in a relationship with a man who had been involved with her since the East-West Highway days. The night she was moved to a nursing home, my sister informed him that my mother was dying from AIDS. He then went back to my mother's room and told her that he knew the truth, and shortly after, she passed away. The truth is he was a practitioner and unalived her with black magic and that is what was set to repeat. Mother was sending warnings from above. They were hoping to get me sick after infecting my past partners if not all in hopes one would unalive me . Only I am not sick by the grace of TMH and the ringleader of all of my betrayal, gang stalking, and the plans to unalive I was the ex's,and family that I spoke of previously. They have infected many of my past partners and then blaming me after sex rituas,but that was partial reason for choosing my ex partners in hopes i would return to one of them. I am not sick and can pull my portal on demand and demand tests. My family has unalived my son which one i am not sure as of yet I believe and it has not been either not discovered by authorities as of yet I only have not had a clear vision on this as we speak, but I know it is coming one or more of my son'shave been unalived one beingmy oldest yes the one i died for is looks up to my mother's past lovers as his stepdad which my sister remained in contact with after my past lovers trusted him, my past lovers trusted my sister all to be betrayed, infected, and possibly unalived. Thetrutb is he is not transitioned he stole the property and the inheritance left to me from my mothers mother inwhich i assumed hated me, but actually cared. He forged my signature switched sexuality sleeping around with cousins and entertaining sex rituals as well brainwashed.This is so deep I must investigate more, but I am determined to find the underlying cause of it all to get the justice they deserve and justice for myself. I have to say WOW as I realize things were never as they appeared. They as well have also been trying to frame me for a murder of whom I have not confirmed yet . They unlived someone's wife and I believe one of my exes who was working with my family and discovered they made them sick at this time needs more investigation, but they buried her in a pond by a cabin in Connecticut. I need more time so I will stick a pin to it for now as it will be revealed soon enough this is why they have been trying to unalive me so many hidden secrets about things stolen, unaliving others to silence me because they stole from me in processed unloved others that knew the truth not realizing it all would be revealed by TMH as I said what is destined is destined.

I've reached a difficult point in my life. My career progression has been hindered by the unfortunate illness of my references, and while my book is available on Amazon, the company's profits far exceed my own. Reaching this stage has been an arduous journey, and I'm yearning for a change. My romantic life is also shrouded in uncertainty; trust is something I can only offer when it's earned. I wouldn't describe myself as particularly happy or sad, but I'm desperately hoping for a positive change in my situation. I'm on the verge of giving up and starting afresh, but the only thing keeping me going is TMH's request that I see this mission through. Things aren't progressing as I'd hoped, and the bills continue to mount.

I've considered offering tarot readings, but I'm unsure of my abilities and wouldn't want to mislead people. I feel blocked and unable to see something, but I'm not sure what. I don't have anyone to confide in these days, having distanced myself from past jobs, FA.N.S., and family. I'm weary of the constant difficulties, like people stalking and watching me, which is unsettling and a complete turnoff. My desire is to be free, at peace, and loved.I pray for change soon, as I'm lonely, broke, and moody. Just when I think things are ending, they repeat. I'm tired of it all and ready to move on; wherever I land is where I'm meant to be. I hear of others' love and accomplishments and know that my turn will come. Everything takes time.

My stepmother and fake father, both with government affiliations, knew I was gifted and have been trying to destroy my potential since I was young. This continued even after I became an adult. As recently discovered I was switched and stolen as my gifts were discovered before my birth and the reason for my parents' una living being was that they stole and made me a live secret experiment of the government. I know it sounds crazy right ? Cults/covens have been around for a long time.My ex-husband collaborated with others in an attempt to frame me for their wrongdoings. This occurred after he contracted HIV/AIDS while incarcerated and spread it through the community and to past partners through sexual rituals as a part of revenge. My refusal to comply with my ex-husband's demands and my consistent payment of child support for eighteen years led to attempts to destroy my reputation and steal my inheritance. These attempts involved spreading lies about my promiscuity and neglect of my children to keep me in poverty. Despite suffering abuse from my son that resulted in hospital visits, I always prioritized his well-being and financial support. My ex-husband's primary goal was to provide financial security for his new family. I was indifferent to this as long as my son was cared for. When my ex-husband realized he could no longer manipulate or control me, he ceased his attempts and joined forces with my family against me. Together, they embarked on a campaign to discredit me, even resorting to attempts to infect me with a disease. I would later discover the disease came from his mistress in which was married under my name took on my identity to file taxes for my son and had him unlived for insurance then unliked my son because of what remained for curse on working with my aunt another ringleader my mother sister yes the one who resided in a one bedroom roach infested apartment and stabbed my mother's her and sister to steal.However, thanks to TMH and my resilience from past traumas inflicted by my family, their efforts failed. Additionally, the military colluded with my adversaries, enabling them to exploit and steal from me over the years. My family has a legacy of military service, with high-ranking members on my paternal side. However, my son's father's family conspired against me. They, along with others they hired - including a recent associate - worked to diminish my self-worth and maintain my low vibration. This associate was sent to exchange energies and steal my talents to heal their coven's affliction, but this was immediately exposed and prevented. Although it took time to fully comprehend, and I may not know everyone involved in the plot against me, The Most High reveals more about their scheme each day as they persist in their attempts, and this revelation safeguards me. My intention in sharing my story is not for fame, but to clear my name and seek justice for the lies and slander against me.

I've faced many challenges in my life, each one connected to the others, creating a chain of events linking my past, present, and future. Some trials were related to family, while others stemmed from former F.A.N.S. who turned my children against me. These F.A.N.S. confused my children about their sexuality, using rituals and hate, and possibly causing them harm. While I can't change what has happened, I am taking control of my future. I'm not accepting any offers right now; everything will resume once this situation is resolved. I can't trust anyone at the moment, as they're still playing games in my life, influenced by the lies of a foolish person and their fake power. Past strategies are no longer effective. Any new attempts to obstruct my path to court will be unsuccessful. I refuse to dwell on past actions and prioritize focusing on my future. I am pursuing new opportunities and have no desire for revenge. I understand that vengeance is not mine to seek, and justice will be served in due time, as it has always been. While I accept apologies, I will not forget the consequences of past actions, including the time stolen from my children, the unjust punishments I endured, and the attempts to discredit me. I have forgiven everyone, but I ask that you maintain your distance from me. There is no need for any further communication.

Those who once took advantage of and dismissed me now act as if they care and want to mend fences. Their empty gestures do not sway me; I see through their lies and betrayal. I want nothing to do with them now or ever. I am healed and will not allow anyone to infect me with their negativity and dishonesty and then try to blame me. I am moving forward and leaving the past behind. I pray that this book will bring justice and expose the truth about the "fake churches" that cover up evil acts, including the sexual abuse of my son. My Sadness that my ancestors' hard work was disgraced and they hoped for victory. The insurance policy-related murders, affairs, and other forms of corruption. The first week at my new house, I was intentionally made ill and hospitalized. During that time, my fake husband, who was supposed to be working for DoorDash (my account had been falsely deactivated the day before), copied my house and car keys. A box-shaped Jeep the neighbor down the hall from me has been stealing my mail from the paid postman, even before I changed my locks. My mailbox now opens easily due to repeated break-ins and mail theft. Despite submitting another change of address, I'm still not receiving my mail.. My stepmother-aunt's son, and roommate from the shelter who were all in relationships with my ex-husband and paid to watch me during my time there and that ladies and gentlemen is the real reason for me being removed from the shelter not because i left thirty minutes early.my ex-husband and my son's father's have been stalking me this entire time.they are connected to something before i was born this is connected to my biological parents and the government some way,now all i have to do is figure it out all conspired to sabotage me. Why?

They paid off my roommate's boyfriend which turned out to be one of the youngest sons' side pieces to destroy my reputation and spread lies.My ex-husband went as far as paying females to get pregnant by him using my identity so he could continue to file child support against me after they left my son. The mistress in which he had a fake belly pretended as she was the mother of our son.They even went as far as to marry off my aunt's son to an immigrant relative for money, and they possibly caused harm.

My intention is not to gain fame or power, but rather to promote peace and justice. I was living my life and not causing harm to anyone. They targeted me with lies, theft, and deceit in an attempt to destroy me. For those who haven't read my previous book, I have given you a brief recap. It wasn't my best work, as I was still piecing together flashes of memory. As you know, I began writing due to my amnesia; it was my way of remembering fragments of my life. These flashes were later revealed to be visions from TMH, angels, ancestors, and guides. Additionally, there were many detractors who tried to undermine my book before it had a chance to be published. I have been silenced for years so my side of the story would never be heard, in fact they never expected me to make it this far. Earlier throughout my story you may have noticed I have always stated how in life we must complete obstacles to get to the next level in life just as the video games taught or board games in order to progress you must complete level after level before moving forward in life pretty much the same applies in life as we believe today closure is presented as FU or I hate you never any conversation anymore. One reason for same-sex relationships is that people refuse to communicate and work through their issues. While it's important to be with someone who understands you, it's also crucial to put in effort if you truly care about the relationship.

Love is a complex emotion with many nuances. It transcends time and space, and past experiences can influence our current perceptions of it. I don't judge others because I've been through trauma myself and once feared intimacy with men due to past hurt. Although I eventually moved on from that fear, I respect everyone's choices because we all have our own unique stories and experiences. It's important to remember this before judging others. My first book may have been confusing due to its lack of organization and direction. Now, with a clearer mind and a better understanding of the visions I received, I have been able to organize them properly. I will dive deeper into these visions and provide a clearer explanation. I've learned to let go of things and accept that not everyone possesses the same abilities as I do. I shouldn't expect others to be like me or have the same opinions as me in order to understand them. Life's challenges are ongoing, and while I'd like to think I'm done with them, I understand that's not the case. However, I've recently come to the realization that I have control over this cycle - who is a part of it and how often it repeats - it's all up to me.

Going through difficult times has changed my perspective. I now know how to endure hardship without compromising my values to help those who have given me nothing but reasons to distrust them. They've done nothing but mock, steal from, lie to, and manipulate me.

I'm continually learning and growing, and things are changing as a result. Although my life seemed chaotic at first, everything that's happened makes sense now. The events of my life – both good and bad – fit together like pieces of a puzzle, and I've come to understand their meaning. My unique perspective allows me to see the world differently, and I'm beginning to recognize my own special abilities. My initial openness about my experiences was met with widespread hostility, which I found confusing. Perhaps it was due to my inclination to reveal hidden truths; I've never been good at keeping secrets and often found myself in trouble for speaking out. I was raised to believe that religion was evil and I have studied many, finding no distinction between them. In the end, there's only one higher power, interpreted differently across cultures and practices.The world is filled with so much hate. I am an omnist; I believe all religions are valid and only differ in their customs, not in their core beliefs. The pieces of my life have finally fallen into place. I now understand the accidents, memory loss, harassment, and abuse. My life was orchestrated: the marriages, children, relationships, co-workers, and family were all manipulated. Some were paid to be a part of my life, while others were paid to ruin it.

The saying "blood is thicker than water" doesn't apply to my family. We're connected only by blood, and that connection is complicated. My research has revealed that my family is full of liars, murderers, and thieves who have done unforgivable things. I was raised to believe that life was full of sunshine and rainbows. That was the world I made up to make myself happy. Others resented my happiness and were determined to destroy anything I had or inherited. Despite the obstacles and lack of guidance, I have risen above their attempts to harm me and continue to stand strong. The things done to take me out to compensate for all of the made up stories, false reports, forging signatures, stealing inheritance, CD, stocks, and whatever was left for me, unaliving my grandparents, parents through blackmagic, poison and abuse, brainwashed my children, lied to the law to have them join forces to cover all the crimes committed under my stolen identity, married under my name using false marriage certificates presenting false death certificates, false adoptions, under fraudulent names, under on names of someone else, slept with family , family stole money from inheritance and splurged unacknowledged insurance policies, receiving funding for social security falsely all while stripping me of everything. If you have seen the movie Trading Places this was my life . A bet on my life and my children and without remorse just laughter. I have endured a lot to secure a place with continued shelter as I have been unsuccessful as I have been chipped as a child. The government tracks me everywhere I go monitoring it all in hopes of me never escaping their matrix. I have been homeless, incarcerated, and separated from my children who have been placed in the system to continue the secret experiment. I have had to complete classes for crimes I did not commit. This all stems from the night at Anacostia Park that I have previously discussed soi believed unbeknownst to me it was lot deeper than told, imagined, or could ever believe of course they want me and others to believe i'm crazy,but that is not true i have been awaken from the lies and illusions placed throughout my life and i am not alone.

My life has been plagued by a long-standing conspiracy orchestrated by my family, including my sister, husband, and others, even before my marriage. I was oblivious to their plans, dismissing strange occurrences as mere coincidence, a belief I now understand to be false. For forty-seven years, I navigated life's hardships, forced lessons designed to strengthen me, while they deceitfully prospered by stealing from others.

My uncle, an insurance agent, played a key role by identifying and eliminating wealthy individuals through spellwork, assuming the identities of their beneficiaries. This practice spanned generations on both sides of my family, and I am just one of their many victims. However, a higher power intervened in my case.

One night at the park, while drinking and smoking with my sister, husband, and his friend, my husband's intense gaze towards my sister and his friend engaging in sexual activity disturbed me. When I confronted him, he tried to involve me, which I refused. Later, my intoxicated sister flirted with my husband, leading to an argument where I injured my hand and ended up in the emergency room. The following morning, I evicted my sister, marking the second instance of her inappropriate behavior with my partners. Years prior, she had attempted something similar with my second son's father while I was pregnant.

During a period of self-sufficiency, my aunt and nephews were unexpectedly moved into my small apartment, legally under my father's name. Despite my own challenges as a minor supporting myself, I felt obligated to care for them. Adding to the burden, my father frequently visited with different women under the pretense of cleaning. Meanwhile, Jezebel, who also resided there, used my home as a drug den and prostitution ring. My checks were stolen, and my tip money was used for expenses unrelated to me, ultimately leading to my eviction and homelessness. I returned from work and school to find neglected babies, a situation mirroring what I had desperately tried to escape. Their actions were deliberate attempts to ruin my life.

The FBI once arrived at my home concerning my case against the Fort DuPont rapist, where I was a key witness who had been wrongly accused of fabrication. My stepfather brought them there and left me, a seventeen-year-old with no parental supervision, to face them alone. Justice was eventually served when the rapist was convicted, a small comfort amidst my difficulties. Shortly after, I was evicted and forced to move into a hotel.

These events following the park incident culminated in the devastating raid on my house. Despite these hardships, I persevered, my faith and belief in eventual justice sustaining me.

The night I lost my home and belongings, the reality of losing my children consumed me. My ex-husband and his partner's conspiracy to destroy me became evident, revealing a pattern of escalating abuse. This realization, coupled with witnessing my mother's health struggles, motivated me to rebuild my life, causing resentment from my sister. My family's long-standing practice of magic and spells aimed to drain my energy and control me, even recruiting past partners for this purpose. I was intentionally kept ignorant of spiritual matters. The betrayal extended to placing cameras in my home to exploit my intimate moments for their rituals, further sickening me. My fake husband hosted orgies at our home, and his partners, along with my sister, poisoned my food and drinks and stole items for death magic. My family's manipulative and deceitful nature had been a constant throughout my life, which fueled my desire to be a positive role model for my children, who were ultimately taken from me. They envied my drive and success, seeking to steal my life and identity.

Growing up with the expectation to surpass our parents, I always hoped for a better future for children. It became clear that many, including family and supposed friends, were draining my energy, resenting my nonconformity which mirrored their own flaws. I learned that inner character is paramount, a truth recognized and protected by a higher power.

Living on Sheriff Rd., I endured an illness inflicted upon me to support lies about me spreading STDs, which was untrue despite three instances of sexual assault. Ironically, the only time I contracted anything was chlamydia from my then-partner during my last pregnancy, which led to our separation. His potential connection with my family further complicated matters.

These orchestrated situations have been recurring since 2001, intensifying around my neglect and criminal court cases, divorce, and the births of my children, all designed to keep me oppressed. The numerous medications prescribed for my physical and mental health, by a manipulative psychotherapist handler, likely worsened my condition. I ended the engagement to this controlling therapist to regain my peace. His behavior mirrored my abusive ex-husband, reinforcing my resolve to avoid such relationships. The constant attempts to exploit my gifts, with everyone around me seemingly aware except myself, and the organized crime-like network profiting from my suffering, only strengthened my determination to break free and reclaim what I had earned through hard work. I learned that possessions gained through effort cannot truly be taken away.

The abuse from my ex-husband left deep scars, yet also forged my resilience. By sharing my story, I hope to offer solace and healing to others. It is time for my suffering to be acknowledged and put to rest.

My former fiancé, who obtained his wealth through illegal means, betrayed my trust by using information from therapy against me, sharing it with my family and others in violation of my privacy and HIPAA. This betrayal endangered me and further fueled my pursuit of justice. Their manipulation aimed to break me, but I refuse to succumb.

Through deception, they briefly caused me to self-destruct, manipulating my relationships and health. A higher power revealed their secret actions. Ultimately, justice will prevail. My marriage was founded on lies, as my husband was already married. They intended to transfer their negative karma onto me through voodoo and hoodoo. My exes and family colluded with those I once feared. Despite reporting identity theft, the perpetrator's position as a social worker allowed him to manipulate the legal system against me. My first ex-husband initiated a smear campaign through false court filings, enabling him to steal my assets, including homes and inheritances, even forging my signature. He currently resides in one of my properties.

He falsely claimed no proof of identity theft existed across various government agencies. My son, also possessing unique gifts, was exploited by institutions for profit without my consent or even notification of his death, with policies in place and potential cloning involved. I challenge the system to DNA testing to expose the lies. My family and fanbase were easily turned against me. My repeated violations included financial exploitation and orchestrated car accidents, one of which in 2005 caused permanent facial nerve damage. A donation received after a DUI accident where I was injured was also taken. I believe I was drugged that night and remain unable to fully recall the events. Without transportation, I endured homelessness, sleeping on park benches to work. My sister consistently lied about me and impersonated me, even having children under my identity for financial gain, part of a larger scheme involving my ex-husband. Their constant interference led to my near mental breakdown. They never anticipated my recovery, but a higher power revealed their deceitful plans, allowing me to reclaim my true identity. My limited contact with my sister and cousin was solely due to familial ties, as I never connected with the rest of my family. My supposed father was not my biological father, and I was never meant to be part of this toxic family involved in the very occult practices I was taught to despise. It became clear I was part of a larger, unknown reality. Their motivations were self-serving, leading them to recruit others and destroy lives to maintain their status.

My sister, despite having better opportunities, consistently made detrimental choices, even enlisting former friends against me. Her jealousy extended to sabotaging my relationships. Unlike her, I faced numerous hardships from a young age, including potential discrepancies in my birthdate that would make the traumas even more profound. I have endured repeated cycles of poverty, death, and survival. My purpose now is to share my truth. Despite their attempts to hinder me, they underestimated my resilience. I am now speaking out against the years of their evil.

I feel compelled to share my story in hopes of finding justice or at least catharsis. Driven by greed and in collaboration with the government, they made multiple attempts on my life, thwarted by deceased loved ones and divine intervention. They not only stole and lied but also took out life insurance policies on me.My reputation suffered, and I lost loved ones and colleagues. I received messages from the deceased, including details of their deaths and invitations to the afterlife.

Despite multiple attempts on my life, I have been assured that the perpetrators will face consequences. I hope my experiences will resonate with at least one person. Eventually, peace will be restored. While companionship is desired, my current focus is on self-healing and moving forward.

My stepmother and father, responsible for my mother's death, have actively worked against me for years, spreading lies and disease and stealing my inheritance. The recent revelation that my grandfather is my biological father ignited further conflict with my siblings. Their betrayal has caused immense pain, and I am determined to expose their wrongdoings.Lacking the courage for direct confrontation, they resorted to theft and invasion of privacy, sending my ex-husband and others to steal my belongings and recording my private moments. They exploited years of trauma to manipulate situations and portray everyone as mentally unstable.

I am appalled that the legality of the footage they obtained was not questioned by court officials. I have learned that footage of me has been posted on the dark web and other platforms.websites in an attempt to humiliate me. As an adult, I am not ashamed of my private life, and it is my personal business. I demand to be compensated for what I am owed, as the recording and distribution of this footage was done without my consent.Unfortunately i will not be shamed or feel embarrassed as they wished as i did nothing wrong i was in the privacy of my own residence not home as home is well peace resides and i have not had that for at least ten years now. I pay my bills to continue to disrespect , violate, and constantly harass.

My former partner and others were involved in a scheme intended to disrupt my life. This scheme was a waste of time and money, and only benefited those who perpetrated it. While some may attempt to blame the pandemic, it had no effect on any policies or procedures in my life. Additionally, my former partner and I were never legally married.This entire operation was clandestine and could not have been executed without the cooperation of corrupt officials. I would like to believe that all the law cannot be corrupt, and I know all involved are not all bad just as magic . You have good or bad . It is who is behind it and the intentions in play. I am playing it safe and remain alone without delays, deception, or games due to jealousy by all means no one wants to work as a team they are greedy and want it all to share with someone else other than me only to feed off my energy all doors have been cleared and locked at this time love does not live or exist anymore a bunch of money hungry Jezebels/gigolos family and F.A.N.S lazy always trying to come up off of others hard work and thought workers who want position not fit for them failed trying to maintain images not earned and F.A.N.S who have who have hated since grade school. I choose a different route all the F.A.N.S., family and exes with new Jezebels trying to duplicate what they could never be you cannot turn a Jezebel into a housewife and anyone who has been in contact with anybody in my family or circle never has to worry about me ever revisiting a relationship or family full of Jezebels, diseases, and murderers may they become caged in prison and never return to society and to those trying to or have sent death spells may it be returned tenfold and pass down for eternity for those with the money spells well guess what TMH is my provider and my wants are unlimited no matter where I have journeyed or placed nothing is ever permanent in my life only what he wants it to appear as. Hear me loud and clear TMH sees all and hears all you are not above him, and I am chosen for he will always reveal for those who need a reminder.

Many people, myself included, pray for the triumph of faith, hope, and love. While some may choose hatred and dishonesty, seeking destruction and rejecting belief in a higher power, their perceived victories are fleeting. I believe that a higher power has intervened, and their plans are destined to fail. I remain dedicated to my purpose despite facing challenges such as internet outages, mail rerouting, and slander, which were intended to disrupt my life. As instructed, I will rise above these obstacles by sharing my story. Lies and deceit will not deter my commitment to truth and justice. I will continue to protect myself by following signs from the universe and using the knowledge that TMH has revealed to me to achieve success. I understand that fate and destiny are never changed, only guided onto the chosen path. By embracing this, fate and destiny will align and find the right path, allowing me to move forward without fear and with the sole intention of success.

I have prayed for change for years, but my life remains the same: monotonous and rehearsed. Happy times have been rare in my past, and they've often led to destruction that I am still trying to repair. Fun has always been followed by consequences, and I long for happiness without punishment. For example, the last time I went on a trip with others, I ended up paying for everyone. While I don't know what true love feels like, I am all too familiar with hurt and hate. I pray for happiness that doesn't depend on having company.People lie so frequently that they believe it's acceptable, but I won't stand for it anymore. It's challenging to trust anyone these days, and I'm starting a new chapter in my life where it seems like justice and love are hard to find. I've completed writing my life's story, from the beginning to the recent drama. All I want is to be loved, but it's difficult to trust anyone.I don't feel isolated, even though others try to isolate me. My life is monotonous and nothing seems important anymore outside my wants and desires in life. I stopped putting myself last because TMH said last will be first and I believe and stand behind that..

It's my second book. It continues the story of my first book and reveals hidden truths that others have neglected to tell.I'm weary of my monotonous routine: work and prayer, with no one to confide in except my angels and TMH. Summer has passed, and I remain alone and broke. Opportunities for change arose, but my priorities lay elsewhere. Bill collectors remain unmoved by my writing pursuits. I'm unable to rent a car, my accounts are overdue, and I lack vacation, money, and privacy. The worry of what lies ahead weighs heavily upon me, and I pray for a swift resolution. Despite my awareness of progress, tangible evidence remains elusive. I persist in prayer and writing, in alignment with my lifelong aspirations. I understand that surrendering and releasing what no longer serves me will bring clarity. The path ahead may involve both improvements and setbacks, but this is intrinsic to the process. Falling precedes standing, and crawling precedes walking. The actions of others no longer perturb me; they have inflicted their worst, and their capacity for harm is exhausted.My life feels stagnant. Despite my seemingly correct actions, those who deviate from the path continue unabated, as if no wrongdoing has occurred. I'm left awaiting divine intervention, as only a higher power possesses the capacity to resolve this predicament.

They changed their fates, and I was trapped in the life I had struggled to escape. I had done the work, but they stole the rewards. Now, I am awake and have reclaimed my life. I have surrendered everything to TMH, trusting him to fight my battles and recover what was taken. I will wait for TMH's decision, as he has the final say and ultimate control. The past two days have been exciting. As I advertise my book and network, I'm running into many people interested in my story. I need to schedule book signings with local stores soon, but I'm taking it one step at a time. I have faith in my leap and am patiently waiting for things to unfold. It's funny how people talk about themselves while helping you achieve your goals. I remember my stepmother used to tell me to learn patience every time she saw me. It's ironic that she was the one who initially encouraged me to meditate. It's sadly humorous how your enemies can unknowingly give you the keys to your destiny while hoping to tear you down. They are so focused on your failure that they don't realize they're helping you rise. My father used to say, "You're so smart that you're stupid," and that saying comes to mind.The phrase "too smart to pay attention" means that overconfidence can lead to missing important details, resulting in mistakes. It is crucial to remain attentive, even when we think we have everything under control.For example, I disregarded my father's advice to apply for social security benefits despite my failing health. I wrongly assumed I could manage without assistance, but this was due to the distractions of illness, abuse, and homelessness. I was not fully aware of the reality of my situation and the solutions that were available to me after discovering I have been lied to my entire life.

Life's most valuable lessons can only be applied when we are truly awake and receptive. One such lesson is the importance of making the best of any situation, even when it seems difficult. Although it may have been challenging initially, I have now gained clarity and am moving forward towards a brighter future. I am actively working to reclaim what has been unjustly taken from me and am excited about the opportunities that lie ahead.

I reconnected with an old associate and sold my television. I'm headed to another job interview today and hoping for a positive outcome. With only five months left in the year, my life feels like it's balancing itself out. I'm planning to either auction, donate, or sell online the rest of my belongings. The idea is to clear out the old and make space for new things to come into my life.Even though I may feel alone, I've learned that pursuing peace and sanity is worth it. There's no point in surrounding yourself with people who lack direction and want to keep you lost, just like them.I have never been one to settle for the minimum. Unlike many who are comfortable with their current situation, I believe that life has more to offer and that something better always exists. I am always searching for growth and improvement. Today's shortcomings can transform into tomorrow's successes. I am determined to move forward, leaving my past behind, towards a brighter future. Each day, I strive to erase the previous day's burdens and focus on growth and expansion. I understand that progress requires removing people and things that hinder my growth from my daily routines.

I've been off for so long that I forgot to double-check my work; it's a crucial step. I'm enjoying my time alone, and I'm focused on justice. Right is right, and this situation is wrong.Now that I know the truth about many people in my circle, I'm more cautious. I don't accept people at face value, and I watch and wait for them to reveal their true selves. I enjoyed my outing today, but I wish I didn't have to be around other people. Not all energy is good energy. Plus, I want to go places that do require a car or money for transportation. I know that TMH has a plan, and things have been looking up lately. I'm no longer accepting things as they are presented, and I'm moving forward. I have a lot planned; this is the calm before the storm, and I'm surprisingly comfortable.

It's Independence Day and fireworks are going off in my life and in my heart. My days aren't as heavy or stressful as they normally are. After working hard to get my book noticed, I've been taking it easy for a few days. I handed out flyers, put them up on bus stops (some were taken down, but I know some were seen), and did everything I could to get it noticed. I know that everything takes time, and I know I'm being watched and blocked from my destiny. I'm going to post some things online for three days. If I get a quick response, I'll take it as a sign. If I don't, I'll donate them to Goodwill or the Salvation Army.I'm exhausted from this journey. It feels endless, and the waiting is agonizing. I'm in control; I can only wait for TMH to decide when it's time for change. Everything happens for a reason, and I must be patient. I shouldn't complain, but the stress and heartache seem never-ending.

I long to escape, to leave it all behind. The stolen items are insignificant compared to my reputation and hard work. I know that trouble doesn't last forever, and this too shall pass. Life has a different destination for me, as always. I've always been the odd one, the 1 in 100. My journey has shown me that my destination is different from everyone else's. TMH's plan for me is unique and painful, but necessary. It hasn't killed me; it has only made me stronger than I ever imagined.There have been days when I felt like giving up, crying and praying for change. I know that tears won't solve anything; only strength can move me forward. That's what keeps me smiling. I take breaks often because I need time for myself. I'm not perfect. I have to manage my time and money carefully these days as I live day by day, hoping for a brighter future. I know things are close. It's calm now, but a storm is coming. I will remain still and peaceful. I find peace in the moment and pray more each day. Although I continue to lose things, it doesn't matter anymore. I work hard to rebuild, but I always end up back at the start, running the same race. I always win, but I'm tired of the constant restarts and replays of obstacles I've already learned from. Material things can be replaced, often with better things. Life isn't exciting anymore; it's just work without joy. Another day, another year, another season will soon pass. We're halfway through another year, and nothing has changed. I prayed to make sure I wasn't off track. I'm not; I just need to wait.

I'm exhausted by the constant drama surrounding me. It's both ridiculous and sad how many people are actively trying to undermine my success. I followed TMH's instructions, and now I'm expected to be afraid? Sorry, but the only one I fear is TMH, because he sees and controls everything. Honestly, I'm bored with the whole situation. I've worked incredibly hard to get where I am today, overcoming countless obstacles without any help. Despite my achievements, many people still view me as privileged and entitled. They've tried everything to bring me down – slander, financial sabotage, even love spells – but I've refused to give up.The individuals responsible for this are deeply troubled and need to seek forgiveness and healing through prayer. I am exhausted and desperately need rest, but find it nearly impossible as my focus remains on escaping this dangerous situation. I strive to maintain composure, but my patience is waning and I am on the verge of snapping. I am not harming anyone; yet, they persist in their attempts to hack my systems, as evidenced by the verification codes I continue to receive on my phone. I am weary of this absurd behavior; these individuals need to mature and accept responsibility for their choices. Their attempts to destroy me will not solve their problems; only through healing and confronting their true selves will they find the answers they seek. True change requires feeling and acknowledging the need for healing; inaction will yield no results.Instead of hindering others on their journey, prioritize your own personal growth and progress. Self-love and acknowledging your shortcomings are crucial for advancement. These concealed flaws, created for self-preservation, are merely temporary solutions that will continually resurface until properly addressed.

I had to block my Facebook page again due to ongoing drama. I only created the page to advertise my book. Unfortunately, some old F.A.N.S. and family members mistakenly thought that a former associate I encountered wanted to rekindle a relationship, which was never the case.. We started talking last year in late summer and it never went anywhere. I quickly discovered he was a player and not just another player out for opportunities and cheap thrills, the type of ninja that thinks if he buys wine you belong to him or owe him something you a nothing type feeling as he is a gift and needed. It is like I stated before reversals in situations nowadays the guy being female and female being the guy crazy only true.I don't think that guys understand the reason why women started being in charge was being they were not, and the relationships show just that same-sex . No problem with it as I once had but who is left to populate and continue generations do, we just say forget the generations before even though I realize many do not want to create due to society and others feel love is love. I feel that way as well, only there is more to it than just that I could get deep as before mentioned about transitioning and different realms as we are returned in many different covers. He thought he was going to re-enter my life trying to piggyback off my success or trying to destroy what I built on my own and alone and discovering trying to create a soul tie through sex and as well was sent in by my family to assault me. I realized he has been one of my many stalkers as actions and expressions never lie. Body language says a lot about a person. Trying to seduce me as trying to project if I were desperate "NOT (LOL)" FOS is what I told him I only went in the store to see if they would let me put my flier up and no other attention not to mention the store he claimed to own only a manager the lies people tell to play big he may be king in others site all I see is a liar and manipulator trying to get what he wants with no cares of others feelings. I was not impressed, especially with a liar. I am financially independent and capable of generating wealth for myself. I am indifferent to the destinies of others, as they are not my concern. Sharing is an option, but it is rare and often leads to control, reminiscent of my controlling and borderline abusive ex-husband. I will no longer tolerate the "tag, you're it" game that others have played in my life, using my hard work and energy for their own gain, as I am aware of my ex-husband's collaboration with my adversaries.This was a case of dishonesty and betrayal; there was no need for anything more than a civil conversation or friendship. The way I see it, if it didn't work initially, and you betrayed me once, there's no reason to believe it would now; you're likely to do it again. I don't know what's happening with my book or accounts as they keep getting hacked, and I'm not seeing any sales.I have applied for a job and have a final interview next week. I hope to get it, as I need the income to properly promote my product. I have already claimed all the blessings and opportunities that TMH has lined up for me, and I know that TMH may step in and elevate me beyond my expectations, as always. In the meantime, I remain grateful for the blessings I have and hope for further improvement soon.I pray something happens soon . As I need necessities for everyday life, I am not worried knowing TMH will always show up on time. I am so sick of the continued harassment of those trying to sicken me from their diseases while paying to keep the court dates pushed up and delay my money being returned while trying to give me STDs to blame me for being the carrier or to unalive me so they can try to steal or profit money. I have worked hard to earn with authoring my story claiming it was their idea saying they inspired me I call it "BOO BOO" As previously mentioned three books were written and stolen before the one, I just published are all lies and them once again seeking attention the one thing they have always accused me of doing. This means not since I was never around it is obvious that I was sought after and harassed with made-up stories and complete lies.Their attempts to manipulate my image, drive me to insanity, and alienate my loved ones only served to strengthen my resolve. I worked tirelessly to uncover the truth behind the lies and deception, determined to clear my name.I am thankful for all the challenges and difficulties I have faced. Because of them, I can now share my stories of resilience and overcome the victim mentality that others tried to force upon me. These experiences gave me the strength to leave behind what was harmful and recognize my true worth, instead of focusing on helping others.Despite their lies and slander, no one can take away my destiny or my accomplishments; this is a universal truth. I won't tolerate this behavior and I'm no longer playing games. If you commit a crime, you will face the consequences. I've been lenient in the past, but I won't be anymore. I'm only interested in friendships, but others seem to only be driven by lust and a desire to steal my time and energy. They even try to frame me for their own wrongdoings. This is all orchestrated by my son's father who got an STD from his stepdaughter and had a baby by her while they are claiming my son on taxes, benefits, and more. The entire family is an entire cult/coven and only helped me to rise. The matriarch is his mother pretending to be loving . Christian turns out to be an evil dark witch for whatever reason possibly in her own life as she was told her mother passed away while giving birth. that was a lie she was taken at birth and her father move on with her mothers best friend they ran/owned a church off Pennsylvania Ave SE, WDC until her stepdad passed and the pastor who is too her friend is a pedophile in fac to the entire is based on incest, pedophila.Trying to frame me will not work because my box is golden and I am celibate not sharing with no one not even entertaining the thought it is all "BOO BOO "I do not have time I am too focused on working on solving my life and my hidden and stolen identity, and find out what has been hidden from me and as I investigate there has been a lot hidden. I am going to reveal it all because I asked everyone to stop playing in my face. I was quiet and now I'm not, as explained throughout my first book this is the continuation of it for the very reason of others stealing my hard work, they have never lived my life and could never walk in my shoes going to jail, psych wards, homelessness, and grieving losing of my children they brainwashed and adopted falsely they are way too sheltered for such a life trust me there is no arrogance just facts and truth. It can all be researched so why lie? I speak from pain, heart, soul, and experience. No sympathy is needed, only justice and peace. I've been through a lot and I'm seeking peace as I work through it all. I know it will take time, but I'm tired of these people getting on my nerves. I confronted the associate about his stalking, lying, accusations, and attempts to set me up or swap destinies. I'm bored with these repetitive games and the constant stream of new players.

Their attempts have been varied, utilizing individuals from all walks of life - young and old, rich and poor, addicts and the homeless. The question is, where will it end? I can only assume that many of them fail to learn from their past and continue to make the same mistakes. I, however, am different. A single instance is enough to raise my awareness permanently. While I might not detect the initial attempt - as evidenced by the fact that I didn't catch on until the third - any subsequent attempts only serve to highlight their foolishness. It's a waste of time, energy, and money, especially if they're paying for this. I've been closely observing my surroundings and have noticed someone following me. This man boarded the bus near my home, claiming he lived nearby, and inquired about laundry facilities in the local buildings, mentioning his unit lacked them. Subsequently, he appeared at the library every day I was there and even attempted to ascertain my residence. I disembarked the bus, recognizing the situation.I was uptown when a drug addict approached me; I'm tired of these encounters. I know the intention is to make me believe that this is all I attract, which is untrue, as I have many options. I choose solitude for peace.

Speaking of, the associate who pretended not to be involved in the nonsense, as they all do, only TMH reveals my enemies and protects me. The associate then became loud, claiming it was his cookie; I laughed as I walked him to my front door. He thought I cared that he was angry and looking for a fight. I've worked too hard to go through any more unnecessary cycles. I tried to be friends, but the devil always shows up out of arrogance. My family somehow retrieved my book and stole my royalties; it was connected to him, as I gave him a flyer, unaware of his connection. I'm not stressing; the universe and TMH see all and will continue to provide for me. All will be returned; it will only be more and better in divine timing.

The landlord continues to underestimate me, assuming I'm naive. They try to manipulate me with letters and three-way calls with workers, pretending we're collaborating. They're trying to pry into my personal life, likely to report back to the community or society about my private information, even discussing CC on emails. This information is strictly for my worker who as well is involved in with receiving compensation from my family as stated DCHA, DOH, DHS,CPS, DOJ,DOT,DMV all working to keep me bonded and continue to gang stalk, delay, all while trying to keep me in a poverty mindset in hopes of becoming homeless once again; the landlord has no right to it. I've been managing my affairs independently my whole life. I wouldn't be surprised if they were recording our conversations or taking notes, but I don't care. This situation with them is over. They even contacted the housing specialist also involved as the guy. that placed me under surveillance and then exploit me on line one of his ex's they all collab together about payment,the delay on the paperwork for my emergency transfer as if They're unaware of the necessary repairs, like my ceiling, that haven't been addressed.The landlord was previously informed me of the need to maintain the dehumidifier to prevent ceiling damage from humidity. This was communicated in an earlier email, before portions of the ceiling collapsed. The landlord is now feigning ignorance, demonstrating the consequences of dishonesty. The lack of repair has led to ongoing delays, despite a false inspection on May 24th, which indicated a 28-day repair window. The landlord has not communicated further but has sent individuals to spy and intrude.I have attached emails and pictures to my response, and I am awaiting a reply. My landlord and the others are colluding to have me evicted and are trying to intimidate me. I have rights and will not be taken advantage of. My landlord is also attempting to obtain my personal information illegally to force me out of my residence and cover up their wrongdoings.

I was completely honest and open with her, emphasizing that only TMH's will matters. Through Him, everything is possible and will eventually come to pass according to His plan. I hope the men I met at the park a few weeks ago will get in touch soon, but I'm not sure if any of them even bought my book. It turns out, no coincidence , they knew I would be there and only wanted information. I'm overwhelmed with managing my emails, phone calls, and electronics, so it's hard to keep track of everything,but somehow I manage to maintain it. Despite these challenges, I'll continue to promote my book as best as I can with the resources I have available. My life is destined for change and requires significant faith and patience as I navigate this challenging journey with the resources TMH provides. As I mentioned, I am currently relying completely on the land for sustenance. While I'm sure some people expect me to return to my old way of life, I have no intention of doing so. Through my experiences, I have discovered alternative paths. For now, having shelter and food is sufficient. However, I intend to embark on a new journey and leave this place soon.I have no money to even get on the train, on foot, and on the bus these days as I continue to pray for a vehicle soon. I know it is for a reason as many have wished death upon my travels sending spell-work in hopes of an accident TMH is protecting me as he continues to reveal plots and plans on my life from others projected towards me unsuccessfully. I pray that one person finds my story and hears me. There is so much going on in life behind my back as it has been brought to my attention how my last son's father has been sleeping with his stepdaughter,my cousin as well as her daughter had a baby by her daughter and I believe I am not aware but that is not the concern. the concern is history repeats itself same as they left me there that night for my uncle to assault me, will the apple doesn't fall far from the tree as she is aware that he is assaulting her daughter but anything for a dollar and a buz it is sick and pray that the truth shines so bright that has been the secret also a possible hidden adoption of our son to be able to receive funds. His kids most before unfit spell caster also worked with his mother to keep an income based upon harvest energy as many in this cult/coven have been doing for years and i was on their agenda. These people are crazy people I do not care just give me my son stop being greedy and you continue to do whatever with whatever family you created along with the diseases obtained while doing so in other words continue to be nasty by yourself don't include me and mine in the "BOO BOO" with incest, confusion of sexuality, drugs, rituals, identity theft, fraud and whatever else. If you chose to sleep with your stepdaughter and other family and associates as said before she is not his biological daughter still creepy as he raised her as his own from birth just nasty but to each their own. They stole my identity to steal money, opened bank accounts in my name to cover the incest, and then did a false adoption saying I was deceased to steal and cover up their dirty laundry. Do yourself a favor and tell the truth and shame the devil who wants to keep it a family secret. Well tell the truth, do not include me and mine in it. This is crazy. I already knew something was going on. They are having a baby together or having sex it may not be his child or children as they are both Jezebels, he contracted HIV/AIDS while doing these rituals, and blaming and framing will not fix this. His mother, another Jezebel, plotted this. His constant drunkenness, cocaine use, and lust trapped him. She held this over his head as if I cared. We separated when my son was two. He kicked me out after she became pregnant around sixteen and had an abortion. Ironically, I was the one who exposed the pregnancy because they were oblivious.They conspired against our relationship as if they'd been practicing black magic for years. No one wanted us together, and they succeeded. I could never be with someone who would even consider such a thing, regardless of their understanding of right and wrong. It's unforgivable. I can forgive, but it's done, and that chapter is closed forever.He wants to bring up the fact that I slept with his friend, but we weren't even together at the time - it was years after we'd broken up. He didn't care about me at all, especially because he thought he had the upper hand since he was sleeping with my cousin while treating me like dirt. The only reason he even knew about my actions was because he saw his friend's car parked in my lot on his way to my cousin's place. His friend was there for me when I needed a friend and had no one. We were friends; he helped me and I helped him as we were both going through a difficult time. We were only friends out of respect for him; I purposely created an argument between us, after researching he too was a part of setting me up to help steal from me. no one can be trusted as well they all leave me but want to return truth be told i intimidate many as i have been on all sides good and bad, street and schooled,up and down i am adaptive no matter what environment is presented i will fit in as i was design and molded that way as i walk by faith not fear. He was playing with my emotions and lying to me about his future intentions while being unfaithful to me with my family and others, which is why he is sick. I have been made aware of similar things he has done with his family as well. I no longer care about anything from my past as I have let it go many years ago, yet I am still trying to hold onto myself as many people before and after are all conspiring against me.

My parents continue to cover up secrets on how they collaborated with my exes and sibling to destroy my life giving my personal information to them so they would be able to file child support, false adoptions, and insurance policies hoping to unalive me for come-ups and remain in places stolen, obtain fancy cars and not worthy of with sex rituals and spell work. I pray the same way they obtained TMH strips it away in the same manner they obtained the same wish shall become their fate as I have returned all projections and closed out chapters that were open far too long out of the love for my children and now my children are grown, I am free from all the "BOO BOO". I'm ready to start a new chapter filled with loyalty, laughter, fun, travel, and everlasting true love. I know it's out there; I'm just waiting for it to arrive, and when it does, I'll be ready.

I've intentionally revisited certain areas of my past to ensure they're closed, with no possibility of return or further delays. I put myself at risk to close out what was no longer good and holding on. I released these things years ago and needed no further closure. I'm done with falseness, illusions, and lies. I provided closure because it was necessary, regardless of others' opinions. The opportunity was given and lost; there will be no second chances. These chapters are closed for me, and if others choose to cling to them, so be it. I followed instructions and did what was needed.

I cared for my children despite the lies and deceit used to gain power. I remained present amidst confusion, kickbacks, and personal destruction. The root of this hate-filled game lies in my identity as an omnist—one who embraces all religions—and my unwavering honesty, which I refuse to be ashamed of. My intelligence, street smarts, and enduring beauty have always attracted envy and resentment, despite the hardships I've faced. They aimed to break me, but years of enduring trials have made me unbreakable, except by the Higher Power I was taught to trust. They fail to realize that their attempts to steal my gifts—my children, men, books, cars, and pieces of my life—stem from a desire to emulate the very person they despise.The ex-lovers were sent in to unalive me for their fake come-ups that will only last temporarily it was not earned so it will not last anything built off what was stolen will fall and TMH has promised me that much. Then you have the ex-co-workers sleeping with the old bosses for a come-up at work watching my home doing rituals outside my home, neighbors listening and recording my conversations. I am not scared or intimidated as they constantly gang-stalked and harassed me daily to try to cover up so many crimes from past and present. My children are trying to manipulate me. One son, who is incarcerated, is sending messages to an account I no longer use, trying to extort me. My other son is sending me cash app requests but refuses to contact me directly, believing it will somehow harm or weaken me. I cut ties with them four years ago when I realized they were trying to harm me, and I refuse to go back to being betrayed and mistreated. I know my own capabilities and I'm not looking for trouble, but I won't hesitate to defend myself if necessary. I've changed so much that I barely recognize myself, and people shouldn't underestimate me.I will continue to ignore all attempts to derail me, through gang-stalking, scare tactics, or any other means. These attempts will not succeed in taking me off my path.

I am learning new and important things on this new journey. The biggest lesson I learned was the power of the word "NO." I realized that my associate was in my life to teach me this. Saying "NO" has often led to traumatic experiences for me, especially with sex. I feared that saying "NO" would be useless and that people would do as they wished anyway, particularly in marriage and relationships. I have allowed others, especially men, to disrespect me out of fear of sexual, physical, and mental abuse. Without realizing it, I have released this fear. I had to learn the magic of the word "NO" and stand behind it, despite my belief that it wouldn't be respected. To my surprise, it was the best feeling I have ever experienced in life. With the help of TMH, I have overcome my fear of assault and recognized that I was prioritizing others' happiness and allowing them to control me. I am not an object to be possessed or played with at anyone's convenience. I am not a rug to be walked on or a door to be opened and closed at will. This chapter of my life is closed, and I am moving forward on a new journey of self-fulfillment and respect.

I am thankful to the TMH for helping me see my trauma and giving me the strength to heal. I feel ready to continue my journey of self-discovery and truth-seeking. I've realized that many people I've helped have used my kindness against me. I taught them, gave them strength, and helped them find their self-worth, but they betrayed me and tried to destroy mine. They will never succeed with deception. I am a teacher, always learning and growing, and I will never give up. I will always get back up, no matter how many times I fall. Life is unpredictable, so be prepared for change. We often postpone our destinies by holding onto things that hinder our growth and prosperity. It's time to let go and move towards our true purpose.

I've received shocking news about my family. The people who raised me are not my biological parents as previously mentioned. My real father was murdered by them by my sibling who i was raised to believe were my aunts and uncle are really sister and brothers. My grandfather is actually my stepdad, and my stepmom is my sister- in-law,my siblings are nieces and nephews. Well I think you get it . Nothing is as it appeared. The woman I thought was my mom isn't my birth mother. Apparently my true mother slept with my grandfather who was either just out there ,an addict or just not fit, not sure.I was switched at birth or stolen and adopted. My medical records were altered due to my deception . Another well hidden secret in the family everyone has known. I was not notified however until all transitions that hold the true details of my story. Information was left to explain when I was younger . Only they concealed the truth and stole what was left for me. They continued doing this through the depths of my life not giving A care so it was not necessary they had far more sinister plans for me. In fact after several unsuccessful attempts on my life they decided to defame me and give others the perception of I am insane.The truth is I was given to the government as part of a secret experiment that everyone has gotten compensated for despite me being the guinea pig crazy but true. The government and my family have conspired together to observe the most different obstacles in life to see how I would respond and if I would remain alive through all things created to create disaster by locking me away as they would a lab rat testing all things creating near death and deadly situations for decades . Apparently I'm not what or who I am. was told. I always knew the government made things. How do you think COVID was created ? Some scientist was experimenting and there are many cases, man and animal half fish. They do these things and I am ladies and gentlemen a part of those creations unfortunately.I'm determined to uncover the truth. My birth mother had an affair with him, and I was taken from her at birth. She was already married to a wealthy man who was unaware that I wasn't his biological child. As the truth was about to be revealed, he was alive. He had already named me in his will, leaving me his estate.I'm confused, but I know I'm close to the truth. There are still some missing pieces of the puzzle. My father unloved by his own daughter same as my grandmother and my brother as we both are not considered blood as he has a different father and I had a different mother and after my grandfather passed away they decided we were not worthy and straight up just took what was left from me after them unaliving my brother My biological stepdad one of which to believed to be grand stepdad my entire life entertained a younger lady who was not considered fit after having having an affair and that I was the result. My sister-in -law along with their offspring and the offspring of those created after decided they were not going to give up the life they created made up of lies for decades . In fact they unlived everyone to maintain it. they even created false deaths, took on identities, and collected off policies. it is scam been one for years but i imagined whom ever created this idea or scheme never expected me to return with the truth as my gifts was switched, swappedout while i fed lies,put in the most dangerous situation the truth behind it all was i hold a gift so powerful that if ever revealed i could destroy them all without even trying which has come to call.i have been able to see those transition as well speak to others in different realms that which to speak or tell their stories and i am sharing those stories right now through the hearts of many that were deceived and betrayed. I am their vessel, siblings and others teamed , and stole my inheritance as well my birthright and the ancestors are furious as they weren't expecting such betrayal, along with others. My race and age were major factors in their ability to take what was rightfully mine.These things have not returned as they continue to live off, live in, and recruit many to unalive me to cover up the crimes for a life never destined for them. The funny thing is as soon as they unalived my father and my brother for wanting to come forward and tell me the truth of it all. They came for me, it was the incident mentioned in my last book. It must be understood these are two separate men, my biological father and the husband of my biological mother, both unloved by family to cover up lies. I spoke of previously while living in Capitol Heights and the visions of Beyonce and other artists thinking my house was bugged, FBI, DEA, and CIA were watching as they sent hitmen into unalive me. This was my biological father letting me know what was going to happen and what had already taken place as well. My son was in the vision having an orgy in fact the entire family was the sex rituals spoken of with my ex's, children and family still my energy and trying to get me to conform to it all. I was on medication so I just knew I was for sure tripping. After all, I wanted to wake up from just the site of it all, an illusion and a vision into the past,present, and current things. i thought nothing of it at the time as they erased my memory but i have always had the ability to foresee things before they occur only i was made to believe i was crazy, it was my imagination despite me knowing for sure i saw it unbeknownst to me they unalived the one person remswith the truth aside them and then came for causing me to try and unilever myself and landing me in the hospital. My fake father came to pick me up on Memorial Day as well. My sister-cousin was celebrating her birthday with things which were stolen. All things continued for years, all lies.. In my last book I briefly discussed the energy swapping of my son as well, I had no idea how serious and real it was from all the medications thought I was delusional this was way before I realized I had gifts.As a child, my gifts were stifled, and I was frequently silenced and mistreated. This was because the truth was being revealed through me, and they didn't want me to understand any of it. I believe I have a twin. There were always rumors of someone having twins, with one transitioning. I don't believe she transitioned; instead, I think we were separated and switched due to my skin color. This was in the 1970s, before DNA systems were in place, so paperwork could be easily falsified. I haven't fully investigated this yet, but I will.The most important thing covered is anything attached to me prospers which is why I was molested and assaulted as a kid so often more than I could remember due to the spell work done on me to make me forget and cover the torture I had been through they all attached themselves to me I believe sexually to live good lives and swapping destinies while I have been in poverty, sick, jailed, and abused the lives all destined for the lives they had chosen before I came along and now it makes since as to why my sister decided to molest me as she more in likely witnessed others doing these things to me sad thing is she hates me thinking I stole her light and attention well she can have the "BOO BOO" I went through I may not remember it all but what I do it is nothing to be jealous of trust me.I am piecing together my memories and realizing that I am blessed. TMH had to love me because no one else ever has; I was treated as worthless and auctioned off to the highest bidder. This is sadly the truth.

It also makes sense that they claim to have found a video at my grandmother's house. I'm only now finding out that she has passed away and that I was never notified. They assumed I would never find out because my grandmother and I barely spoke after what they did to my mother. They went through her belongings and are aware of everything I'm talking about, yet they neglected to tell me about their actions to steal the trust and inheritance my grandmother left for me. My family has stolen multiple inheritances that were rightfully mine, including a house and vehicle left by my grandmother, and possibly CDs and stocks from my paternal grandparents. Additionally, I inherited a home from my biological father and potentially something from my biological mother's husband. Despite my family's claims that I am incompetent and unwell, I am actually financially secure due to these inheritances. Observing me you would not know that as I have never had access to anything, everything I have is earned despite their interceptions to keep me in poverty. They have used lies and deception to steal from me while living in my home, driving my vehicle, and withdrawing from my accounts.The incoherence of their claims is baffling. How can they declare me incompetent, unable to work, file taxes, or manage social security, while simultaneously claiming I'm incapable of self-care and according to them I transitioned? Well I am alive only under the name given, but so much has been altered and accepted.They lived with me in my home until I had them removed, and I was the one taking care of them. Then, they turned around and filed life insurance policies on me, falsely claiming I had passed away. This is utterly illogical and contradictory.. I laugh at how ignorant and greedy people truly are. This has been the reason for making me sick, incarcerating, trying to drive me insane all the make me disappear if I and, I was any of these things I would not be traceable allowing them to continue to reap the proceeds a lot of people involved to make this happen which is not difficult due to the many rankings in my family law officials, doctors, nurses, military, there are so many I could go on for days. I am bringing this to light. I did not have all the details but thanks to my passed over loved ones, related and unrelated as well, high ranked officials that were unalived have come and told all the tea for their justice and mine. They have paid so many to be a part. We have mayors, politicians, judicial all with acknowledgement of all these things done and have done nothing all paid to be silent and overlook things for payment and their own self gratifications. I always knew something was wrong. After unaliving my father with spell work and black magic and discovering they were not included in the will and estate they decided to take me out to collect mine and theirs too if anything was even left to them. I'm fairly certain I wasn't the only one my father left something to. I have been a secret for a long time so I have siblings who know me, but I'm unaware of their identities as of today I am not sure of my own identity.

There was a joke as a kid that when my grandfather passed away, my father wouldn't inherit anything because my grandparents raised all his kids and helped their moms. However, that was only partially true.I do have a sister, but I saw online that she passed away in 2012. However, due to my brother's connection at the funeral home, she may still be alive. If so, she and my brother could explain why my mail has been intercepted, as he is the supervisor at the post office and has held that position for years.

This has been an ongoing issue for four years, and I have escalated my complaint this year. Instead of going to the postal inspectors or postal manager, I went higher up. I am waiting to see the outcome and hoping for a resolution. Unfortunately there have not been any changes. They only give me what they feel necessary for worries as the bill continues to build as employment is limited due to them calling places of employment. To ensure my mail reaches its intended destination, I have started taking it outside of my neighborhood to mail it, rather than using the mailbox in my building. The government has failed to stop criminals from faking deaths, collecting money, stealing policies, and committing murder. This is both sad and sickening. Despite my numerous reports to the FTC and other government and law enforcement agencies, these activities persist.

Suspicious activities around my home between 12-5 am have prompted me to change my sleep schedule to keep watch. Additionally, there have been attempts to hack my email throughout the night, and I'm constantly receiving verification requests.I am not changing anything else this time except my password and adding the verification code as part of the verification process and only I can view it. They do this to keep me with no communication and since I know everyone is watching, including the FEDS, let them keep doing it as I have faith TMH will make it all known in time. I know all law officials are not corrupt. I still am careful; this must end.I have been under attack for the past four to five years. They have cast numerous spells to silence me and force me to give up. They have blocked my finances, hacked my emails, and gang-stalked me to prevent me from receiving job offers and prospering. Despite their efforts to sabotage my income, including the sales of my book, I remain unbothered.TMH sees this and I wait for him to show up and show out soon. I am up early awaiting the Salvation Army and Mary's Center to pick up these donations. I should be sleepy only. I am not. My heart is set on revealing everyone that was involved. They may be able to stop my communication online, but not physically even though I am also being followed, constantly gang stalked, and harassed. I am under attack by at least twenty-five individuals, all driven by different motives. My ex and their associates are enraged that they can no longer control me, manipulate my finances, or dictate my life. They have taken out loans and insurance policies in my name, abducted my children, and misappropriated funds intended for them, including tax refunds, benefits, and child support.

My family has stolen the inheritance left to me by my father after his and my mother's suspicious deaths. Additionally, my son's father, along with his family and associates, have engaged in fraudulent adoption practices and stolen the settlement check from my 2005 accident. This accident resulted in memory loss, a coma, nerve damage, and facial plastic surgery. The associated paperwork and legal cases have mysteriously vanished, leaving me without recourse or a proper investigation. I have done nothing to deserve this relentless persecution. I simply walked away from a toxic and abusive situation. I have never sought revenge, choosing instead to rely on prayer and faith. Despite their ongoing attempts to harm me and my loved ones, I remain hopeful that justice will prevail. I will continue to document my experiences in the hope that an official will uncover the truth and hold those responsible accountable. I do not feel safe, but I trust in TMH and my guardian angels. They have protected me through multiple attempts on my life and allowed me to share my story. Through these trials, I have come to realize how truly blessed and favored I am.

This isn't just happening on the outside; it's also happening behind bars and around the world. They are trying to destroy my second son's , his father whom I will always consider my first love. I began dating him shortly after breaking up with my high school sweetheart.We used to hang out, go to hotels, and I was often at his house or on the block with him late at night. He always encouraged me to stay in school, and when he was arrested while I was pregnant, I took care of everything on my own. I kept his books straight and prepared for our son. He taught me not to put all my eggs in one basket and never rely on anyone to treat you the same as you treated them. He taught me that it's every man for himself and that love loves no one. No matter how much time, effort, or loyalty you put into love, it can all be wiped away in an instant. He taught me never to get attached and to expect that everything can change at any moment. They have ordered a hit on me, tried to plant drugs and weapons they used to commit crimes in my home, and collaborated with my son. He is incarcerated, angry about his life, and easily angered like me. He was never silent, always a fighter. He is working with them out of anger and feels like no one cares. I spoiled my children, unaware of what I went through to make everything possible for them. I gave them time and devotion to keep them safe because I knew my family. He is also being extorted in jail. They are using him to get to me. Some Days I wish I would have never entertained getting my oldest son when they returned him allowing them access to me. I forgot to mention the reason for his return was due to the same thing that happened to me as a kid incest my cousin's daughter was touching him at least that is what he expressed to me upon his return and then would later tell my second son I did not care about them based on the brainwashing he received while residing with the demons. I have always loved and provided for them generously, even when I had nothing left for myself. I made sacrifices to ensure they had everything they needed, including money for education and other expenses. Unfortunately, they did not reciprocate this love and understanding when I was no longer able to maintain that level of support. Instead, they focused on the material things I had always provided. They took advantage of my generosity, even stealing from me and portraying me as incapable. Despite this, I continued to support them financially, along with other family members, F.A.N.S., and friends. In 2015-2016, shortly after my probation ended for falsely accusing my second husband of assault and my son was released from prison, I opened my door to him, hoping for a different outcome than the one that had repeatedly disappointed me. Unfortunately, my actions led to my second son's current incarceration for stealing a vehicle and committing a robbery at a gas station. My sister has never disguised her dislike for me, frequently announcing it to family members from the moment I arrived. Her hatred stems from the fact that I worked hard to achieve the life she wanted for herself but chose a different path. I'm tired of the lies, projections, and delays, so I'm telling my story. To clarify the half-truths that have been spread, here is a brief recap from my previous book before moving forward. I was embarrassed and didn't want to say anything about it, but I'm 43 and it's time to tell the truth. You can't assume something is okay just because trusted family members (like my sister, uncle by marriage, and many others who were paid off) said it was. They led me to believe they were showing me love, but now I look back and question those years. I had a son at 14, and I wonder why. My sister used to molest all of us, me and my cousins' boys and girls or exploring as she would say it didn't matter, she was in that line of work(prostitution) and the oldest, so everyone followed her and since we never got caught in a mindset between the ages of seven to thirteen it was okay. When it started, I did not have a clue what I was doing, did not even know anything could be inserted in the hole until my uncle showed how that worked after molesting me for years and then finally one day just said forget it and just rammed his wand in me as I was virgin and I was only thirteen and he had to be about thirty-five or something I do not know all I remember is the pain from it all. I said that to say that if I had never been exposed to any of that if I had never been exposed to too many situations throughout my life in the first place maybe I would have said something instead of nothing this is just what people do to show the love they cannot mean to hurt me because we are family which left an open door for a predator like my oldest son's father and many others because thought it was okay because no actions were ever taken. My sister has been hurting me for years. I finally got to the point where I am just not accepting any more of her "BOO BOO," the list goes on and on. Calling the police, having the police come to my home not once but three times, and stealing my identity so many times. I am so tired of it that I just cut off everybody because no one loved me or even cared they wanted me to fail so many times because they were using my identity all these years seven years of back and forth with the government that was working with her because they changing my paperwork and writing in the reports that weren't true. My sister is fake as usual pretending she cares when we all know I am the last person she wants to help or to be happy. This has been a problem for years but I thought my last straw was when she took my kids and kept them for her own selfish needs instead of being a big sister and helping me in a bad situation even finding out the truth still stabbed me repeatedly in my back remember my kids were removed during the raid yeah well that lasted all of seven and a half years before my second son was molested and sexual assaulted while in foster care is what I was told as get back for all the years she could not beat me so she teamed up with others that were jealous and haters because at some point I told them to kick rocks as well all had their cards pulled at some point and did not want to admit that they needed me I helped and they abused it so when I cut everyone off they hated me for not carrying all their weight with my hands being tied I had been already dealt with how they wanted it to be and I steal win with a full house every time despite all the poker faces. They would return damaged goods to me, shifting the blame onto the person who had been supportive, maintaining peace, and taking care of everyone. Knowing the outcome wouldn't benefit any of us, I should have simply let it go.

Returning to our previous conversation, she asked me to accompany her to the grocery store, which I did. Upon returning home, I found my son and his friend terrified. I had put my son out a few days prior for breaking my rules. They were scared, looking out the windows, and although I sensed something was wrong, I couldn't quite identify it at the time. He had been asked to leave previously due to his constant rule-breaking, which included staying out until 2-3 am, stealing from the house, and selling my medication. The day I saw the fear in his eyes, I knew he had done something wrong. I demanded to know the truth, warning him that he would have to leave if he didn't confess. He denied any wrongdoing, but a mother knows her child. I insisted he leave my house that day. My sister and I arrived home to find a suspicious van parked outside. She joked that I'd better hope my son hadn't done anything wrong. A few days earlier, my son had noticed a man taking pictures of our house, but I didn't think much of it at the time. However, my son was arrested a few days later, despite my warnings that his actions would land him back in jail. I even offered him my fare card, but he continued to drive around in the same stolen vehicle. The day before my birthday, my home was raided. I didn't realize at the time that this was another setup.The police arrived at my residence with a warrant to conduct a search. However, due to my past experiences with raids on Queen Street, I had learned the importance of verifying the warrant's validity. Upon inspection, I noticed that the presented warrant lacked the necessary signature. Despite their premature entry into my home, I firmly prohibited them from touching any of my belongings. During the raid, my psychotherapist was present and engaged in a disagreement with one of the officers after lighting a cigarette indoors. The officer demanded that he extinguish it, a request they had no authority to make, especially considering all my doors and windows were open in the subzero temperature. I was in no mood for further confrontation. He left, and I waited for over an hour and a half for a signed warrant to continue the search. During this time, PG County was called in for a robbery on the MD side. They completed the search and found a gun under his mattress, along with stolen IDs and credit cards that were likely placed there while I was out with my sister as they had retrieved his keys which were given to me after the search.

This all makes sense now; they were trying to set me up again, assuming I was still on probation, which I had completed less than a week before the raid. This would have resulted in my arrest. They had already arrested him earlier, and they thought I would be joining him.The vehicle that he had stolen was the reason for PG coming to my house he had robbed someone he had gone to someone's home and homicide was committed on New Year's my son informed me he was going to get back at some guy for a stupid Obama phone and a cheap under armor coat told me while he was intoxicated he had gone into the gas station to get something and when he came back the guy left he was determined to get him back and I told him it was not worth it to leave it alone, My money was funny at the time being sick from all the spell work and black magic being done at the time. He was impatient, and I was doing my best. While I was out of town for New Year's with my ex-partner, he called and told me he was going to the club with his friend. My son was later charged with robbery, possession of a stolen vehicle, and accessory after the fact. He was caught near my house with the stolen car, ID, and gun from the incident. As a result, he was sentenced to fifteen years in prison.

This was another setup intended for me, but it landed him back in jail. He had just been released from federal prison, and now he was in a Maryland state prison. They paid him to set me up, and it's all starting to make sense now that my memory is slowly returning.I've endured many hardships without recognizing the hidden dangers around me. I believe that both my son and I were targeted due to our giftedness. They've attempted to dim his light as they did mine, but he's still young, reckless, and angry – much like I once was. Despite my struggles, I never resorted to stealing, unlike him. Perhaps different standards are applied based on gender. They targeted him knowing he'd protect me, as he always has. However, at his age, money seemed to solve everything. Both his father and I are guilty of making life appear easy – I spoiled him, and his father showcased a life of luxury without consequences. This explains his materialistic focus, even though material possessions are ultimately meaningless and have led him to his current predicament. He should not be in maximum security for the crimes he committed unless there's something I don't know about. As far as I'm aware, he was an accessory; someone else pulled the trigger. If stealing a car puts you in maximum security, that's news to me. My ex likely gave him the gun. My sister, as usual, sent the police after me as I would later discover they were sleeping together behind my back and had prior connections, the same as many she sent in to sabotage my life. I just went through lock-up, homelessness, and classes for defending myself, and only took a plea deal on the advice of my public defender. I recall the day she picked me up in a brand new, shiny red Kia Rio, a replacement for her old Caprice with the blown motor. As I opened the car door, she was on the phone with my aunt via speakerphone, giving instructions on what to write "so I can notarize it." She abruptly ended the call, saying, "Well, I'm here now picking up CC, so I'll call you back." I could sense they were talking about me.

Moreover, that week everyone seemed to get a new vehicle: my cousin a white Infinity, my father a new Tesla, and her son a Kia (I don't recall the model). I find it peculiar that this all happened right before my marriage and right after my father's death. They were all driving new cars while I was still doing DoorDash and paying for a rental car just to get to my 9-to-5 job. My family is strange and dysfunctional. It's sad that they can look at themselves in the mirror and still live with themselves. Every holiday, my youngest son's father would show up unexpectedly, pretending to let me spend time with my son. The truth was to stop any plans I had knowing I would never turn any of my children away.. This was their way of ensuring that my special days were ruined. They were determined to create trauma and prevent me from being happy.

One year, on my birthday, he appeared and we went to his father's house. At that time, I wasn't fully aware of their deliberate attempts to sabotage my happiness and success. They used distractions to keep me from speaking out about their betrayals. They knew I would always prioritize my children, who are my everything. For a long time, my life revolved around my love for them. I realized that I needed to break the cycle of allowing their fathers to control my life through my children. It was a painful decision, but necessary. I knew it would hurt my son, but I had learned from past experiences that they were using my children to manipulate me while they continued their unfaithful pursuits. I had erased the identities of those who had betrayed me from my mind, refusing to acknowledge their true nature. But TMH reminded me and intervened to protect me once again. The individual everyone envied after seeing my pictures online, showcasing our constant travels and leisure, provided me with everything I desired. However, the price was his escalating irritability, fueled by snooping and accusations aimed at provoking me. He failed to realize that my time in the shelter, coupled with counseling and anger management classes, had equipped me to handle such situations calmly. I felt calm in the knowledge of my innocence. Approximately a week following the raid, my ex-husband called and wanted to take me out. We ended up at a girl's house off South Capital St, SE, WDC, and MLK Ave SE. He was trying to provoke a fight after she commented that I was pretty then stated with confusion and anger, "I thought she was dead." As she became irate, I left and we returned to his mother's house around the Pinnacles. He knew I hated being there because of my childhood trauma, but my son was there so I stayed. Unbeknownst to me, it was all a setup. He lied to his friend about me being sick and abandoning my son. Despite this, his friend and I ended up talking and spending time together. Then, he would cut off communication with my son and try to intimidate me by coming to my house. I was no longer afraid, so this didn't work. The painful disconnection was necessary. Afterward, they sent another hitman who feigned interest. I ended the relationship when I discovered he was dishonest, inconsistent, and married but separated. He had told me he was recently divorced, but this was untrue. Ultimately, they sent in my second husband to conclude the situation. another hitman sent in to poison me or unalive me while sleeping which while cleaning my house out preparing to move and packing his things would discover a machete above the bed on the side which he slept, poisoning my coffee every morning to make me sick after having his mistresses in and out of my home as well poisoning my food, drinks, stealing items to try to later frame for a "M" committed earlier before him coming in to propose to me part of the reason for the proposal and him constantly trying to keep me under the same illusions from my past by constantly bringing thing up as well as feeling privy to my new life in which was obtained through the hard work of classes and counseling, not to mention me being homeless after my arrest for assaulting him due to self-defense which would explain my medical records being tampered with at the time of my arrest all my paperwork from doctors were there as I had been applying for social security for years and have always been denied funny how he and his Jezebels could claim it and this is the law will live by.

I feel like the world is against me as I continue to face more and more adversaries. Even people I don't know, along with a group of deceitful men who have joined forces with my exes, are targeting me based on lies. They are motivated by greed and the desire for an easy, luxurious life that they haven't earned. Despite these challenges, I trust that TMH will ultimately turn things around.It's disheartening that so many people seem to have nothing better to do than meddle in the lives of others. As I reflect on the stories I've uncovered about past and present relationships, both within my family and beyond, I'm struck by the sheer number of unhappy individuals. It's true what they say: misery loves company. I'm not worried, despite everyone having their own hidden agendas. They're all disloyal and will eventually betray each other to save themselves. The truth will come out eventually. Although I'm uncertain about the future, I sense that it will be positive and wonderful once everything is revealed.

I don't know exactly what was taken or stolen, but it involved PPP loans. My ex-husband asked me about it before I kicked him out, suggesting that I would be okay with the scheme. He mentioned that his associate had someone on the inside and had already received two loans. As an accountant, I know that everything leaves a digital and paper trail. He wanted to use my account, but I refused.Regardless, I was ready to move on and leave everything behind. None of this makes sense. The destruction, delays, and cover-ups stemmed from crimes, lies, and envy. They assumed I'd repeat past mistakes and take on others' karma. Instead, I chose a different path, regardless of potential losses. I was accustomed to starting over; if necessary, I'd leave, and I did.

Despite facing unexpected challenges, I remain optimistic. My perspective on life has shifted. While my book sales and profits haven't met expectations, my purpose lies in the message—to expose corruption, inspire change, and guide others. Setting boundaries with my landlord has been essential in maintaining my autonomy. I haven't received a response to my message, as usual. Despite the ongoing struggles and behind-the-scenes issues, I'm focused on my happiness and freedom. I'm continuing to work on my book and have an interview tomorrow for a job that doesn't align with my desired income. Although I'm not where I want to be financially, I remain hopeful and patient, trusting that things will work out in time. I'm awaiting TMH and praying that everything I'm working on grows. I've decided to focus on the important things in life. Although my days feel overwhelming at times, I know it's not as bad as it seems. I'm hoping for a new vehicle to expand my marketing efforts, but I trust in TMH's plan, which is often greater than my own, despite the negativity that comes my way. I'm considering removing my eBook from Amazon due to their profit margins and adjusting the prices of my paperback and hardcover to see if that improves my earnings. My love life remains unfulfilling, as all my current options seem motivated to destroy, slander, and embarrass me. I've felt alone for years, even in relationships. I've given up on love because it's been a constant disappointment. I love myself more, and if TMH intends for me to have a partner, he will provide one. My phone will be disconnected again soon. I had hoped to earn enough to cover my personal and daily expenses. I will continue to pray and have faith that TMH will provide, as he always has.

I've reached a point where I only feel safe within the confines of my home, despite the constant surveillance both inside and out. These desperate individuals, with their empty lives, are relentless in their attempts to sabotage me. Their goal is to make me abandon TMH and my journey, but I've come too far to turn back now. I have a different strategy in mind. I've found ways to share my story on various platforms, hoping to reach a wider audience. I need to have faith and trust that everything will work out as it should. The universe will guide me and keep me safe if I follow my path. Everything happens for a reason, and I must pay attention to the signs around me. If I stay positive and focused, I will succeed.I am always able to rise above challenges because of my faith. TMH will never let me fall or give up, and I'm always pushed to reach my full potential. I used to question why people pushed me so hard, but it was because they saw something in me that I couldn't. I am truly blessed and favored.

I know that I can only fall so far, and even when others might see it as a failure, TMH allows me to learn and grow from the experience. Things are not always as they seem; they are simply challenges that lead to destined change. I remain silent and faithful, waiting for my turn. I know a breakthrough is near because things seem more difficult than ever. But troubles don't last, and "this too shall pass." Everything will happen in its own time.

So many forgotten memories are flooding back to me now, maybe because of the retrograde or maybe because I released my book along with all the negativity that was attached to it. I remember meeting another associate sometime around 2008, after my last son's father took me out and I ended up at my aunt's 7-Eleven in Fort Washington, MD - a place I truly hated. Our relationship was casual, yet he consistently appeared during my times of need, offering either conversation or assistance. It wasn't based on sex; it was a genuine friendship. When another person mentioned him while I was struggling, we reconnected and hooked up a few times. However, due to my personal challenges, we disconnected again. Despite this, we always found our way back to each other, regardless of the time apart. We both had our own separate lives and never held any expectations. We were simply cool with each other. He always showed up when I called, unlike many men in my past. I never had any expectations; everything just flowed. When I became engaged, I promised my ex-husband that I would not contact anyone from my past. We were both supposed to erase all contacts, but he kept his – along with all his nasty videos and naked pictures of his "Jezebels" that I would discover after marriage; so much deception. After my divorce, I tried to contact him on Facebook, but he's rarely on social media, and I couldn't remember his phone number. We hooked up and chilled, but not too much. He was an independent contractor, and I was an accountant, always moving around. He was younger than me and I think he realized I was married, so he moved on. He was kind and driven, which made him desirable as a partner - I admired those qualities in him. He was also very focused on his career, just as I was. Many things have been erased from my memory, either due to head traumas or my family's involvement with black magic. Every time I've come close to happiness, it's been interrupted by illness or having to move. Everyone I've been close to has come at a price. I can't find happiness in D.C., and I need to go somewhere where no one knows me or my past. I want a relationship where we remain connected even when separated. I want to walk in parks, have picnics, take endless pictures, have lunch dates, party together, go on vacations, and make passionate love. I want to have everlasting fun and make up for all my lost years and memories, many of which were planned and not true. I want to make new memories with someone as special as me, with matching energy. I often imagine laying under the stars, making love all night long until the sunrise by the water.

Back to reality and the anxiety that comes with a scheduled job interview. My days have been chaotic lately, and writing helps to pass the time while I reorganize my life. I'm removing what doesn't serve me anymore and focusing on what does. It's like having a box of mixed-up puzzle pieces; it'll take time to sort through and solve, but things are gradually becoming clearer each day to create a full picture.The truth about my parents remains a mystery, a puzzle for which I have only a few pieces. I know we're all connected, but only time will reveal the full truth. I'm still unsure about the number of enemies involved. Money has a powerful influence, causing both harm and destruction; it is one of the seven deadly sins, alongside greed, gluttony, and jealousy. I, however, have never been afflicted by these sins. I've never felt the need to chase what isn't meant for me. If something requires excessive effort to attain, it's not part of my destiny. Growth requires work, something these people don't believe in. Their only knowledge lies in stealing and killing.

I reflect on the countless individuals I've assisted. They achieved their positions using my resume and knowledge as a foundation, despite having minimal qualifications. I shared my resources and education, expecting nothing in return except for them to succeed. Ironically, they now use their success to appear superior, concealing the fact that their accomplishments were built upon the generosity and knowledge that I selflessly provided.I supported them through their abuse, encouraging them to find jobs and become independent so they could escape the life I had lived – a life of abuse and hardship. Life has a way of humbling you when you start to reject things you once accepted. The problem is that others expect you to remain stagnant, never evolving or growing. People are happy to use, abuse, steal from, and manipulate you, but the moment you put a stop to it, they try to act superior and destroy everything you've built, only to claim it as their own. They have no understanding of the journey that brought you to your breaking point.I continue to pray for the healing of those who have hurt me, instead of feeling anger towards them. I also pray for those who are covering up their pain.

There are also those who were never around, but still want to be included for the wrong reasons. They spread lies and piggyback off of others to fit in. They are clout chasers that lack self-image and identity, and are camouflaged to blend in with others. These people are often referred to as energy vampires, which are different from shapeshifters who can blend in with anyone, anywhere. I believe that if I leave my current situation, I will be able to focus on new beginnings in a new environment. My landlord is intentionally harassing me. They're coming on Friday to cut my ceiling and check the pipes, then they're talking about putting up a tarp until next week. If they're going to cut the ceiling on Friday, why not just repair it over the weekend instead of making me uncomfortable? They have to make the repairs by the 29th anyway.

I'm also sick of the nosy person who keeps texting me the same questions over and over. I ignored her this time. She's still trying to invade my space and spy on me, asking about my medical insurance again as if I'm incompetent or trying to change or snoop in my records.Several individuals have attempted to interfere with my housing situation and coerce me into sharing   information. These actions are unwarranted, as my personal information is confidential. They seem to expect my silence and compliance in the face of these invasions; however, I will not be intimidated. I am honest and transparent, and I document and report all relevant information, regardless of whether I am in danger. Dishonesty only exacerbates the situation and increases risk. In recent months, I have had to establish boundaries with numerous individuals who have repeatedly taken advantage of my kindness.Many people try to disrespect me now, but they wouldn't have dared when I was younger. That was before I healed and learned to control my reactions. I've grown to understand that acting out of anger or upset leads to poor decisions and severe consequences, especially when drugs and alcohol are involved. It's amazing how much life experience, time, and maturity can change a person.I was once reckless and uncaring due to anger and loneliness. I believed that being loud and combative was the only way to be heard. Life, however, has taught me the value of silence. Silence has a different impact, leaving others to reflect and reveal their true selves. I've stopped feeding into others' egos and learned to simply breathe and walk away from triggers. This signifies that those who haven't healed have overdue work to address.Many people, like me, have used alcohol and drugs to mask their pain. While occasional fun is okay, and some may find relief from anxiety through these substances (believe me, I've been there), true healing comes from addressing the root causes. Issues don't resolve themselves; they worsen over time. That's why prayer, in any religion, is crucial. It provides solace and guidance. Even I struggled with the pain of losing loved ones, including my mother and grandparents. I stopped going to church and praying . I could not understand how he could allow things to happen and why he removed those that I loved and cherished so much . That was far from true; he didn't take them; he accepted them after they were unalived. Only it was not of TMH it was of the evilness within those surrounding churches, families, and associates' things we least expect. Why? It is because it is secure, feels right, and comfortable where the devil dwells in your comfort zone . If you don't believe me, walk away from it all and see just how many will follow and agree . Or will they shame you, continue to feed you things to destroy, criticize? But most of them will bring up the one thing they know you fear most, but that is your friend and family, right? No that is your foe and been kicking it with all this time sleeping, drinking, and dragging you down like a flat tire including unnecessary weight. Walk away, accept and love yourself or no one else will. It is not a great feeling only as soon as you realize your place and ask if it is for you or against you. Be true to yourself and I promise after there will be no shame in being yourself, we all must learn, and trust me it was all prepared long before taught or you are recognizing it all.

Another part of my journey has been revealed which was unexpected and disturbing all at the same time. At the time my mother was transitioning, she was in a relationship with the same guy for East-West Highway. When they moved her to the nursing home the same night a lot more happened than what was told to me. My sister told me she had let him know that my mom was dying from AIDs and the story was he went back to my mother's room and told her he knew the truth and at that time she transitioned. The truth is he was a practitioner and unalived her with black magic and that is what was set to repeat mother was sending warnings from above as he too has been in the plot of getting rid of me and stealing my inheritance. They were hoping to get me sick after infecting my past partners if not all in hopes one would unalive me only, I am not sick by the grace of TMH and the ringleader of all my betrayal, gang stalking, and the plans to unalive I was my ex-husband that I spoke of previously that had sex and possibly a baby with either my so-called best friend and contracted HIV/AIDS she blamed it on me saying he must have gotten it from me as this story continues to circulate and untrue I am not sick and the only sickness I had was projected to make me appear sick to maintain lies but as you can tell if you were to see me I am not sick I haven't been to the hospital since I left Sheriff Rd. I was sick from all the poisoning and black magic I remember before I kicked him out him still trying to project only, I had been to the doctors as usual for my physical and I remember the CDC calling me only I thought it was referencing the new vaccinations in which I refused to take and was advised not to due to medical conditions. He kept trying to get me to answer the call only I laughed and said that all my tests came back negative I showed him my portal and continued to laugh I said why you worried about it we have not been had sex since our honeymoon only he knew he had been creeping so he was aware then that he was sick and trying to tell me or project it either way I my not sick my cookie is clean nothing but flowers and candy there. Same as my husband before him saying to his man that he sent to my house that I had something. I laughed at him too and showed him my portal. They all knew I was not sick but still spread lies and then made me sick to make it appear that way. They have infected many of my past partners by blaming me. I am not sick and can pull my portal on demand and demand tests. My family has unalived one or more of my children I believe and it has not been discovered by authorities as of yet I only have not had a clear vision of this as we speak, but I know it is coming this is my firstborn son I believe as he was one who is which looks up to my mother's past lovers as his stepdad and remained in contact with my aunt my mother's sister which my sister remained in contact with after her past lovers trusted him, my past lovers trusted my sister as well all to be betrayed, infected, and possibly unalived. This is so deep I must investigate more, but I am determined to find the underlying cause of it all to get the justice they deserve and justice for myself. I have to say "WOW" as I realize things were never as they appeared. They as well have also been trying to frame me for a redrum of whom I have not confirmed yet they unlived someone's wife and I believe one of my exes who was working with my family discovered they made them sick at this time it needs more investigating, but they buried her in a pond by a cabin in Connecticut. I need more time so I will stick a pin to it for now as it will be revealed soon enough this is why they have been trying to unalive me so many hidden secrets about things stolen, unaliving others to silence me as I can communicate beyond and they stole from me in process unloved others that knew the truth not realizing it all would be revealed by TMH they thought they ended my gifts as I said what is destined is destined.

My career is at a standstill. My references are not responding, as they are also involved and have hindered my career advancement. Additionally, my book sales are not meeting expectations; Amazon is profiting more than I am. It has been a difficult journey, but I have come too far to give up now. My love life is also uncertain; trust must be earned.I feel ambivalent and desire change. I'm tempted to abandon everything and start anew, but I'm too close to the end. TMH asked me to finish the mission, but progress is slow, and bills persist. I've considered focusing solely on tarot readings, but I'm uncertain about my interpretations for myself and unprepared to read for others due to the fear of misinterpretation and the responsibility that comes with it.I haven't been able to come up with a plan, and I need more practice. Something is being blocked, but I'm not sure what TMH wants me to see. I don't have anyone to talk to because I've cut off all ties with people from past jobs, friends, and family. I'm tired of the never-ending difficulties and the creepy feeling of being watched and stalked. This makes relationships, friendships, and intimacy impossible. I just want to be free and loved. I pray for change soon because I'm lonely, broke, and moody. The more I reveal, the longer it seems to take. Just when I think things are coming to an end, the cycle repeats. I'm sick of it and ready to give up. Wherever I land will be where I end up. I see others' love and achievements, and I wish for that someday. Everything takes time.

After asking for clarity as I have said many times, things never are as they appear in life. My youngest son's father along with my ex-husband, family, and F.A.N.S. sent in past and present decided to lie to Muslim/Islamic societies which many are a part of to have them gang on me along with my children. This is not only a huge disappointment it is sick the truth has been revealed. I am not dead; I am well and enjoying life as they have faked their deaths and mine for financial reasons, as I said there are so many after me for material things. I didn't even have a clue about any of this until TMH revealed my enemies and plots after isolating, meditating, praying for guidance and truth on all that participated in constant attacks on my life. I asked TMH to reveal all that were causing destruction and delays in my life and it saddens me that my own children would do that to me, only not shocking after all look who their fathers are a bunch of lazy, drug addicted, and sex crazed individuals and let us not forget the one person in which joined forces to cause my demise no one other than my parents who which really are not and ever have been just was a continued auction on my life they worked so hard so many years to destroy my life and they did that by hooking up with the weakest links from my past whom I have shared cords with through past relationships and my children with and the middle man and which my thought to be siblings which really are my nieces/ nephews all to maintain in positions and maintain gifts stolen and obtained by stealing my identity, slandering, purchasing, and creating fake profiles, using past mistakes many before I was twenty-five still young and dumb without any guidance in hopes that I would never figure out who played a part in these things.My path to success was not always clear. It took years of abuse, loss, repeated cycles, jail, wards, and fights for me to realize that my life wouldn't change until I changed my perspective. I covered my pain with drinking, drugs, and sex, but once I ripped the bandage off and faced my healing by letting TMH in, I was able to feel it and heal it all. I received a new beginning, but others, out of hate and envy, tried to destroy it by projecting their own desires and choices onto me. Despite their attempts to derail me, I persevered and found a new path. I express my gratitude to TMH for their unwavering support, which enabled me to uncover hidden aspects of my life that I would have otherwise overlooked. Without TMH, I would not have been able to navigate through life's challenges, both positive and negative. I was constantly in motion until TMH helped me pause and recognize what I had been too preoccupied to see. I had been focusing on fixing external problems, when the true solution lay in fixing myself. Once I made that internal shift, everything else fell into place and became easier to manage. Some issues didn't even require direct action, but simply a change in mindset. As we were once taught, "a mind is a terrible thing to waste," and this holds true. The way we think shapes our reality.

Each day brings its own mix of experiences, but I am always grateful to TMH for guiding me through. By TMH's grace, I am still here. Even my landlord joined the gang stalking against me, but I refused to be intimidated. I stopped and blocked it. The date and time suddenly changed, no worries. I believe TMH has a greater plan and will be moving soon. The money paid to maintain this illegal organization must be stopped. The truth about my inheritance, trust, fake marriage adoptions, and many other things has been revealed. I was kept in poverty so that others could prosper, and this needs to stop. The amount stolen from me is more than I imagined, not only did my stepdad leave me an inheritance in his will, but my grandmother – who I thought despised me – also left me a trust and inheritance. They didn't even inform me of her passing. They have been stealing from me for a long time, and I have been struggling without any acknowledgment while they enjoyed the life that was meant for me. My stepmother and fake father, who had connections to the courts and a judge (more likely my aunt than my uncle), both abused their government powers to turn things in their favor. They knew I was gifted and tried to destroy my potential, both when I was younger and after I became an adult.My ex-husband and his mother conspired to destroy my life. They falsely accused me of spreading HIV/AIDS, a disease he contracted in prison and spread through the community and past partners. Their goal was to ruin my reputation, steal my inheritance, and keep me in poverty. They claimed I was promiscuous and a neglectful mother, using my son as a pawn in their scheme. My ex-husband's and his baby mother never acknowledged me as his mother to my son until he was fifteen. Even then, he attempted to control the situation by manipulating my son into lying to get money from me, although he was receiving child support and tax benefits.

They intentionally caused me to become homeless, hoping to portray me as an unstable parent. Their actions led to my son's abuse, which resulted in multiple hospital visits for me. Despite the constant turmoil they caused, I continued to pay child support for eighteen years in which I recently spoke to him in the realms they had him set up for insurance money as well. He has been trying me to a spot in the woods where i believe he is buried didn't even have enough love to bury him after my ex husband spoke to me as well because of all the lies led to her believing she has authored not only did she steal what was left for my son her, my aunt,and my sister conspired to unalive him to steal what was left for him using my identity. Meanwhile discovering the son in jail was alive during a riot in jail and passed away they poisoned him as well. These are the situations which have been overlooked and covered by the same government that has been watching and stalking me for decades to keep what was left to be covered. These are true crimes and I am seeking justice. Only no one will assist me after the defamation of character and multiple lies. These people in my family work in the government and have worked with government officials for decades not just against me but those who I loved and loved back.

Ultimately, I decided to prioritize my son's well-being and financial stability. I chose to focus on providing for him and maintaining a relationship with him, hoping that everything else would eventually fall into place.My main focus was my son's well-being. I dismissed the situation with him as unimportant; as I felt he was not in danger it simply wasn't worth the emotional turmoil, especially given my ex-partner's inability to manipulate or control me anymore. He had aligned himself with my family, and together they became a united front against me. His tactics shifted to using others to inflict past diseases they tried endless time to spread onto me. However, this strategy failed due to my resilience, faith, and the strength I had gained from overcoming past traumas, thanks to my family's support. It took me a moment to put it all together and I may be missing a few players in the game to end me, but each day TMII has revealed the more they attempt the more will continue to be revealed for my protection from it all. I am not telling my story for fame only to clear my name and receive justice with all the lies and slander to block and stop all involved from doing this to anyone else as they continue to have babies and marry for sacrifices.

I have encountered countless trials throughout my life, each connected to the past and future. Some stemmed from family, while others arose from former F.A.N.S. who turned my children against me. They confused my children's sexuality with rituals and hate, inflicting lasting damage. All I can say is I cannot change the past but going forward in my future changes are being made. I am not accepting any offers at this time. All will resume when this is over. At this time no one can be trusted as they continue to want to play tag in my life based on the lies of the biggest dummy ever known with his fake power chasing ass ninjas in my life. It may have worked in the past but not any longer. Preparing a new attack to stop me before court and it is going to be a "NO" for me. I do not want to hear all that has not been around while I was going through and decided money was more important to remain in that same energy, I promise I will. I am seeking new things in all areas of my life. I have no plans for revenge, as I know that vengeance belongs to the Most High. Justice will be served in His timing, as it has been many times before. I accept all apologies, but I will never forget the years I spent in poverty with my children, the undeserved punishments for crimes I did not commit, and the times I was admitted to facilities to make me appear incompetent. All is forgiven, but please stay away from me. No conversation is required or needed.

Previously, there were outsiders who took advantage of me and my energy. They shared details of my life with others without my consent and showed no respect. Now, they are attempting to come back into my life under the guise of affection.

Any connection or relationship that existed before has been severed. I am awake and aware of the betrayals and unkindness. I refuse to engage in any drama - past, present or future.I am not feeling anything or anybody I am healed and you won't be infecting me and then placing blame on me keep the dirty "D" and fakeness over there with their fake churches to cover covens that were received from people who worked hard to make all possible to obtain positions in life and were well loved to turn it into evil trying to cover up the truth it is a sad how my ancestors a lot of ancestors worked hard in establishing and maintaining for it to end up a disgrace. I pray that this book brings some justice for all as I love all, and victory shall be. They even covered up the sexual abuse of my son after I reported it to CFSA in PG County and past lovers the one I met at the mall years ago killing children for insurance policies one of mine may be included only he is of me so his soul will return if that is the case, and the pastor's wife my son's godmother as having affairs with my son's father and might have touched my son, his sister sneaking and creeping with other spouses while married, police officers that name I won't mention but begins with a "W" with false reports, warrants, and arrest, incorporating past lovers from years ago its a group thing they all sleep together including children to swap energies not to mention the men who they as well sleep with to create cords and vice versa. During my first week at my new house, I became ill and was hospitalized. While I was in the hospital, my deceitful partner was supposed to be working for DoorDash; however, my DoorDash account had been falsely deactivated the day before. My partner took advantage of the situation and made copies of my house and car keys. This allowed them to access and steal both my car and the contents of my house.

Additionally, a box-shaped Jeep, one of which is a board of the HOA, has been repeatedly stealing mail from my mailbox. Even after I changed the locks, my mailbox continues to be easily opened and my mail stolen. Despite submitting another change of address request, I am still not receiving my mail. Not only did they pay my roommate from the shelter who turns out to be the niece of the fake friend who set me up in the hotel and was sleeping with my son and her partner to sabotage me, but they also sought to destroy my reputation. Even my aunt's son was involved; he married an immigrant relative of my sister- in-law for money, and now he's dead. The list goes on and on.

I'm not sharing this for fame or power; I'm seeking peace and justice. I wasn't bothering anyone, yet they targeted me with lies, theft, deceit, and attempted destruction. Now, I'm clearing my name and sharing a vital lesson, hoping the world will listen. Although I thought it might rain, the sun is shining brightly, so I decided to come to the park and enjoy it. I almost brought my laptop, but I'm glad I didn't. I think TMH wanted me to take a break. The universe is sending me signs of love, but I don't know what's coming. Since no one from my past can contact me, it must be someone new, but it doesn't really matter. I'm bored and wish I had someone to talk to. Everyone around me seems to be with someone, but I guess it's better this way to avoid heartache and pain. I have a few dollars, and the movie theater is right here. I haven't seen a movie in years. The breeze feels good. If I had a car, I could have gone to the beach.I packed lunch and water, and headed out. I listened to the sounds of the city – the street, airplanes, music from passing cars – as I handed out flyers for my book.

Despite the number of TMH downloads yesterday, I still need clarification. I'll head home to edit my new book. It's a lovely day, not too hot, with a gentle breeze. I'm at one of my favorite spots by the water, grounding myself. Whether walking or sitting in the grass, looking at the water or sky, it's just peaceful. Sometimes there's relaxing music from the nearby restaurants.It's funny that I should say I need a break from work, as I'm still working right now, sitting here at the park. Work never stops for me. I'm determined to get away, if not today, then one day soon - I pray.

I patiently await answers, hoping to avoid further decline. My income streams are compromised, leading to another job interview today. Despite efforts to silence me, I am determined to share my story. They've isolated me, hoping I'll succumb to their cruelty and lies, but they underestimate my resilience. I am close to uncovering the truth, hence their desperation to destroy me. I wonder how much longer TMH will allow this. I've endured many hardships, longing for a seemingly unattainable reward. I've done my part and am ready for positive change. TMH said I wouldn't be given more than I could handle, yet it feels endless. Though hope dwindles, my faith remains unwavering, even if I lose everything and end up where I never wanted to be. I trust TMH hears me and will intervene at the right time. These are difficult times, with many opposing me as I reveal unwanted secrets and truths. This opposition only arose when they spread half-truths and lies to ruin my reputation and work. The future is uncertain, but I continue to pray for timely change.

Memories of yesterday surfaced as I noticed two recurring cars near my home: a silver Ford with tents and a black Kia Sonata. These belong to my fake husband and my cousin, the daughter of the family involved in abuse. Their constant surveillance is pathetic. I recall pre-awakening statements revealing my opposition. My family has long been two-faced and scheming, starting with my deceitful husband. When we faced financial difficulties and I sought my sister's help, he remarked, "It would be a shame if that was your money." My sister-in-law's wedding compliment was, "You look like an Egyptian." My brother's comments were often cryptic, but one stood out: after I cut my hair, he said, "You are going to live a long life." My family has known about my gifts for a long time and concealed them for exploitation. I recently learned that the ex-husbands of my children's fathers, as well as my third son's father, now have stepdaughters. I suspect my ex-husband of impregnating his stepdaughter, though both are capable of fake marriages and adoptions after learning hidden secrets.

The adoptions are invalid because my ex-husband tricked me into signing away my rights using false adoption papers. My family, connected through his current wife's friendship with my sister and aunt, provided the necessary information. Despite being blood relatives, they are hostile towards me and have used my children as pawns, paying him to destroy my life. He was also a handler, as were they all—devoid of loyalty and heartless. I was forced to pay child support while enduring severe abuse, including physical and sexual violence. Despite all this, he was compensated and aided in stealing my third child after I had already lost two, all while I was battling court cases and homelessness. Interfering in someone's life, especially with children involved, is morally reprehensible. They caused immense and unforgettable suffering. I remained silent, hiding my scars and focusing on getting my children back. I suspect their involvement in obtaining necessary documents after my last fight with my first husband in 2004, when I hastily left behind the marriage certificate. My ex-husband (my son's father) is spreading lies and threats about potential interest in me. They are united in their feelings: they don't want me, but they don't want anyone else to have me either, hoping I'll succumb to their lies and manipulation. This requires further investigation. I am no one's second option. I have no contact with them and will maintain it. They can continue trying to ruin my life and keep me single. However, those "potential interests" are the backbone you allow another man from my past, with whom I have no contact, to dictate your life. That's some true cowardice. I am surrounded by such people, along with bitter, older women resentful of their life choices, which have nothing to do with me. They are angry because I keep my personal life private. They assume I have no responsibilities because my children live with their fathers, as if our roles were reversed and I was the neglectful father. People should mind their own business. Many are upset that my children had fathers I could leave them with. Despite having multiple children, I always knew their fathers. There was never a DNA request or complaint about my provision until I was completely out of the picture. So, they can spare me their complaints; I didn't have the option to collect welfare or child support. I chose to work and leave my children with their fathers, who benefited from me through tax filings and government assistance. Our roles were reversed, which is the truth. My tax records will show I never claimed them once they lived with their fathers; I don't even have two of their social security numbers. People should mind their own business and be grateful for their leisure. I do more than most neglectful stepdads, and their fathers need to stop lying. I excused them from child support in court based on agreements they later disregarded, becoming comfortable with government funds and tax benefits at my children's expense, uncaring of the trauma inflicted. Now that the children are grown and can no longer benefit them, they still target me. I tell them to leave me alone or engage in their usual activities of manipulation and lies. Tell the truth and shame the devil. Their efforts will fail as the truth will be revealed; I have no need to lie. There will be no more exploiting me and my hard work. I remain stuck. They stole everything, and now it's gone. As I told them, they need me, but I am unavailable to any of them. They should pray about it; TMH can help them better than I can. Everyone needs to grow up and get a life. Until then, I will remain single, awaiting someone who is not afraid to stand up for what is right, as I am not interested in someone who cannot stand up for themselves or me. I'm not advocating for conflict, but for fighting for what is right. I am tired of fulfilling both roles in relationships, which is why I choose to stay single—the best decision for self-care. If this continues, I may remain alone.

Today, I plan to call for my maternal grandmother's records and possibly conduct offline research at the library for more information. Everything is unnecessarily difficult without funds, as they continue to block my money and love life through spiritual manipulation, which also hinders new opportunities with my book and work. I find just enough strength to continue investigating for the truth. This is why I also work on my book; I will not give up.

Talking to an old crush brought back memories. He was surprisingly open, but that chapter is closed. While our connection was unique and special, I can't explain it and will go with the flow. We both tend to be guarded. Around 2010-2013, my psychiatrist recommended admitting myself to George Washington Hospital, a chaotic three-day experience I recently recalled. Upon arrival, I was denied a shower and food for 24 hours and only given a room after a long night in the community room. This, along with resurfacing memories, suggests long-term manipulation. In my room, I began telepathically communicating with my ex-husband, hearing him talk to nurses and then having a mental conversation about my son's betrayal—another illusion from spiritual manipulation and waning medication. That night, I felt paralyzed, unable to breathe or move, as if possessed. After freeing myself, I went to the nurse's station, already skeptical due to rumors about the hospital's connection to the Exorcist movie (ironically, I now live nearby). The rude nurses refused my medication. Despite my request to move, they placed me across from their station, where I heard them laughing and planning to withhold my medication the next morning. I filed a report with the doctor. After friends and family called to complain, I was laughed at and ignored until my release. I was denied medication after my doctor recommended admission for suicidal thoughts, fueled by ongoing spiritual attacks intended to make me harm myself. I've been admitted to various hospitals in the city—Washington Hospital Center, Providence, Howard University, and Prince Georges Hospital, among others I can't recall. I couldn't understand my feelings then, but now I realize it was due to external negative influences meant to destroy me. At the time, I thought my experiences were isolated and not harmful, believing they helped me vent, heal, and realize I wasn't alone. Others had similar, even more profound, stories. Now, I question that isolation. Their attempts to isolate me may have inadvertently helped me cope with life and anger, teaching me to release it or take action.

I chose to let go by writing, which helps clear my thoughts and move forward. I've accepted my flaws and strengths and healed, recognizing that everyone is imperfect despite outward appearances. Everyone has a story shaping their present. I used to avoid discussing these experiences due to embarrassment and fear of being perceived as crazy. However, acknowledging and releasing negative experiences has prevented others from projecting harm or self-destructive curses onto me—crucial when one's vibration is low, as mine was during a coordinated group effort to inflict harm. Looking back, I see how often TMH sheltered me, like the "FOOTPRINTS" analogy. When I was weak, he carried me, unaware of the danger, saving me from myself and others. During these hospital stays, no one checked on me, except for one fake visit to maintain appearances.

My life has been full of twists and turns, all intended to stop me from revealing the other side of the story that has been suppressed. I recall a story of my father-brother being expelled from the hospital, supposedly after myI'm also preparing for my landlord. She thinks she can just come and go as she pleases to disturb and spy on me. I'll make it clear that as soon as the repair people arrive, she needs to leave with them. There will be no lounging around as if this is a chill spot. I'm sure they're purposely extending the repair process. My specialist hasn't responded, so she's also working with them. They seem to add on new issues every day. I'm sick of it all and wish I could get away from here. I'm tired of the same scenery and the same things day after day. This must end, and change must happen soon. I'm bored and lonely, and only continue to pray and write to pass the time.

My work is being impeded by ongoing attempts to erase my edits. While frustrating, these delays are only minor inconveniences. Although it's challenging, I refuse to become discouraged or angry. Despite frequent disregard and assumptions about my life, I remain peaceful and content. I've discovered ways to progress without external effort. The only overtures from others seem to be for sex or other things that no longer hold my interest. Perhaps I've been alone for so long that I've adapted and no longer feel the need for much.I've lost my sense of humor and I'm not sure if that's good or bad, or if that was the intention of others. I no longer find joy in things I used to overlook, and nothing seems funny or fun anymore.

I just want to get away from here, so I'm focusing on how to do that.I'm convinced that leaving is the only way I'll ever find happiness. I've contemplated packing a bag and leaving for any destination I can reach, even if it means resorting to hitchhiking or walking the entire distance. I'm desperate to escape this place, especially this residence. I once believed death would be my only way out, but I was repeatedly prevented from it. Although some may doubt my seriousness, I assure you I'm completely sincere. I yearned for a fresh start, a new life and identity where I wouldn't be recognized, sabotaged, or destroyed. However, TMH had different plans for me. It seems that as soon as one chapter ends, another begins; the stories are never-ending. I released these stories decades ago and they no longer hold any space in my heart. Despite this, the blame always seems to fall back on me.I don't know who I am. My age, birthday, and name are all lies. The only way to fix this is a restart, and it's nowhere in sight. I know I'm usually positive and have faith in everyone, even the unseen. But only TMH can fix this. Who will hear my prayers? I force myself to smile to mask my sadness and despair. I'm tired of fighting to regain what was unjustly taken from me. Those who stole from me continue on as if nothing happened, while I'm left with nothing. They've even taken everything I've worked so hard for. I have nothing left to sell, not even enough for a bus ticket. I have no one to turn to, and those who have connections only laugh at my plight. But I know a higher power, and when he reveals himself, everyone will know.

I feel betrayed and hurt. I'm the only one who was foolish enough to care for those who never had a heart. This experience has left me hesitant to ever care for or help anyone again. But I know that's not the right response. I need to be more cautious and discerning in the future.I was always taught that if you have nothing good to say, then it's best to remain silent. However, life has shown me that hiding my feelings can do more harm than good. So, I will continue to express myself and fight for what I believe in. Yet, it feels contradictory to move forward while also sharing my story. How can I tell my story without acknowledging the reason I'm writing it in the first place?.I don't understand why this burden falls on me, especially after everything I've endured. But I trust that TMH has a plan, as He always does; He has never let me down. I'm moving and will be taking a break from writing as I adjust to this new chapter in my life. I'm always adapting to change, but I long for a moment of stillness - a time without thoughts, writing, or stress. Just peace and rest, for once.

II had a restless night and woke up to a letter from my incarcerated son. He's always trying to get under my skin and pry into my life. Although he's hurting, I've stopped blaming myself. He was raised to know right from wrong, and his choices were his own. We were never wealthy, but I always provided for them. He idolizes his father, who's a terrible role model. Some people never learn until it's too late, and I hope he changes his ways before it's too late.Perhaps this is connected to my earlier visions, since both individuals in my visions are also incarcerated. Time passed quickly, and I contacted an old crush. We chatted briefly, but he was working and I didn't want to disturb him. I wouldn't mind seeing him, but I don't want him to get the wrong idea or to repeat our past mistakes - that and my drug use was what ended our communication last time. It's challenging to talk to people these days; no one can be trusted. I'm assessing my water situation carefully, as my options are limited.Due to past betrayals and the prevalence of diseases, I'm not looking for sex right now. It's been a long time, and I haven't even been dating. I've been focused on my writing and finding myself. I guess it will be that much greater when I do decide to give it up to someone I feel is worthy. What I'm really seeking is intense intimacy and passion, not a quick session. I'm looking for a night of passion, something I've never felt. I'm not sure if it's wrong or right, but I've noticed that my old crush is the only number left in my contacts. He's made it clear that he'd rather be single, and I'm not looking for anything right now except laughter and fun.I'm hopeful that I'll soon meet the right person. My current companion is enjoyable company, although it took him two years to open up to me. I was surprised when he finally started sharing more than just a greeting. He's usually shy and can be mean, which is a strange combination. I told him he reminded me of the grind and attitude. I know he listened to my ex and believed the "BOO BOO" lies. I'm waiting to see if he'll be honest with me. I always give people time to tell the truth, and I could be wrong. Maybe he heard the lies but didn't believe them. One thing is for sure: he expresses himself differently now. I don't dwell on things or hold grudges. I'll go with the flow, and if I'm pushed in a certain direction, I'll let it go as always.

I couldn't sleep, so I decided to write. I confirmed that my old crush is still the same; he's only interested in attention and can't be trusted. I don't want to give him the satisfaction of getting attention from me – it's immature and unattractive. We're talking, and he's showing everyone our texts like he's in high school, just like before. Whatever lies have been told will be exposed.

Honestly, I've been testing my intuition, and that's one of the reasons I reached out to him earlier today. I felt like he was hiding something, and I was curious about his role in this game they think they're winning. Meanwhile, I'm sitting back, observing, learning, and getting rid of all my enemies along the way.I am discovering more of my gifts and how to use them to my advantage every day. One gift I am grateful for is my ability to shield myself from negativity before it can affect me. This is beneficial in protecting me from harm. A recent example is when someone tried to trigger me with my son. This person, who was talking about taking a break from smoking and selling drugs, was confused and tried to hurt me by acting as if they hated me. Deep down, they knew this wasn't true, and they couldn't maintain the facadeMy landlord is sending another minion on Monday, as part of his ongoing attempt to get me out. I won't be deterred; I'll continue to speak the truth. I'm learning that truth is more powerful than anger. Engaging in back-and-forth arguments is a waste of time and energy. People expect me to lash out and fight, but I simply state the facts, which ends the conversation. This applies to other situations as well, such as the old crush and the associate who continues to try and cockblock by threatening others because he was a boxer. Neither situation is worth my energy; silence and no forward movement are the best responses.They are already aware of their actions and will simply vanish and operate behind the scenes. They are too cowardly to confront me and fear that I will expose their secrets. They pretend to end things while reversing the situation. I don't care what they do, but if they're going to act that way, they should leave me alone and stop threatening sincere people by claiming to have cut me off. Their behavior doesn't make sense.This is the final round; I will not be reaching out to anyone after this. This is not a bad thing, as I have made space for new opportunities. I am proud of myself and grateful to TMH for giving me the knowledge I needed, especially since I haven't felt my best lately with more problems arising. I keep asking myself how many more problems there will be and how much longer this will continue. It feels never-ending, yet it also feels close to ending as I continue to reveal the truth. I know this makes me a threat, but I don't care, as TMH will continue to protect me as I expose those who have wronged me and others. I felt bad at first, but after their masks were removed, it made sense why TMH had to show me the truth and protect me. I am grateful to be favored.

The world has changed, especially since the pandemic. Rules and laws seem irrelevant; it feels like everyone is only looking out for themselves. I try to do the right thing, but I wonder if anyone else does. It's disheartening when people's jealousy or misfortunes lead them to sabotage others. What's the point of laws if they're so easily disregarded? The youth of today express their pain and apathy towards reflection. This destruction and lack of concern are evident in their actions and attitudes. The traditional roles of family members have been distorted. Grandmothers are young, between twenty and thirty years old, while mothers are overwhelmed and resort to desperate measures to survive. Men neglect their responsibilities as fathers, prioritizing self-indulgence and exploration. Furthermore, there is confusion and dissatisfaction surrounding sexuality for both men and women.When a person's position in life is disregarded, minimized, or ignored, it can lead to disastrous outcomes. In today's society, many individuals have succumbed to feelings of resignation, influenced by their upbringing or a fear of being trapped without making an effort to change their circumstances. This societal breakdown manifests in various ways, including young mothers who teach their daughters how to manipulate men, and men who teach their sons to mistreat women. While not a universal truth, it is a prevalent issue that necessitates introspection. We must all take a step back, examine ourselves, and question whether we are truly content with who we are and what we see reflected back at us. In doing so, we must also remember to love ourselves, because without self-love, it is impossible to receive love from others. We are all reflections of our desires and needs, and others, especially our children, follow our lead. It's deeply troubling that those who do right and work hard are ignored and trampled upon, while rules and laws are broken without consequence. This didn't start with the pandemic; it's been happening since long before then, perhaps even since my birth.

Every day, I pray for justice and truth, and I know TMH hears me. I believe others hear me too, but they don't care because they see my problems as personal, when the issue is much deeper and beyond me. It's not about me; I've been through a lot, but I started writing because of my amnesia and discovered more corruption than I expected. So, I share my story, wondering how many others have had their lives detoured and delayed because of their gifts, strengths, and truths. I know it's frightening when you consider who I'm up against, but I have no fear. They have wiped me out; I have been erased and I no longer exist. My employment has been terminated, and everything I've built and stood for has been destroyed, starting with my precious children. I stand alone.

I don't care anymore. I am determined to spread the word about all the betrayals I have endured, all remembered and erased.The only reason I have the strength to continue is because of my faith. I have been guided to tell my story, even though I don't fully understand why. I know that what was taken from me will be returned and that my struggle will be worth it in the end. It's a shame that I've had to fight this battle for over forty years. I'm tired of the secrets and lies. Why is the truth so important to keep hidden? Is it only about maintaining positions of power and money? Despite the devil's wishes and schemes to make me believe otherwise and give up, I know that TMH has a plan for me. I have never been one to quit or fight strongly, but they join forces to stop me before I could even remember or begin. However, they did not anticipate my return after the continuous, nonstop torture I have endured in my life for as long as I can remember. They are determined to keep me blind and down, but I keep getting back up, and I have TMH to thank for that.

Even before I understood my gift and the revelations that have recently come to light, I never surrendered. Despite facing spells and magic, I persisted in fighting, working, and strategizing to surpass my previous limitations. I have broken free from the deception and illusions, and although victory is only the first step, I believe this will bring justice to the many who remain silent in fear. I will be a voice for all; this must end. Let me clarify something that has recently been brought to my attention. The angels have provided some clarity regarding the story of my father being banned from Howard University Hospital. The reason behind it makes a bit more sense now, as it turns out I was switched at birth with a deceased baby. Apparently, when I submitted my DNA sample to Ancestry, I shared the results with only one person, a co-worker. Unbeknownst to me, he was collaborating with my family. They manipulated the system, and since results are monitored by the government, the results came back indicating my death, as the DNA associated with my name doesn't match mine. This is the most egregious corruption I have ever witnessed. I will pause here for now, as I know you are just as shocked as I am. The lengths they are going to to conceal my identity are astounding. The question is, why? I wanted to share this information, as I hope my audience is following along.

They have been conducting spiritual warfare against me every night for the past week between the hours of 2 and 5 AM. This involves an ongoing battle against supernatural evil forces, often seen as demons or fallen angels, that are believed to interfere with human affairs and hinder spiritual growth. Despite their attempts to silence and discourage me, I remain resolute in my beliefs. The TMH's revelations are true, and I am slowly recovering what was taken from me. As I await the release of my book, I continue marketing my first book through various strategies, including price adjustments and unpublishing the eBook on Amazon. I am also developing new promotional flyers and persisting with on-foot advertising.

Although I prefer direct expression, I am thankful for the Lord's daily blessings and the chance to share my experiences. I trust that He will end the suffering and bring a new era. Ultimately, the Lord has the final say, and I will patiently wait. With unwavering faith in Him, I know I will not fail. My journey continues with guidance and support from a higher power. Despite negativity and discouragement from external forces, I remain protected and positive, thanks to divine signs and the presence of my angels, ancestors, and guides. They shield me from harm and destructive thoughts, allowing me to embrace each new day with purpose and anticipation. The challenges I face are mere illusions; my faith remains steadfast, and I know I am on the right path.

My landlord recently arrived with roofers but hasn't provided any updates. However, this isn't my primary concern, as I don't plan on staying here much longer. I believe that TMH has something better in store for me. The excessive rent and the pre-existing repairs that my landlord was aware of are all part of a game that has now come to an end.The lack of response from my worker speaks volumes. As I mentioned, numerous individuals are involved in this situation. The potential consequences of their actions far outweigh any perceived gain. They will undoubtedly regret their dishonesty. I have unwavering faith that justice will be served and I pray for a swift resolution.I was always instructed not to talk about my dreams upon waking, or they would come true. As a result, I was cautious not to do so. Since discovering my gifts, I understand why I was taught this - it's simply the truth. I have a rare gift of seeing things before they happen or appear.

Even my mother, the woman I grew up believing was my mother, recognized some of my gifts. Many people did. But this particular gift was brought to my attention early in life. I don't believe she was aware of the hospital switch and loved me as her own. She wasn't perfect, but who is? As parents, we learn along the way, often referencing what we were taught by our parents. This isn't always correct, and she had a difficult upbringing as the oldest of four. I witnessed her still being treated as a child rather than a grown adult. To think she married at sixteen to escape her family, only to return. I felt her pain then, and I understand it better now, as they tried to trap me in the same scenarios. The difference is that I've never been a follower, which is why I've always been the black sheep.

Well, I've been having a vision that has been bothering me, and I really didn't want to speak on it. I was simply hoping it would go away, but it continues to reappear. As I continued to connect the dots and uncover the hidden connections between all these people, I realized that there are at least seventy plus people involved against me. I must be honest, I don't like what I see, but it has to be addressed. I've mentioned my grandmother in my first book as well as this one, and I'll pause here for a moment. I recently learned from TMH that my maternal grandmother passed away and left me a trust and inheritance. This news made me think back to March 2024 when I visited the cemetery to celebrate my other grandmother's birthday. While there, I also visited the graves of my other relatives, including my grandfather, great-grandmother, and mother. My grandmother paid for everything in advance. When I went to the office, the clerk told me that my grandmother already had a headstone there even though she hadn't passed yet. We started talking, and she explained that my mother, grandfather, and cousin were all buried there together. I told her that two of them were still alive, to my knowledge. She joked that my grandmother was better than her because she wouldn't want her name in the cemetery if she were still alive. My grandmother must have known she was close to death and prepared accordingly. Around 2021-2022, my sister and aunt argued about who would prepare my grandmother's food. Shortly after, my sister started coming to my house during the day with my niece. She tried to stir up old memories, but I stopped her visits after the first day. They've always tried to keep me trapped in the past, but I was awakening to the betrayals that were being revealed. She claimed to be having repairs done to her apartment and did not want to go over my grandmother's because her and my aunt were beefing over her preparing my grandmother's food and she wanted me to believe that my grandmother's boyfriend at the time the military veteran wino I mentioned previously in my other book had been looking at my niece and my aunt was supposed to have found pornography with children on it and said he was going to the playground looking at kids there. I did not believe it because it did not make any sense, just something to trigger me to go off as I cared deeply for my niece. It did not make sense in the beginning, only it does now in the beginning of my vision. I kept seeing a law official who was my grandmother's boyfriend.

There was also talk of the ancestors of someone being unloved and buried. I think they unalived my grandmother by poisoning her meals and once discovered the house that my aunt had been waiting years for to receive most of the reason for her assistance in unaliving my mother. This is the aunt I mentioned before in my first book that resided in a one-bedroom apartment her entire life being hateful and evil, as well as my grandmother left instructions with her boyfriend and when he was about to reveal the truth, I believe he also was believed to prevent from finding about the inheritance and the truth about my biological parents. My grandmother had no living relatives and we were never close, so I would only check on her occasionally. I assume they figured no one would know or tell if they did something wrong. I think they either buried her somewhere other than her plot or cremated her, even though I know she paid for her funeral in advance. I went to the cemetery in March 2024 and there was no ending date on her headstone, which makes me think something is off. I hope they didn't do something terrible, especially since she had no remaining family. I'm worried they may have done this for the money. I wanted a wellness check from the authorities only my ancestors informed me it was not necessary. This situation is incredibly distressing and bewildering. It's unfathomable that they're capable of such actions. This pattern has persisted for decades within my family, originating with my grandmother. She labeled me as evil, but I believe she was involved in witchcraft. Although I'm reluctant to say it, karma spares no one. She imparted her teachings to the wrong individuals, and I'm uncertain of her motives. Her actions were malevolent and misaligned with the principles of TMH. There was no one present to offer support or defense at the end. However, I am here now and refuse to remain silent, regardless of the harm inflicted upon my mother and the intentions they had for me.I have been advised to pray and leave the situation with TMH. I have surrendered it all to him, and interfering will only prolong matters or warn them. Therefore, I will remain still and obedient, trusting that TMH will resolve everything better than we ever could.

Okay so as I put the pieces together it is disturbing as it began when I was younger a baby my biological mother who is of another race I believe Caucasian possibly Egyptian with royal blood was married to a wealthy man same her and while married had an affair with the help which would be my father as she doesn't like afro- American s but loved black wands if you know what I mean she became pregnant and at the time of her giving birth of me I was switched and stolen by my biological father. These are all stories heard throughout my upbringing, never knowing they had any truth behind them. The family concocted a scheme to conceal the child's true paternity due to their disapproval of my skin tone and my gifts. I investigated the possibility that I was one of two non-identical twins with different fathers, one light-skinned and one dark-skinned. I, the dark-skinned twin, was given to another family who raised me as their own. This switch was facilitated by the lack of stringent verification processes for medical records at the time. Although not officially confirmed, I believe my family acknowledges the truth of this situation. I am biracial, not fully African American, and I should never have lived the life I have. My mother was wealthy, or so she thought, until her husband discovered the truth after all these years. He left me his inheritance and, from what I heard, left my mother nothing. This is why they were both murdered - my father and her husband. The killers then came after me out of greed. They spoke of privilege, but it was all based on things that didn't belong to my mother.

I was raised to believe that they murdered anyone who could reveal the truth, as well as anyone who interfered, all to keep their secrets hidden and to maintain their wealth and power. They felt I was undeserving of the inheritance due to my age and race, leaving me in poverty. However, they never expected me to rise up and expose the truth. My biological parents harbored such intense hatred for me that they were willing to go to any lengths to destroy me. They considered me different, an outsider, while embracing others. They even resorted to redrum to maintain their control and protect their secrets. When my biological father fell ill and wanted to reveal the truth of my parentage, they silenced him to prevent me from claiming my rightful inheritance.

For decades, they concealed the existence of a will that included me as a beneficiary. My father's children, whom I had grown up with as a family, became resentful when they discovered my inclusion in the will. They had always seen me as distant and uninvolved in their lives. Years ago, after the passing of my grandparents, I had distanced myself from the family, unaware of the deception and the inheritance that awaited me.

Driven by greed and a desire to maintain their control over the inheritance, they conspired with others to betray me. They even enlisted the help of family members and others who disliked me due to my inherent goodness and light, which contrasted with their darkness and evil. Unbeknownst to me, I had been surrounded by a family of witches and warlocks who used their dark powers against me. I have always been different. They spread rumors to my sister-cousins, who then decided I was too privileged and received too much attention. They felt the need to destroy me and everything I had built. They wanted to ruin my independence and success. They tried to control everything I worked for or was given, aiming to make me disappear and seem worthless and needy.

I proved them wrong, which is why they're meeting behind closed doors with corrupt judges, abusing their power to withhold what's mine. They try to convince everyone that I'm incompetent, irresponsible, and reckless, but I've overcome all the obstacles they've put in my path. I've continued to rise instead of fall, receiving everything I've asked for in prayer, and they're furious! They've even interfered with my mail and employment to prevent me from attending court and to make me seem unemployable. But I continue to succeed with TMH. My grandparents left me an inheritance of CDs and stocks years ago, but my family kept it hidden from me.After my grandmother (my mother's mother) passed away, they continued to conceal the inheritance and steal from me once again.

My exclusion from the will was insignificant. My sister, cousins, and other relatives devised a plan to torment me by exploiting my love for my children. Initially, their tactics were successful, but they evolved into hiring assassins and sending men to abuse and exploit me. These men, some carrying sexually transmitted diseases and involved in moon rituals, were intended to infect me or cause my death, allowing them to collect on another insurance policy, morbidly echoing a previous one. Their desperation overshadowed morals and honest means. They wrongly assumed I would remain stuck in the past; the reality I faced was far worse than imagined. While I engaged in promiscuous behavior, it was solely with those I believed genuinely loved and cared for me, unaware they were all paid actors in an orchestrated deception. What began as a small scheme escalated with the family's greed, leading them to recruit friends and acquaintances. Jealousy over attention and the mission caused some recruits' partners to turn against me. Oblivious to this intricate web, I felt my world crumble.

The time spent in the shelter served as a harsh awakening. I realized the director and others were paid handlers, explaining my sister's continued contact under the guise of help, despite her long-standing hatred. My world had been shattered, and I was adrift in a haze of drugs, alcohol, and sex, having lost my sense of self and my values. TMH intervened, helping me remember my true desires and goals, initiating my journey to reclaim my life and identity. I needed to discern the truth behind false appearances. Having endured the worst, I witnessed the greatness of TMH. A chance encounter with a wise older gentleman served as a reminder of how angels use others to send messages and offer solace. He shared his own survival story, having been shot multiple times, yet bearing no visible signs. He, too, had been given a chance to share his experiences. TMH is benevolent; when deemed worthy, survival and success are ensured, even when others have written you off. Adversity is transformed into good fortune, exceeding expectations. We all possess unique gifts, but righteousness is the key to unlocking lasting peace, happiness, and joy—rewards that must be earned and proven internally, as outward appearances can be deceiving.

Recent days have brought unexpected peace and joy. I refuse to let anyone or anything steal this tranquility. Despite being physically free, I recognized my self-imposed isolation, an unintentional consequence of constant mental and physical battles. Though attacks persist, I've learned their impotence; no weapon can harm me. I've ceased acknowledging ignorance—a past failing. Now, provocations will be met with silence. Over the weekend, I intentionally disconnected to relax. My silence has always been unsettling to others, prompting attempts to disrupt my peace. My landlord has been testing my boundaries since last Thursday, met with continued silence. Her texts have gone unanswered. When altering the inspection date failed to elicit a reaction, she attempted to provoke me by withholding communication after the roofer's visit, hoping for an outburst. That didn't work. Next, she fabricated an unusual smell emanating from my unit through the bathroom vents. When ignored, she requested my next-door neighbor's occasional use of my parking space, to which I firmly replied he would be towed.

Those with control issues will receive no response from me. Their attempts to provoke me stem from the realization that roof repairs are necessary for rent payment. When this failed, the harassment continued with unwanted video calls, also ignored. TMH is aware of everything, and when their schemes collapse, they will face the consequences. I have invoked judgment and surrendered everything to TMH; the battle is no longer mine. There will be no more arguments, complaints, or anger, only composure. I recognize the progress I've made and now seek justice, not compromise, confident in its imminent arrival. I remain grateful for the present and the future, acknowledging the unseen. I trust and pray for this difficult period to pass, believing in a brighter tomorrow. I am fed up with mail tampering and privacy invasion and will contact my council member, as this has persisted for too long. My patient silence has endured gang stalking and harassment. This situation is unprecedented, and my only expected help was from TMH. Only my prayers are heard but currently unanswered, for reasons unknown but within TMH's plan. Though weary and frustrated, I strive for calm amidst continued theft, delays, and betrayal. My prayers continue as I await a response. My silence intensifies their agitation. I adhere to the principle that it takes two to argue, rendering their mission incomplete. Threats, lies, and betrayal will be ignored, regardless of the source—friend, fan, or family. My emotions have dulled. Self-help is paramount now; I can no longer be relied upon, having been manipulated too often. It's time for change.

I have urgent matters to attend to and am tired of waiting for the return of what was stolen. Love no longer holds its previous meaning, and my feelings have shifted. Material concerns have diminished as I focus on self-discovery and purpose. The question arises whether to continue helping others when my own life seems disregarded. While I don't mind sharing myself to bring joy to others, I see little value in spreading a message that is met with hostility, adding to my existing burdens. Some days, the desire to give up feels overwhelming, yet encounters with inspiring individuals offer renewed hope. Recent weeks have brought such connections, leading me to believe that some people enter our lives as messengers with vital lessons.

As my book gains attention, interference with my mail and banking prevents any financial gain. I am denied peace and privacy, merely trying to live. I maintain faith that the current adversity will amplify the eventual good fortune. Despite changing account numbers and opening new ones, I only receive select mail, such as bills and letters from my son, intended to undermine my happiness. Thirteen books have generated a mere penny in profit. The constant interference is exhausting. I know sales have been greater, but there's no profit, even after removing my eBook. This injustice is undeserved. Speaking my truth, as guided, is what I've done. Everyone has had their opportunities; now it is my turn.

My second book is nearing completion, delving deeper into the themes of my first. While I trust my story will eventually be heard, the lack of funds hinders self-publishing and hosting a book signing. Unable to create resources from nothing, I must seek alternative income. Considering hairdressing, I hesitate due to the chaotic energy in my home and the problematic individuals already present. Selling meals from a car is an option, but I lack transportation. Cutting grass is unfeasible during winter with minimal snow. While numerous ideas exist, I am reluctant to revert to past livelihoods that yielded inconsistent results, especially since I no longer have reliable transportation. Finding a new income source is essential, even with the demands of writing. A recent job interview was missed due to lack of internet access for reserving a study room.

I need TMH's intervention to remove negative influences and facilitate my progress. I have no interest in others' personal lives, focusing solely on myself. Years of successful isolation have followed my last employment in March 2024. Time is passing, and it seems respite will only come when others have moved on. I wish them well, but the principle of "live by the sword, die by the sword" applies.

Initially, I believed this applied to me, but I've been made to forget much. My actions have been consistently helpful, yet upon my exhaustion, I faced betrayal and the recruitment of others against me. I am finished with the conflict, having surrendered to whatever unfolds without resistance. This decision allows me to relax and find peace. I trust in TMH's ability to resolve this. My prayer for a miracle will be followed by patient faith in TMH's intervention. My day was surprisingly peaceful, dedicated to organizing my mail and banking. Persistent efforts to contact higher authorities for follow-up and investigations appear to be yielding results. I successfully changed all my account numbers and requested new ones, though an incorrect address requires further verification. An attempt to redirect my request was thwarted. The resolution of the last banking issue remains uncertain until my next deposit next month. Notification of my Bank of America account closure was received, in contrast to my other open accounts, likely to prevent further deposits. I will investigate this at the branch on Thursday.

After four years of complaints, I finally contacted The Advocate of Consumer Affairs. The initial response was fraudulent, omitting crucial details, likely intended to discourage me. Undeterred, I visited my local post office with identification and relevant information. Following multiple transactions at the library for upcoming interviews and submission of necessary documents, I continued working on my book. A call from a USPS manager informed me of a few days' processing time and a test letter with tracking. At the post office, I found it noteworthy that the only change of address on file was for last year's P.O. Box. Given the numerous individuals involved, I will contact the council member if no change occurs within fourteen days, believing I have taken all necessary steps. At the post office, a postal worker acquainted with my family contacted my cousin, who claimed a past relationship with a family member (unspecified) and knowledge of everyone, including my great-aunt, potentially explaining my mail issues as another instance of a family-paid employee. She insisted I speak with the clerk who assisted me; time will reveal the truth. I have become more attuned to the angels around me, delivering guidance and illuminating important messages from TMH in various forms, for which I am grateful. There is always more to learn. We often overlook our blessings, focusing instead on our perceived lack. Fixation on desires can overshadow appreciation for TMH's unexpected gifts, whose answers to prayers may be missed due to differing expectations.

I needed to remind myself of gratitude. While I didn't come this far with anyone's help; I made it here with TMH and the heavens above. Don't mistake my smile for weakness; it's a warning to back off. Throughout my journey, I've proven to be strong, not only to others but to myself. I know tomorrow will be busy, so I won't stay up too long. I'm ready to move in any direction anytime. The landlord and I will no longer be communicating unless a worker is present, as no workers showed up again today. I'm waiting for DCHA to inspect and have posted a notice on the entry door with my contact information, although they should already have it. The new associate may or may not be involved, but as a recovering addict, he is unreliable and enjoys tricking people. Right now, I can't trust anyone and won't let anyone delay my plans. I intend to meet with housing, visit the shop, and work tomorrow.The man downstairs continues to cause delays and distractions, including interfering with my book royalties. I received a sales notification but no payment. They want me to give up, but I know I'll eventually be paid what I'm owed.For my next book, I'll use a different publisher, not Amazon, and already have a new plan and a few publishers in mind.

My day began with a frustrating delay as the bus was late. To my surprise, I saw my ex-husband's cousin on the bus, which added to the unexpectedness of the morning. The bus was late arriving at the station, but once I reached work, everything went smoothly. Later, while on the train, I received a concerning text from my landlord. She stated she was entering my residence as an emergency due to a notice from the Department of Housing to replace the fire alarms. She failed to mention the ceiling and roof damage or that she had 15 days to comply. I believe she was intentionally trying to provoke me. I responded honestly and directly, without anger. Despite our Sunday morning conversation about the issue, she texted that she would be entering with a contractor to repair the smoke detector without my permission. I simply replied that the police would be notified if she entered without my permission, and followed up with an email to the worker.

I am tired of the bullying, lies, and scare tactics. I have remained calm and said that I would fight fire with fire if necessary; I am simply matching her energy. I know my rights and am not in violation of anything. She has been doing this for a while, and I'm sure she has done this to previous tenants. I have an email to prove it. They have managed to delay my mail again, as expected, and I will be reaching out to the Postal Inspector again. I will not stop until I receive my mail. The next letter will be sent to the council members. This is going to stop; I am tired of it all. I remain hopeful, and know that everything happens for a reason. This too shall pass.I arrived at the food bank early on Sunday, despite the weather. The line wasn't very long, which I attributed to the weather conditions.

I'm confident that I'm close to receiving my blessings, even though the man downstairs continues to frustrate me with his tactics. He sends every man he can to bother me, but I'm not worried. I've been in this situation many times before. The closer I get to my blessings, the more difficult it becomes, but the fewer complaints I have, the faster they arrive. It's a true test of my faith and patience. I pray that this is my last trip to the food bank for a while. I don't like the energy here; there's too much drama, and I try to avoid it. I only come here when it's absolutely necessary. Since I started working, I haven't been able to go to Bread for the City because the time conflicts with my schedule. I'm low on food until next Sunday, so I'll use everything that I was given last Friday.

Speaking of which, that landlord received a well-deserved tongue-lashing, and she continues to try and bully her way back into my residence. I'm eager to turn my phone back on so I can access more information and respond more efficiently. Everything will go much smoother, I hope. I also hope the storm will end soon, as it has been a hellish tornado. Yet, by the grace of TMH, I still stand; my strength and faith were under attack, and I see no justice being done as I continue to be attacked. They are definitely stealing all my royalties, which is next on my list to address. I may need an attorney, but I will get what is due to me soon enough.

I can feel my breakthrough is near, no matter how much they try to destroy my faith in TMH. It will not happen, as I have endured many struggles and battles in my life and yet I am still here, standing strong in faith. Today ended up being an encouraging and joyful day. I ran into some interesting people while waiting in line at the food bank - just as prophetic as me, all different ages and religions. It proved what is written in the book: we are at war, but we were all on the same page despite our differences. The messages remain the same, no matter the religion or the culture, as long as they are from above. People are placed in our lives for a reason, sometimes it's a message, a sign, or resources. Either way, all things are done for a reason and for the season.

The only thing I don't understand is why my accounts continually change; however, I am noticing more credit and my credit score has been updated. I'm getting closer to my goals; things are changing quickly. I'm losing patience with my landlord and housing situation, but I'll start a more thorough search once my internet is working again this week. I aim to finish my second book by September or October, but I'll set the goal for October. I'm merging elements for a powerful message; my purpose is never money, only justice for myself and to help others through my experiences. I had no guidance on my journey, and I hope to provide that for someone else. My journey didn't go as expected, but it's all part of a higher plan. I'm grateful for the understanding, encouragement, strength, and appreciation that have come from everything that was stolen, hidden, and perceived differently by others. Despite my many falls, I am where I am today I continue to move forward, even though I may have to unpublish my book on Amazon. There are many other ways to spread the message. I put in the work, and I feel like I'm being robbed if I'm not receiving any royalties. This will all come to an end soon, as I've done the work and only have a little more research to do. I'm still living and learning, facing new challenges and new levels. I will survive, as this is not my first rodeo. Every obstacle I overcome only makes me stronger.

My days become more interesting as my pressure lessens. I've let go and let TMH take control, while I focus on finishing the second half of my book. Many are interested in my story, and my neighbors have purchased my first book and given me a few reviews. I write what I feel as it comes to me. My first book may not be as interesting as the second half, as it is only an introduction of how I made it this far. It is my story, and people are entitled to their opinions. My job's been going well, reaching new levels. I'm unsure why people envy me, especially when so many others are more deserving and have earned the distinction of being disliked.

At this point, it doesn't bother me much, as I've endured enough ridicule to simply pray for those who have nothing better to do than find faults and create problems that don't concern me.

I've been resting and waiting for things to ease up. My landlord is very ill, fixated on control, and housing refuses to help with my transfer. My goal is to get out of the system soon, as I've lived without it for 40 years and managed, but there's no rush. I know a higher power is working to move me soon, so I'll wait. As expected, my mail is being rerouted again, and nothing has been returned when it comes to my heart stent, but that's fine. I'm blessed to know that the best provider is TMH. I pray He'll show up soon, and I know He's always on time.

Things have gotten easier. I dreamt last night of recovering over $700,000, so it's coming soon. Tomorrow is Friday, and I have plans to meet with their property so I can get out of this place, as I see my ceiling is about to collapse at any moment.I will use every resource available to prosecute if necessary, and everyone involved has been notified. Things are falling into place, even those beyond my sight. I can feel a shift, and I'm grateful for the positive changes in my life. Today was interesting and happy; I entertained a friend who showed interest, but I don't expect things to progress further. I think I've found someone on my level – mentally, spiritually, and physically. He's a true gentleman, and I'll proceed cautiously, aware of past experiences with deception. I value honesty. I plan to work on my book, finish cleaning my house, and prepare for tomorrow. I pray for a successful day and week.I'm focusing on what I want, not what I've lost. I want to change everything going forward, but I can only take one day at a time. Things are not always as they seem.

I'm taking a break from thinking about past experiences because I know they'll just manifest as thoughts. Instead, I'm manifesting all positive and good things to come. I decided to take the day off to catch up on the book work. It's great, but I feel like I haven't vented in a while because I've been so focused on my job. I have to remember the first lesson I learned: throughout my journey, things are not always as they seem.I need a break from work; I might stress others out since I make everything look easy. Every venture, every attempt in my life is solely mine. Someone was sent to harm me, but the Most High blocked it and gave me the necessary awareness. My landlord keeps playing games; there was a notice about roof repairs starting today, but no one has shown up. I'm tired of the cover-ups and corruption; no one can be trusted. I'm isolated again, remaining patient while accepting my faults. I'm going to start typing again since I've learned more details today. I'll be so happy when all this ends and I can rest peacefully without worrying about tomorrow, but then I remember that tomorrow isn't promised and I should make the most of each day. I'm exhausted, and TMH knows I'm ready to rest, but I'll keep going until I reach my goal. My life is close to a breakthrough; I'm on the edge and I feel it. Everything is possible in divine timing; TMH is good and I'm grateful.

The quiet and rainy days mirror the tears I've shed, yet I wake up feeling lighter.

As I rest and reflect, life's conclusion becomes clearer. Each day, I choose a different path, praying for a breakthrough amidst the shifting energy. This feeling isn't quite freedom, but it's close to the finish line. Too much has been lost and disturbed by hate. Looking back reveals nothing but the discovery of a life stolen, adopted, trafficked, and unraveling. I stand here to tell my story and reveal hidden truths, closing out years of hate-filled disasters.They continue to send spies and try to end my curiosity. I'm tired of the constant back and forth, the ups and downs, and the betrayals. I close myself off, remain silent, and pray for peace. I know brighter days are coming; I can feel it in my soul. This time, I'm trusting my intuition and walking by faith. No matter how far I fall, I'll never truly land; TMH has always caught me at my lowest.

Many believe I'm lonely and hurt, but I see it differently. I see peace and progress. Every day, I pray for peace and forward movement. I've had to relax, let go, and let TMH. At this point, I've done all I can do. I just want to move far away, where there's no judgment and lots of love. Some days feel long and monotonous, while others simply flow. I believe everything happens for a reason. Destiny cannot be changed, delayed, or destroyed by decisions. Only those for whom destiny is set have the ability to change it.Throughout my life, I have faced many disasters due to high expectations from others and myself. In trying to meet these expectations, I have often caused harm to myself. However, this is not a flaw, but rather a different perspective. I have never desired much from life – only family, true love, loyalty, and respect. None of these have I received without payment; I have been judged and misunderstood, but never loved. Wisdom transcends the mind.

Things are looking up; the days aren't as harsh anymore. I know when he gets quiet and at ease like this, something big is coming. I've been here many times before; it could be good or bad, depending on the energy I put out. I'm finding more peace these days, even though all I want to do is rest. That hasn't been an option for a while, but I'm praying that changes. I need to break free and take a long vacation, without any worries waiting for me when I get back.When I look back on my life, I see that for every occasion everyone enjoys, there are probably five to ten behind-the-scenes responses that no one knows about. Well, my energy, mindset, and soul have been renovated and are under new management.It's a shame that these days I'd rather be alone than deal with foolishness. All I've ever wanted was a normal, prosperous life with a loving family. Family was always there for me growing up. Big Mama always had gatherings, and there was never any doubt about the love. I wanted my kids to have that, and for a while, they did—until things changed.

I can't blame anyone else because I allowed and accepted everything, good and bad, without complaint. Like I've said before, everything in my life has been a lesson, and I have no regrets. Without those trials, I wouldn't have a story to tell. So, I'll take this time to express my gratitude for all the blessings.I am truly blessed and highly favored. I am grateful for my new path. I feel more relieved and relaxed now; less stressed, not angry, and happy with life as it is. The most high continues to bless me with another day of life and breath. I know my haters are lurking in the shadows, but hopefully, I will be moving soon. I put in an application far away and I am praying that it will be accepted. As I wait, everything seems to be speeding up. Each day a little more is brought to the light. My family is insane, but sadly, they are not really my family. I try not to stress. My work helps relax my mind with travel, puzzles, and challenges. I have to admit that I need a break though. My landlord continues to get on my last nerve, but I don't feed into it. There is too much going on. I'm ready to pack up the kitchen this weekend and have the junkman pick up the rest. Nothing really matters these days.I'm going with the flow and choosing the path of least resistance. People are fake and get on my nerves, but I won't let it happen anymore. I choose peace and respect—if you don't have those, get out of my face and leave me alone. I don't have time for that anymore; I've spent enough time catering to others and imprisoning myself. It's time to love myself like no one else can.

Three more days left in this week, and I don't think we have Columbus Day off. I might work, but it doesn't matter. It's a cool job with good energy, but I need a break from it all. I need to have some fun. I'm tired of lame people with their fake love; it's understandable, though, because how can you give what you don't have? Everything in life is a reflection; we mirror each other. If you're angry, you'll attract anger; if you're sad, you'll attract sadness. The question is, how do you change that? It's simple: put yourself first. Think good and positive thoughts, and let go of the bad and negativeAbove all, always trust your gut. Your first answer is usually the best choice. We all have intuition, especially women, and it's amazing how often it's right. Sometimes we know the answer but aren't paying attention. Relax and think; you'll realize you already know it.

These past few months I've been reflecting on how lucky I am. I'm still able to stand strong after all my falls, and it's only because of my strong heart. Every fall may have scared me, but I'm still alive.I'm exhausted by the constant obstacles, even though I understand that everything happens for a reason. It feels like every time I take two steps forward, I get pushed one step back. Despite feeling blessed and grateful, I'm also tired and just want to switch off. It's been years since I've been able to breathe; even the brief moments of respite are fleeting. All I know is to keep going; I'm not sure what else life holds for me. I feel trapped, and I desperately need a break to clear my mind, energy, soul, and body. It's a shame that this is a never-ending struggle for so many, and they don't even realize it.

Over the past few months, I've felt like no matter how much I expand or sacrifice, nothing seems to work. The more I rise from setbacks, the more challenges I face. I'm so tired of dealing with landlords and their issues. It's been months since my recertification, and everything was in order, but now that I'm finally able to move, there are more delays. Part of me just wants to scream and cry; I've been patient, loyal, and obedient, and yet nothing has changed. Despite all I've been through, I've always believed that the Most High is the only one who has guided me. I believe no one is higher, yet the devil and his minions continue to test my strength. I feel weaker due to the constant delays, distractions, and obstacles that hinder my path to love, finances, family, and peace. I just want peace, and an end to all this. I am not the Most High, so I have nothing to say but to pray that He comes soon to show me the way, as I am lost and confused. I see that nothing has been or will be explained until after it's all over. I just want rest, stability, and no more struggle.

My mind feels clouded and overwhelmed right now. To be honest, it's been a lot to handle, and it feels like there's constantly more being added. I'm tired of playing games with immature people. I know that others often turn away from what makes them uncomfortable, and that they fear those who are different or express themselves freely. But that's why we have freedom of speech, isn't it? I refuse to be quiet. I've been expressing myself for years, and I'll continue to do so. You are you, and I am me.It doesn't matter to me how others perceive me; love me as I am, or leave me alone. I don't change, and I don't expect others to change. Everyone has a story, and I may not agree with all of them, but I am fair. Many adults today are stuck in a time with no clear guidelines or limitations. It's sad to say that I've been through a lot, and it seems there's more to come. After so many blows, they become softer. I know something big is on its way; it's too quiet, almost too peaceful. I've learned not to ask questions, just to go with the flow.

In the past few months, so much has come to light; I'm shocked. It was unexpected. As if the beginning of this story wasn't enough, now I understand why names and positions in our family were important. It was tradition, and tradition never changes. What's written is written; there are no take-backs. I have found peace and safety within myself. Nothing else matters as much anymore.The only thing that matters to me now is finding peace, understanding, and moving forward. I'm tired of punishment and lessons. I just want to breathe and smile. I need to move, and although I don't know how it will happen, I trust that I will be guided.

Today is a new start at work, as we've moved offices across the street. I like the new environment better, but I'm not getting too comfortable, as my contract ends in mid-November. The uncertainty of contracting is always unsettling. . I'm starting to realize that my family tends to discard anything that doesn't fit their idea of perfection. I was removed from my mother at a young age or possibly at birth. This was due to my mother being in an unknown situation - more research is needed.

All of this angers me. I wish I knew my true identity and where I belong. I don't care about love these days; there's too much going on. My landlord continues to disrespect me by entering my home without permission and leaving my door unlocked. I need to move before something happens. My ex continues to stalk me with others. I know they are watching, stalking, blocking, and projecting, but I don't care anymore. I'm not paying attention to any of this nonsense. The only peace I get is at work. I hate coming home these days. I'm tired of the constant disrespect and back and forth. Even when I feel a little relaxed, I'm not comfortable. I haven't been writing due to writer's block, but I cleared some of it away yesterday when I rearranged my living space. There's always drama, and I'm tired of the same old life and things. I just want change, peace, and financial stability.

Everyone wonders why I'm alone, but people are crazy. I don't have time for any more games. There is no peace, and I'm so fed up with life itself. I'm tired and ready to say forget it all, move, and start over somewhere new. I'm not sure where or how, but I'm thinking every day of something new.I've tried to shift my energy, but I'm not feeling it these days. I'm angry and frustrated. Every day, I pray for a better day and try to smile, but it's hard to keep up. Smiling only seems to bring trouble, and I don't want to have to resort to violence I'm tired of waiting for the truth to be revealed and for what's rightfully mine to be returned. I've earned it - all of it, no matter how big or small. Everyone tells me to speak up and take action, but that won't work in this situation. Only the truth will be understood and supported which I expressed many times with no response. Instead I told the person who loves to be truly TMH and I left it there.

I'm ready to leave this place. I'm grateful for everything, but I'm miserable without peace and privacy. I'm sick of the constant disrespect from everyone. My story is all over the place, but it makes sense because I've been exposed to this my whole life. There are so many snakes around, but they can't block my blessings. I need a moment to relax. Change is always difficult, and I'm not sure I can keep going like this. It's time for change in all aspects of my life—work, home, and my overall lifestyle. I've been down for too long. I haven't fallen, but anything is possible these days. There are no rules or laws anymore. I can't trust the justice system; it's all corrupt. They're allowing crimes to happen without any intervention. They've been playing games with my life to cover up crimes I wasn't even aware of until I woke up—or should I say, was reborn.It's ironic that they didn't just let things die down after partially accomplishing their mission. But as humans, that's what we often do. Read about the seven deadly sins - many of us fall into those categories.

People never get enough, no matter how much they pray for peace. I feel at peace in all aspects of my life except where I lay my head. You should always feel most comfortable where you arAt this point, it's unbelievable how much you think you can disrupt my life without facing consequences. I dream of owning a home with a front and back yard, porches, a tall fence, and a gazebo bathed in moonlight. I'd add a patio, a barbecue, and a two-car garage. Inside, I envision two or three bedrooms, a home gym, a home office, and a basement movie room. I picture myself driving home from work in my new BMW i4 M50 to a delicious seafood dinner, just enough for two.

I know that I'm blessed, and wonderful things are coming soon. I've worked too hard to give up now. All the negativity, betrayal, and hardship will soon fade, and I trust that a higher power will have the final say. I'm starting to think that perhaps there's no reason for what never happened. Maybe, but I don't believe there's a chance anymore. The last experience was the final straw. No one chooses, and love will only come with Divine timing. No more games with my life. I didn't go through all that just to catch a disease or get pregnant by some loser. They all hang out and communicate in the same place, and there's even a club for them on Instagram and Facebook. They're all part of the same group.

With about eight days left in this month, I'm just watching and noticing. Not much has changed since this time last year, just a little more peace and the same drama. Jealous family and haters still surround me. My contract will end soon, and then I'll get back to writing and publishing my second book. I am still faced with the same challenges of being hacked. This makes me sick as I feel rushed to tell my story before those who stole will present before I can once again steal my work this time online . As I have been involved in multiple projects while trying to finish my book, I am defending my messages from TMH online in hopes of clearing my name and retrieving what belongs to me. It feels as the more revealed the further I become from receiving as they are set on silencing me. I will resume work next week as I am exhausted mentally and physically. I've given up on love; it seems I'd rather be alone. No one is worthy of my friendship these days; no one can be trusted. This has been going on for about ten years, so I don't care anymore. I'm just ready to publish my book and move far away from these fake people. I pray things will continue to get better.

I'm headed to work as usual; nothing has changed. There's only constant work and no family, friends, or love. I can only expect something from above. Enough is enough until it's all revealed and over. I've reached a point where I need to isolate myself and prioritize my own well-being. I'm tired of the constant drama that comes with dealing with people who are only interested in using others, seeking attention, or causing conflict. I'm close to 50 and I realize that life is too short to waste on negativity. I've lived my life to the fullest, with all its ups and downs. The world is a confusing place, and it seems like many people are struggling with self-love and authenticity. I refuse to be dragged down by the anger and trauma of others, especially when it's rooted in their past and has nothing to do with me. It's clear that they need to focus on their own healing.

I understand the importance of self-care and prioritizing myself, especially after facing my own challenges. I'm tired of the dishonesty and disloyalty that surrounds me. I choose to protect my energy and distance myself from negativity. I want to be left alone and am tired of people who are untrue or disloyal. I didn't ask for these intrusions into my life; they were sent and paid to interfere. I prioritize my safety and well-being, and I'm tired of people who only want to use and disturb my peace. For too long, I've endured neighbors' games, stalking, and violations of my privacy. People have been sent to sabotage me, create false relationships, and steal my children. I'm tired of the lies and manipulations surrounding my family. As I reflect on my life, I realize that my family is not what it seems. The relationships are all based on lies, meant to sabotage and infect me. My entire life has been a lie, including my parents and everyone connected to them.

You are who you are, and that will never change. You attract what you think and feel. The energy you put out will be received, good or bad. Over the years, I've noticed how people perceive me. When I was younger, I was seen as a crybaby. As I've grown and healed, I don't have to cry anymore. I take care of myself, so I don't have to ask, want, wait, or think about what I need. What I have is either earned, not given, and maintained without help. I've learned to trust only the highest power. People you consider true friends often disappoint when things get tough. That's why I work hard for what I want and need.

I really need a car these days. It's dark when I leave early in the morning and late at night. But I have to do what's necessary to keep going. I'm praying for a break soon. I want to be free, at peace, and left alone. We all need to grow up. What's been done cannot be undone. It's forgiven but not forgotten. There's not much that can distract me from my plans. I just want to relax without constant delays and chaos. I'm choosing a drama-free life.I'm so close to achieving my goal; I can feel it deep down. I won't let anything from my past – the headaches, despair, and betrayals – negatively impact me now. I've worked hard to get where I am, and I'm not letting anything stand in my way. I'm alone, and that's how it will stay for now.

Life has presented constant challenges, marked by unreliable transportation, physical discomfort, and persistent drama. Despite past struggles with addiction, heartbreak, and negative influences, I've learned resilience, echoing Big Mama's wisdom about rising above circumstances. My experiences, both positive and negative, have shaped my perspective and inform my writing. While life holds beauty, there's also significant suffering. I refrain from judgment, acknowledging everyone's unique story. However, many lose sight of their agency, forgetting their power to shape their own narratives. It's taken me a lifetime to realize that my destiny rests in my choices, guided by a higher power. Every event, good or bad, holds a purpose, requiring thoughtful reflection before choosing a path aligned with my true desires.

Currently, I find myself alone by choice, seeking peace amidst overwhelming chaos. Solitude offers respite from the constant drama I've endured. Simple pleasures, like visiting the pandas on a beautiful day, are welcome. However, ongoing issues, such as the unaddressed roof repair, create frustration and a sense of displacement. The violation of my personal space adds to the desire for justice and a fresh start far away from this environment. Despite the desire for immediate escape, today is about personal focus and forward momentum. Lingering on unfulfilled promises is futile. Sleep offers the only solace. Perhaps I'm old-fashioned, but there's always the prospect of another lifetime, though I will miss this one. For now, I find comfort in old-school music, while the negativity from my neighbors is simply ignored. Their attempts to intrude and judge are tiresome. My past attempts to help were unsuccessful. Understanding their motivations, even without external validation, is enough. I'm aware enough of the truth to navigate their denial.

The longing for justice has been a persistent theme. Despite outward appearances of strength, I am weary. The world is filled with irrationality. My simple desires for love, respect, joy, and peace have been met with pain and betrayal, which I will no longer tolerate. Self-love dictates a boundary, and I extend prayers to those grappling with their own limitations and choices, trusting in the eventual return of karma.

Resentment simmers beneath the surface, perhaps intentionally fueled to harden me. If so, why not fulfill that expectation? The harm inflicted upon me and my children, devoid of remorse, will face judgment. While I value fairness, endangering innocent children is unforgivable. The desire for my downfall, envisioning imprisonment or damnation, has only strengthened my resolve. Despite enduring abuse, I persist, as do my children. May divine mercy guide the consequences for those who inflict harm. Appearances are deceiving; true understanding lies beneath the surface.

Yesterday was spent in quiet rest, as divinely guided. Today involves cleansing and preparation for change. Intermittent internet and nighttime disturbances do not cause fear, trusting in divine protection and gratitude for safety. New revelations continue to surface, presenting a complex puzzle. It's remarkable how clarity emerges through divine intervention. My faith provides constant support, especially when others falter. The journey has been arduous, filled with obstacles, but the lessons learned have fostered strength. While others focus on negativity, I embrace each day as part of my path, actively seeking to cleanse myself of negativity and attract positive energy as I anticipate moving forward. The process of writing my second book continues, acknowledging ongoing personal growth. I trust in my ability to handle whatever comes my way. With increasing mental clarity, the reliance on external comforts diminishes. My energy is now focused on sharing the love and positive change I believe is approaching, needing only an escape from my current circumstances.

At times, I feel as though everyone and everything from the past is against me, some perhaps from the very beginning, despite my lack of awareness or intention. My fundamental desires have always been genuine peace, love, and respect, which I consistently offer but rarely receive in equal measure.Experiences have taught me that betrayal often comes from those closest to you, echoing my mother's cautionary words about the transient nature of friendships. While people may come and go, the truth invariably surfaces. I am accustomed to bearing blame, but not in the current situation. A suppressed childhood memory shared by my nephew hints at long-standing issues, now gaining clarity. Past incidents and choices are acknowledged without dwelling on them. The focus is on change and moving forward, a familiar pattern of rebuilding after loss. Learning to release inhibitions and embrace life is the current focus. Uncertainty about the starting point exists, having never truly experienced freedom, with past events and timing always acting as constraints. Now, the desire is to break free and soar.

Despite the recurring challenges in my living situation, seemingly orchestrated to impede my escape from constant surveillance, the shared experience of discomfort among residents is notable. The persistent intrusion and disruption of my peace, even in my own home, are maddening. Former partners, seemingly stagnant and resentful, attempt to undermine my progress. While past attempts to derail me have occurred, this time feels different, as their actions are becoming apparent. My current writing remains unrecorded for its protection. Exhaustion from constant disruptions and negativity is overwhelming. The need to release the past and cease anticipating further betrayal is paramount. Hope for positive change sometimes wavers, but I ultimately entrust my future to divine will. A loss of appetite and readiness for fasting reflect a desire for a shift. Packing remains unfinished, as the prospect of moving seems distant, regardless of my efforts. Everything unfolds in divine timing.

My life has often prioritized the happiness of others, while my own needs are consistently deferred. Lifelong patience has yielded little change. I feel trapped in an unwanted situation stemming from circumstances beyond my control or knowledge. Discontent with the current reality and a desire for a simpler connection with the divine are present. The drawn-out moving process, fraught with miscommunication, continues to disrupt my life. Attempts to maintain calm are challenged by the daily upheaval. The impending intrusion into my home feels deliberately irritating and potentially harmful energetically. Physical limitations prevent further packing. Seeking external help for junk removal is planned due to growing frustration. Reaching out to housing authorities has become necessary due to the prolonged inconvenience affecting only me. The suggestion of emergency shelter feels inappropriate given the completed and approved paperwork. Delays are attributed to the lack of urgency of others, leading to a refusal to further accommodate their needs at the expense of my well-being. Trust in divine intervention remains strong, with a growing sense of impatience for the situation to resolve.

The imminent arrival of an ancestry kit coincides with further disruptions, interpreted as deliberate inconveniences. The response is to seek refuge and security elsewhere, incurring additional expense and potential health risks. A decision to assert control over my personal space is made. Indifference and a sense of displacement in my own home prevail. Readiness to move is absolute, with plans to declutter and simplify. Temporary accommodation is sought for safety and peace. The protracted process of housing recertification, despite approvals, highlights ongoing frustration with bureaucratic delays and excuses. Trust in divine support remains unwavering. Awareness of negative intentions and rituals directed towards me during specific lunar cycles fuels a sense of preparedness. Despite the slow progress, the ultimate goal remains in sight. Prayers for favorable conditions and safe passage are constant.

Weariness from constant disappointment is palpable. The lack of a car is compounded by housing issues and a new contract, all shrouded in a sense of falsity. A feeling of being denied the natural stages of life – childhood, adulthood, seniorhood – persists, marked by premature responsibility and current infantilization. The absence of peace fuels a desire for a radical fresh start, a clean slate devoid of current existence and suffering. For 46 years, life has been a relentless struggle without support. Now, external forces seek to control my life. Faith, though consistently practiced, is wavering amidst persistent turmoil and inexplicable daily negativity from various sources.

The value of rules and efforts for improvement is questioned in the absence of tangible change, only increased drama. A sense of losing control and feeling unsafe prevails. Speaking truth through writing has resulted in harassment and instability. The fundamental desire is a peaceful life free from threats. While believing in protection, the constant attacks raise questions about the purpose of enduring such hardship despite consistent prayer and hope. Years of unfulfilled promises and a sense of preferential treatment for others breed resentment. A recurring feeling of being disliked and the questioning of my existence lead to a longing for a spiritual home. The notion of past agreements to return to this life is met with disbelief and a persistent desire to depart.

Despite periods of improvement, life remains chaotic, marked by family animosity stemming from an unknown inheritance. Experiences of trafficking, energy siphoning, and karmic burdens contribute to a feeling of being overworked and underappreciated. Returning to writing and introspection leads to the fundamental question of identity. The revelation of non-biological family ties and ongoing manipulation by others intensifies the turmoil. Grief over unresolved issues and unreturned belongings persists. The same individuals continue to inflict harm through various means. Interactions with authorities feel manipulative. Trust in divine timing for eventual consequences remains. Protection from negative influences and past acquaintances is sought. Solitude after prolonged betrayal is the current state. Rest is essential for reflection and the need for constant adaptability. Readiness to leave now is paramount.

Home no longer provides sanctuary due to constant accessibility and privacy violations, a lifelong pattern. Weariness from ongoing manipulation is profound. While not desiring isolation out of fear, trust in others is eroded. New connections lack depth and shared understanding. A sense of a predetermined, overly structured life breeds discontent. The desire for normalcy and simple enjoyment clashes with constant scheduling and routine. The fundamental need is to be left alone, free from external control, reputational damage, and lifelong deception. Confusion rather than anger prevails, tinged with a sense of expectation. A long-held awareness of familial issues was met with non-judgment and physical and emotional distance. The childhood lesson of unconditional family

At this point, I trust no one and nothing. It's amusing that people are paid to destroy me, but it's at my expense. Love exists, but it will have to find me. I've never experienced it, so I assume it's not meant for me, or that it will come when the time is right. To be honest, I don't really see my purpose. I was asked to tell my truth, and that cut everyone off. Now, I don't trust anyone. I'm left trying to figure out other people's problems. This is the closest I've come to peace, and I'm not willing to mess it up for anyone. I'm not telling anyone where I stand, I'm not going out to be left stranded, and I'm not having sex to be given diseases. What is meant to be will be.

I'm exhausted by the constant disappointment of reaching out to people who only want to steal my energy for their own benefit, whether it's personal or professional growth. I'm done with the endless cycle of betrayal, lies, and wasted time. I'd rather be alone until I find someone who genuinely cares for me, even if that means being alone forever. I'm tired of being used and manipulated. If being kind only leads to being taken advantage of, then I'll choose silence and solitude. At least that way, I can protect myself from being played, betrayed, or used. I'm weary of trying to help others, only to be misunderstood. My energy is precious and sought after by many, but it's a divine gift with a purpose. Even if I don't understand that purpose yet, I trust that God has a plan for me.

Moving and packing by myself left my arms and hands sore. The movers only took the large items, leaving me to load the rest alone. I'm glad I had the strength to finish, but it reinforces the feeling that I'm meant to be alone. People are fake, and I don't have time for relationships. Right now, faith and prayer aren't enough.

I've discovered that the last time I had contact with them, they were being fake and brought someone in to see if she could copy or needed my energy. The endless disrespect is ridiculous. At this point they brought her in hopes of dimming my light not realizing the destruction it will bring.I was on a four-month contract, though I never planned to stay beyond the initial three months. I didn't realize what I was involved in at the time.

The company hired a Reiki healer from YouTube, who also claimed to work in accounts receivable, at least that's what they wanted me to believe. When I started, I only received a desk and a notebook. However, she was hired on the spot with a paycheck and a catalog to order whatever she wanted.I knew the company was deceptive, so I intentionally sabotaged the contract by requesting a raise for my duties had been extended and at the timeI was unaware of the recruiter's involvement and only discovered his participation after I accepted a contract at VOA. Unbeknownst to me, my family, who was working with VOA at the time, was trying to destroy what I had built. On my first day, no one showed up. After waiting an hour, the recruiter returned my call and claimed it was a mix-up, a "boo-boo." I played along and responded truthfully, as always. I stated that I hoped for the same understanding if the roles were reversed. To prove my point, I did not show up and canceled my contract. I couldn't believe that both the recruiter and the Comptroller reached out to me; they were desperate for my energy. That same week, I received many contract requests, but no one showed up. As I've said, I don't argue or chase, I walk away. I saw clearly what they had been doing for years.

In contracting, the recruiter gets a percentage of the contractor's earnings. In this case, they were reversing this and paying me more than half of my earnings. My pay was $40 per hour, and they were paying me $25. They were doing this with many companies I worked for, mainly non-profits or government contractors, including Altumint, Catholic Charities, Cyprus Air, and many others. This was done so that they could get contract extensions with the government and other companies. My contract ends in three days, just before Indeed, and I hope that God will punish this company. Two other companies requested my information as if I had been hired, to get my identification and banking information once again. I feel unsafe and pray that TMH will show up soon because my resources are limited. They took my taxes again this year; first it was child support, then school loans, and now unemployment that I never received and have been paying off since 2008. I went to the hearing and they began taking payment out of my check from then. I am cornered, and only TMH can fix this. For my birthday, I rented my dream car, a BMW X2, and went to the casino to watch the game and had a few drinks. When I came back home, I was met with more complaints of smoking, even though I wasn't even home. The harassment and gangstalking continues. They falsely accused me of smoking when I was simply burning sage to cleanse my surroundings. In just one week, I lost my contract, narrowly escaped a fraudulent one, and received news that I won't be getting my tax refund. My savings, which were meant for future living expenses and bills, will now have to be used sooner than expected. Despite everything, I remain hopeful, although I'm unsure how I've managed to hold onto what little I have left. But I know that it's the only reason I'm still standing.

I understand now that my purpose was to bring judgment upon them, and that judgment will be delivered. TMH will deliver retribution to those who exploit others to the point of losing their benefits. He guided me away from that situation, and I can no longer be deceived or defeated. I will not accept projections or destinies, nor will I allow my energy to be manipulated. I know that I intimidate many people, even those in high-ranking positions. There simply wasn't enough room for me, especially when I outshine others. This does not concern me, as I explained that a significant pay cut would not discourage me. I had a court appearance upon my return.I had hoped she'd be discouraged and not show up, but TMH had other plans. Unlike my previous company, I was able to work from home, with higher pay, and in a position that matched my requested description. I wasn't given additional duties that didn't pertain to the position. However, you get what you pay for. This company had inconsistent payment schedules and the workplace was chaotic. I often found myself doing unnecessary work due to a lack of organization and communication. Deadlines were frequently changed, and additional tasks were added unexpectedly. I give it 30 days before everything falls apart. I felt taken advantage of because of my ability to meet tight deadlines and produce accurate work. While others slacked off, I remained focused and dedicated. Despite the challenges, I consistently delivered high-quality results. However, there were issues with payroll, including a lack of oversight and instances of overpayment. Although these problems weren't my responsibility, they added to the overall frustration of the work environment. Ultimately, I decided to leave the position because I felt undervalued and underrated. My contract was completed sucessfully.They expect me to stay, which is already terrible, but my supervisor was only giving me a ride to steal my energy. They don't realize that anything built from my energy, good or bad, will reflect on them later. If they harm me to gain my energy, it will ultimately backfire - you could call it instant karma. As God reveals those who laughed, smiled, and hurt me, I'm slowly putting it all together. They will face consequences in due time.

They may have joined the others, but that's alright. The show is ending, and I'm finding peace. No more drama from the woman who was here before me and believes I desire the man they fired upon my arrival - a demon in disguise, another bum. He and his girlfriend created drama when he returned to drop off equipment after I arrived. From what I could tell, he seemed to be nothing more than a clown. He had a stroke and mentioned wanting to meet for drinks sometime, so I gave him one of my flyers, always advertising. He took my flyer and gave it to his wife or side piece, whoever she was, to make her jealous, and the hate train started immediately. She came over from across the street, pretending to be cool with me and asking for my phone number. I don't discriminate; everyone gets one shot. If that trust is betrayed, there won't be a second chance. The main issue wasn't that I took her position; it was that she didn't understand the inherent respect the accounting department commands in any company due to its control over finances. Ironically, she was someone from my past that I didn't initially recognize.

This situation brought back memories of my mother's late-night drives to Maryland to collect my sister. It's funny how I don't know her friends and have never had any desire to. I remember them as small and cute, but they're adults now, unhappy with their life choices and resentful of my punctuality and responsibility. They weren't working with my sister; they were collaborating with my ex-husband and his associates. This situation continues to escalate. I assume they all dislike me, but only as a way to hide their criminal activities and thefts. She mainly felt I overshadowed her, a common sentiment that doesn't bother me because I don't view it as a competition – I'm simply there to do my job. Many people expect you to want a permanent contract, but I disagree. I've been contracting for over two decades, been told countless lies, and been taken advantage of as an inexperienced worker. However, I get paid to finish the task, and that doesn't necessitate friendship or competition. At the end of the day, when the contract ends, it ends.

The offered pay rate was considerably lower than what I've earned in the past—I haven't been paid $25 an hour since 2008, when I made $27 an hour. I saw the position as a temporary favor, not a permanent solution, and we discussed this before I accepted the job. As agreed, I left the position when I planned. If I had stayed longer and allowed them to continue taking advantage of my lower rate, I might have finished my book by now. Regardless, I'm still on track. I'm used to balancing my work, studies, writing, and personal life despite the challenges that come my way.

I've recently uncovered and resolved many challenges in my life. Through research, I discovered a plot involving my grandmother's boyfriend and my aunt, who intended to harm him for insurance money. Additionally, I've realized that my work contracts have been exploited to auction my energy to the highest bidders, as they are all connected to secret societies and cults. The organizations I've worked for my entire life are now using my jobs to harm me, and I no longer feel safe. My only comfort comes from my faith and the belief that a higher power is protecting me. They retaliated against me by harming one of my children and withholding my paycheck, which was delivered to my previous job in 2022, because I refused to manipulate people into leaving town. The paycheck was delivered to the job I left in 2022. I believe I know where my supervisor suddenly got a Tesla, given by the secret societies, companies, cults, and covens that would have secret meetings to cover up stealing. Other IT coworkers only had new Hondas, as I observed after quitting. I would like to have a car since there are so many things in my name that I don't know about. The companies that recently hired employees from my former company are connected to a cult and coven majority contractors. These contractors were already receiving a percentage of my pay and have been underpaying me. As a result, I've decided to remain an independent contractor.

I am pursuing legal action against my family and the government for the harm they have caused my children. My son is currently incarcerated, and I believe they are intentionally harming him and my other children in an attempt to manipulate fate. I reported this to Child Protective Services, but they failed to investigate due to a conflict of interest involving one of my ex's girlfriends, who works there, as well as all branches of the government involved. My son's father recently asked about my blood type, which raised my suspicions. I believe they are attempting to use my blood to create another child with my abilities and pass them off as me. However, I have a rare blood type and special abilities that cannot be duplicated. Instead, they used my third son's test results to steal additional benefits. They have been successful in obtaining benefits by placing my last son's information on my third son's results, changing all the names, and replacing them with the desired mother. As a result, they are filing child support and having me pay for it out of my taxes and through my check without my permission and consent.The government desperately needs to be audited, and the corrupt employees need to be replaced with those who follow the rules and their oaths.

I've discovered that many clones are pretending to be me, but they wouldn't match my DNA if tested. They're focused on deception, while I'm focused on revealing the truth. I've asked TMH to expose everything, and now they will face the consequences as I reveal their true identities.

Despite receiving threatening and harassing emails, texts, and phone calls as early as 6 a.m. due to my initial complaints, I have been patient, understanding, and cooperative regarding many issues as a resident here. My cooperation, however, has been misinterpreted, and I can no longer ignore these problems. They require my immediate attention. I have made multiple The agency's acceptance of substandard repairs from landlords allows landlords to exploit the system. This practice of temporary fixes has become recurring, further evidenced by the landlord's insistence on a temporary solution in this case. Landlords are able to continue collecting government funds by pressuring and harassing tenants who object to these inadequate repairs, while the agency's inaction perpetuates the issue.

My rights as a tenant in low-income housing under the HOA through DCHA were clearly violated. I requested an emergency transfer, which is no longer necessary as I have moved. Unfortunately, similar issues have arisen at my new residence. My current neighbor is my former neighbor's sister and the property manager's sister. The board member and property manager are part of the L, B, T, G+Q community, as was my previous landlord. The maintenance man, also a member of this community, had access to my residence, which made me feel exploited and uncomfortable.
His presence in my residence was unwanted and unnecessary. I have lived in properties where this was not required and would have preferred all communication to be via email. The constant text messages I received disrupted my peace, which they were aware of and took advantage of. Due to ongoing hacking and mail theft since my arrival, I've had to purchase several new phones.

I was encouraged to get Wi-Fi, which I believe was an attempt to monitor me. Additionally, I was told to switch electricity providers upon moving in, which was done without my consent. I've since received a $747 electricity bill for two months, despite never having a monthly bill over $100 in previous residences. I believe they are attempting to provoke me, but they will not succeed, as I am focused on moving soon.I believe these actions are unjust and discriminatory. No one should be subjected to such disruptive and unfair treatment. I request that you investigate this matter and take appropriate action to protect my tenant rights.

I spent the day clearing out anything that might harbor old energies. Everything is packed and ready for trash removal next Saturday. Although they were able to postpone my move, they couldn't delay my faith. The final decision rests with TMH. I admit there were times when I thought my life would never change, but now things are less stressful since I've learned to let go of anything that makes me uncomfortable. This time I choose to wait on TMH, as nothing I pick or choose seems to be good. I know there hasn't been much activity, partly due to my protection, but also to see where I've grown. I'm impressed at how far I've come along this deep, dark road paved for me long ago by the government's MKUltra and secret societies with their secret experiments. While I remain distrustful of the government, I recognize that there are both positive and negative aspects to it, just like anything else in life. Everyone is capable of knowing right from wrong and making their own decisions. We all possess common sense and a basic moral compass, irrespective of our upbringing. Even without parental guidance, we have an inherent ability to distinguish between right and wrong, a divine gift that many choose to disregard.I'm going to call it a night, having achieved a lot today. I feel lighter after releasing so much negativity. I'm done with making excuses and tolerating negativity; I'm letting go of all baggage and burdens. I've dealt with all I'm willing to handle; I won't be burdened any further, not today or any other day.

I will always focus on myself and accept whatever TMH provides. This lesson, along with love and discernment, was taught well. I had to endure loneliness and craziness, but it was a lesson for me and justice for my loved ones who have passed. I await the day I see them again. Many readers are curious about the details, but they will have to wait for the conclusion, just like me. I have asked TMH to review my case, and he is diligently working on it. The situation here is the same as in other realities.

One of my family or crazy partners infected my son, possibly his own father, to swap energies during a sex rituals before he returned to me in Capitol Heights, where they also molested and confused the young to cover up their desire to infect me, as they did to my son. I have been equipped to treat HIV patients by working in clinics. You are made to attend preventive classes so I was never in any fear of any transmission, the same as my mother never discriminating as I loved them both aside from their sickness. I knew and believed if it was meant to be it would be based only on TMH.They incarcerated and released him at their convenience to monitor and destroy him, making it appear as if I was the cause. My son was born healthy, weighing 10 lbs 12 ozs. The only sickness he had was asthma, the same as me.

They tried to hide the fact that they were using underage runaways and neglected children in their rituals by portraying me as promiscuous. They orchestrated a scheme with my drug-addicted second husband to falsely accuse me of crimes, spreading diseases, and incurring debts with drug dealers. This was all an attempt to destroy my reputation. Despite their efforts, I always paid my debts promptly, even when the money I was given was stolen. I was known for being a good payer and never owed anything to dealers. In fact, they often gave me more than I purchased because of my reputation for hard work and dedication. Their ultimate goal was to portray me as unsuccessful and desperate.

Since 2001, I have been clean from selling drugs, a past I lost everything to due to lies. Although I occasionally smoke marijuana, I would never sell it. I've learned from my mistakes and channeled my entrepreneurial spirit into my education, something I funded through my previous activities, though others have tried to undermine this as well. I've always been a hustler, understanding that success in any endeavor requires effort and a plan. For instance, DoorDash, like selling drugs, involves a constant hustle for similar daily earnings, but it's legal and has more customers. The same principle applies to doing hair or selling food. It's crucial to avoid the trap of believing drug dealing is the ultimate goal. The government will get its share one way or another; I prefer paying taxes to serving prison time.

Since 2001, my family and I have faced obstacles in securing permanent housing and stable employment, yet I remain hopeful. I believe I am watched over and that perseverance will lead to a better future. Today, I'm home, trying to secure the $1,351 needed for a move I've been planning for months. I was counting on relocation assistance during my unemployment, but now that I'm working again, I need to find the funds myself. The delay in processing the assistance is frustrating, as it wouldn't have put me in this situation otherwise. Despite my frustration, I trust everything will work out. I am angry because, despite my efforts, people continue to create problems, costing me time and money. Though I feel like giving up because it seems pointless, I will never give up on TMH. I surrender everything to TMH, who is the only one capable of fixing everything. I am tired of the negativity and being single. I followed instructions, but now I'm being asked to revisit a closed chapter. Attempts have been made to contact me, but all accounts and numbers were erased as directed. This feels unfair; following TMH is never wrong. They fabricate stories unrelated to me. I am ready for a new home or heaven, as my current situation feels unchanging and endless. I am weary of facing so many alone.

Throughout the week, I focused on personal growth and avoided distractions. I am moving forward with my relocation and will complete my current job. Some colleagues have become judgmental and envious, perhaps more significantly than I initially thought. They misunderstand my intentions and are needlessly fearful. I am here to work, not to replace anyone. I observe much, even when I seem unaware. I will seize a good opportunity and move in a new direction. The 'crazy warlock' tired upon my arrival, along with his partner ('the witch'), are monitoring me. They are connected to the new employee (a reiki healer and the Comptroller's girlfriend) and were all part of FOP, DOJ, DEA, and FBI within the company. They collaborated with my family and my first ex, my high school sweetheart, whom they later murdered after he discovered a larger conspiracy. The warlock's partner worked with my sister, a high school classmate at Blair HS. My sister and family were involved in something bigger than I could have imagined, possibly with influential connections, but at a great cost, as greed is detrimental. I trust God to provide; wants are okay, but cheating for them is not worth sacrificing one's soul. Hard work yields lasting rewards.

Past experiences have taught me not to carry others' burdens, which angered them. People cope in various ways, but I refuse to compromise my integrity or remain in a negative environment. Not all my desires are harmful; energy is constant, and everyone is entitled to their opinions. Some are intimidated or confused by me, but continuing engagement is not in line with my father's (TMH) wishes. Despite corrected work, I won't proceed if my creativity is taken for granted, overworked, and underpaid. Others often criticize based on limited understanding, masking their confusion and anger. My time has come. The energy felt positive, despite underlying tension. I never expected to stay this long and took a pay cut due to my supervisor's favoritism after a period of isolation following my last book.

I needed to refocus on my goals, but some mistook my kindness for weakness. They sent a 'creepy neighbor' claiming to be a lawyer (actually a web designer who helped my family exploit me and has been watching me) to interfere. My sister's former Lyft driver was also involved, attempting intimacy with roses, but I was aware of their surveillance. I am celibate and will not take what isn't mine or form unhealthy attachments. My focus has always been on learning and growth. Past mistakes will not be repeated, and I refuse foolish games. I pray for the success of the well-intentioned and swift justice for those who have wronged me by The Most High. Wickedness hinders growth. I am working hard and progressing, but peace will only come with a change of my current situation, though it's not my final destination.

For five years, I've endured illegal surveillance, gang stalking, mail fraud, and harassment. I need peace and privacy. I cleansed my home and myself today, Saturday, a day when rituals, projections, and the evil eye are often directed. Know that actions have consequences. Many have opinions on my last book, good and bad. Please understand I was under severe attack from black magic and projection at the time, without a job, internet, or phone—completely disconnected. The first book was my attempt to understand it all, even pawning my laptop for the cover and ISBN, as TMH knows the truth. My life is often perceived as privileged, but this is a cultivated image. Only prayer and my inner self know the truth; without them, I wouldn't be here. Judging by appearances is common, but inner beauty and the soul are what matter. Treat others with care, as their history and connections are unknown—you could be interacting with an angel, a childhood lesson.

Some may call me crazy, but the truth will eventually emerge, and I can only imagine the karmic repercussions for wrongdoers. I was sent to expose hidden truths and bring justice within the government and on the streets. Actions reveal more than words, and the heart is truthful. Some 'bad' actions can lead to justice, depending on the context. Balance is essential. All choices have significance, depending on presentation and execution. Will you follow or forge your own path? Arrogance, believing oneself above a higher power, is a common mistake; even the devil was once an angel. Be mindful of interactions and seek healing through experiences to avoid detours. We all have free will. If wrong, seek guidance and forgiveness, which will be granted. I must rest before they use voodoo dolls and projections to cloud my judgment; it will be returned to them. They mistakenly believe keeping me awake will weaken my resolve; my strength comes from above.

They were aware of my homelessness and the need to walk or take the bus all night to stay awake for work. Previously, I lived in my car for almost a year to save for a house in Capital Heights, MD, which was later destroyed. My son's father and grandfather remain angry about my car being repossessed after our separation, as it left me without transportation for work and daycare. I chose to leave my son with his father, ensuring his shelter. I could endure hardship, but it was unfair to my sons. My exes anticipated this decision and were pleased, as it meant I would return to their control, reporting to my family and engaging in destructive activities for payment, sustaining their lifestyle while destabilizing mine with false accusations and documents, leveraging their connections. They had access to all resources, while my sons and I had none. They believed hurting my children would hurt me, but my love for God surpasses even my love for my children. Though they brought me low, it never stopped my progress, as I knew my children were safe.

While my choices weren't always ideal, I did what I felt necessary for my family and myself. Shortly after, I began losing everything: my car, house, and mental well-being. They were Masons and Eastern Stars and believed they could control me. This is not a condemnation of all Masons and Eastern Stars, but rather the actions of those in higher positions. They paid his son to take my child and ruin my life while I was struggling. He wanted me to suffer, assuming I would always bear burdens, observing my difficulties with my other children's fathers and expecting his turn next. However, that was not to be. I learn from my mistakes and move in a different direction; repeated ineffective approaches are futile. Thus, despite obstacles, I was never truly stuck, merely detoured.

They expected me to beg, but I have never done so, not even from my own child. Everything I possess was earned, despite the existence of easier paths. Life has never been easy for me, and I've never sought the easy way out. My choices weren't always the best, but I had to navigate life's lessons without guidance or spiritual awareness for much of my journey. However, I have no regrets for these experiences; I now understand their purpose and how they ultimately led to blessings once I learned from them.

I met his father's ex-girlfriend's sister, who had infected him with HIV. She was my stylist, explaining how they obtained my hair. She introduced me to her brother, and that's how everything started. I was simply trying to get back on my feet, and had they not been so hateful and had given me what was rightfully mine, I would have reciprocated the help I received. They sought to play God (TMH), control my life, and destroy my destiny and my children's destinies. Their actions were driven by greed despite the abolition of slavery. My recent move has only resulted in more drama. The property manager, who is connected to the Masons and the LGBTQ+ community, has turned the lawn guy against me. This happened after I reacted to his lies and attempts to force something onto me. As a result, I've been wrongly accused of smoking sage, which is another form of gangstalking created by the psycho-psychiatrist. The constant stalking is all part of my ex-husband's society, and I'm sure he's behind it. They all share his dumb ways, which is an instant turnoff for those sent my way. He is determined to keep me alone while he engages in promiscuity and spreads diseases. Besides, who follows behind another grown man? That's just strange and unattractive.

People frequently misunderstand things they don't know, and this can cause a lot of confusion. For instance, my first ex-husband went to great lengths to conceal his illegal adoption, insurance fraud, and child support fraud. This involved paying people to impregnate me and then take my children away, all in an attempt to secure funds and drive me insane. For years, I was broken, lost, confused, and angry at the world. Thankfully, I eventually woke up and removed myself from the situation, reclaiming my energy from those who tried to destroy me. I'm tired of the haters, those who project negativity, and those who try to tie me down. Money isn't everything, and evil people who acquire wealth remain evil. A lot of my energy is currently focused on the downlow, where most of the cult involved in these activities – including their kids, fathers, ex-husbands, mistresses, foes, and partners – are engaging in illegal activities to steal from me.

Despite facing numerous challenges and attacks against me, They managed to keep my businesses, vehicles, houses, credit cards, and accounts afloat under my identity and the government connections. However, TMH will soon deliver retribution for those who have crossed the line. They may have thought they were invisible, but their actions have been observed, and karma will catch up with these disgruntled, undisciplined individuals. They should seek support and guidance through prayer because their actions will have consequences. My absence will likely lead to blame and finger-pointing, but my cousin, who was involved in stealing my inheritance and associated with my abuser, will also face unexpected punishment from TMH. This punishment will include the spread of diseases and the abuse her daughter has suffered. The daughter of my uncle's next-door neighbor, who later died mysteriously, was falsely presented as my uncle's biological daughter. My sister used to date this neighbor's brother, who was involved in stealing my money and was later unalived. My ex-husband was aware of this deception and opposed my claim to the inheritance.

The fake husband's plan to marry and then murder me, using either spellwork or poison, was unsuccessful. He had intended to stage a fight with my uncle and/or my uncle's children, assuming I would intervene and be arrested. Fortunately, I didn't fall for his setup and declined. I had to work and so did not have the privilege of going on cruises, vacations, and constantly posting on FB from 2016-2022, unlike others. Eventually, I was blocked from pages and made to delete my memories and connection to my FB page, as it was hacked. I lost a lot of my children's and family's history collected over the years - marriages, graduations, and self-portraits. I was raised in a family full of photographers, as my grandfather would say, "capture the moment in time, which you can never return." Instead, they were using my pictures for rituals and dark things, such as exploitation, photoshopping, and putting them on dating sites. This is why the guys coming or being sent in assumed a was out there.

All of this being noted, as there will be a lot of suits filed at the end of this. It amazes me that the law is fully aware of the abuse I have endured and has yet to do anything about it, so I prayed to TMH and asked him to intervene, and now I wait. During my marriage, my spouse took out a life insurance policy on me and plotted to kill me, either by hiring assassins or poisoning me, to make my death appear natural. When these attempts failed, and after I ended our relationship upon discovering he was married, he sought revenge by sending the lawn guy to install cameras in my home for the purpose of revenge porn. Later, he colluded with my ex and my son, who was his acquaintance from our old neighborhood. They used this connection to enter my home on Sheriff Road while I was at work, leaving a window open and taking my belongings, including knives, clothes, and shoes.

Additionally, he betrayed me by receiving tax money and overtime pay from a job that my sister had obtained using my resume and credentials, while we were not in contact. Subsequently, my son reconnected my sister and me, and I agreed to help her with reports she couldn't complete in exchange for payment. The family involved in the cult and coven with my family were trying to frame me for a crime they committed before my marriage. This crime was most likely the accident my sister was involved in. This occurred shortly after I lost my home to foreclosure, which followed a three-to-five-year period where I lived in a home owned by the brother of the hairstylist whose sister, who died from AIDS, was the lover of my son's paternal grandfather.

I have never experienced true love in my life. I am a government experiment, which began after my stepfather and my aunt discovered my abilities when I was younger, recorded me, and sold me to the government for study. They then auctioned me off, just like in the movie "Get Out," when I was younger after revealing my abilities. They have blocked my abilities since there is a video circulating of past sexual abuse from my grandmother and mother figure, who used this abuse to harvest my energy. They also allowed others they knew or were connected to, to have relations with me to harvest my energy.

For decades, I have been subjected to exploitation and harassment due to my unique abilities, which I will not disclose for safety. This has included the theft of my mail and personal belongings, gang stalking, and harassment by my past landlord, property manager, and neighbors at my previous residence. Their cult-like conspiracy stemmed from the belief that I didn't belong in the community. This is similar to how whites have historically exploited and stolen from African Americans, including the harvesting of energy through rape, as they could never achieve what African Americans inherently possessed. They aimed to isolate me, obstructing my path to destiny. As the truth about me unfolds, many, swayed by falsehoods and assumptions, have turned cold and distant. Around 2007-2008, a DC Superior Court hearing granted her guardianship of my son, who had graduated early due to his intelligence and hard work. Despite this, he wasn't living with her. I lost my job because she failed to provide financial support for his graduation, prom, and other essentials. She had transportation to Delaware, and I was excluded from seeing his dorm room, while she was welcomed. Roughly a year later, she sought a paternity test for my son. I recently recovered the motion while researching neglect case records for my story, as my ex-husband had destroyed my records between 2002 and 2004. It's peculiar that all other documents were missing, as they should have been archived.. She requested past benefits, claiming she was the guardian after his father was murdered around 2014-2015. However, it was discovered that she was involved with him even after learning about my second son's release from prison. They orchestrated his release as a distraction and controlled his actions due to his dissatisfaction with prison and my residence in Capital Heights. During this period, I was not in contact with my family due to a previous betrayal.

I was not informed of the hearing. Due to false testimonies from her friends and other paid individuals, including members of an AA group who had received DUIs, funds were unjustly allocated. I was treated with disrespect and condescension, and what rightfully belonged to my children and me was wrongfully taken. As a result, I lost my home, he was rearrested, and I was subjected to abuse and imprisonment. My sister and his father had taken out an insurance policy on him. Instead of "unaliving" him at the hospital, they were determined to silence him through imprisonment. He was later released from the hospital and "unalived." This was a setup by his father and childhood friends who worked at the jail. I still have not been notified of his death, as they stole my identity, showed up at the morgue as me, and received his belongings and documents that hold the truth. I am not sure if he was buried properly. That is two of my children that I am aware of who have been "unloved." One took drugs that were laced with something and overdosed; the other was set up and "unalived." I am not sure what my last son is doing, as they have brainwashed him. He is currently trying to come up with a plan to poison me. It will not work. I have called judgment upon him, as I love no one more than God and myself.

I was placed on probation, but everything was orchestrated to make me appear crazy, unlawful, incompetent, and dangerous as a distraction. She spied on me, taking photos while pretending to care and assist me. She pretended to give me money that was obtained illegally. They stole my inheritance from my uncle's will after he passed away in 2014, and used money they stole from me to pay off debts and everyone else back. They're trying to portray me as unable to care for myself, and have been going to court to prove it. I've been taking care of myself since I was fifteen years old. I've always had to work for everything, and I've never been loved. They've done all of this to make me disappear—to make me homeless, abused, admitted, and locked up.

The previous company I worked for was managed by a cult-like organization that consistently overworked and underpaid me, and engaged in identity theft and wage theft. When I resigned, I was falsely assured that I had resolved the CFO's issues and asked not to quit, yet the company requested that I mail in my laptop the next morning. I was never officially fired; they lied to me. They wanted to steal my energy and identity, a pattern that has followed me to almost every job I've had. I was used as a scapegoat, and I learned that they all worked together against me - my family, exes, and even coworkers I was talking to for a short time all planned and staged he was to come in to record so they could later humiliate me with cameras watching me illegally on top of me having cameras previously placed in my last two residences by the maintenance, family, fake hater, ex-lover whomever which would explained while moving all eyes were on me everybody appeared that day property manager, the stalker parled in between car on the a motorcycle rude nosey neighbors, maintenance men these mason, islamic, muslim, jewish, and government societies all trying to take me out due to man inheritance my biological father. The truth will be revealed as TMH and my angels expose the fakeness in my final contract. Many have judged me after reading my book, but

I'm not worried. The truth will always shine through and be known, because people often judge what they don't understand.

I have been putting the finishing touches on my book by editing and adding to the conclusion, while also going on job interviews so I can stay afloat. While both interviews show promise, only one offers the career advancement that I've been striving for. My ability to connect with people on a deeper level makes me stand out from my colleagues. I am confident that this will help me excel at my interviews and land the job. As the saying goes, "you shouldn't judge a book by its cover."

The shocking truth is that my family has been manipulating and controlling my life from behind the scenes for as long as I can remember, all driven by greed and power. My sister and cousin, who are involved in a dangerous cult, even had me followed. They've recruited people from my past—exes, bosses, and even enemies—to spread rumors and damage my reputation, making me feel isolated and worthless. They've even contacted my former classmates, all the way back to elementary school, asking for them to assist for money. These individuals are heartless, lack self-respect, and have clearly made a deal with the devil - not that they care. Furthermore, I've uncovered a hidden family and a potential destiny that I was completely unaware of. Driven solely by greed and the pursuit of wealth, they lacked loyalty. I refuse to follow their example and compromise my values. For instance, my other cousins, who lived with my aunt in a one-bedroom apartment for forty years, were waiting to inherit my grandmother's house—or anyone else's—through insurance fraud or other dishonest means. The thief's daughter, my other aunts' children, and the rapist's son apparently robbed my son's paternal grandfather, or Southview guy who was also the co-defendant of Rafal Edmunds which one i am unsure as they both were against me and they both have the same name. Meanwhile, they were trying to obtain power of attorney over me to steal my inheritance, property, land, and anything else left to me. They claimed that I had transitioned and were receiving benefits on my behalf. I am in court but cannot show up because apparently I am sick, incompetent so they can maintain payments for someone who is deceased. Which one was the last time I checked ? I am still standing all liars. I then discovered that my workplace affair was never genuine. I had quit due to constant harassment from a secret society within the company, who held meetings and ranked members. They had accessed my akashic records before hiring me. This was all part of their plan to steal my energy, time, and money and keep me trapped in the last cycle.

During a night out at the bar, I met with my cousin who was angry with me for a guy choosing me over her. I later realized he was another handler sent to interfere. She frequented The Hideaway bar near my last son's father and they often plotted against me. She would share my secrets with him, and vice versa. We had a falling out due to his lies about her brother, but I later reconnected with her while living in Southview. During this time, I was distancing myself from my family. My sister and a close friend betrayed me, using spellwork to make me sick and dependent on them. They pretended to be caring while taking advantage of my energy.

Eventually, their scheme fell apart due to financial issues and an inability to maintain their lifestyle. My cousin also experienced rental problems around the same time, which wasn't a coincidence. These repeated cycles were due to unbroken curses and illusions that still clouded my judgment, preventing me from recognizing my enemies and fully utilizing my gift.

I was deliberately placed in an underpaid, dead-end position by my family and the government as a means of control and suppression. This strategy, however, was undermined by the rampant jealousy and envy it fostered in my workplace. My role was essentially to cover for the assistant comptroller's incompetence, all while being exploited by my own family and ex-husband. He, along with various government officials, lawyers, judges, council members and mayors, was involved in numerous affairs both inside and outside the office. These relationships were used to exploit me and others, who were often paid to keep silent.

I was met with widespread animosity from my colleagues, who actively worked to undermine my relationships within the company. Unbeknownst to me at the time, my co-worker was interested in me, I only discovered this after leaving the company. His mistress, who was involved in witchcraft with the Google witch and her grandmother, used Santeria to cast illusions over the company and its employees. They both were a part of something more corrupt as both were lovers of my ex-husband and received payment. This was done to prevent me from taking her position and to turn employees against me. These actions also served to conceal her own thieving and the fact that she was only there to steal time, money, and other resources. Furthermore, I encountered bias from both the company president and the CFO. The president believed she was beyond criticism, while the CFO initially seemed to be under mind control, but was later revealed to be involved in the same cult/coven as my ex-husband. This group consisted of high-ranking individuals with addictions who had taken an oath and operated outside the law in exchange for payment. They, in turn, attempted to label me unfairly. I admit that I occasionally drink wine - mainly for the aroma - and anything else makes me sick. I don't get drunk; I sip and relax. I may also smoke marijuana recreationally or to clear my head, but I am not an addict. I have successfully completed numerous narcotics and alcohol classes due to the lies orchestrated by many. I have never judged, only they know their actions and that I was vulnerable after losing my children. Between that and the abuse from the handlers, I am fortunate not to be an addict. Thank God, who had a plan for my life and lifted me from those dark places, allowing me to see the light within myself and reach my full potential.

During the 2023 holiday season, when I left the company, a check was issued to me. However, a group of individuals conspired to steal this check. This group included the company president, CFO, my supervisor's mistress, my son's father, and members of a secret society. They shared my digital signature and banking information with my family and the secret society.

Furthermore, certain individuals deemed my inheritance insufficient and attempted to discredit me and my accomplishments. They resorted to posting videos on the dark web and creating distractions to avoid my attention. Additionally, funds intended for a specific account were diverted into various other accounts, none of which belonged to me. Instead of providing me with my rightful assets, they used the money for personal expenses like travel, cars, hairstyles, clothing, and accessories, without any intention of helping others.

A couple, who felt wronged after being exposed in my book, sought revenge by spreading falsehoods, stealing royalties, and manipulating book sales for their own financial gain. At the same time, they took advantage of my energy at a company where I was initially contracted for only three months. The company, misled by others, extended my contract to exploit both me and the projections based on my work. Despite being underpaid by my agencies and many other companies, I stayed with them to survive until I realized that TMH is my provider. Ironically, my ancestors revealed that these companies used their own employees' information to support their business, although this is unrelated to me. Driven by my love for numbers and the need to catch up on bills after a period of isolation, I embraced the contract and fulfilled my job duties both spiritually and physically. I never feel pressured, even when others expect it. I am always blessed and favored, never lacking anything essential. TMH will always provide for my needs, so I work to fulfill my wants, not my necessities.

My family, including my late husband's ex-wife, have been conspiring against me and my son since 2001 to defraud us of our inheritance. They fabricated documents and engaged in a scheme to control me, including attempts to impregnate me. I've discovered that many presumed dead individuals have assumed new identities, and these people were aware of my unique gift, similar to my aunt's, which made me a target. My family was poisoned, and as the sole survivor, I've been continuously targeted. My parents exploited my gifts, selling me for government and other experimentation, pimping me out, subjecting me to sexual abuse, and exposing me to demonic influences. My rare sexual energy was exploited for profit by adults through various relationships, including during my youth, and I was trafficked. Many built their wealth by exploiting my energy and absorbing my negativity. These assaults were incentivized with bonuses for ruining my life. Despite this horrific abuse, I have persevered and exposed their lies.

Many individuals from my past, such as my sister, her children's fathers, and others, have harmed me. In Red Springs, NC, my sister used me as a sacrifice for herself and her son's father, who were possessed and sought to steal my positive energy. Her ex-husband, still alive and working as an insurance agent, has been part of this long-term conspiracy, causing deaths for insurance money. My sister's oldest son's father, a PG County police officer, and my nephew, a Fairfax Police Department officer, have covered up evidence. This lack of accountability has had severe consequences. Additionally, my first husband and my mother's cousin's daughter had an affair and a child. To conceal this, child support was redirected, and my deceased son never received it. My second husband illegally sold my books, and now his ex-wife and my aunt are collaborating on a book using my stolen work, which they have no right to do. I am prepared to take legal action to stop this exploitation of my intellectual property.

I've also uncovered surprising family connections. My fake husband's supposed mother is actually his deceased sister who never transitioned. She is also the sister of the woman my son lived with and the woman who adopted my oldest son. A relative has a child with my ex, who was never meant to be my second fake husband. There is also conflict involving my aunts, a will, and my second husband's brother. This is connected to my incarcerated son, who was the target of an attempted sexual assault by this brother. I believe they tried to extort my son to gain leverage over me, involving prison staff, childhood friends, and organized crime. I am distancing myself from this negativity and focusing on my children, refusing to support those who repeatedly harm me, regardless of family ties.

My son, who is bisexual and sometimes cross-dresses, has been committing crimes disguised as a woman, influenced by brainwashing and manipulation to believe he is me or superior. My other children and family are involved in this scheme and have also brainwashed my youngest son, a genius. I have also been subjected to MK Ultra. I am still trying to understand my family history, particularly my connection to my next-door neighbor with whom I grew up. Other neighbors who knew my grandmother were aware of this potential link, possibly explaining my grandfather's dislike for the alcoholic's father. I wonder if they were in a relationship or if they simply assisted him with his veteran's or disability benefits. Many unanswered questions remain.

In 2020, a life insurance policy was purchased for my biological parents and me. Two years later, my nephew's father was at a club where my biological parents were "merged." My son's father staged a custody test after a problematic individual from North Carolina appeared. Devil worshipers stole from the Chief of Police. My son's father and his friend conspired to harm me by revealing my secrets. His friend paid the lawn guy, my aunt's husband's nephew, who then interfered in my life, attempting to ruin my relationships and finances.

I experienced severe privacy violations, including cyberbullying, deletion of my contacts, and responses made as if they were me, all to destroy my life. During our last conversation, I expressed my anger towards the disrespect of him coming to my home to steal and harvest my energy for his sister and her coven, who were also my ex-husband's sex ritual partners. They were all infected and tried to infect me. I warned him, but he shared our conversation, leading to further attacks. I ended the connection, disgusted by the thought of being with anyone from my past or family. They also tried to coerce me into threesomes or polyamorous relationships, which contributed to the hate I faced in the LGBTQ+ community, despite my own past bisexuality. My landlords from the 90s, who are also my ex, are working with my abusive ex-husbands and my sister-cousin and a psychotherapist to disrupt my life following a successful contract completion, as they owe a favor.

Furthermore, my second son's father has collaborated with my aunt (whose family has a history of rape), a former crush, and others to cause catastrophic events in my life, aiming to steal a house, continue receiving payments, and conceal past crimes committed in my name. They even hired a fake actor and attorney to monitor me and intend my complete destruction.

Many people, including my youngest son's father, have falsely accused me of crimes to illegally collect funds for my son through other women via taxes and government benefits. My son knows the woman he was deceived about wasn't his biological mother, and she retaliated by having him set up. He was harmed, and my ex-coworker witnessed him tormenting me but then slept with him and became part of the gangstalking and theft, aligning with his supposed second wife who assumed my identity. There was constant infidelity and swinging. They were angry because he still loved me and devoted time to me.

I would never participate in stalking an ex. The mistress of my ex-husband stole my son and my identity and hypocritically claimed to be Christian. She never loved him or my son and later contracted HIV/AIDS. Life should be lived fully as TMH approaches. Those who have caused harm will face karma. My decision to leave my son's father was due to infidelity and abuse, not illness. Their malicious attempts will fail. While I advise against casual relationships, the choice is personal. Evil exists in many forms and can affect anyone. Superficial appearances are deceiving; it's important to look beyond them before judging. They have been using my married name, which I haven't used in over two decades since my forced marriage to my handler, who obtained my accounts and tried to have me committed. They stole my inheritance with the help of family and enemies. The baby's father from Building 529 and the police chief, my sister's baby's father, were involved in the stolen goods.

The stolen art, a ring, and my parents are all connected to my past. The police and insurance agents, some of whom were involved in targeting beneficiaries for large payouts by killing them and assuming their identities, had access to these items. I am speaking out for my living and deceased family members to stop this. Vengeance belongs to the Lord, and I am his instrument for those lost to violence and spells, and for myself. TMH will have his way. TMH is real, and I am proof. After surviving multiple attempts on my life, I fell and "died," but now I rise for justice.

My life has been plagued by the theft of cherished possessions, leading to broken relationships. A safety report was opened without my consent, which I believe is used to keep me impoverished, similar to tactics used against my cousin. I've witnessed the destructive power of these spells but was spared a similar fate. Despite my family's government connections, they've profited from my identity while I contributed to the government. My stepmother and aunt forced me to move and constantly surveilled me. After I moved, my ex, the lawn guy, conspired with people from my current and past jobs and the police to have me falsely imprisoned to cover up his actions or because he felt slighted. My family members also conspired against me out of jealousy when I was attracted to someone, making harassing calls, showing him a video, and attempting to poison my food. They also used dark magic against me.

The judge in my case is the sister of a former boyfriend with connections to my aunt's daughter and my fake husband's sister's child. My fake husband believed in harmful sex and incest rituals used to disrupt my life. The woman who stole my land and identity, pretending to be me and supposedly deceased from cancer, faked her death and is living under my name in South Carolina, possibly having harmed their mother to assume her identity as well. They are drug addicts who exploited my kindness towards her brother, using him to manipulate me. While I regret the pain this will cause his family, I don't regret helping him as my intentions were genuine. They will face the consequences of their actions.

They were also connected to my last contract. The witch involved believes someone wants her partner. The main person behind the attacks appears innocent, while her best friend, my sister, and my son's father, another lover, have been involved in destiny swapping and tracking children within a church setting, a cover for a secret society that exploits the vulnerable. A large group, including my aunt's husband's nephew, my sister's ex, my second son's father and his family, conspired against me, feigning friendship. A former one-night stand, also involved with my ex-husband, was sent to harm me.ything from my past. I await something new that hasn't been tampered with. They continue to project and do poverty spells, hoping I'll lose my home and everything else. I'm putting the final touches in place and praying this ends soon. I'm tired and need a vacation.

I had hoped to spend this summer at the beach, but I'm stuck in D.C. instead. The cult keeps sending its followers after me, but with divine intervention, I remain calm and collected. I'm shocked as I piece everything together for the conclusion; it's truly horrible what these people have been doing. Though I was close to the truth, TMH is now confirming everything. I will continue to share secrets and speak out until the right people are in office – those who will actually honor their oaths and serve and protect, rather than spreading lies for profit. The truth will always come out; nothing and no one can hide from TMH. What is hidden today will be revealed, whether it's tomorrow or years from now. Right now, I trust no one and will remain vigilant until TMH says otherwise. My story is almost complete.

I feel my hope dwindling as I work tirelessly without seeing any results. Although things are shifting, I know I'm close to something important. However, TMH continues to allow projects and blockages to stand in my way. Despite my efforts to break free from negativity and harmful influences, I'm still held captive. Even my home feels like a prison due to constant surveillance and monitoring. I try my best to please TMH, but it's never enough. I remain trapped in bondage, even though I freed myself from it years ago. I'm tired of trying to figure everything out. The truth always evades me, yet others can easily find me to cause harm and steal from me. I don't understand why TMH allows this to continue, but I'm no longer concerned. This situation has disrupted my life countless times, no matter how hard I work. It's a never-ending story. I can only advise you not to be disappointed; you may have a true destiny awaiting you. Unfortunately, I cannot say the same for myself, as I've worked tirelessly without results. Perhaps your outcome will be different, as no one seems to have as many adversaries as I do. My origins and identity are irrelevant. The important thing is that I've learned valuable lessons. I pray I've helped at least one person avoid enduring the hopeless life I've lived.

Stay positive and observant, and remember that things aren't always as they appear. Believe in yourself, and success will follow. Everyone's journey is unique, but for me, I see no way out except death. Given the unexpected level of detail and interest, there will definitely be a third book. The truth is complex and remains unresolved, so I'll continue in the next book. For now, I'll need to update my findings, which is taking longer than expected due to the sheer number of people and government entities involved. This weekend has been a whirlwind. I've uncovered so much information and still have more research to do. I now realize it's going to take longer than I initially thought. I will be writing another book because this one is already quite substantial. I haven't delved into the truly terrible details yet because it hasn't been addressed. From what little I've heard, I don't think I'll be able to handle it because the truth about my family is both sickening and disturbing.I came across one of my old acquaintances from The Pinnacles, my safe haven when I was younger. He was someone I could confide in and he would listen, as he knew my story almost as well as I did. He was one of my sister's exes and also a friend of my oldest son's father. He showed up in my readings, and I'm not sure if he's alive or not. I believe he may have passed away, which is saddening because I never would have known that my son's father had passed either. But, as I've said, I don't believe in death, so he'll be back around eventually.

Discovering that my family has been involved in incestuous relationships has been deeply shocking and disturbing. They have been sleeping with each other, including exes, children, aunts, and uncles. I want no part in this behavior and choose to remain single. It's true that people often don't appreciate you until you're gone; the loudest person at a funeral is often the one who cared the least. I believe love should be given freely and unconditionally. Many people have been involved in this situation since my childhood, including friends, family, coworkers, associates, F.A.N.S., and exes. I've never been close to many people, which may explain why I don't feel hurt. I left to protect myself, constantly moving and losing many people along the way. I believe this is how God intended it to be. The only people who stayed in my life for any length of time were either unloved, removed, or cloned. Most of them were never meant to be in my life, which is why it ended.

I've decided to conclude this book now, as I've spent more time on it than anticipated. Also, this is the same as the last book at risk of being stolen, as they've managed to hack all my accounts again. I'm being completely transparent with you all. I hope that closing this book will also close this chapter of my life. I will write another book after I comb through the most recent details provided from above. I will reveal the behind-the-scenes events in the next book, hopefully with closure. As I see it, this has no conclusion anytime soon. There is too much corruption and no one is bold enough to stand up for what is right, as money is more important than another life, especially when telling the truth would interrupt whatever is being received. People don't realize that TMH's blessings are much greater than material and tangible items.

I close with love and respect to all. Remember to pray, and that thoughts form into reality. Believe and achieve it all.

www.ingramcontent.com/pod-product-compliance
Lightning Source LLC
Chambersburg PA
CBHW070344090426

42733CB00009B/1275